THE
SELF-INFLICTED
WOUND

THE
SELF-INFLICTED
WOUND

ৰ৽

by Fred P. Graham

The Macmillan Company

Chapter IV was originally published in *Violence in America*, Chapter 13. Copyright © 1969 by Fred P. Graham. Chapter V was originally published in *Harper's Magazine*, September, 1970, under the title, "Black Crime: The Lawless Image." Copyright © 1970 by Fred P. Graham. The quote on p. 169 is from the article, "Arrest, Detention, Interrogation and the Right to Counsel: Basic Problems and Possible Legislative Solutions," by Bator and Vorenberg and is reprinted by permission of the *Columbia Law Review*, vol. 66, p. 62. Copyright © 1966.

The Macmillan Company
866 Third Avenue, New York, N.Y. 10022
Collier-Macmillan Canada Ltd., Toronto, Ontario

Library of Congress Catalog Card Number 79-129750

First Printing

Printed in the United States of America

Contents

PREFACE   vii

I   CRIME AND THE SUPREME COURT   1

II   THE POLITICS OF CRIME   10

III   THE DUE PROCESS REVOLUTION   26

IV   THE MATHEMATICS OF CRIME   67

V   NEGRO CRIME AND THE SUPREME COURT   86

VI   RE-TRYING THE CONVICTED   102

VII   POLICING THE POLICE   122

VIII   *Miranda*: SELF-INFLICTED WOUND   153

IX   SEARCHES: FROM CONFUSION TOWARD A RULE OF REASON   194

X   IDENTIFICATION: LAWYERS AND LINEUPS   221

XI   POLICE EAVESDROPPING: LAW-ENFORCEMENT REVOLUTION   247

XII   HANDCUFFING THE POLICE   276

XIII   REVOLUTION AND AFTER   305

NOTES   333

LIST OF CASES   355

INDEX   361

FOR MY PARENTS
Otis L. Graham and Lois Patterson Graham

Preface

It was mid-spring of 1965 before they noticed that the Supreme Court had been left out of the District of Columbia telephone book. The section for "United States Government" contained eight tightly packed pages of listings, ranging from "Academy of Sciences" to "Zoological Park." But somebody had neglected to list the Supreme Court. No one will ever know how many visitors came, searched and were persuaded that their school texts had been grossly off the mark.

When the oversight was brought to the attention of Banning E. Whittington, the Supreme Court's official spokesman, there was some unbelieving shuffling through the pages, some surprised chuckling and a resolve to correct the omission in future years. (They did.) But that the Supreme Court had not been listed, and further, that it had made so little difference, said much about the odd insularity of the third branch of the Government at a time in which it was approaching a climactic point in a revolution in the nation's criminal procedures.

To a large extent, the fiction was being maintained that the Supreme Court spoke through its opinions only to the nation's lawyers and judges, about matters of their special concern. The Justices were, indeed, issuing legal opinions as they had done for 175 years. But the impact on the world beyond the cozy profession of the law was certain to be pervasive, and in some ways traumatic, as the Supreme Court moved to reinforce the constitutional rights of those accused of crimes.

The Justices of the Supreme Court had decided four years before that the time had come to make the major restrictions of the Bill of Rights that apply to criminal procedure enforceable against the states. By the mid-1960s they were still considering what the new constitutional standards should be. But whatever the new rules were to be (and they proved to be more drastic in several respects than many people thought the country could safely stand), they would require wrenching adjustments in law enforcement methods in every community in the land. Prior to 1961 each state had virtually gone its own way on criminal procedure, administering criminal justice with the degree of punctiliousness or muscle that suited the style of its people, and with little regard for the Constitution and courts of the United States. The Warren Court had undertaken to bridle that process, to make it more humane and evenhanded. Almost necessarily, this would also make it less effective—or at least to appear so— and this was certain to make it a matter of deep public concern and political importance.

Yet circumstances combined to cloud public understanding of this process. The Supreme Court maintained its traditional discipline of speaking only through its own opinions. The best of these did well if they explained, in terms that nonlawyers could comprehend, what was being done and why the Constitution required it. This left unexplained such matters as why the revolution suddenly sprang from the pages of the Bill of Rights, unchanged since 1791, into a crime-plagued society, and what the impact might be upon the public, the police and the Supreme Court itself.

In a Government in which the Pentagon spent $27.9 million in a single year on public relations, the Supreme Court's actions were explained officially only by Banning Whittington, who appeared to operate under orders not to say anything that was not on the record or already known. The persons who understood the situation most thoroughly were the lawyers who were involved in the controversy. But being advocates, their public statements and writings were designed more to win converts than to explore the problems and educate the public. Attorney General

Nicholas deB. Katzenbach, a liberal, tried the latter, was pilloried by the defense advocates for taking a law enforcement position and thereafter shunned the controversy because he said it had become too polarized to serve any enlightening purpose. The lawyers' obfuscation was surpassed only by the performance of the politicians, who manipulated crime statistics, flirted with the white backlash and used the crime controversy to settle old grudges against the Supreme Court.

The Supreme Court press was shackled by the daily-story format, which largely restricted it to describing the procedural trees, as they emerged from the Court's decisions, rather than the constitutional forest. Some excellent articles were written about various aspects of the due process revolution, but the tyranny of the 750-word piece too often asserted itself and prevented a broad discussion of what was taking place. So the one group of neutral observers who were close enough to what was happening to understand and explain it were restricted by their medium from telling the complete story.

This book is an attempt to provide what has not been available so far; a full exposition by a neutral observer of what the Supreme Court has done and why—and what the outcome is likely to be. To the extent that it succeeds, it is due in large part to several persons who contributed to its accuracy and understanding, but deserve none of the blame for its faults. Walter V. Schaefer, Robert B. McKay, A. Kenneth Pye, G. Robert Blakey, Jerome Daunt and Marvin E. Wolfgang read parts or all of the manuscript. I am grateful for their advice and suggestions, and my confidence is bolstered by the fact that it has been reviewed by persons as expert in these matters as they. Linda Stores, Angelina Gomez, Helen Westwood, Adrianne Burke and Olivia Harrison typed the manuscript, often under pressure of odd hours and close deadlines, and always in good humor. Christopher Edley of the Ford Foundation provided a grant that permitted me to spend the summer of 1969 at the Appellate Judges Seminar at New York University Law School, where much of the research for this book was done. My wife Lucile cheerfully adjusted her own life, and that of three energetic children, to give me the time, and often the quiet, needed to work on this book.

I would not have had the opportunity to write this book but for the friendship of two persons. They are Tom Wicker and David Halberstam, who once practiced journalism on the staff of *The Nashville Tennessean*, as I did until I strayed into the practice of law. They later persuaded me to return to my first calling, journalism—as Supreme Court correspondent for *The New York Times*. I thank them most of all.

Fred P. Graham

THE
SELF-INFLICTED
WOUND

I

Crime and the Supreme Court

Justice . . . has become a mere game in which the defendant's counsel play with loaded dice.

WILLIAM HOWARD TAFT

For all of their traditions of democracy and independence, Americans take comfortably to government by judges. The ink was barely dry on the Constitution (which gave the Supreme Court only the seemingly innocuous "judicial power") before the Justices assumed the authority to nullify laws passed by Congress and the state legislatures. The Justices have never looked back, and today the Supreme Court of the United States is easily the supremest court in the world.

Power of this nature—when exercised by isolated men with limited political experience, lifetime tenure and long black robes

—can create an aura of Zeus. It would happen even if the Justices were merely uncommonly powerful arbiters of the law, but the Supreme Court has acquired a moral function as well—a duty, as Felix Frankfurter put it, to ascertain the conscience of society.

For the most part, Americans have embraced this idea. With Congress and the Presidency as sensitive as they are to the voters' self-interest, it has seemed a good thing to have a third branch that is geared to reflect the nation's idealism. So the public in general applauded when the Supreme Court outlawed legal segregation in 1954 and unfairly apportioned legislatures in 1964, although neither move was politically feasible through the legislative process at the time. There were fewer cheers when the Court outlawed prayers and Bible reading in the public schools, but when Congress moved to reverse the rulings by amending the Constitution, the public did not respond and the idea was dropped. Wrongs done to Communists do not stir most Americans' indignation, but even here, when the Court made it almost impossible to convict, register or even fire one, the public remained sullen but not mutinous.

This latter revelation—that the Justices could not always touch the public conscience merely by exercising their own—suggested the pitfalls that come with the splendid powers that have devolved upon the Supreme Court. "The power of the Supreme Court is immense, but it is power springing from opinion," Alexis de Tocqueville observed; "They are all-powerful so long as the people consent to obey the law; they can do nothing when they scorn it. Now, of all powers, that of opinion is the hardest to use, for it is impossible to say exactly where its limits come. Often it is as dangerous to lag behind as to outstrip it. The Federal judges therefore must . . . be statesmen; they must know how to understand the spirit of the age, to confront those obstacles that can be overcome, and to steer out of the current when the tide threatens to carry them away."

If constitutional law, like politics, is an art of the possible, then the hazards of being the keeper of the nation's conscience are obvious. The Court's idealism can carry it off in one direction, while public opinion moves in another. If the distance becomes too great, the result can be a constitutional crisis of serious proportions.

This is no mystery to the Court, for an important element of its folklore dates back to a series of lectures given at Columbia University in 1928 by former Associate Justice—later Chief Justice—Charles Evans Hughes. He warned that the Court has found its fortress in public opinion and it has fallen into error when it moves counter to the public will.

"In three notable instances the Court has suffered severely from self-inflicted wounds," Hughes warned. The first was the Dred Scott decision of 1857, when the Court demonstrated that it had become "the citadel of slavocracy" by refusing to free a Negro slave who had crossed from slave to free territory. The decision was greeted with "derision and contempt"; the Civil War was required to reverse the decision, and many years passed before the Supreme Court "was able to retrieve its reputation," Hughes said.

The second incident that "brought the Court into disesteem" was the legal tender case following the war. President Ulysses S. Grant needed the power to print paper money in order to pay off the war debts, but the Court ruled, 4 to 3, that the legal tender act was unconstitutional. On that same day Grant named two new Justices to the high bench and the newly packed Court promptly reconsidered the case and declared, this time 5 to 4, that the law was constitutional after all. Hughes recalled that this "shook popular respect for the Court."

The third incident came in 1895 after the Court had spared the new income tax law and then executed a quick turnabout and declared it unconstitutional. Initially the eight-member Court had been divided 4 to 4 and so had declined to rule on the issue. Then one Justice switched his vote, the case was reconsidered, and the law was struck down. The ruling made a constitutional amendment necessary before incomes could be taxed, and "aroused a criticism of the Court which has never been entirely stilled," Hughes said.

It was against this background that the Warren Court undertook in the 1960s to limit the powers of the nation's police. No one could have known, when the Court began this process in 1961, that it would coincide with the most troubled period of violent crime and racial unrest that has occurred in this century. As it turned out, the cycles of legal reform and rising crime and racial tensions moved in uncanny rhythm. The Supreme Court's reform movement got under way in 1961, when it first began to make the Bill of Rights enforceable against state and local police. It rose to a period of greatest judicial activity in 1966, and was already slowing down when Chief Justice Earl Warren retired in 1969. In 1962, the Federal Bureau of Investigation's crime index swung upward, after several stable years. By the mid-1960s, record crime increases were being registered each year and waves of Negro riots were raking the cities each summer. By the end of the decade the annual rate of increase in reported crime was in a slight decline, and massive ghetto riots had become rare.

History has played cruel jokes before, but few can compare with the coincidence in timing between the rise in crime, violence and racial tensions in the United States and the Supreme Court's campaign to strengthen the rights of criminal suspects against the state. In retrospect, it seems obvious that the Warren Court reformed the criminal law when it did as a natural outgrowth of its civil rights activities, and because the differences from state to state in the treatment of persons who ran afoul of the law had become intolerable in a nation where state lines had come to mean so little. The Court's reform effort could have come at almost any time in the recent past, and it is intriguing to consider how the course of events might have been altered if it had taken place in the period before World War II, or in the decade immediately after it, or at some other period when it could have taken root before crime became the problem that it has become. As it was, the Supreme Court's reform campaign eventually encountered a monumental incongruity—the Court had announced the most rigid legal limitations that any society had sought to impose on its police at a time when the United States had the most serious crime problem of any so-called advanced nation in the world.

It was almost inevitable that the Supreme Court's reform of the nation's system of criminal justice would appear to be a radical process, because there was so much to be done. In 1961 defendants who could not afford counsel were still floundering through jury trials against seasoned prosecutors, then serving long prison terms as the price of their courtroom inadequacies. Police were still flouting laws against illegal searches and wiretaps and courts were accepting the fruits of their lawlessness as evidence against its victims. "Dragnet" arrests were used to round up possible offenders, in hopes that interrogation would show who, if any, were guilty. Throughout, there was an absence of outrage in many communities that implied an acceptance of the proposition that justice is worth what the defendant can afford to pay.

Most of the criminal prosecutions in this country are conducted by state and local officials in their own courts, and they had been left by the Supreme Court to go their own ways, virtually untouched by the Federal Constitution, until shortly before World War II. Even then, the Supreme Court's concern with criminal law was very slight, so that when the Court began to move on the states in earnest in 1961, it came as a shock. *United States Law Week*, a publication that provides a rapid reporting service of Supreme Court decisions, reported five opinions for the 1938–1939 Supreme Court term under the index heading of Criminal Law. Three decades later, in the final year of the Warren Court, it reported twenty-six opinions under the expanded heading, Criminal Law and Procedure. The Supreme Court usually writes opinions in about 115 cases each term, so criminal law had come to consume almost one-fourth of the Supreme Court's efforts, with an inevitable impact on the nation's system of justice.

Under the circumstances, the Supreme Court might have been expected to tread lightly, spending its good will carefully in an effort to bring the crime-conscious country around to an acceptance of the new constitutional restrictions on its police officers' authority.

The Warren Court did nothing of the sort. It plunged ahead with its criminal revolution, bringing the state and local courts within the effective coverage of the Bill of Rights, and simultaneously tightening up its interpretations of several key provisions of the Bill of Rights so that they keep a tighter rein on the police. Contrary to the impression that this created, the Court did not invariably make things more difficult for the authorities and easier for defendants. In some respects, police were given more freedom to search, and they were provided a constitutional basis for using wiretap evidence in court. But the Supreme Court was influenced by three general principles in its efforts to reform the criminal process, and each was volatile and controversial enough to assure that the process as a whole would disturb law enforcement.

Basically, what the Court did was to refine the meaning of the due process requirement of the Constitution, which until then required only that states observe "fundamental fairness" in criminal matters. The Warren Court changed the due process requirement to demand absolute compliance by state and local police with the key provisions of the Bill of Rights. For a process that was accomplished in less than a decade, this could properly be called a "due process revolution," and it was inevitable that it would create much confusion—even if it did not, as Felix Frankfurter warned, "tear up by the roots much of the fabric of law in the several states."

In the process, the Warren Court reinterpreted some of the major provisions of the Bill of Rights, with emphasis on the privilege against self-incrimination and the right to counsel. Its purpose was to strengthen them as safeguards for the individual, but the rapid changes in meaning, added to their sudden application to the states, inspired the widespread complaint that the Court was "making" law, not "interpreting" it.

Finally, the Court infused the entire process with the egalitarian principles that dominated much of the thought of the Warren Court. For the most part this was long overdue, for the criminal justice system had frequently seemed to work properly only for those who could pay to make it work. But egalitarianism proved to be a slippery principle when applied to the Constitution's privilege against self-incrimination; the ability of strong-willed, well-lawyered suspects to muffle their shortcomings in protective silence seemed to call for affirmative efforts by the state to give less resourceful defendants the same protection. As Attorney General Nicholas deB. Katzenbach once put it, with a marked lack of enthusiasm, "if one can beat the rap, all must beat the rap."

On June 13, 1966, with the F.B.I.'s crime index pushing the top of the crime charts, and the second annual "long, hot summer" under way in the urban ghettos, the Supreme Court wrapped all three of these principles into a single remarkable package in the confessions decision known as *Miranda* v. *Arizona*.

This decision said that no statement made by a person being held by the police could be used in court unless the suspect had first been offered and had turned down the assistance of a lawyer —who, the Court conceded, would undoubtedly tell the suspect not to say anything. The decision has probably been praised and damned more than any other ruling since *Dred Scott*, which helped start a war. Its declaration that rich and poor alike are entitled to counsel during interrogation satisfied the highest standards of equality and fair treatment of criminal suspects. But in combining the three major principles of the due process revolution, it also provided a concise catalogue of the features of the Warren Court's criminal-law decision-making that had most rankled its critics: It saddled the police with what appeared to be drastic new restrictions, based upon a reinterpretation of constitutional provisions that had been on the books for most of the nation's history. It overturned well-established precedents by a vote of 5 to 4. It was frankly "legislative," containing a detailed code of post-arrest procedure, similar to a statute that a legislature might enact. It implied that local police, judges and juries would violate suspects' rights unless hemmed in by the Supreme Court. Finally, it appeared to undermine the truth-finding role of criminal courts in order to carry out the Supreme Court majority's concept of a social good. "The proposal that we must condition questioning on the presence of counsel is, in effect, really saying that there may be no effective, immediate questioning by the police," protested Judge Henry J. Friendly, one of the country's most respected Federal judges; "I submit that that is not a rule that society will long endure."

As it turned out, the *Miranda* decision has earned neither the initial accolades of its admirers nor the outrage of its critics. Liberals now grumble that most suspects waive their right to counsel and talk to the police, and some law enforcement officials say that the ruling has improved law enforcement by making the police rely more on "hard" evidence. But at the time, the announcement of the *Miranda* decision was a critical turning point in the Supreme Court's campaign to reform criminal justice.

Prior to *Miranda*, the Court's outpouring of criminal law decisions was so complex that even many lawyers could not say with confidence if the Court was to be blamed or praised. In

1964 Barry Goldwater had failed to strike a spark with campaign speeches deploring "violence in our streets." But the announcement of *Miranda* v. *Arizona* in 1966 provided an example of the due process revolution that a critic of the Supreme Court could get his teeth into. Senator John L. McClellan, an old-fashioned law-and-order advocate, later delivered an arm-waving, table-thumping oration in the Senate on behalf of his bill to revoke *Miranda* and return to the previous "voluntariness" test for confessions. It gave some idea of the emotional head of steam that a critic of the Supreme Court could generate, contemplating *Miranda* v. *Arizona*:

> I know good men and honest men can disagree, but I say to the Senate, and no man here will dispute this, that the answer is, if this confessions provision is defeated, the lawbreaker will be the beneficiary, and he will be further encouraged and reassured that he can continue a life of crime and depredations profitably with impunity and without punishment. If it is defeated, the protection of society and the safety of good people—of the innocent throughout the land, your constituents and mine—will be placed in ever-increasing peril as the crime rate continues to spiral onward and upward to intolerable heights of danger.
>
> Yes, Mr. President, if this effort to deal with these erroneous Court decisions is defeated, every gangster and overlord of the underworld; every syndicate chief, racketeer, captain, lieutenant, sergeant, private, punk, and hoodlum in organized crime; every murderer, rapist, robber, burglar, arsonist, thief, and con man will have cause to rejoice and celebrate.
>
> Whereas, if it is defeated, the safety of decent people will be placed in greater jeopardy and every innocent, law-abiding, and God-fearing citizen in this land will have cause to weep and despair.
>
> You tell me it is not a law-enforcement measure? Our Government operated under it, and the courts operated under it, from the time of the founding of this Republic to the Miranda decision.

In 1965 the Gallup Poll had found that 48 percent of the public believed that the courts were too lenient with criminal defendants. Three years later, in 1968, 63 percent felt that way, and two persons out of three thought the Supreme Court had made a mistake in restricting the police in questioning suspects and obtaining confessions. The Supreme Court's trumpet call for justice had been heard as a call for permissiveness in dealing with criminals, and *Miranda* v. *Arizona* became the cutting edge of a political thrust against the Warren Court.

The Supreme Court continued to decide more cases for criminal defendants than for the prosecution, but a series of political developments on the outside left no doubt that the due process revolution had peaked with *Miranda* v. *Arizona.* In 1968 Congress voted overwhelmingly to include in the Omnibus Crime Control Act a provision that purported to reverse *Miranda* in the Federal courts. Abe Fortas was denied confirmation as Chief Justice, with the critics of the criminal law decisions leading the way. Richard Nixon won the Presidency after promising to appoint Justices to retract *Miranda* and other decisions. Finally, Earl Warren was replaced, upon his retirement, with Warren E. Burger, a judge who had criticized much that the due process revolution had produced.

Whether the Court's decisions as a whole merited this public rejection—that is, what the rulings actually did and why they were made—is the subject matter of much of this book. But how the Warren Court came to risk a self-inflicted wound as it did under such unpromising circumstances merits a close look at the start. For it throws a revealing light on the powerful forces that tend to press the Supreme Court toward the hazardous business of attempting to police the police, and it suggests the conflicts that may remain in store if the nation's judges are left to carry that responsibility alone.

II

The Politics of Crime

*If you walk out of this hotel tonight and some-
one knocks you on the head, he'll be out of jail
before you're out of the hospital, and on Monday
morning, they'll try the policeman instead of the
criminal.*

GEORGE C. WALLACE

If legal folklore has a more honored axiom than that judges
follow the election returns, it is that proposals for fairer court
procedures are certain to be met with cries of alarm about rising crime. King Charles I warned Parliament that the Monarchy
would crumble if Parliament insisted on demanding that "no free
man be detained in prison without cause shown." (Parliament did
so anyway.) William Howard Taft was so concerned over the
increase in the number of defendants' peremptory challenges in
jury selection that he predicted that lynchings and murder "will
increase unless the criminal laws are enforced with more cer-

tainty, more uniformity, more severity than they now are." When the governing fathers of New York State considered—briefly— in 1938 a proposal to suppress from trials any evidence obtained by illegal searches or wiretaps, a member of the constitutional convention prophesied that "from far and wide all the racketeers and murderers and embezzlers will collect into the City of New York to celebrate this famous victory of the forces of evil, so that they can be protected by the Constitution of the State of New York."

So the Supreme Court could hardly be faulted if it went about its criminal law reform, to all appearances oblivious to the steady rise of the F.B.I.'s crime index. The F.B.I.'s statistics had a bad name among liberals anyway, because the figures had frequently appeared to exaggerate crime needlessly. But about the time of the *Miranda* decision in 1966, the evidence became convincing enough to persuade most of the leading criminologists that the crime index rise represented far more than just J. Edgar Hoover crying "wolf."

During the period of the Warren Court's most active criminal law reform—from 1960 to 1968—the annual number of reported murders increased by 52 percent; reported rape rose 84 percent; robbery, 144 percent; aggravated assault, 86 percent. By the middle of the decade, the murder rate in the United States was twice that of our nearest competitor—Finland—and ranged from four to twelve times that of a dozen other "advanced" countries, including Japan, Canada, England and Norway. For other violent crimes, the picture was about the same, or worse. Rape was twelve times as prevalent in the United States as in England and Wales; the robbery rate was nine times as great, and aggravated assault was twice as frequent.

These were statistics of reported crimes, and the experts warned that they were treacherous. Yet even the experts who questioned the accuracy of the F.B.I.'s statistics had ceased to deny that crime was in fact rising rapidly, and as the index continued to climb, crime replaced communism as the hobgoblin of American politics.

In 1968 alone there were five separate Congressional investigations of various aspects of crime. There were not enough crime-fighting subcommittees to go around, and crime investigations were conducted by such unlikely units as the House Post Office and Civil Service Committee's Subcommittee on Census and Statistics, the House Government Operations Committee's Subcommittee on Legal and Monetary Affairs, and the Senate Select Committee on Small Business. Altogether, various subcommittees held 49 days of crime hearings in that session of Congress, published the results in 3,919 pages of prose, and enshrined about 23,000 new statutory words on crime in the United States Code.

With the crime issue packing so much political clout, it was inevitable that a venerable law of politics would assert itself: That if a situation stays bad enough long enough, it can ultimately be blamed on somebody. In 1968, the members of Congress had only to look across the street, at the Supreme Court.

If any proof was needed that the time had finally come when courts ignored alarums about crime at their peril, it came that spring, when the Senate voted on the Omnibus Crime Control Bill. When it came time to take up the heavy-handed set of proposals designed to reverse *Miranda* v. *Arizona* and a few other decisions and to strip the Supreme Court of much of its criminal jurisdiction, Senator McClellan propped up in the rear of the Senate chamber a huge facsimile of the F.B.I.'s crime graph. The titles of key Supreme Court decisions were marked at the peaks along the rising line, to show the embarrassing parallel between Supreme Court activity on behalf of defendants and the crime rise. As the Senators debated the bill, the graph loomed over their shoulders. Senator McClellan let it speak for itself until the last few minutes before the vote. Then he swung around, shook his fist at the chart, and bellowed: "The Supreme Court has set a low tone in law enforcement, and we are reaping the whirlwind today! Look at that chart! Look at it and weep for your country—crime spiraling upward and upward and upward. Apparently nobody is willing to put on the brakes."

The vote to include the anti-Supreme Court section in the crime bill carried, 51 to 31.

As if it were not unfortunate enough, from the Supreme Court's viewpoint, to have a revolution in defendants' rights coincide with a crime scare, both developments are complicated further by their subtle connection with the problem of the Negro. The Supreme Court was drawn into reforming the criminal law when it set out to give Negroes equal rights before the civil laws and was faced with the absurdity of leaving them with no effective constitutional rights before the criminal law. Having outlawed Jim Crow, the Court had to humble John Law. Many of its landmark decisions on behalf of criminal defendants involved Negroes, often after they had been caught up in that ultimate of racial trials, a prosecution for raping a white woman.

Thus it was apparent that a moving force behind the Supreme Court's efforts to safeguard criminal suspects was its commitment to protect the rights of Negroes. Abe Fortas once expressed the relationship between the civil rights revolution and the Supreme Court's refinement of the criminal law as a parallel process, part of an overall effort by society to civilize itself. "I believe," he said, "that if you think of the developments in the racial field, you will see a parallel which similarly, in my opinion, indicates that in the past generation, we as a people have been moving forward towards a better, a greater and a nobler conception of the rights of man, and I think *Gideon* is part of that movement." The case of *Gideon* v. *Wainwright*, which he saw as part of a broad civil rights movement, was a criminal law ruling that required states to furnish counsel to indigent defendants in the trial of all serious criminal offenses.

Whether it was intentional or not, the Supreme Court emerged from this process with a strong pro-Negro image. It was no coincidence that the Reverend Fred L. Shuttlesworth, a lieutenant of Dr. Martin Luther King, Jr., became the all-time record holder for successful Supreme Court appeals. Rev. Shuttlesworth has appealed to the Supreme Court seven convictions arising out of civil rights activities. The Justices have reversed six of them.

There is considerable irony in this, because "crime" has come to mean "Negro" to many whites, and the willingness of people to be disturbed by the crime index reflects a widespread fear of Negro lawlessness. Some of this fear is justified. The national arrest rate among Negroes is already five times that of white people, and for violent crimes the ratio is much higher—as much as ten times higher for some crimes. These national figures actually underplay the seriousness of the situation in the cities, where the crime-in-the-streets issue got its name. There, the arrest rate for Negroes is ten times that of whites for assault, eleven times greater for rape, sixteen times greater for robbery and seventeen times greater for homicide. For a bleak insight into the future, the statistics for teen-age offenders show that the Negroes' ratios are much, much higher still. Studies show that most of this crime is directed at other Negroes. But they also reveal a trend that has not been lost on white people—that the frequency of crimes by Negroes against whites seems to be increasing, and the level of violence in Negro crimes against whites also seems to be turning up.

The average white person may have no knowledge of the figures, but he knows the potentialities of Negro violence because they have been brought out into the open in the form of ghetto riots. In 1967 there were disturbances that could be characterized as Negro riots in 75 cities, leaving a total of $664.5 million lost in fire, theft and pillage and 84 persons dead. Since then the incidence of large-scale Negro riots has declined, but the Negro arrest rate has not and many Americans appear to have begun to doubt if the police, working within the traditional framework of rights, can deal with Negro lawlessness.

Neither of these factors—the rising violent crime or the Negro unrest—were visible when the Supreme Court began its criminal law revolution in 1961, although both were very much in view when the Court handed down *Miranda* v. *Arizona* in 1966. By then it was clear that the public reaction to both was shaping into a powerful force, and that those who wished to lay responsibility for it at the Supreme Court's door were being heard.

"We mollycoddle young criminals and release unreformed hoodlums to prey anew on society. The bleeding hearts, particularly among the judiciary, are so concerned for young criminals that they become indifferent to the rights of law-abiding citizens." This statement in 1964 by J. Edgar Hoover, director of the F.B.I., reflected the tone of much of the criticism of the Court. To its critics, the Justices were taking the side of the forces of evil, to the peril of the good people. "What the Supreme Court is doing," former New York City police chief Michael J. Murphy used to say to the delight of enforcement-minded audiences, "is akin to requiring one boxer to fight by Marquis of Queensbury rules while permitting the other to butt, gouge and bite."

It could not have been beyond the imagination of the Justices that a candidate for President would say, as Richard Nixon did in 1968:

A cab driver has been brutally murdered and the man that confessed the crime was let off because of a Supreme Court decision. An old woman had been murdered and robbed brutally, and the man who confessed the crime was let off because of a Supreme Court decision. And an old man had been beaten and clubbed to death, and the man who committed the crime was let off when he was on a spending spree in Las Vegas after he confessed, because of a Supreme Court decision.

And I say, my friends, that some of our courts and their decisions in the light of that record have gone too far in weakening the peace forces as against the criminal forces in this country.

Those who defended the Court found themselves leaning on the wobbly crutches of logic and psychology while the treadmill of crime and racial disorders accelerated. Not surprisingly, they made considerable sense but little impact on public opinion. "Court rules do not cause crime," insisted Ramsey Clark, the most outspoken defender of the Supreme Court. "People do not commit crime because they know they cannot be questioned by police before presentment, or even because they feel they will not be convicted. In the long run, only the elimination of the causes of crime can make a significant and lasting difference in the incidence of crime." He ended his tenure as Attorney General as a whipping boy of the Republicans and a lesson to future administrations that Attorneys General cannot appear to be soft on criminals. His father, Justice Tom Clark, argued ᵗhat "to say that a bank robber reads our cases before he robs the bank, in order to develop a loophole to his conviction, is ridiculous." But this was said after he retired from the Supreme Court, where he had been one of the most frequent and indignant dissenters against court decisions that curb law enforcement. Former Attorney General Nicholas deB. Katzenbach, the chairman of the National Crime Commission, concluded at the end of his group's eighteen-month study that fighting crime by reversing liberal court decisions "would be like putting a band-aid on a cancer." But seven members of his Commission were so distressed at the trend of the Supreme Court's rulings that they filed a separate

statement, asking "whether some of these rights have been interpreted and enlarged by Court decisions to the point where they
now seriously affect the delicate balance between the rights of
the individual and those of society. Or, putting the question differently, whether the scales have tilted in favor of the accused
and against law enforcement and the public further than the best
interest of the country permits."

Many of those who looked askance at the due process revolution seemed to see the fault in intensely personal terms. To them
the five liberal Justices of the Warren Court appeared to be
afflicted with a sort of judicial nymphomania, a compulsion to
bestow the favors of justice too freely, which the critics saw as a
weakness of liberal thinking. Senator McClellan delighted in
reeling off the distinguished names among the twenty-eight Justices whom he said had rejected the *Miranda* thesis in past decisions, before the five liberals on the Warren Court finally decided
otherwise. Richard Nixon campaigned on the premise that if the
next President were to name "strict constructionists" to replace
the aging liberals, then law enforcement would get back on the
track.

Personalities did shape the Court's actions in reforming the
criminal law, but strong constitutional currents also pulled the
Supreme Court toward the rigid rules of police procedure that
finally turned the country against the Court.

The essence of the due process revolution was an attempt by
the Supreme Court to reform American justice—and particularly,
to police the police of the nation—by imposing rigid constitutional rules from the top and requiring that they be followed in
all cases. It replaced an earlier approach that had given state
and local officials wide discretion to follow their own procedures, so long as the overall results were fair and just. It was not
altogether accidental that the switch came during a brief era of
immense national faith in the capacity of enlightened and powerful men—especially in Washington—to accomplish reform. By
the end of the decade, many thoughtful reformers were advo-
cating decentralization of power and local control, but in 1961
the New Frontier of President John F. Kennedy had undertaken
to put into effect the prevailing liberal view that the ills of the
country could best be redressed by able men wielding power in

Washington. President Kennedy had given the Warren Court its five-man liberal majority when he appointed Arthur J. Goldberg from his Cabinet in 1962. The others who made up the "Warren majority" were also well attuned by background to the prevailing faith in the power of strong men in high office to do good. Earl Warren had been a reform Governor of California. Justices Hugo L. Black, William O. Douglas and Abe Fortas (who later replaced Goldberg) were graduates of the New Deal. William J. Brennan, Jr., was the son of a Democratic party stalwart in New Jersey. The idea that the Supreme Court and the inferior Federal courts could police the police of the entire country had never before been tested, but to these activists, gaining a majority on the Supreme Court at a time of high activity and idealism in Washington, it may well have seemed unquestionable that the police could be controlled by the courts, if the Supreme Court had the courage and determination to demand it.

Furthermore, the Supreme Court's doctrines had been inching toward that course for many years. As written, the Bill of Rights shielded people only from oppression by Federal officials. But long before Earl Warren's day the Supreme Court had held that some of the guarantees were so fundamental—freedom of press, speech and religion were obvious ones—that state officials were required to respect them also. In its effort to standardize and upgrade justice at the local level, the Warren Court simply extended this "fundamental" list to apply to the states most of the provisions of the Bill of Rights that regulate the conduct of criminal justice.

The importance of this was that most of the provisions of the Bill of Rights were written as absolute limitations on official conduct. This meant that when they were made binding on the states, they had to be obeyed in every case, regardless of the circumstances. When the provisions governed the in-court procedures of criminal trials, this absolutism proved to be a boon to the state and local officials because it told them exactly what was required by the Constitution. Once they knew that defendants must have lawyers in all felony cases, that juries must be granted in all but petty cases, that defendants must be permitted to confront their accusers at trials, it was not difficult to comply with those requirements.

If the Justices saw any differences between the effect of re-quiring absolute, unvarying compliance with the Bill of Rights' provisions as they applied to in-court procedures, and the exten-sion of similar inflexible rules to cover the fluid, unpredictable world of police investigation, they did not discuss them in public. But events showed that while absolute rules were tolerable in the well-rehearsed rituals of courtrooms, whenever they were extended to cover in-the-field operations of the police, serious problems developed.

One of the details that had been overlooked by the framers of the Bill of Rights was what should be done when the police overstepped. Because the prohibitions were absolute, it was dif-ficult for courts to shrug off violations by the police and to rule that the evidence could be used anyway against the victim of the unconstitutional act. That would permit the state to profit from its own unlawful conduct. Furthermore, a strong policy argument could be made for suppressing evidence obtained by means that violated the Bill of Rights—that an absolute rule forbidding the use of unconstitutionally obtained evidence would tend to deter the police from lawless actions. The Supreme Court had adopted this rule as far back as 1914 with regard to illegal searches and seizures, but had applied it only to the tiny percent-age of criminal cases prosecuted by the Federal Government. Several state supreme courts had done the same regarding illegal searches. But for the supreme court of a nation to undertake to police every officer in the country by laying down a series of rigid procedures for criminal investigation and declaring invalid any evidence obtained in violation of them, was something that had never occurred before.

The Warren Court became the first national supreme court to try. It was strongly influenced by the absolute nature of the Bill of Rights and its own members' confidence in the power of the national government to reform the grass roots. But sprinkled throughout its opinions is a suggestion that another factor might have been equally important: that all other attempts to police the police had failed, and that the Court would not leave the people without effective recourse against police lawlessness. So the Warren Court developed a rule that any breach by a state or local law-enforcement official of key provisions of the Bill of Rights served to bar from evidence any information

obtained by means of the violation. This "exclusionary rule" became the heart of the Warren Court's efforts to reform law enforcement—and ultimately the reason for the charge that the
Supreme Court was "coddling criminals" and "handcuffing the
police."

The Supreme Court could have been under no illusions that
its use of the exclusionary rule could pass without vehement
opposition. To be an effective deterrent, it had to be applied in
every case—no matter how seemingly unintentional or minor the
constitutional violation, or how important the evidence or heinous the crime at issue. Ultimately, the Supreme Court was to employ the exclusionary rule to enforce its procedures governing
four typical law enforcement situations: arrests, searches (including illegal eavesdropping), interrogations and lineups. This meant
that the Court would be vulnerable to outrage from communities across the country, where its exclusionary rule might require
the dismissal of prosecutions against notorious defendants.

Two courts had gotten ahead of the Supreme Court in using
the exclusionary rule, and both had been badly burned because
of it.

The United States Court of Appeals for the District of Columbia demonstrated the possibilities when it gave an expansive
interpretation to the Supreme Court's 1957 ruling that Federal
courts could not accept confessions obtained by police during
unreasonable delays between arrest and arraignment.

The case that probably made more Congressional blood boil
than any other concerned James W. Killough, who was picked
up by the District of Columbia police on October 18, 1960, after
the blood-spattered car belonging to his wife was found. Killough was questioned for about two hours that night, and after
questioning resumed the next day, he confessed that he had
choked her to death "in a fit of rage" because she had been seeing another man. He then took the police to the dump where
he had hidden his wife's body, and later gave a written statement
about the crime. When he was finally arraigned before a U.S.
Commissioner and advised of his right not to make a statement,
he had been in custody for more than thirty hours. The following day he confessed the murder again to the police intern who
conducted his "classification interview," and later in the day he
went over the crime again in detail with a detective.

At his trial the first confession was excluded because of the delay between arrest and arraignment. But the second-day confession to the detective was admitted, and Killough was found guilty of manslaughter. The Court of Appeals reversed the conviction, holding that the second confession was obtained as a direct result of the tainted one. Killough was tried again and convicted again, this time on the intern's report of his confession. Again the Court of Appeals threw out the confession and the conviction, holding that nothing said at a classification interview should be used against the interviewee in court. Since there was no evidence left to connect Killough to the corpse of his wife whom he admittedly killed, he was set free. Over the years so much Congressional bile flowed over the mere mention of the "Killough case" that attitudes toward restrictions on police interrogation were soured long before the Supreme Court got seriously into the act.

The Supreme Court of California found itself in similar straits after it anticipated the drift of the Supreme Court's confessions doctrine and issued a *Miranda*-type decision more than a year before the Supreme Court did. The California court's troubles had actually begun on an August afternoon in 1963, when Fausto Edward Flores sat in his cell in the Los Angeles jail and discussed murder with his cellmate, a man named Miranda.

"I tried to smother her with the towel," Flores explained; "and then she said 'I—I—I—Sonny, I can't breathe. You're trying to kill me. Scream—I'll scream.' I told her, 'Shut up.' "

"She quit screaming, huh?"

"Shut up, shut up. She shut up, the bitch. She no longer made a fuss. She shut up. She was shut down."

There was more, but this in itself was enough to prove that Flores, who had denied to the police any part in the murder of his sixteen-year-old mistress, was indeed guilty of murder. But the police did not have enough evidence to convict Flores and he knew it. He was in a relaxed and talkative mood; he knew they would soon have to let him go free.

It happened, though, that the police did have enough evidence —Miranda was a police agent. The cell was bugged. A jury heard the tapes of the cellblock conversations and even though there was little other evidence against him, found Flores guilty of murder in the first degree.

The friendly-cellmate ploy had been used so often that a seasoned jailhouse veteran like Flores should have suspected and
should have been on guard. But where confessions obtained by
trick had always before been accepted as valid evidence, on the
ground that an uncoerced confession was about as reliable as
evidence could be, Flores' confession was thrown out in 1965
when his case reached the California Court of Criminal Appeals.
It was held that it violated the state Supreme Court's confessions
ban and the United States Supreme Court's then-embryonic
rule against police interrogation outside the presence of legal
counsel. Flores' conviction was overturned, and the murder
charge against him was dropped for lack of evidence. Six similar
dismissals of charges against self-confessed killers followed, generating so much public indignation that a campaign to deny re-
election to Chief Justice Roger J. Traynor almost succeeded at
the next election.

So the Supreme Court had ample notice, when it announced
its *Miranda* decision, that the public reaction could be extreme.
"In truth," says Robert G. McCloskey, a perceptive observer of
the modern Court, "the Supreme Court has seldom, if ever, flatly
and for very long resisted a really unmistakable wave of public
sentiment." That it chose to take the risk of doing so on the subject of confessions was undoubtedly the crucial decision of the
due process revolution. It crystallized the opposition to the
Court's criminal rulings, produced a quick string of public re-
bukes to the liberal wing, and demonstrated that the Supreme
Court is more vulnerable to political reprisal than even its enemies had realized.

Whether the Court paid too dearly to make its point on confessions is more than an academic question, for the reaction
against it may affect events for many years to come. Surprisingly
few suspects have asked for lawyers' assistance, and many have
given incriminating statements to the police. Yet the shock effect of *Miranda* on the police, and its overall tone of repugnance
toward confessions, may have accomplished much that the legal
formula did not. Police reliance upon lengthy incommunicado
interrogation appears to have diminished in many communities.
Prosecutors' reliance on the confession as the keystone of the
typical case seems on the way out.

One irony of the Supreme Court's hard line on confessions is that during the same period the Justices were being less than militant about other constitutional values that could arguably be said to be more relevant to the present time. The Court's concern with confessions dated back to the 1930s, when a succession of men who had been beaten and bullied into signing confessions appealed to the Court and shocked the legal profession into a realization that the criminal justice dished out in many communities was based on brutal methods of wringing confessions out of unfortunate suspects. These famous "third degree" cases convinced a generation of thoughtful lawyers that the first goal of justice must be to outlaw the rubber hose. Eventually this produced a Supreme Court majority so suspicious of police interrogation that it was willing to take great risks to curb it.

But by the time the Court moved in the 1960s to restrict police questioning, it was dealing with a problem that was already fading into the past. As Chief Justice Earl Warren acknowledged in the *Miranda* opinion, physical brutality had already virtually disappeared and had been supplanted by psychological tactics. These ranged from the unsavory to the respectable, but the Court condemned them all as inherently coercive when used by the police against arrested suspects—a conclusion that Congress was quick to contradict.

Yet the threat to individual liberties in the second half of the twentieth century may well be Big Brother and not the third degree. The horror of George Orwell's *1984* was the pervasive fear that Big Brother's government was always watching—even though the police of *1984* were capable of using force to obtain admissions · nd did, in the end, resort to a physical atrocity to coerce a confession. If government surveillance rather than backroom interrogation is the threat of the future, then the Supreme Court committed the bulk of its prestige and attention to a battle against the wrong evils of the police state. For while the public furor raged over *Miranda*, the Court handed down a series of decisions that enshrined the system of government informers in the constitutional system, broadened the authority of police to search for evidence, and laid the groundwork for the constitutional use by police of bugging and wiretapping.

The Supreme Court has never conceded that it intentionally compensates for a tough decision on one point by handing down a soft ruling on another, but its actions occasionally give that impression, and it was openly suggested that this should be done to cushion the impact of the *Miranda* ruling. The next important issue to come before the Court after *Miranda* concerned the constitutionality of the widespread use of government informers and police agents to deal with consentual crimes such as bribery narcotics traffic, gambling and espionage.

This informer system had been under a constitutional cloud as a result of rulings that had strengthened the privilege against self-incrimination, the guarantee against unreasonable searches and the right of privacy. Many lawyers had thought that when the Supreme Court finally dealt with the question of informers and agents, it would clamp down sharply on their use by police.

The matter came to the Court in the form of three appeals— one by Teamster President James R. Hoffa, convicted with the aid of a government "spy" of bribing jurors; his lawyer, Z. T. Osborn, Jr., found guilty, through the use of a government agent "wired for sound," of attempting to bribe the jury in Hoffa's jury-bribing trial; and Duke Lee Lewis, a Boston dope peddler who had admitted a narcotics squad detective into his home and sold him drugs in the belief that he was an addict. The informer system was the most important police investigative technique to come before the Supreme Court since the confessions curb, and the law-enforcement world was watching to see if the decision would reveal a knee-jerk antipathy to the police. Holding its nose over the use of informants, but citing the importance of their work to law enforcement, the Supreme Court upheld the three convictions and created a judicial climate that is certain to encourage the use of government informers and agents in the years to come.

At about the same time, Judge J. Edward Lumbard, chief judge of the United States Court of Appeals for the Second Circuit and chairman of the American Bar Association's highly regarded special Committee on Minimum Standards for Administration of Criminal Justice began to argue in speeches and Congressional testimony that police wiretapping should be legalized in order to compensate for the strictures placed on the police by *Miranda*. Whether such considerations played any part is unknowable, but in a 1967 decision, *Katz* v. *United States*,

the Supreme Court gave a sign that it would uphold such a law—
and within six months Congress had passed it.

Whether or not the Warren Court consciously leaned harder
on the police when the rights of poor, black suspects were at
stake, the fact was that the Court's indignation quotient over
police activities tended to subside when it was organized crime
that was being policed. Some of the practices that the Warren
Court struck down seemed pale when compared to wiretapping and police spying—techniques best adapted to police efforts
against organized crime. The Warren Court kept its powder dry
to deal with police threats to the poor and unprotected; it
seemed to go out of its way to uphold techniques used by the
police against organized crime.

Finally, in the two years following the *Miranda* ruling, the
Court backpedaled in the area of constitutional limitations on
police searches. In *McCray* v. *Illinois* it authorized police to
search individuals on the basis of purported tips from anonymous
informers. In *Warden* v. *Hayden* the Court dropped its half-
century-old "mere evidence" rule that had permitted searches
only for the purpose of recovering instrumentalities and fruits of
crimes and not merely to get evidence. In the "stop and frisk"
decision of 1968 the Court opened a gap in the Fourth Amendment's restrictions against unreasonable searches, by authorizing
the police to stop persons on suspicion and frisk them for weapons.

These decisions were commended by some lawyers, and condemned by others. But the fact remained that the right of citizens
against unreasonable searches had been substantially reduced
under the stress of the backlash from *Miranda*, and the average
individual might well wonder if he had not lost ground as a result.

A final irony of the due process revolution did not come into
focus until the Court reached the stop-and-frisk question. The
irony was that for all of its potential to cast the Supreme Court
in a bad light, the exclusionary rule could not effectively police
the police. Often the police managed to ignore, bend or violate
the rules and obtain convictions anyway. Increasingly they did
not care—when dealing with lawlessness in city slums, they were
frequently content to disarm and harass rather than convict. Having paid such a high price in its efforts to make the exclusionary

rules tough and rigid enough to keep the nation's police in line, the Court struck an almost poignant note when it conceded in the stop-and-frisk opinion that "the exclusionary rule has its limitations . . . as a tool of judicial control" and could not be applied to shield citizens from police "frisking" on the streets.

This meant that unless some other force emerged to police the police, the Supreme Court could well be faced with the same problem again in the future. Next time, another, more effective technique than the exclusionary rule would have to be employed to police the police, and the battle over "coddling criminals" and "handcuffing the police" would have to be fought out again.

III

The Due Process Revolution

*While unconstitutional exercise of power by the
executive and legislative branches of the government is subject to judicial restraint, the only
check upon our own exercise of power is our own
sense of self-restraint.*

HARLAN FISKE STONE

Most Americans had never heard of the term "wheeler-dealer"
until 1962, when a Texas preacher named Billie Sol Estes was
discovered overselling his stock of soybean fertilizer tanks to his
friends and neighbors in West Texas. Very few Americans had
ever seen an actual criminal trial on television, either, because
only two states permitted television coverage of trials. But it
happened that Texas was one of the states that did (Colorado
was the other), and since Estes' Texas-modern style of dishonesty
intrigued people in other sections of the country, his trial became
the most widely televised criminal prosecution in American history.

Being on television tends to make people overdo whatever role earned them their moment of pervasive attention. The mere appearance of lights, cameras, cameramen, commentators and other television paraphernalia has been known to turn a stolid picket line into a fist-shaking tantrum and an urban incident into a riot. So Estes' lawyer, seeing the same electronic accouterments crammed into the courtroom in Tyler, Texas, cried "foul." His client stood accused of being a uniquely rascally wheeler-dealer, charges that could only gain currency with the jury by the daily presence of the men and equipment from the networks. Even though Texas court rules permitted television coverage of trials, he insisted that the cameras' presence violated Estes' right to due process of law, as guaranteed by the Fourteenth Amendment to the United States Constitution.

Obviously irked, Texas state judge Otis T. Dunagan snapped:

> This case is not being tried under the Federal Constitution. This defendant has been brought into this court under state laws, under the State Constitution. . . .
>
> I took an oath to uphold this constitution; not the Federal Constitution but the state constitution; and I am going to do my best to do that as long as I preside on this court.

He ruled that the cameras could stay.

Even if hindsight did not show that Judge Dunagan had committed an historic legal boner (the Supreme Court reversed him so decisively that the opinion virtually banished television from American jurisprudence), the Tyler incident would stand as a classic illustration of why the Supreme Court has felt compelled over the past decade to carry out a due process revolution —and why its impact on the nation's criminal laws has been so great.

The fact was that a convincing argument could be made that Estes could not get a fair trial with television in that Texas courtroom; that the jurors could not be expected to bask each day in the attention of television coverage and not be impressed with the District Attorney's blandishments that a West Texas boy had become the Barnum of corporate flimflam. Yet assuming that television coverage made the difference between a fair and unfair trial, Estes was being made to suffer because of a legal accident that had nothing to do with his offense. Since only two states permitted television coverage of criminal trials, he was being denied a fair trial by the accident of state lines, an intolerable circumstance in a nation so shrunken by modern communications that its television watchers could follow the day-to-day proceedings in an out-of-the-way Texas courthouse.

There was no public outcry in 1965 when the Supreme Court reversed the conviction and ruled that this use of courtroom television violated the United States Constitution. Few states were affected, and the new rule did not make it more difficult to enforce the law or convict the guilty. But Judge Dunagan's testy rejection of Estes' constitutional claim demonstrated the deep-seated belief of many state judges that their states' procedures were the last word in criminal law, and that the United States Supreme Court had no legitimate power to interfere.

As recently as four years earlier this would have been true, with minor exceptions that did not make much difference in practice. But in 1961, in the case of *Mapp* v. *Ohio*, the Supreme Court had ruled that the states could no longer use evidence obtained in violation of the Fourth Amendment's prohibition against unreasonable searches and seizures, and in so doing had signaled the beginning of a due process revolution that was to transform the rules of state law enforcement and criminal procedure and provoke the current protest that the Supreme Court is coddling criminals and handcuffing the police.

Never before had a country's judiciary undertaken to change the law as drastically as the United States Supreme Court did during this period. As Erwin N. Griswold, then one of the Court's most effective defenders, wryly put it in 1965, "some things have recently been found in the Federal Constitution that were not previously known to be there." In any country, adjusting to such sweeping changes would have been an awkward process. But in the United States a unique system of legal diversity made the Court's change of direction as painful as turning around in a briar patch.

American justice is administered in two layers, in the Federal courts and in the state judicial systems. The Federal courts handle a thin crust of relatively specialized offenses, most of which involve Selective Service violations, criminal activity across state lines or narcotics offenses. Even prior to its current activism the

Supreme Court had settled all questions of procedure or evidence in these prosecutions not set by statute. This was done as part of its general supervisory power over the Federal courts, based upon the guidelines laid down in the Bill of Rights. Thus, long before the Supreme Court entered its present expansive phase in criminal law it had already developed a model of how a well-ordered system of justice should be run.

The vast majority of crimes are dealt with by the states, which have the responsibility for maintaining public order and preserving the security of persons, property and normal commercial transactions. This is done in the "state courts," an umbrella term used to denote the kaleidoscopic court arrangements that operate under the authority of the various state constitutions, and actually serve as local courts. They include the county courts, municipal courts, traffic courts, juvenile courts, and justices of the peace, which enforce the laws passed by the state legislatures, county boards and city councils.

Statistics on criminal trials are almost nonexistent in this country, but the Federal Bureau of Investigation estimates that some 7.3 million people are arrested each year for nontraffic offenses. Since only 30,714 criminal cases were commenced in the Federal system in a recent year, upwards of 99.6 percent of the criminal cases in the country are handled by the states. Outside of the District of Columbia, where all of the courts are Federal courts, and with the exception of the many interstate auto theft cases and narcotics trials that are handled in the United States courts, Federal cases tend to involve tidy white-collar offenses that represent considerable chicanery but very little street crime. The states' 99.6 percent of the offenses include almost all the rapes, murders, muggings and other forms of violence. To some extent, what the Supreme Court has done is to superimpose on these courts and police the restrictions and exclusionary rules that it had previously developed in dealing with its relatively tame .4 percent of the offenses.

The cries of "handcuffing the police" often boil down to the protest that these methods are too legalistic to deal with the hurly-burly of big-city crime. Rules designed to be enforced by law school-trained agents of the Federal Bureau of Investigation in pursuit of errant bank clerks—where the emphasis is likely to be on durable, documentary evidence—are said to tie the hands of the urban cops who must often deal with messy crimes that have to be proved, if at all, through questioning of witnesses and searches of suspects.

Revolutions have a way of modifying form more than substance and of generating more outcry than change, and this one is already showing signs of accommodation to old realities. But it has been carried out in a remarkably short period of time and has attempted no less than the elimination of the laissez-faire arrangement that the states had felt to be the necessary concomitant of their primary responsibility for keeping the peace.

The idea that states were sovereign in matters of law enforcement and criminal justice died hard because it had gone virtually unchallenged since the nation was founded. The Constitution as drafted in 1787 delegated a number of specific powers to the Federal government, but the power to safeguard individuals from unjust state law enforcement was not one of them. Under the constitutional scheme any powers not specifically delegated to the national government could not be exercised by it, and the framers emphasized their understanding that this power had not been given to the Federal government when they added the Bill of Rights that prohibited specific oppressive police action by the Federal government, but did not mention the states.

Chief Justice John Marshall never blushed to stretch the power of the Federal government and the Supreme Court, but even he unequivocally refused when asked in 1833 to rule that state justice was subject to Federal constitutional limitations. In *Barron v. Baltimore* he rejected the assertion "that the Constitution was intended to secure the people of the several states against the undue exercise of power by their respective state governments." As for the contention that the Bill of Rights restricted state as well as Federal action, he answered: "Had the framers of these amendments intended them to be limitations on the powers of state governments, they would have imitated the framers of the original Constitution, and have expressed that intention. . . . These amendments demanded security against the apprehended encroachments of the general government—not against those of the local governments."

This left state officials free to enforce the law as they pleased.

If individual rights were trampled in the process, only the states, and not the Supreme Court or any other arm of the Federal government, could interfere. In theory, this arrangement had much to recommend it, so long as the country remained a sprawling aggregation of relatively isolated communities. The problems of criminal suspects' rights are ultimately exercises in balancing the freedom of the individual against the needs of law enforcement, and the local communities whose security and liberty were at stake could best judge the methods necessary to achieve a proper balance.

The theory foundered, as American principles so often have, over the problem of the Negro. After the Civil War the rest of the nation realized that the Southern states could not be trusted to deal fairly with the newly-freed slaves, so the Fourteenth Amendment was added to the Constitution. It declared that:

No State shall make or enforce any law which shall abridge the privileges or immunities of citizens of the United States; nor shall any State deprive any person of life, liberty, or property without due process of law; nor deny to any person within its jurisdiction the equal protection of the laws.

With the adoption of the "privileges and immunities" clause the claim was immediately made that legal laissez-faire had been eliminated; that the Supreme Court could now supervise local law enforcement to see that individuals' basic rights—at least those set forth in the Bill of Rights—were not violated by state officials.

Realizing that this would require national standards of procedure for state justice, supervised by the Supreme Court, the Justices quickly demurred. In the *Slaughter House Cases* of 1873 they ruled that the "privileges and immunities" protected by the Fourteenth Amendment encompassed only those few rights that had traditionally been considered Federally protected rights, and not the wide range of relationships between citizens and police that had been the sole province of the states. Faced with the choice of imposing the commands of the Bill of Rights—and itself as arbiter of their meaning—on the states, or of ruling that the "privileges and immunities" clause meant nothing, the Supreme Court buried the clause so deep that even the more venturesome present-day Justices have not seriously attempted to unearth it. To this day, the clause means almost nothing.

But the Fourteenth Amendment also forbade the states to deny persons life or liberty without due process of law or to deny anyone the equal protection of the laws, and over the years the Supreme Court has woven two competing theories of the due process clause together with the equal protection clause, to form a legal fabric that now covers all areas of state law.

For a half-century after the *Slaughter House Cases* the Supreme Court gave the states a free hand. Finally, in 1923, it cautiously seized upon the due process clause to begin supervision of state justice.

If that clause had any meaning at all, the state of Arkansas had to have violated it in *Moore* v. *Dempsey*, the 1923 case. Five Negroes had been convicted of murder and sentenced to death in a 45-minute trial that was dominated by the presence of a mob inside the court room. It was obvious that if the Negroes had been acquitted they would have been lynched on the spot. The jury deliberated five minutes. Justice Oliver Wendell Holmes declared—without much analysis of the reasons for the finding—that such a trial had to be subject to attack under the due process clause. He thus moved the first pebble that was to lead to the constitutional avalanche of the 1960s.

It was nine years before the Court again invoked the due process clause to attack a state conviction, this time in the case of *Powell* v. *Alabama*. The Court held that Alabama could not execute the "Scottsboro Boys"—five illiterate young Negroes convicted of raping two white girls—because the boys had been denied effective counsel at their trial. Four years after that, in *Brown* v. *Mississippi*, the Justices threw out a state confession for the first time. Since the statements had been beaten out of two Mississippi Negroes by deputies wielding metal-studden belts, there could be no doubt that, whatever due process was, this was not it.

In those barbaric early cases all a Justice had to employ was a sense of outrage to determine if due process had been denied. The Supreme Court got along well enough with a visceral process that resembled the one later used by Justice Potter Stewart to identify hard-core pornography: "I know it when I see it."

But having insisted that there were limits to the states' free discretion to deal with criminals, the Court was forced to face up to the necessity of defining those limits—the process which has now led to the charge that the Justices have shackled law enforcement.

This danger was foreseen by the Justices, and in an effort to avoid it they first promulgated a generous standard of conduct designed to let the states continue to prescribe their own procedures, so long as state officials did not violate fundamental principles of justice. This "fundamental fairness" standard was stated in its classic form by Justice Benjamin N. Cardozo when he posed the test for determining if a given state action denied a citizen due process of law: "Does it violate those 'fundamental principles of liberty and justice which lie at the base of our civil and political institutions?' "

Over the next three decades, the Supreme Court groped for a more useful definition of fundamental fairness. Felix Frankfurter, realizing that the Supreme Court would be forced to impose rigid rules on local officials unless it could articulate principles that they could apply in practice, floated a series of trial balloons in the hope that one definition would click. Fundamental fairness was said to be any action that offends "those canons of decency and fairness which express the notions of justice of English-speaking peoples even toward those charged with the most heinous offenses"; it was tactics that "offend the community's sense of fair play and decency"; conduct that "shocks the conscience."

The definitions grew shorter, but not more precise. None of them revealed in advance what due process permitted, so in all but the most brutal instances it was impossible to know if due process had been denied until the Supreme Court itself reviewed the facts and disclosed whether or not the sensitivities of five or more of the Justices had been offended. Then, as now, the Supreme Court had complete discretion to grant or deny petitions for certiorari (review) of state court decisions, and until recently it customarily included less than a half-dozen state criminal cases among the 200-odd appeals it agreed to consider each year. For defendants the result was a form of judicial roulette. Thousands would be convicted each year for every one whose appeal reached the Supreme Court for a definitive ruling as to the constitutionality of his conviction.

The result was also a Federal standard of constitutionality that in light of today's values seems to have tolerated too much. Volumes 356, 357 and 358 of the *United States Reports* contain the Supreme Court decisions for 1958—a typical year when the fundamental fairness doctrine was in full flower. They include such rulings as these:

—In Illinois a man was accused of killing his wife and three children. The state tried him for killing the wife, but introduced evidence of all four deaths, and the jury gave him a twenty-year sentence. The state went for the death penalty again, prosecuting him for killing one of the children. This time he got forty-five years. At the third trial, for killing another of the children, the jury finally sentenced him to death. The Supreme Court held that his double jeopardy argument was irrelevant, since the Fifth Amendment did not apply to the states. Otherwise, the procedure did not seem fundamentally unfair, so the death sentence was affirmed.

—A New York businessman was subpoenaed to testify before a state grand jury investigation into labor racketeering. He was given a grant of immunity from prosecution on state corruption charges, but he still refused to testify, pointing out that he might incriminate himself under similar Federal labor racketeering statutes. The state judge nonetheless gave him a thirty-day jail sentence for contempt of court, and the Supreme Court affirmed on the ground that the Fifth Amendment does not apply to the states.

—A New Jersey man was tried for the robbery of three persons in the course of a tavern stick-up. None of the three could identify him, and although a fourth patron did, he was acquitted by the jury. The state then tried the defendant again for the robbery of the patron who said he could identify him, and this time the defendant was convicted. The Supreme Court let the conviction stand on the ground that the double-jeopardy clause does not bind the states.

—On the advice of his attorney, a New Jersey murder suspect turned himself in to the police. They isolated him in an interrogation room and questioned him for seven hours, refusing to let the lawyer see or advise him until after he confessed. The Supreme Court upheld the confession, finding it voluntary.

—A Los Angeles man was arrested on charges of having murdered his mistress. During the fourteen hours between his arrest and his confession he asked repeatedly to be allowed to call his lawyer, but was refused until after he confessed. His death sentence was affirmed by the Supreme Court.

It was the Court's inability to deal effectively with the problem of confessions that made the impotence of the fundamental fairness approach so apparent. Having declared in 1936 in *Brown* v. *Mississippi* that confessions must be voluntarily given to satisfy due process, the Court found that it could not pin down the definition of "voluntary." Its attempt to delineate the circumstances under which a confession must be considered involuntarily given proved to be a case-by-case exercise in frustration. The question was not so much whether there had been coercion —a term almost impossible to define beyond physical force— as whether or not the will of the accused had been overcome by his interrogators. This proved to be a most subjective test. Physical violence or threats were out, but beyond that, voluntariness was determined by such factors as the length of interrogation, the age, race, sex and sophistication of the suspect, and the tactics of the police.

In the three decades between *Brown* v. *Mississippi* and *Miranda* v. *Arizona*, the Court delivered thirty-six opinions on the voluntariness of state court confessions. They covered a wide variety of circumstances; some confessions were upheld and others were thrown out. The result was that state courts could examine the case-by-case authorities of the Supreme Court and could find authority for affirming or rejecting almost any type of confession.

In 1963 H. Frank Way, Jr., a political scientist at the University of California, studied the 126 state appellate court rulings on allegedly coerced confessions that had been reported in a previous seventeen-month period. He found that the Supreme Court's subjective test "provides no substantial yardstick for the states," and that only a handful of the opinions even referred to Supreme Court confessions decisions. As an example, he noted that all six of the confessions reviewed and upheld by the Texas courts during this period included elements of heavy-handed justice. He described one appellant's case as follows:

Here then is an accused who made a confession after being twice arrested without a warrant, after being illegally arraigned on a false charge under a fictitious name, and after being illegally held and questioned intermittently during a two-day period, with the final interrogation continuing throughout the night. Of course, he had no legal counsel during this period. Collins was described by medical experts as being of low intelligence, with an abnormally low tolerance for stress—a man who had the character of a three to six year old child. With the use of this confession, Collins was convicted of murder and sentenced to ninety-nine years of imprisonment.

The other five cases included: (a) a defendant who was illegally arrested and, according to undisputed evidence, beaten until he confessed; (b) a Mexican-American who was arrested without a warrant and questioned intermittently for three days before he confessed and was arraigned; (c) a Negro who was sentenced to death on the strength of a confession given after intermittent all-night questioning, including, he claimed, beatings; (d) a robbery suspect who was questioned for fifty minutes and confessed because, he claimed, he was sick and the police refused to take him to a hospital until he talked; (e) a twenty-two-year-old man with a sixth-grade education who was never arraigned, and who was denied counsel during his interrogation and also at his trial, which resulted in a five- to thirty-five-year prison sentence.

Thus by the early 1960s it was clear that the subjective fairness test had not provided a coherent confessions standard for the states. Yet the Supreme Court was unlikely to choose confessions as a vehicle for a breakthrough to a more rigid state standard, and for a good reason—the Justices' efforts to solve the same problem in the Federal courts had brought them nothing but grief. In 1957 the Court had made a stab at settling the matter in *Mallory* v. *United States*. It ruled unanimously that Federal officials must take arrested persons before a committing magistrate without unnecessary delay, and that any statements taken during a period of unnecessary delay would be inadmissible. The storm of criticism that followed *Mallory* was proof

enough that police interrogation was not a promising area for experimentation with state law. But the same did not seem true
of another area of police activity—searches—and it had been apparent for years that when the Court finally made its move to
clamp down on state criminal justice, it would be on the matter of
searches by police. Of the eight constitutional amendments that
make up the Bill of Rights, the Fourth is by far the most
specific. It says:

> The right of the people to be secure in their persons, houses, pa-
> pers and effects, against unreasonable searches and seizures shall not
> be violated, and no warrants shall issue but upon probable cause,
> supported by oath or affirmation, and particularly describing the
> place to be searched, and the persons or things to be searched.

Unlike the matter of confessions, where there is still a bitter
dispute over the true meaning of the Fifth Amendment's privilege against self-incrimination, there has always been virtual
unanimity among Americans that the Fourth Amendment means
that officers cannot search individuals or private premises on
caprice or suspicion, but only with a warrant based upon a showing that evidence of a crime will probably be found. There are
exceptions to this rule, but the rule itself is well settled. The early
Americans were not soft on criminals, but in the Fourth Amendment they made a calculated decision to sacrifice some of the
evidence-gathering capacity of the police to enhance individual
privacy and dignity. With the exception of the modifying term
"unreasonable," the wording was unyielding, and the mystique that "a man's home is his castle" made it the most durable of
the legal safeguards. Periodic crime scares have brought demands
for dilution in privileges ranging from the right to remain silent
to the presumption of innocence, but it has never been fashionable to call for expanding policemen's authority to enter and
search.

This may have been partially due to the fact that only Federal officers were effectively covered by the Fourth Amendment, and the average citizen's security from crime rested on
the effectiveness of local police. State and local police, who had
the primary responsibility for enforcing the law, played the
game by different rules. Each state had a version of the Fourth
Amendment in its constitution or laws, but there was a crucial

distinction between most of them and the Federal law. The U.S. rule against warrantless searches was enforced by a strict exclusionary rule that precluded the use of any evidence obtained in an illegal search. Most of the state courts had declined to put such formidable teeth in their laws, so their police searched without warrants when it seemed expedient.

Stripped of its legal trappings, the situation was that Federal officials, who were bound by the Fourth Amendment, could not search an individual's person or his premises (a man's office and car were also considered his castle) based on suspicion. To obtain a search warrant, they had to produce enough evidence to persuade a judge that the search would probably turn up certain items of contraband or the fruits or instrumentalities of a crime. They could search without a warrant only in situations involving "hot pursuit" by the police, moving vehicles, consent of the person searched or as an incident to a lawful arrest, which again required proof that a crime had been committed and that the suspect probably did it. Yet most states permitted their police to search on suspicion and use the fruits in court, so long as the circumstances were not shocking.

This double standard was distressing enough in the abstract; in practice, it permitted cynical whipsaw tactics between state and Federal enforcement officials that made a mockery of the Fourth Amendment. State policemen could stage illegal raids and, so long as there was no showing of collusion with U.S. officers, the evidence could be used in Federal court.

By 1949, even though the Supreme Court was still dominated by enforcement-minded Justices who had no stomach for a wholesale reform of state law, the Justices were so miffed at the situation that they carried out one of the oddest maneuvers in the Court's history. One of the oldest principles of the Supreme Court is that the Justices do not issue advisory opinions. When the Constitution was new and the law unsettled, President George Washington had asked the Court for guidance on what it might rule if certain situations arose on the high seas between British and American ships. He was told he would have to wait until the situation occurred and cases growing out of them reached the Supreme Court in proper form.

Yet in 1949 the Justices warned the states by indirection that if they did not see fit to exclude the fruits of illegal searches, the Supreme Court would do it for them. In *Wolf* v. *Colorado* the Court held that the Fourth Amendment is binding on the states —but it ruled that the Federal Constitution did not preclude the use in state courts of evidence gathered in violation of the Amendment. The implications of this weird ruling were well understood in legal circles: If the states did not rapidly adopt exclusionary rules to bar evidence obtained in violation of the Fourth Amendment, the Supreme Court would eventually do it for them.

Five years later there had been little change, so the Supreme Court issued another warning. In *Irvine* v. *California* the Court again upheld a warrantless search by state officers, but this time Justice Robert H. Jackson dropped an impatient hint that time was running out. In the *Wolf* decision, he noted, "as we pointed out, thirty-one states were not following the federal rule excluding illegally obtained evidence, while sixteen were in agreement with it. Now that the *Wolf* doctrine is known to them, state courts may wish to reconsider their evidentiary rules," he suggested.

By 1961, when *Mapp* v. *Ohio* reached the Supreme Court, roughly one-half of the states had gotten the message and had adopted exclusionary rules designed to bar the use of evidence obtained in illegal searches. In some states the judges were generous about excusing the police's failure to observe all of the Fourth Amendment's niceties, but at least in these states the official legal policy was to follow the Federal standard. Yet this only made the need for a universal Federal standard all the more compelling. If a person had driven across the country at that time from New York to San Francisco, he would have passed through four states (Indiana, Illinois, Missouri and California) in which the police would have been unlikely to search him or his car without probable cause, since their courts would not have permitted the fruits of the search to be used in evidence. In eight others (New York, New Jersey, Pennsylvania, Ohio, Kansas, Colorado, Utah and Nevada) officers could have made a search which did not measure up to Fourth Amendment standards and could have used the findings against the traveler in court. In a nation where state lines had otherwise become so unimportant, this checkerboard of human rights had to be short-lived.

One of the states where the motorist would have been legally most exposed to police overreaching would have been Ohio, where the State Supreme Court had given its blessing to warrantless searches, even in situations when search warrants could have been easily obtained. A victim of one such search, a Cleveland woman named Dolree Mapp, appealed her case to the U.S. Supreme Court. The summary of her case in the Supreme Court's opinion showed how much police abuse some state courts would excuse:

On May 23, 1957, three Cleveland police officers arrived at appellant's residence in that city pursuant to information that "a person [was] hiding out in the home, who was wanted for questioning in connection with a recent bombing, and that there was a large amount of policy paraphernalia being hidden in the home." Miss Mapp and her daughter by a former marriage lived on the top floor of the two-family dwelling. Upon their arrival at that house, the officers knocked on the door and demanded entrance but appellant, after telephoning her attorney, refused to admit them without a search warrant. They advised their headquarters of the situation and undertook a surveillance of the house.

The officers again sought entrance some three hours later when four or more additional officers arrived on the scene. When Miss Mapp did not come to the door immediately, at least one of the several doors to the house was forcibly opened and the policemen gained admittance. Meanwhile Miss Mapp's attorney arrived, but the officers, having secured their own entry, and continuing in their defiance of the law, would permit him neither to see Miss Mapp nor to enter the house. It appears that Miss Mapp was halfway down the stairs from the upper floor to the front door when the officers, in this high-handed manner, broke into the hall. She demanded to see the search warrant. A paper, claimed to be a warrant, was held up by one of the officers. She grabbed the "warrant" and placed it in her bosom. A struggle ensued in which the officers recovered the piece of paper and as a result of which they handcuffed appellant because she had been "belligerent" in resisting their official rescue of the "warrant" from her person. Running roughshod over appellant, a policeman "grabbed" her, "twisted [her] hand," and she "yelled [and] pleaded with him" because "it was hurting." Appellant, in handcuffs, was then forcibly taken upstairs to her bedroom where the officers searched a dresser, a chest of drawers, a closet and some suitcases. They also looked into a photo album and through personal papers belonging to the appellant. The search spread to the rest of the second floor including the child's bedroom, the living room, the kitchen and a dinette. The basement of the building and a trunk found therein were also searched. The obscene materials for possession of which she was ultimately convicted were discovered in the course of that widespread search.

At the trial no search warrant was produced by the prosecution, nor was the failure to produce one explained or accounted for. At best, "There is, in the record, considerable doubt as to whether there ever was any warrant for the search of defendant's home." The Ohio Supreme Court believed a "reasonable argument" could be made that the conviction should be reversed "because the 'methods' employed to obtain the [evidence] . . . were such as to 'offend "a sense of justice,"' " but the court found determinative the fact that the evidence had not been taken "from defendant's person by the use of brutal or offensive physical force against defendant."

Faced with this appeal, the Supreme Court stood at a crossroads in constitutional history. (Much to the surprise of Miss Mapp's lawyer, who had based his case on the claim that the items were not obscene.) The Court could sustain the conviction, as it had in *Wolf* v. *Colorado* and *Irvine* v. *California*, with stronger words of warning that *next* time it would make the Fourth Amendment effectively binding on the states. But a third warning, more than a decade after crying *Wolf* in 1949, would have made the Court appear impotent and ridiculous. The only other course would carry the Court beyond the point of no return along the path that a minority of the Justices had been urging as an alternative to the fundamental fairness approach.

The second theory of the Fourteenth Amendment's due process clause called for the specific limitations on official power which are set out in the Bill of Rights to be made binding on the states. Where the fundamental fairness technique permitted the states to fashion their own procedures and voided only those actions that failed the subjective fairness test, the Bill of Rights approach would impose in advance on state police and courts detailed and objective procedural standards—and would void all convictions obtained in violation of these rules.

Both had their flaws: The fundamental fairness approach asserted that Federal rights existed, but generally failed to protect them; the Bill of Rights technique would provide more objective rules, but posed the threat of a virtual take-over by the Supreme Court of state law-enforcement standards—and if the rigid rules dictated by the Supreme Court majority should prove unwise or unworkable, the result could be calamitous for justice and for the Supreme Court.

For years the intellectual thrust behind the fundamental fairness approach had been provided by Justice Felix Frankfurter, the brilliant, irascible former Harvard professor who championed the doctrine of "judicial self-restraint"—the theory that the Supreme Court should move with mincing steps, prodding, cajoling, inspiring the other branches and levels of government to undertake necessary reforms, but never taking over the job itself.

The leading critic of this view was Justice Hugo L. Black, the passionate, populist-minded former Senator from Alabama, who felt that today was already too late to implement all of the Constitution's promises to all Americans. He believed that the genius of a written Constitution was its capacity to anchor the rights of the people and limit the power of judges. To Black any "fairness" consideration by Justices was unconstitutional; it could only result in either hedging on the Bill of Rights or inflating the power of the Supreme Court. Since he felt that the Fourteenth Amendment had made the entire Bill of Rights binding on the states, he believed that these rights should be literally enforced in all courts, thus assuring that the people would have no fewer rights than the Constitution promised—and that the judges would have no more.

Realizing that the future of criminal justice in this country would be determined by one of these competing principles, in 1947 each Justice argued his case in long opinions rendered in a case called *Adamson* v. *California*. In California and five other states the law permitted a prosecutor or judge to comment to the jury on the inferences of guilt to be drawn from a defendant's failure to take the stand in his own defense. Adamson had been convicted of murder and sentenced to death after he declined to take the stand and the prosecutor argued that this was a sign of guilt. Since this was proper under California law, the sole question was whether the Fifth Amendment's privilege against compulsory self-incrimination was binding on the states and if so, whether the prosecutor had infringed that right by making light of the fact that Adamson had invoked it.

Hugo Black argued in his opinion that the conviction should be overturned because Adamson's Fifth Amendment rights had been violated:

I would follow what I believe was the original purpose of the Fourteenth Amendment—to extend to all the people of the nation the complete protection of the Bill of Rights. To hold that this Court can determine what, if any, provisions of the Bill of Rights will be enforced, and if so to what degree, is to frustrate the great design of a written Constitution.

Conceding the possibility that this Court is now wise enough to improve on the Bill of Rights by substituting natural law concepts for the Bill of Rights, I think the possibility is entirely too speculative to agree to take that course. I would therefore hold in this case that the full protection of the Fifth Amendment's proscription against compelled testimony must be afforded by California. This I would do because of reliance upon the original purpose of the Fourteenth Amendment.

It is an illusory apprehension that literal application of some or all of the provisions of the Bill of Rights to the States would unwisely increase the sum total of the powers of this Court to invalidate state legislation. The Federal Government has not been harmfully burdened by the requirement that enforcement of Federal laws affecting civil liberty conform literally to the Bill of Rights. Who would advocate its repeal?

Felix Frankfurter replied in his concurring opinion that:

A construction which gives to due process no independent function but turns it into a summary of the specific provisions of the Bill of Rights would, as has been noted, tear up by the roots much of the fabric of law in the several States, and would deprive the States of opportunity for reforms in legal process designed for extending the area of freedom. It would assume that no other abuses would reveal themselves in the course of time than those which had become manifest in 1791. Such a view not only disregards the historic meaning of "due process," it leads inevitably to a warped construction of specific provisions of the Bill of Rights to bring within their scope conduct clearly condemned by due process but not easily fitting into the pigeonholes of the specific provisions. It seems pretty late in the day to suggest that a phrase so laden with historic meaning should be given an improvised content consisting of some but not all of the provisions of the first eight amendments, selected on an undefined basis, with improvisation of content for the provisions so selected.

The arguments of Justice Frankfurter carried the day. Adamson's conviction was affirmed, 5 to 4, and Hugo Black was left to express his views in a dissent—a familiar situation for him in those days. He was never again able to marshal so many votes for the proposition that all of the Bill of Rights' guarantees had been incorporated wholesale into the Fourteenth Amendment.

Yet by the time *Mapp* v. *Ohio* reached the Supreme Court in 1961 the groundwork had been laid for a piecemeal, clause-by-clause application of the most important provisions of the Bill of Rights to the states. This process has been called "selective incorporation," "absorption," "inclusion," and other names by various legal scholars, who have been unable to agree on a label for the theory because the Supreme Court has never explained it in detail in a majority opinion and thus has had no occasion to give it a name. While this is only a minor embarrassment to the Supreme Court, it permits critics to point out that, however handy or beneficial the "selective incorporation" theory has been as an instrument of legal change, there seems to be no clear constitutional rationale for it.

In 1965, when the process was well along, the Court decided unanimously that the Texas courts had violated the United States Constitution by convicting an accused robber on the strength of a transcript of a witness' pretrial testimony, taken when the defendant had no lawyer to cross-examine the witness —a procedure that violated the Sixth Amendment's guarantee that the defendant and his counsel may confront his accusers at the trial. But having all agreed on the result, the Justices could not agree on the reason. The case produced four separate opinions that rehashed the familiar arguments of *Adamson* v. *California*, but failed to explain satisfactorily why the Constitution regulates state justice in this way.

What the Warren Court has done is to accept the principle behind Hugo Black's "incorporation" theory without risking the constitutional indigestion that would come with swallowing the theory whole. The majority wished to move beyond the impotent fundamental fairness approach to one that would bind state justice in advance to rigid standards. For this, certain provisions of the first eight amendments were ideal. Some of them were explicit and others had been given definite meanings over the years by judicial interpretations handed down in Federal cases. Others were potentially troublesome anachronisms that the Supreme Court would prefer to leave buried in the fine print of the Bill of Rights. Fortunately for those Justices who wanted to pick and choose, there was already some precedent for a selective application to the states of certain Bill of Rights' provisions.

The availability of these precedents to undergird the Supreme Court's new course after Frankfurter's death is a classic study in the venerable Supreme Court technique of keeping one foot in each of two legal worlds until the Court is ready to make the jump from the old world to the new. In 1908 the Court had considered, in *Twining* v. *New Jersey*, whether the Fifth Amendment's self-incrimination clause was binding on the states as a necessary element of due process. The Court considered the question thoroughly, and, with only one Justice dissenting, declared that it was not.

Soon the Court began to waffle; some guarantees of the Bill of Rights seemed too fundamental to permit their violation by any public official. The result was a string of decisions that adopted the substance of Black's position without accepting it in principle; the Court, as one Justice commented about a similar Supreme Court exercise on another constitutional point, reacted as did Lord Byron's Julia, who "Whispering 'I will ne'er consent,'—consented."

In 1925 the Supreme Court, in affirming New York's conviction of the socialist political leader, Benjamin Gitlow, had declared almost in passing that the First Amendment's protection of freedom of speech applied to state as well as Federal action. Over the next two decades the Court developed the idea that the rights contained in the First Amendment were "preferred freedoms" that could not be infringed by officials at any level of government. As a result the First Amendment's guarantees of religious freedom, free press and the right to assemble peaceably were also made binding on the states, even though the Amendment begins: "Congress shall make no law. . . ."

By 1937, *Twining* v. *New Jersey* had been so thoroughly riddled with loopholes that the Supreme Court took its pulse to see if the doctrine was still alive. In *Palko* v. *Connecticut*, the Court again considered whether the states should be bound by the Fifth Amendment; this time, by its double-jeopardy prohibition. Justice Cardozo wrote an opinion that undertook to say why some provisions of the Bill of Rights had been applied to the states, while most had not. He concluded that those rights "implicit in the concept of ordered liberty" had been applied to the states by a "process of absorption" into the due process clause. Since the Court in *Palko* did not find the double-jeopardy clause that fundamental, it was held not binding on the states. But the "ordered liberty" standard was a subjective one, which meant that the Supreme Court could justify binding the states with the various criminal procedure provisions of the Bill of Rights as soon as a majority developed that wished to do so.

Thus in 1949 it was only a short leap for the Justices to take the position in *Wolf* v. *Colorado* that the Fourth Amendment was so fundamental to American liberty that it must be considered a requirement of due process. But so long as the Court maintained the inconsistent position that only the state courts could act to prohibit Fourth Amendment violations by state officers, the Justices had not yet crossed the all-important line between a brooding and occasionally-vented displeasure at state justice and the imposition of rigid rules of procedure that states must follow in all situations.

In *Mapp* v. *Ohio* the Justices moved the Supreme Court across that line. The decision was by the narrowest of margins, made possible by a coincidence of the personal and philosophical predilections of two vastly different men.

Tom Clark had risen to the Supreme Court through the ranks of the Justice Department; he was by experience a law-enforcement man. But emotionally, he had been deeply impressed by his first Federal case, when as a twenty-three-year-old beanpole in Dallas, he had undertaken to defend the son of his family's Negro maid. The son's home had been ransacked, without the benefit of a search warrant, by state officers, who found a jug of moonshine liquor. That led to a Federal prosecution under the Prohibition laws. Young Tom Clark tried an unusual maneuver for those days. He filed a motion to suppress the liquor from evidence on the ground that it was obtained in violation of the Fourth Amendment. The law then provided that evidence obtained illegally by Federal officials was excluded by the Fourth Amendment, but under the "silver platter doctrine," objects seized illegally by state police, who were not covered by the Amendment, could be used in Federal trials. The trial judge admitted the jug of liquor and, irked at young Clark's effrontery, gave his client the maximum penitentiary sentence. He came out a chronic troublemaker, and was ultimately convicted of murder. The injustice of it cut deeply into Clark's beliefs. Years later his eyes narrowed with remembered anger as he said that "I couldn't see then, and I can't see now, any reason why it made any difference which police violated the Fourth Amendment—the fruits of the search shouldn't be admitted."

Justice Clark's determination to expand the Fourth Amendment to cover state officers didn't extend to other safeguards of the Bill of Rights, which made his position almost the mirror image of that of Hugo Black. Black wanted to apply the entire Bill of Rights to the states, but he would have given the Fourth Amendment less enforcement there than the other safeguards. His reasons were doctrinal. As an absolutist, he read the Fifth and the Sixth Amendments as forbidding courtroom use of evidence obtained in violation of the privilege against self-incrimination or the right to counsel. But he saw no exclusionary rule in the Fourth Amendment which forbade the use of items seized in violation of the Amendment.

It was clear, though, that if the Bill of Rights was to be made enforceable against state police officers, the process would have to begin with searches and seizures. Black decided to go along. Clark wrote the Court's opinion, declaring that every search by every police official was subject to the standards of the Fourth Amendment, and that if those standards were violated in any search, the fruits of the search could not be used as evidence in court. Chief Justice Warren and Justices Brennan and Douglas joined. To provide the fifth vote, Black wrote a concurring opinion, explaining that the exclusion of illegally-seized evidence was required by the Fifth Amendment's self-incrimination guarantee, in tandem with the Fourth Amendment.

For the first time in the nation's history the Supreme Court had effectively imposed detailed constitutional restrictions on the actions of the state's law-enforcement officials in their handling of their 99.6 percent of the criminal offenses. It was a milestone in criminal law that eclipsed John Marshall's performance in *Barron* v. *Baltimore* and the Supreme Court's second no-thank-you in the *Slaughter House Cases*—for beyond the Fourth Amendment was the complex of constitutional limitations on police action contained in the remaining articles of the Bill of Rights. Some were relatively innocuous. But two of them— the Fifth Amendment's privilege against self-incrimination and the Sixth Amendment's guarantee of the right to counsel—could, as the Warren Court was soon to show, bring almost the entire range of state police action within the detailed control of the Federal judiciary.

Once *Mapp* v. *Ohio* breached the precedent against supervision by the Supreme Court of the nuts and bolts of state justice, there was only one reason why the Court could not proceed to dictate a top-to-bottom reform of state procedures: A five-man majority, led by Felix Frankfurter, was fearful of the results and satisfied with the status quo. This reason was removed in 1962 when Felix Frankfurter retired.

In retrospect, the appointment of Arthur J. Goldberg to Felix Frankfurter's seat was one of the most far-reaching acts of John F. Kennedy's Presidency. For without Frankfurter, the other eight Justices were equally divided between four who were eager to get on with the business of imposing a new standard of conduct on the states, and four who were leery of further incursions by the Court into state criminal justice.

In the future, those who ponder the impact of men on events may savor the ironies that created the bold and liberal "Warren majority" in the year 1962. If the five-Justice majority that carried out the due process revolution had not fallen into place until, say, 1968, when the tides of racism and crime had made ambitious experiments in defendants' rights hazardous, then the Warren Court's idealism and public credit might have been channeled more into other legal fields. The Court might, for instance, have felt secure enough to consider the constitutionality of the Vietnam War draft; it might have tried to deal with de facto school segregation and unequal spending by states on slum schools; or perhaps it might have moved sooner to reform the many contractual and procedural rules that make life precarious for the poor.

But law enforcement was in bad odor in 1962: Dr. Martin Luther King, Jr., was leading his demonstrations against the laws of Birmingham, Alabama, and Police Commissioner Eugene "Bull" Connor was becoming a symbol of justly defied police power. (It was in a later era, 1967, that the Supreme Court finally consigned Dr. King to jail for his actions in Birmingham—and then, because he had disobeyed a judge.) The criminal law was widely viewed as an oppressive force, to be thoroughly changed if not selectively ignored. Into this uncharacteristic national recoil against law enforcement came a reform-minded—and in some ways, radical—new Supreme Court majority.

Still at the intellectual helm of the activist bloc was Hugo Black, in 1962 a tennis-playing, seventy-six-year-old sprite of a man who had waited long if not patiently to realize the prophecy of his *Adamson* v. *California* dissent. Born in Clay County, Alabama, in 1886—Scarlet O'Hara would have been forty-one-years old—he had joined the Ku Klux Klan so casually that he later compared it to his Rotary Club membership. Then as a Justice he helped strike down segregation with obvious relish, inspiring wags back in Alabama to quip: "Hugo Black used to go around in white robes, scaring black people. Now he goes about in black robes, scaring white people."

To some it was almost a miracle that Black was around in 1962 to complete the liberal majority; in 1956 he had appeared so peaked that a worried *New York Times* reporter had updated the Black obituary, writing that "In December of 1956 it was noted that he appeared frail although he retained much of what was described as his 'alert and springy bearing.'" As it developed, Hugo Black was sufficiently springy to mastermind the due process revolution of the mid-1960s and then to become one of the most eloquent of those who warned later that it had gone too far. Throughout his life Black had been attracted to extremes, and in 1962 he was to have the long-awaited opportunity to take the Supreme Court with him on the major issues of criminal justice.

Yet the "Warren Court" was in truth the Court of Earl Warren, the burly, genial Chief Justice who had been the father-figure of American justice since he marshaled a unanimous Supreme Court behind the school desegregation decisions of 1954. Warren was one of those political men of goodwill but ambivalent performance in elected office who had been liberated by the robe. As a prosecutor and later as Attorney General of California he had been accused of endorsing some of the heavy-handed police practices that were later to be outlawed by the Court, and as Attorney General and Governor of California he had insisted upon the removal of the Japanese to concentration camps. As Chief Justice he became famous for resolving great issues of constitutional law into the simple question: "But is it fair?"

By 1962 his answers to this question had brought an end to legal racial segregation and had made Earl Warren an historic figure in his own time. It had also made him the object of intense hatred by segregationists and conservatives. Yet Warren had learned to live with this and perhaps had been stiffened by it to discount the clamor that invariably greeted controversial decisions. Those who observed him as Chief Justice sensed that he wished in his time to reform the criminal laws as he had the racial ones, and that public displeasure would not greatly affect his course.

William O. Douglas, a brilliant man and an unfailingly liberal Justice, disproved the adage that consistency is a quality only of small minds. When he was named to the Court by President Roosevelt in 1939 Douglas was one of the bright young lights of the New Deal. He had his eye on the Presidency, and Roosevelt seriously considered picking him for Vice President rather than Harry Truman in 1944. Even in 1948, when dump-Truman fever rose among the Democrats for a time, Douglas had hopes that Presidential lightning might strike. But it did not, and Douglas, with a lifetime appointment to one of the highest offices in the land, was liberated from the last influence that might have prevented him from translating into law at every opportunity his passion for individualism.

Douglas was an outdoorsman, a nature-lover who believed so deeply in freedom that he rarely voted to uphold an appellant's conviction, regardless of the circumstances. He almost always discovered a reason why the conviction should not stand. "As presented by Justice Douglas, not a single case is hard enough to perplex a right thinking man," one of his critics wrote in 1964; "a case does not present a tangle of competing principles, but a single transcendent principle—for instance, free speech or religious freedom—which need only be identified for the solution to be plain." (A civil liberties group later studied the appeals from 1957 to 1968 that involved claims of individual rights and discovered that out of 483 cases, Douglas voted against the individual only 22 times.) This instinct insulated Douglas from the scholars' concern that some of the Court's major interpretations were legally indefensible, as well as from the pragmatists' charges that they were unwise. Even when the other eight Justices bowed to reality in 1968 and upheld the police's power to "stop and frisk" dangerous-looking suspects, Douglas dissented. He remained unashamedly an automatic liberal in judicial robes, indispensable to some of the close major decisions of the due process revolution, and unchanged after the thinking on the Court began to shift.

Of the four Justices who made up the liberal wing of the Court, William J. Brennan, Jr., was the youngest and most pragmatic. Brennan was an oddity among Supreme Court Justices —a judge who had come up through the ranks. He had started as a trial judge in New Jersey, and had moved up the state judicial ladder to the state Supreme Court. There, he impressed Chief Justice Arthur T. Vanderbilt so much that when President Eisenhower offered the aging Vanderbilt a seat on the Sueme Court, Vanderbilt demurred and recommended Brennan.

Brennan's success story was almost a carbon copy, in judicial terms, of the Irish-boy-makes-good formula that had become a classic pattern of elective politics; he was smart, hard-working, affable and—in an era in which the basic movement of events was toward liberalism—he was a liberal. To Brennan, judicial liberalism meant that the Supreme Court should get out in front of events and attempt to draw the nation into progressive paths. But he had a sense of the possible and his liberalism proved to be correspondingly flexible. (A lifelong guardian of free speech on the bench, Brennan withdrew the appointment of a law clerk in 1966 after the young man came under fire in the Southern press for his protest activities at Berkeley.)

It was Brennan who, only one week after the *Miranda* decision had been announced, left the Warren bloc and cast the deciding vote in *Schmerber* v. *California*. This case held that the police could, over an individual's protest, take a sample of blood, test it for alcohol content, and use the results against the person. It proved to be a turning point in the development of the Fifth Amendment's privilege against self-incrimination—and, in retrospect, the first sign that the high water mark of the due process revolution had been passed.

Of the four more-conservative Justices, John Marshall Harlan was clearly the "Mister Conservative" of the Warren Court. Harlan looked like a Supreme Court Justice—he was gaunt, gray and calm—and indeed he was born and bred to be one: his grandfather of the same name had been the lone dissenter who had insisted in *Plessy* v. *Ferguson* that the Constitution should be color-blind. Harlan the younger was a product of Princeton, Oxford, New York University Law School and a Wall Street law firm. He had inherited Felix Frankfurter's mantle as the apostle of judicial restraint, and he clung to the fundamental fairness view of due process long after the majority had applied most of the Bill of Rights to the states.

Tom C. Clark was both a Texan and a former Attorney General, and his opinions preached a no-nonsense brand of law and order. Even in the days before the Warren majority jelled, when the Court would overturn an occasional conviction, Clark was frequently a lone dissenter, insisting that jury-trial convictions were entitled to more respect. Yet on unpredictable occasions Clark could come down emphatically on the side of the liberals, as he did when he declared in *Mapp* v. *Ohio* that "There is no war between the Constitution and common sense."

But over the years Clark voted on the side of law enforcement in the vast majority of cases, and the liberals' desire for a significant shift in the balance of power between the individual and the policeman could not have been accomplished if it had depended on Clark for the vital fifth vote.

Potter Stewart had been cast as a conservative from the time

President Eisenhower appointed him in 1958. The son of a former Republican member of the Supreme Court of Ohio, Stewart bore the stamp of Hotchkiss, Yale College, Yale Law School, Cambridge, and corporate law practice in New York and Cincinnati when President Eisenhower appointed him to the Court of Appeals for the Sixth Circuit in 1954. When he arrived in Washington and was asked if he was a liberal or a conservative, he replied, "I'd like to be thought of as a lawyer."—which was taken by most to mean that he was a conservative. Later in his career Stewart took bold positions against obscenity regulation and the Supreme Court's refusal to review the constitutionality of the Vietnam War draft. But throughout the crucial years when the Warren Court was attempting to change the scheme of criminal procedure, Stewart was usually on the other side.

President Kennedy's first appointee to the Supreme Court, Byron R. White, provided one of the first public hints that the young men of the New Frontier were not necessarily as radical as the country had been led to believe. White's dashing image was largely a product of his nickname, "Whizzer," which he had picked up as an all-American collegiate football player and later as a professional halfback. He has rarely been called "Whizzer" to his face since.

White was a bright, orthodox judge who seemed to take satisfaction in writing long and definitive opinions on such subjects as government contracts, and who had occasional bouts with stomach ulcers. He had been Deputy Attorney General before he came to the Court in 1962, and he had great sympathy for the lot of those who were charged with enforcing the law. It was clear from the start that White would take no part in generating from the Supreme Court a revolutionary change in law-enforcement procedures.

There is always a danger of oversimplification in sorting Supreme Court Justices into "liberal" and "conservative" (terms they abhor) categories. Yet on the broad question of the future of criminal suspects' rights, it was clear after Felix Frankfurter left the Court that the remaining eight Justices were neatly divided, 4 to 4. Thus President Kennedy decisively changed the direction of the Court when he appointed Arthur J. Goldberg in August of 1962.

Men have been known to perform in surprising ways after they donned the lifetime robes of a Justice, but Goldberg was clearly not one of them. He had never been a judge, but he was known to be a liberal in the political sense—he had been a labor union lawyer and a Democratic Secretary of Labor—and he was an innovator by nature.

As a lawyer he had delighted in the daring stroke. Once when he was attempting to mediate a labor dispute for President Kennedy and the negotiators suddenly became hostile, Goldberg soothed them by passing along President Kennedy's invitation to the White House for cocktails. The negotiators relaxed and accepted, and Goldberg rushed word to the White House that he had invited himself and them over in the interest of industrial peace. On another occasion he stated during a television interview that President Kennedy had written a certain letter to the principals in a labor dispute. He then quickly had the letter typed, rushed it over to the White House, and persuaded Kennedy to sign it.

As a Justice, Goldberg was equally unattached to old and safe ways. He promptly aligned himself with the Warren group, giving the liberals a five-Justice working majority that held fast in most of the important cases involving individual rights that came before the Court during Goldberg's three-year tenure there.

This remained so after Goldberg resigned in 1965 to become U.S. Ambassador to the United Nations, because President Johnson appointed in his place Abe Fortas, a man who proved to be remarkably like Goldberg in judicial philosophy. Fortas was a successful businessman's lawyer, but he was also a libertarian who represented persons accused of being security risks during the McCarthy antisubversive scare. He had a unique flair for blending fat cats and underdogs into the same clientele, and his Washington law firm flourished in the service of both. In 1963 Fortas had become a national figure when he argued in the Supreme Court for Clarence Earl Gideon in the famous right-to-counsel case, *Gideon* v. *Wainwright*. As long as he remained a Justice he continued as a consistent and persuasive champion of the rights of the individual against the state.

In a span of seven years after the appointment of Arthur Goldberg, the process of applying the Bill of Rights to the states was almost completed. Between 1962 and 1969 the Supreme Court applied to the States most of the remaining key safeguards of the first Eight Amendments:

Fifth Amendment

"No person shall . . . be subject for the same offense to be twice put in jeopardy of life or limb. . . ." (*Benton* v. *Maryland,* 1969)

". . . nor shall be compelled in any criminal case to be a witness against himself. . . ." (*Malloy* v. *Hogan,* 1964)

Sixth Amendment

"In all criminal prosecutions the accused shall enjoy the right to a speedy and public trial. . . ." (*Klopfer* v. *North Carolina,* 1967)

". . . by an impartial jury. . . . (*Duncan* v. *Louisiana,* 1968)

". . . to be confronted with the witnesses against him. . . ." (*Pointer* v. *Texas,* 1965)

". . . to have compulsory process for obtaining witnesses in his favor. . .ᵉ" (*Washington* v. *Texas,* 1967)

. . . and to have the assistance of counsel for his defense." (*Gideon* v. *Wainwright,* 1963)

Eighth Amendment

". . . nor [shall] cruel and unusual punishments [be] inflicted." (*Robinson* v. *California,* 1962).

By 1968 Justice Black could pronounce the struggle between the inclusionists and the proponents of fundamental fairness to be a rout. Speaking at Columbia University School of Law, as Charles Evans Hughes had when he warned about self-inflicted wounds, Black reeled off the major provisions that had been applied to the states. As proof that his theory had been accepted in substance, if not in form, he noted that *Twining* v. *New Jersey,* the classic expression of the principle that the states are not bound by the Bill of Rights, was itself expressly overruled in *Malloy* v. *Hogan* in 1964. "Obviously, I am not completely happy with the selective incorporation theory," Black said;

since it still leaves to the determination of judges the decision as to which Bill of Rights' provisions are "fundamental" and thus applicable to the States. . . . But the selective incorporation process, as it is now being used, does limit the Supreme Court in the Fourteenth Amendment field to specific Bill of Rights' protections only and keeps judges from roaming at will in their own notions of what policies outside the Bill of Rights are desirable and what are not. And it has the virtue of having worked to make most of the Bill of Rights' protections applicable to the States. For these reasons I have supported the absorption process as an alternative, although perhaps less historically supportable than complete incorporation.

Today, of the twenty-five specific safeguards of the Bill of Rights that restrict government action, all are now binding upon the states except the Second Amendment's guarantee of the right to bear arms, the Third Amendment's prohibition against the quartering of troops in private homes, the Fifth Amendment's requirement of grand jury indictments for all capital or infamous crimes, and the Eighth Amendment's bar against excessive bail. There is one further provision that does not concern the police power and which has not been applied to the states: the Seventh Amendment's requirement that jury trials be allowed in all civil suits involving twenty dollars or more.

Chief Justice Earl Warren said at a press conference at the time his retirement was announced that he did not expect two of these—the Seventh Amendment's twenty-dollar rule and the grand jury indictment requirement—ever to be applied to the states. The twenty-dollar ceiling on nonjury trials would wreck the petty claims courts and arbitration systems that many states use to dispose of minor civil cases. Some states also use a device called an "information"—a formal charge initiated by the prosecuting attorney rather than the grand jury—as a substitute for grand jury indictments. Procedures in those states would be upset if informations were declared unconstitutional. Prosecutors usually control grand juries anyway,. so there is no strong constitutional reason why the prosecutors should not just sign the charges themselves.

Thus the Justices adopted the spirit of Hugo Black's position, if not his absolutist reasoning. Then they proceeded to take the best of both worlds by also continuing to follow the fundamental fairness theory when it suited their purposes. Much to Black's disgust, the Court has continued to invalidate state actions that strike the Court as grossly unfair, even though the action might not violate any specific provision of the Bill of Rights. This was so in the Billie Sol Estes case, in which the Clark opinion simply ticked off all of the bad effects of the television coverage and concluded that such outrages must be unconstitutional. The classic example of this was *Rochin* v. *California*, in which the Supreme Court was faced with a conviction based upon narcotics that had been pumped out of the defendant's stomach, at the cost of much pain and vomiting by the defendant. This was an outrage that the Founding Fathers had not anticipated in the Bill of Rights, so the Supreme Court had no choice but to let the conviction stand or throw it out on the ground that it shocked their consciences. They threw it out. A few other decisions have been almost as intuitive, but usually the Court prefers to stretch the meaning of some provisions of the Bill of Rights to cover an unfair situation—resulting in some elastic interpretations of the Bill of Rights, as Frankfurter warned in *Adamson*.

For good measure, the Court has found in the equal protection clause of the Fourteenth Amendment a third layer of consitutional regulation that state justice must observe. This doctrine forbids procedures that give wealthy defendants access to procedures that poor people might not be able to use. It was first announced in 1956 in *Griffin* v. *Illinois*, in which the Supreme Court held that if the state permitted a convicted person to appeal only if he had a transcript of his trial, the state must furnish a free transcript for any defendant too poor to pay for one.

The application of these three doctrines to state justice quickly brought into operation a fundamental dilemma of the constitutional system that invariably appears when the Supreme Court exerts new powers. Article III of the Constitution gave the Supreme Court the authority to wield the "judicial power" of the United States. Since John Marshall's time the Supreme Court has used this inscrutable grant of power as authority to exercise "judicial review"—to examine the acts of other branches and levels of government and declare invalid those that do not square with the terms of the Constitution. But the Constitution and most of its amendments are written in broad terms that permit almost any interpretations that the Justices are willing to give them.

"The meaning of due process and the content of terms like liberty are not revealed by the Constitution," Felix Frankfurter once pointed out. "It is the Justices who make the meaning. They read into the neutral language of the Constitution their own economic and social views. . . . Let us face the fact that five Justices of the Supreme Court are the molders of policy rather than the impersonal vehicles of revealed truth."

In effect, the Justices define their own powers while sitting in judgment of others. Thus Americans have taken as revealed truth Charles Evans Hughes' famous confession that "We are under a Constitution, but the Constitution is what the judges say it is."

For the Supreme Court, this virtually open-ended grant of power presents a dilemma: The Court can move almost wherever the will of five Justices dare to take it, but it can never clearly refute the charge that those five Justices have overstepped their proper role.

In the early stages of the due process revolution the Supreme Court was blessed with critics whose charges were often misdirected and whose motives were suspect. The Council of State Governments, alarmed at the threat to state sovereignty, circulated a proposed constitutional amendment that would have set up a "Court of the Union," composed of all fifty state chief justices, which would have the final word on constitutional interpretations. The Conference of State Chief Justices, who had been unaccustomed to having their criminal law rulings—good or bad—reviewed elsewhere, issued a rebuke to the Court for permitting individual Federal District Judges to overturn convictions that had been approved by the full Supreme Court of a state. Finally, the political figures who denounced the Justices' criminal decisions tended to be the same Southern politicians who were nursing hurt feelings because of the school desegregation decisions.

From this the impression was created in the early 1960s that criticism of the Supreme Court's current vigorous course was simply a measure of whose ox had been gored. As one eminent law professor, Philip Kurland (who disagreed with much that the Court was doing) put it, "it is difficult not to help resist attack from racists, from the John Birch Society and its ilk, and from religious zealots who insist that the Court adhere to the truth as they know it."

One unfortunate by-product of the gored-ox character of the early criticism of the due process revolution was its tendency to reinforce a sense of judicial infallibility that surfaced among some of the Justices of the Warren Court in connection with their interpretation of the Bill of Rights. Much of the Supreme Court's success has been due to its Olympian willingness to make far-reaching decisions, to grasp and wield authority at the point where, as Harry Truman put it, "the buck stops." But there is a crucial difference between the aplomb that befits the exercise of final decision-making, and the conviction that the decision must be correct because it is being made by the supreme decision-maker.

Criticism based on the effects on law enforcement of Supreme Court decisions would indeed have been irrelevant if the function of the Justices were to "find" the law by a process of inductive reasoning from settled precedents. This was the English theory of the judicial process, as preached by William Blackstone, and even in this century some American judges have professed to believe it. Justice Owen Roberts said as recently as three decades ago, apparently with a straight face, that the judges' role was simply to "lay the article of the Constitution which is invoked beside the statute which is challenged and to decide whether the latter squares with the former."

But the Justices have made too many changes lately in the meaning of what Cardozo called the "great generalities" of the Constitution to permit them to insist now that they merely "find" and apply pre-existing law. Of the 133 times that the Supreme Court has reversed itself in its 180-year history, 45 of the reversals—more than one-third—were made by the Warren Court. Rather, there is an understanding—usually unspoken but occasionally expressed, as by Frankfurter and Hughes—that the Justices often properly "make" law by reading their own ideas of what the law should be into neutral constitutional language.

Despite this understanding, some Justices tended to identify their own views of the Constitution with the binding hands of the Founding Fathers. Justice Jackson had once cautioned his brethren that "we are not final because we are infallible, but we are infallible only because we are final." Yet being final, the Warren majority occasionally clothed its emerging constitutional doctrines with an inevitability that chilled rational discussion of the issues and infuriated the Court's critics.

How close this thinking could come to Owen Roberts' side-

60 · *The Self-Inflicted Wound*

by-side theory of constitutional decision-making emerged in Hugo Black's 1968 television interview with CBS News reporters Eric Sevareid and Martin Agronsky. Asked to comment on the public clamor over the decisions that had allegedly restricted the police and aided criminals, Black said:

"Well, the Court didn't do it."

"The Court did not do it?"

"No. The Constitution makers did it. They were the ones that put in 'no man shall be compelled to convict himself.' They were the ones that put in every one of those amendments. . . . And so, when they say the Court did it, that's just a little wrong. The Constitution did it."

This attitude was apparent in the *Miranda* decision. The Court brushed off arguments stressing the potential adverse impact of the ruling and the dearth of empirical data, with the comment that on constitutional questions the Court "does not take a poll." The following year, Byron White, who had dissented vigorously in *Miranda*, took the same line in defending it before the Conference of Chief Justices. He questioned whether the decision had handicapped law enforcement, but added: "Whatever the true facts are, is the seriousness of the impact of *Miranda* of any relevance whatsoever in determining the proper scope of the Fifth Amendment's privilege against self-incrimination? Is it important in a constitutional sense whether fewer confessions or convictions were obtained?" There was a hint of future trouble for the Court in this reasoning. The Warren Court was moving for policy reasons further and faster from the understood meanings of the Constitution than any Court had ever moved before, yet in answer to others' concern about the results, there was a tendency to fall back on the traditional mystique of the Robe. It was as if the Justices had perceived the need for new activism in criminal law, without acknowledging to themselves that their new role would take them beyond the protection of the old shibboleths. If the Court was going to legislate on the subject of criminal procedure, then the results would have to be rationally defensible. The Justices' tendency to wish away this fact boded trouble on the volatile issue of crime.

Whether the Court had been lulled by the quality of the early criticism or by its occasional Delphic view of its own role, the results show that the Justices were not receptive when, in the year before the *Miranda* decision, three of the most distinguished legal scholars in the United States publicly warned the Court to take care.

If the American legal profession had been polled as to the two state justices most respected for their intellectual power and liberal views, the answer would almost certainly have been Chief Justice Roger J. Traynor of the Supreme Court of California and Justice Walter V. Schaefer of the Supreme Court of Illinois. Chief Justice Traynor's court had anticipated several of the Supreme Court's libertarian decisions, and Chief Justice Warren declared in the *Miranda* opinion itself that Justice Schaefer was "one of our country's distinguished jurists" (citing a ten-year-old Schaefer lecture—not the recent one that warned against the move that was made in *Miranda*). If the legal profession had also been asked to name the most distinguished Federal judge below the level of the Supreme Court, the majority would probably have named Henry J. Friendly, a judge of the U.S. Court of Appeals for the Second Circuit in New York.

Judge Friendly was the first to speak out. In a lecture to the State Bar of California in September of 1965 he warned that the Supreme Court was "moving too far too fast"—that it was a mistake for the Court to rush forward to establish a detailed code of criminal procedure in constitutional terms, "allowing no room whatsoever for reasonable difference of judgment or play in the joints." As an example, he posed a hypothetical but routine situation involving the arrest and conviction of a narcotics peddler. Then he identified ten points upon which the defendant might well have won his freedom by appealing to the Supreme Court.

Anticipating that the Supreme Court might soon impose new restrictions on police questioning, Judge Friendly declared that there was no constitutional basis for such a rule and "no social value in preventing uncoerced admission of the facts." Finally, he reminded the Court of the near-debacle of the Nine Old Men and raised the spectre of another self-inflicted wound. "In the long run," he said, "the people could hardly be expected to be more tolerant of judicial condemnation of reasonable efforts by state governments to protect the security of their lives and property than they were of nullification of efforts to advance their economic and social welfare" in the 1930s.

The following spring, after the Supreme Court had heard the arguments in *Miranda* but before it had decided the case, Justices Traynor and Schaefer both warned in public lectures that the Court would be giving criminal suspects too much if it should rule as it eventually did in *Miranda*. Both judges pointed out that such a rule, combined with existing decisions, would give each suspect a constitutional right to refuse to explain to the police the circumstances that led to his arrest, plus the right at the trial to decline to take the stand—and that no comment could be made to the jury by the judge or the prosecutor that the defendant's wall of silence might imply guilt. They argued that there was no basis in the history of the Fifth Amendment for thus handicapping reasonable efforts to discover the truth.

In the legal world, where Supreme Court Justices are revered as the high priests of their cult, it was a striking occurrence that three of the most respected lower-court judges spoke publicly in anticipation of a Supreme Court ruling, asking the Court to stay its hand. They felt that the problem of police questioning was too complex to be decided in terms of a rigid constitutional rule that would have to be applied in all cases (as the Supreme Court, sadder but perhaps wiser, was to conclude in the 1968 "stop and frisk" ruling), and that a compromise would have to be worked out to permit brief periods of police questioning, with built-in safeguards against coercion.

Dean Griswold of Harvard and other defenders of the Court had justified the previous sweep of its decisions on the ground that the Court had been forced to act by the default of everyone else; that the states had not faced up to such problems as illegal searches and lawyerless defendants, so the Court had no recourse but to announce such cases as *Mapp* v. *Ohio* and *Gideon* v. *Wainwright*. Here, all three judges pointed out that the American Law Institute, an organization of leading lawyers, judges and professors, had undertaken to draft a recommended model code of pre-arraignment procedure to be enacted by the states, and that after several years of work, it was nearing completion. The Court was not, then, being forced to act by others' refusal to grapple with the problem of confessions. It was under pressure to clarify the constitutional status of confessions vol-

untarily given but without warnings of rights by the police—
over 100 appeals on the point came to the Supreme Court in the
eighteen months that followed the inconclusive *Escobedo* ruling
—but the Court had recently demonstrated how nimbly it could
avoid ruling on such pressing matters when it wished. When it
was being pushed to decide if the Fourteenth Amendment guaranteed Negroes equal use of public accommodations, it stalled
until Congress declared in the Civil Rights Act of 1964 that
they did. In *Gideon* v. *Wainwright* the Court had left undecided
whether or not the right to counsel applies in misdemeanor
trials, and despite a succession of appeals on the point, and the
millions of trials that have been held without counsel each year
since, the Justices have not yet seen fit to answer that extremely
pregnant question.

In the public accommodations situation, the Court had been
pleased to wait because it agreed with the course that Congress
was expected to take. But the American Law Institute's draftsmen had prepared a tentative draft of a code that would have
sanctioned up to three hours' questioning in the police station
outside the presence of counsel (but with some mechanical "witness," such as a sound recording or video tape), and this compromise clashed with the prevailing absolutist thinking on the
Court. Also, several years would have passed before the A.L.I.
could have completed its code and before it could have been
enacted and tested in a few states. In terms of the history of the
country the time would not have been long; but the men who
made up the five-man Warren majority then averaged sixty-
eight years of age, and they were not disposed to wait.

The Court's action in *Miranda* becomes more understandable
when it is viewed, as the Justices saw it, against the impressive
backdrop of *Gideon* v. *Wainwright*. *Gideon* stood as a glittering example of what the Supreme Court could accomplish by
insisting on unbending compliance by the states with a rigid
constitutional rule. In *Gideon*, only three years prior to *Miranda*,
the Court had been faced with another subjective standard that
had proved unsatisfactory—the fundamental fairness technique
of deciding on the circumstances of each case whether or not an
indigent defendant should have had a lawyer appointed to represent him at his trial.

Despite the dire warnings that the states could not provide

lawyers in every felony case, the Court ruled in *Gideon* that the Sixth Amendment required it. The result was overwhelmingly beneficial: public defender offices sprang up across the country; a new concern for defendants' rights was evident throughout the nation; the Court was relieved of the burden of numerous right-to-counsel appeals; and the Supreme Court was venerated for sounding its call for equal justice for the poor.

Yet the Gideon's-trumpet image of the Supreme Court also had its hazards. It tended to create an impatience with ad hoc decision-making; a feeling that the Supreme Court could settle nagging problems of justice if it would only lay down the law in the form of objective absolutes. It belittled the hazards of a public backlash against the Court and cultivated the belief that once the Supreme Court moved, the country would lift its vision and follow along. It also disregarded the crucial distinction between rigid constitutional rules laid down for judges to follow in the calm of the courtroom, and ironclad procedures imposed on policemen in the streets. But in the glow of *Gideon* these limitations on the bold judicial stroke were easily overlooked.

In the Supreme Court, the votes of four Justices are sufficient to grant a petition for certiorari and bring an appeal before the Court. Assuming a full Court, the votes of five are enough to decide the case. In Warren, Black, Douglas, Brennan and Fortas there were five votes, so the appeal of Ernesto Miranda and three companion appeals were granted (the identities of those who vote to grant certiorari is never disclosed) and, by a vote of 5 to 4, the new doctrine became part of the Constitution.

In recent years the Justices have delighted in quoting Justice Schaefer's statement that "the quality of a nation's civilization can be largely measured by the methods it uses in the enforcement of its criminal laws." But Justice Schaefer did not contend that a civilization could be improved by an insistence on careful procedures; nor, on the contrary, that a society can afford to adopt more gentle procedures only after its members have civilized themselves. He simply said that the two occur together; it is yet too soon to judge from the results of the due process revolution which interpretation is correct.

What does seem clear is that *Miranda* marked the peak of the Supreme Court's revolution in criminal procedure. A year later the Court did declare, in *United States* v. *Wade*, that suspects were entitled to counsel at police lineups. But the presence of lawyers at lineups proved so ineffectual (and rare—few lawyers bothered to go) that the decision only highlighted the limitations of landmark Supreme Court decisions in securing individuals' rights.

Meanwhile, the Court—under withering criticism because of *Miranda*—gave ground on electronic surveillance, informers and searches. Furthermore, it surprised most observers by countermanding liberal lower courts that had declared it to be unconstitutional "cruel and unusual" punishment for the law to convict, rather than to attempt to cure, chronic alcoholics.

The climactic test came in 1968 when the Supreme Court considered the one other police practice that rivaled interrogation as an emotional issue—the "stop and frisk." Like interrogation, the police technique of "frisking" suspicious persons is usually directed at Negroes and the poor, and it had long been assumed that when the Supreme Court finally dealt with the practice it would take steps to curb it. But by June of 1968, when the Court ruled on the practice in *Terry* v. *Ohio*, public resentment against *Miranda* and other rulings had boiled up in the form of the anti-Supreme Court amendments to the Crime Bill. Furthermore, experience with *Miranda* had showed that despite the furor, it had not greatly affected police interrogation habits.

Two years after *Miranda*, it was apparent that on-the-street frisking by police would not be brought nicely within clearly defined limits by rigid procedures issued from the Supreme Court. Chief Justice Warren had chosen to write the Supreme Court's opinion when it made its grand attempt to police the police in the *Miranda* case. When it came time in the stop-and-frisk case to concede that the protective power of the Supreme Court had its limits, Warren again wrote this opinion of the Court. He said that police may search persons "on suspicion"—without the probable cause that is specified in the Fourth Amendment—if this seems necessary to discover weapons and protect the police.

Three weeks later, President Johnson announced that Chief Justice Warren had tendered his decision to retire. In a subsequent interview, Warren declared that he intended to devote most of his time after retirement to the improvement of criminal procedure, a task that he felt could no longer be dominated by the Supreme Court. The Supreme Court had settled most of the major constitutional issues, he said, so that now "the most important job . . . is not to decide what the substantive law is," but how to handle the mounting case backlogs and long trial delays. He believed that this would have to be done by institutions outside the appellate function of the Supreme Court.

IV

The Mathematics of Crime

The land is full of bloody crime and the city is full of violence.

EZEKIEL VII:23

On a rainy night in June of 1968, a "frost notice"—a word-of-mouth warning system used by the United States Marines to inform personnel of emergency situations—went out to all Marines in and around the Washington, D.C., area. It concerned the fashionable Georgetown section of residential Washington, a stately neighborhood of tree-lined streets and expensive town houses where such citizens as Allen Dulles, Averell Harriman, Dean Acheson and Abe Fortas have their homes.

"It would be inadvisable to frequent the Georgetown area currently," the frost notice warned the Marines, "and in general exercise caution and restraint in Washington." The reason for the warning was that in the early hours of that morning, June 5, two young Marine lieutenants had stopped in Georgetown for coffee in an all-night hamburger shop, had exchanged remarks with a trio of black militants who had come from California for the Poor Peoples' Campaign and had been shot dead. Only three nights earlier an eighteen-year-old high school senior had been shot to death after a bumping incident with a stranger outside a pharmacy two blocks away. In the six weeks before that, the area had been plagued by a series of vicious muggings.

The spectacle of Marines being warned away from Washington's most prestigious neighborhood (all the crimes were within shouting distance of the familiar town house from which John F. Kennedy had announced his Cabinet appointments in 1960) was only one of a number of bizarre incidents that seemed to show that violence had become more prevalent and threatening than ever before. Bus drivers in Washington and Baltimore had gone on strike in protest against being required to carry change, because a number had been beaten and one had been killed by robbers. An all-night grocery chain in Cleveland had issued free food vouchers to policemen so that their comings-and-goings would frighten away potential robbers. Pistol practice had displaced ladies' bridge clubs as the center of social activity in some suburban communities. A book by a former ice follies performer on judo and self-defense for ladies was selling briskly, along with such titles as *How to Avoid Burglary, Housebreaking and Other Crimes*, and *How to Defend Yourself, Your Family and Your Home*.

Small wonder that in the summer of 1968 the Harris Poll found 81 percent of the people believing that law and order had broken down, and that all of the Presidential candidates were promising to do something about it.

"Crime and violence have increased ten times faster than the population" was a stock punch line of Richard M. Nixon's all-purpose campaign speech. Vice President Humphrey noted that the annual number of homicides was lower than it was in 1930, but he, too, campaigned from the assumption that the crime rate was getting out of hand. George Wallace never failed to warn his listeners that they might get hit on the head on the way home by a thug who would probably be out of jail before they got out of the hospital.

With most Americans from the President down believing that crime has risen to emergency proportions, there has emerged a puzzling paradox: Many of those who have given the subject the most study have, until recently, concluded that it is not so.

Attorney General Ramsey Clark became the whipping boy of the 1968 campaign because he had expressed the belief in an unguarded moment that "the level of crime has risen a little bit, but there is no wave of crime in this country." In 1968 Robert M. Cipes, a lawyer and consultant to the President's Commission on Crime in the District of Columbia, published a book, *The Crime War*, which proceeded from the thesis that there was no crime wave, but rather that "current statistics simply reflect the fact that we are digging into the reservoir of unreported crimes." Intellectuals who were not specialists in the field also tended to accept this view. Dr. Karl Menninger, founder of the famed Menninger Clinic of psychiatry, concluded after writing a book on crime and punishment:

No crime statistics are dependable; most crime is not reported. Most violent crime takes place in the home. Most nonviolent crime takes place in department stores. My own belief is that there is less violence today than there was 100 years ago, but that we have a much better press and communications to report it.

The President's Commission on Law Enforcement and Administration of Justice, reporting in 1967, could not say after an eighteen-month study if the crime rate was higher than it had been before, or if Americans had become more criminal than their counterparts in earlier times.

At the center of this controversy had been the ever-rising crime index of the Federal Bureau of Investigation. This index, which has been widely accepted by politicians, policemen and editorial writers as the official barometer of crime, has also been described by Harvard crime expert Lloyd E. Ohlin as "almost worthless—but it is the only thing there is." Thorsten Sellin, the dean of American criminal statisticians, has been quoted in *Life* magazine as saying that the United States "has the worst crime statistics of any major country in the Western world." *The New*

York Times quoted Sophia M. Robison of the Columbia School of Social Work as saying that "the FBI's figures are not worth the paper they are printed on." Other experts were quoted to the same effect in the press.

Until the last few years, it was fashionable for criminologists to debunk the crime index in this vein when periodic flaps over the F.B.I.'s figures erupted and the news media solicited the academicians' views. However, their quoted statements were decidedly more critical than the articles that these same experts were writing for their fellow professionals. Whether they were being quoted out of context (as some claimed) or whether they were victims of betrayed innocence by reporters who did not bother to cushion the professors' true opinions in qualifying padding, the outcome was that the academicians' criticisms of the F.B.I.'s statistics were overstated in the mass media. The result was that while the general public tended erroneously to accept the crime index as gospel, the sophisticated readers who delved far enough into news articles to find the scholars' comments were usually persuaded that the statistical proof of rapidly-increasing crime was almost certainly wrong. Most of the academic experts did not intend to go that far—but the most respected ones agreed, at least until 1967 or 1968, that the F.B.I. had not proved its case.

This division of opinion was most pronounced with regard to violent crimes. The President's National Crime Commission stressed repeatedly that while thefts and other property crimes were rising rapidly, the increase in the type of violent crime that most people fear was lagging far behind. All of this doubt and division cast an aura of unreality about the political dialogue over such suggested reforms as Nixon's demand for changes in the Supreme Court's confessions decisions, Humphrey's call for a tenfold increase in law-enforcement spending and Wallace's suggestion that Federal judges' lifetime tenures be ended.

So long as some of the most thoughtful crime specialists in the country questioned whether violent crime was rising at an unusual or unexpected rate, there was every reason to hold back on any institutional changes, and especially such drastic ones. But since the National Crime Commission issued its report in February of 1967, events have occurred which have convinced most of the previously skeptical experts that violent crime has been rising dangerously, and that the increase can be expected to continue for a decade, at least. The exact nature and extent of this rise is still blurred. But that it is occurring—that the dark prophecy of the crime statisticians and the politicians is coming true—is no longer disputed by the experts.

This has come about in a curious way. In the early 1960s the academicians could see that a crime scare was being launched on the basis of questionable conclusions drawn from unreliable statistics. Many of them committed themselves publicly then to the proposition that the statistical "crime rise" was overblown. The Crime Commission hinted as much, although it stopped short of laying the blame at the doorstep of J. Edgar Hoover and the F.B.I., where most of it belonged. Yet after the Commission issued its report in early 1967, crime reports from around the country and special studies in key urban areas have satisfied the most serious doubts of the academic skeptics. In effect, these data have confirmed the conclusions about rising violence that Mr. Hoover had been drawing all along—unjustifiably, the experts thought—from the earlier data.

Despite the circumstances, the justification of J. Edgar Hoover and his crime statistics is certain to have a profound impact on the future of the "law and order" controversy, and possibly on the Supreme Court. Most of the erstwhile academic critics of the F.B.I.'s statistics are conceding, if not that he was right, at least that events have transformed illusion into reality. The controversy over the mathematics of crime will continue over the meaning of the statistics and the manipulations and distortions to which they are subjected, but the frame of reference has shifted in a dramatic way. Crime—violent crime—is increasing rapidly, and few criminologists will now deny it.

There were three good reasons why, prior to the release of the crime statistics for 1967, thoughtful crime experts bridled at the assumption that violent crime was in a dangerous spiral. First, history shows that there has been a rhythm to criminal violence in the United States, and that its rate has probably been higher at times in the past than it is now. Second, the crime scare had been generated by crime statistics that were so questionable and by distortions and exaggerations of those statistics that some critics considered them unworthy of belief. Finally, even those statistics didn't show an alarming rise in violent crime until 1968, when the figures for the previous year became available.

Attempting to put the recent spurt of lawlessness in perspective, the Crime Commission said:

> There has always been too much crime. Virtually every generation since the founding of the Nation and before has felt itself threatened by the spectre of rising crime and violence.
>
> A hundred years ago contemporary accounts of San Francisco told of extensive areas where "no decent man was in safety to walk the street after dark; while at all hours, both night and day, his property was jeopardized by incendiarism and burglary." Teenage gangs gave rise to the word "hoodlum"; while in one central New York City area, near Broadway, the police entered "only in pairs, and never unarmed." A noted chronicler of the period declared that "municipal law is a failure—we must soon fall back on the law of self preservation." "Alarming" increases in robbery and violent crimes were reported throughout the country prior to the Revolution. And in 1910 one author declared that "crime, especially its more violent forms, and among the young is increasing steadily and is threatening to bankrupt the Nation."
>
> Crime and violence in the past took many forms. During the great railway strike of 1877 hundreds were killed across the country and almost 2 miles of railroad cars and buildings were burned in Pittsburgh in clashes between strikers and company police and the militia. It was nearly a half century later, after pitched battles in the steel industry in the late thirties, that the Nation's long history of labor violence subsided. The looting and takeover of New York for 3 days by mobs in the 1863 draft riots rivaled the violence of Watts, while racial disturbances in Atlanta in 1907, in Chicago, Washington, and East St. Louis in 1919, Detroit in 1943 and New York in 1900, 1935, and 1943 marred big city life in the first half of the 20th century. Lynchings took the lives of more than 4,500 persons throughout the country between 1882 and 1930. And the violence of Al Capone and Jesse James was so striking that they have left their marks permanently on our understanding of the eras in which they lived.

No comprehensive crime figures were collected prior to 1933, but studies of individual cities have been made, and they show that crime characteristically has its ups and downs, rather than a steady growth along with the population. James Q. Wilson, a crime expert at Harvard, has said that the early studies "agree that during the period immediately after the Civil War the rate of violent crime in the big cities was higher than at any other time in our history." Almost all of the available data also indicate that the crime rate rose rapidly during the post-World War I period and the economic boom of the twenties, and that it nosedived within a year or so after the bust in 1929. Crime was already in a steep dive when the F.B.I. began tracking the curve in the early thirties. It bottomed out in the early forties, and has risen almost every year since then—giving some credence to the impression that crime rates, like women's skirts, go up in periods of prosperity.

However, when the F.B.I. publishes its crime charts for public consumption, it usually slices off the downward years, which seems to bear out its claim of "record highs" in crime, even in mild years. One reason for this is that the F.B.I.'s statistical system was overhauled in 1958, and the Bureau doesn't consider the pre- and post-1958 figures to be entirely fungible. Yet as a result of slicing off the earlier years, the F.B.I. gives a skyrocket impression with its crime charts that the facts do not fully support.

The crime index has given "law and order" an important element in common with the other political issues that have stirred the emotions of the modern electorate—the proposition that things are bad and are likely to get worse can be demonstrated by statistics. Figures on paper were not always a *sine qua non* of scare politics. The prosecutions of the Mormons were not supported by statistical evidence that polygamy was deleterious; there were no figures to support the Red Scare that led to the Palmer raids in 1919; and nobody thought it necessary to show on paper that the Japanese-Americans were a threat before the Nisei were rounded up after Pearl Harbor. But since World War II Americans have not easily been persuaded that evil threatens unless the threat could be reduced to figures on paper. One of the pioneers of statistical politics, Senator Joseph McCarthy, demonstrated that this requirement need not cramp a statesman's style. For so long as the figures are sufficiently obscured that they cannot be absolutely refuted ("I have in my hand a list of fifty-seven names of known communists in the State Department. . . ."), they usually satisfy the public desire for quantum proof. That this was not some political witchcraft peculiar to Senator McCarthy was later demonstrated by John F. Kennedy during his missile-gap stage and still later by Lyndon B. Johnson, who discovered an alarmingly large category of the "poor" and then substantially reduced its size, all by statistics.

According to behavioral scientists, the reason why statistics are so willingly swallowed as adequate food for thought on public issues is that society has a gift for accepting and then turning into emotional symbols those statistical indicators that confirm and reinforce existing conceptions. People believe those statistics that tell them what they already believed. This, according to sociologist Albert D. Biderman, is the key to the great prestige of crime statistics in the United States. "The crime index," Professor Biderman says, "shares with many indicators the property of owing much of its credibility and popularity to its being consistent with beliefs formed by everyday experience. . . . It serves as a short-hand certifier of beliefs, rather than as a shaper of them."

This once became so galling to Attorney General Nicholas deB. Katzenbach that he is said to have seized a sheet of crime statistics one day, pounded his desk and growled: "It's bad enough to lose the war on crime, but to lose it five times a year is too much!" The offending paper was one of the most predictable of government documents—the latest report by the Federal Bureau of Investigation on crime. These compilations of crime statistics from local police departments, released to the public in the form of four quarterly reports and a fifth annual recapitulation, are known as Uniform Crime Reports. For the past decade they have been truly uniform in at least one sense—they have invariably declared that crime is rising at a terrifying rate.

By 1966, the year of Mr. Katzenbach's outburst, the periodic crime increase announcement had become a familiar Hoover's Comet that burst upon the national scene at regular intervals, always followed by a trail of indignant editorials and Congressional speeches deploring rising crime. In 1968—a typical year— the reports produced these headlines in *The New York Times*: March 15: "Major Crimes up 16% in '67: F.B.I. Puts Year's Rise at 23% in the Big Cities"; June 25: "First Quarter Rate of Crime is up 17%"; August 26: "Serious Crimes in U.S. Rise 16%"; September 20: "A 21% Rise in Crime is Reported by the F.B.I."; December 12: "16% Rise in Crime Reported by F.B.I." After a decade of this steady drumbeat of crime rises, many, if not most, Americans have become conditioned to feel that as a function of the law of averages, their chances of escaping rape, murder or mugging much longer must be about to run out.

As the Federal official primarily responsible for contending with the problem of crime, Mr. Katzenbach had good reason to be irked, for the F.B.I.'s stewardship of the nation's crime statistics has resulted in a hysteria that seems more beneficial to the F.B.I. as a crime-fighting public agency than to the people's enlightenment. Three elements appear to have combined to puff the crime picture out of shape, and the F.B.I. could at least have ameliorated two of them.

First, the figures themselves are easily the most suspect statistics published under the imprimatur of the United States Government. They are highly susceptible to reporting vagaries, do not allow for built-in increases due to shifting age ratios in the population, and do not clearly separate crimes against property from more serious offenses against people.

These flaws are built into the system and the F.B.I. is not necessarily responsible for them, but in its zest for bearing bad news the Bureau has compounded the mischief that is inherent in the system. The F.B.I., with its flair for publicity, has managed five times a year to wring the maximum amount of public terror out of a statistical system that was conceived (by the International Association of Chiefs of Police) as a technique for keeping lawmen informed of the trends of their trade. It has consistently emphasized the alarming implications of the statistics (even in good years, such as 1959 and 1961, when violent crime *declined* in relation to the population), and has not adequately pointed out their inadequacies.

Finally, the F.B.I.'s statistical image of a rising national crime rate has been translated into a personal threat in the minds of many Americans through the instantly shared experience of television coverage of a few spectacular crimes and riots. The Crime Commission found that this has created a pervasive "fear of strangers." It noted the interaction between crime statistics and vivid exposure of a few events:

Many circumstances now conspire to call greater attention to crime as a national, rather than a purely local, problem. Concern with crime is more typically an urban than a rural phenomena and the rural population of the country is declining. At one time, for a majority of the population, reports of crime waves related only to those remote and not quite moral people who inhabited cities.

Now, also, more people are informed by nationally oriented communications media and receive crime reports from a much wider territorial base. In recent years news of the violent and fearful mass killing of eight nurses in a Chicago apartment, five patrons of a beauty shop in Mesa, Arizona, and 13 passersby on the University of Texas campus in Austin received detailed coverage throughout the country. The fear of the people of Boston in 1966 of the brutal attacks of the "Boston Strangler" must have been sympathetically shared and understood in many homes across the land. Some part of the public fear of crime today is undoubtedly due to the fact that the reports of violent crime we receive daily are drawn from a larger pool of crime-incident reports than ever before. But perhaps most important has been the steady stream of reports of rising crime rates in both large and small communities across the Nation. From all this has emerged a sense of crisis in regard to the safety of both persons and property.

The political effects of this have already been profound. During the 1968 Presidential campaign a reporter for *The New York Times* polled the citizens of Webster City, Iowa, which calls itself "Main Street, U.S.A." He found the overriding issue to be "crime in the streets," with particular concern about riots and unruly demonstrations. But when the interviewer inquired about crime in "Main Street, U.S.A.," the complaints were that youngsters were drinking beer, driving fast and breaking an occasional window. Pressed further, the city fathers complained that trucks hauling turkey feathers through town were unlawfully failing to cover their cargoes to keep from littering Main Street. Another reporter, who found the citizenry of Garnett, Kansas, up in arms over crime, discovered that there hadn't been a rape there for twelve years, nor a murder for twenty-one, and that the only person in jail was a seventeen-year-old hot-rodder.

To understand how this exaggerated image of "crime" gained currency, long before the academic experts agreed that violence was climbing, it is necessary to comprehend the mechanics of the Uniform Crime Reports. Local police departments voluntarily report to the F.B.I. the volume of crimes known to the police, offenses cleared by arrest, persons held for prosecution, and persons released or found guilty of offenses. Of the twenty-nine different crimes reported, the F.B.I. uses only seven in its crime index. The "index" crimes, chosen because they are serious and are thought to be bellwethers of criminal activity, are murder, forcible rape, robbery (muggings, armed robbery and theft by threat of force), aggravated assault (assault with intent to kill or seriously injure), burglary (breaking and entering to steal), larceny of $50 or more and auto theft. From this the FBI publishes the famous Crime Index, which is simply the rate of these offenses per 100,000 people.

The Uniform Crime Reports are naturally suspect because the F.B.I.'s crime index reflects only *reported* crime. There is known to be so much crime that is either not reported to the police, or not reported by them to the F.B.I., that only slight changes in reporting habits could have a yo-yo effect on the effect on the crime index. The Crime Commission learned from house-to-house surveys that the volume of unreported crime is far greater than anyone had imagined—double, triple and even ten times the volume of offenses that are actually reported, depending on whether the crime involved is the type that shames the victim or whether it is the kind the police are thought unlikely to solve.

Since there is so much unreported crime, it is theoretically possible to have a "crime wave" on the index charts, when in fact nothing but reporting habits have changed. Thus a crime scare could result from victim sophistication—a realization that only reported thefts can become valid income tax deductions or insurance claims, or a new willingness by nonwhites to report crimes to the police.

The same crime "rise" can occur when the police become more diligent in reporting crime. For years the police of Chicago reported many times more robberies than the City of New York, which has more than twice as many people (in one year, Chicago reported eight times as many robberies). Finally, in 1949, the F.B.I. stopped including New York's statistics because it didn't believe them. New York has since been reinstated, but periodically its police have slipped back into their old ways of neglecting to report painful facts.

There seem to be two principal reasons for this tendency by the police to fudge on crime reports. One is that much of the crime occurs in Negro neighborhoods, between Negroes, and there has sometimes been an easy-going tolerance of it by the police. It was neither investigated nor reported as carefully as crime was elsewhere. The other reason is that increasing crime is political trouble for city administrations, and they like to give the impression that it is under control. Ambitious police officials realize that their superiors want crime kept down, with the result that complaints sometimes get "lost." The Crime Commission found a secret "file 13" in one city containing a catalogue of complaints that were not officially reported, and a single precinct in Philadelphia once had 5,000 more crime reports on file than it had officially recorded.

Some experts suspect that both motives for under-reporting are losing their validity, and that a good portion of the crime bulge in certain cities is due to the new official willingness to tell all about crime. In recent years more Negro policemen have been hired and more attention given to ghetto crime. This concern has probably dissipated the feeling that Negro complaints are not worth reporting. Also, with the Supreme Court and not the police being widely blamed for the increase in crime, some resentful policemen are said to be reporting crime with a vengeance. The late Police Chief William Parker of Los Angeles once startled a visiting Federal official by his candid discussion of the huge chart on his wall depicting the rise of crime. Each crime peak was topped with the title of a Supreme Court decision in favor of defendants' rights. Chief Parker explained that the police had seen, years before the Court issued its landmark rulings, that a crime boom was coming despite their best efforts—and that they had been lucky to have the Supreme Court to serve as a lightning rod for the criticism. He said that this was partially responsible for his decision to begin making speeches and writing articles about the connection between crime in the streets and judicial decisions.

Jerome Daunt, the chief of the F.B.I.'s crime statistics operation, concedes that some of the index crimes are subject to wide reporting fluctuations, but he points out that some are not. Mr. Daunt, a lean, serious man who learned his crime statistics on the job as an F.B.I. agent, makes the point that certain crimes by their nature are almost always reported: bank robberies, because none are too insignificant to report; assault by gun, because the law requires physicians to file reports; murder, because there is a body to be explained.

Bank robberies have increased even faster than the general index, with a rise of 248 percent from 1960 to 1967. Assault by gun rose 84 percent in the five years from 1962 to 1967. Much has been made of the fact that criminal homicide has actually declined by 70 percent since 1933, but Mr. Daunt has an explanation for this: "Police response, ambulance response, and improved medical techniques," he says. "It's like the decline in the relative number of war wounded who die—because they get better, quicker treatment."

"Trends—it is the trends in crime statistics that count," declares Mr. Daunt, "and we have been right on the trends." The F.B.I. has indeed been right on the trends (except that its gloomy projections of future crime levels have invariably fallen short of reality), and this has been due in some part to its painstaking efforts to eliminate error—especially by checking for reporting failures whenever reports began to run suspiciously counter to expectations. But part of this success must also be attributed to the melancholy fact that in dealing with crime, if one predicts disaster long enough, events will finally bear him out.

The most valid complaint against the F.B.I. is not that its figures have been soft, but that the Bureau has not presented them honestly to the public. When the F.B.I. first began to sound the alarm about rising crime a decade ago, the overall increase was small and the violent crime rate was actually frequently in decline. In 1961, for instance, the crime rates for violent offenses *decreased* across the board. Murder, forcible rape, robbery and aggravated assault all declined. Yet the overall crime index rate rose by 3 percent because of a modest increase in property crimes. J. Edgar Hoover darkly announced that "major crimes committed in the United States in 1961 have again reached an all-time high," adding that during the year there were "four serious crimes per minute." The reason for the rise was that then, as now, about nine out of ten offenses included in the crime index do not involve violence, so that even a modest rise in property offenses was enough to lift the entire crime index. Currently, murders, rapes and assaults make up only 8 percent of the crimes reported in the index.

If robberies are included as "violent crimes" (about one-fourth of them result in injuries to the victims), it is still true that more than four-fifths of the index crimes are nonviolent thefts of property—burglary, larceny of $50 or more, and car theft. Since the crime rates for these offenses were, until recently, consistently higher than the rates for violent crimes, they inflated the overall crime index and gave the impression that violent crime was rising faster than it actually was. This has led to the charge that the F.B.I.'s crime index is really a gauge of "joy-riding" by youngsters in other peoples' cars. In any year the number of auto thefts in the crime index will far outnumber all of the violent crimes taken together, and since nine out of ten stolen cars are recovered and returned to their owners, the fearsome "crime rate" is far less a reflection of the pain of victims of rape and assault than the temporary aggravation of those who left their keys in their cars.

Another complaint about the F.B.I.'s crime reporting system is its tendency to tempt exaggeration, oversimplification and even manipulation of the crime increase. By taking the population increase (the rule-of-thumb figure is 1.5 percent per year) over a given stretch of years and dividing it into the percentage of crime increase, it can be said that crime is growing many times faster than the population. For instance, if the population increased by approximately 11 percent over an eight-year period, but the number of reported index offenses grew by 122 percent, it could be said that crime "outstripped our population growth by over eleven to one"—J. Edgar Hoover's assessment of the crime rise of the 1960s.

Once announced, this roughhewn calculation from the highly suspect crime index can be cited as government proof that "crime is growing eleven times faster than the population." And when the public recalls that only two years earlier Mr. Hoover used the multiple of seven to describe the increase, and that two years before that he used the figure five, it is given an avalanche impression of "crime"—the threat of attack by strangers—that is puffed out of any relation to the actual threat that any individual will become a victim of violent crime.

An even more warped impression is given by the "crime clocks" that the F.B.I. publishes each year. This baffling presentation, year after year, of the shrinking average interval between the commission of various offenses across the country, seems to have no purpose other than sheer terror. Since the population is growing, the interval between crimes would necessarily narrow each year, even if the crime rate wasn't increasing. Thus the hands of the F.B.I.'s "crime clocks" invariably show fewer minutes between crimes than for the previous year. The "crime clock" device lends itself to shocking conclusions that mean nothing, as a published interpretation of the 1966 figures show: "An American woman is raped every 12 minutes. A house in the United States is burglarized every 27 seconds. Someone is robbed every 4½ minutes in this nation."

By reducing crime to these terms, the "fear of strangers" syndrome is justified in a way that is not borne out by the risks of everyday life. Statistically, the fear of attack by strangers is one of the least likely hazards that the average person encounters. The risk of death from willful homicide in any given year is about 1 in 15,000, and almost three out of four murders are committed by family members or friends. So out of about 13,650 reported homicides in a recent year, some 3,500 were committed by strangers. In that same year, 55,200 Americans met violent deaths in car wrecks. The result is that the average person's likelihood of being killed in a car crash is more than fifteen times the chances that he will be murdered by a stranger. His risk in any given year of being attacked by a stranger and hurt badly enough to require any degree of hospitalization is about 1 in 4,500—and this is an average possibility: If he lives away from high-crime areas his risk is much lower. As Ramsey Clark used to put it, the average individual's chance of being a victim of a crime of violence is once in 400 years, and Clark always added that if one wished to improve his odds he could avoid his relatives and associates—since they are statistically the most likely to do him harm.

What this shows is that extremely subjective conclusions can be drawn from the basic crime data in this country and that the F.B.I. has consistently presented it in a way that tends to make little old ladies stay indoors and strong men look over their shoulders. As one observer pointed out, rather than publishing the fact that some unfortunate individual is murdered every forty-eight minutes, the F.B.I. could have told the country that the average citizen's chances of becoming a murder victim on any given day are about 1 in 2,000,000, and that then he might well be willing to brave those odds without hedging on personal freedom of movement or the country's traditional scheme of personal rights.

As slippery as these figures can be in the hands of crime experts, politicians can turn them to quicksilver. During the 1968 Presidential campaign Richard Nixon observed that crime had increased 88 percent under the Democratic administration. Attorney General Clark went on television with the reply that crime had risen 98 percent during the Eisenhower period. Aghast, the Republican Task Force on Crime fired back with this statement:

. . . crime in the eight Eisenhower years between 1953 and 1960 did not increase by 98 percent. That charge is simply inaccurate.

Crime reported in 1960, the last year of the Eisenhower administration, was 63 percent greater than in 1952, the last year of the Truman administration.

This, of course, covers eight years. If the experience of 1967 holds true this year, the eight-year Kennedy-Johnson record will show a whopping 118 percent increase for the comparable period, or almost double the rate under a Republican administration. Parenthetically, if only a seven-year frame of reference is used, they fare even worse. During the first seven years of the Eisenhower administration the crime increase was 43 percent, less than half of the 88 percent recorded during the seven years thus far under Kennedy and Johnson.

Vice President Humphrey said he deplored this crime numbers game—and added that if he were inclined to play it he could point out that the eight states with the highest crime rates all had Republican governors.

Because the F.B.I.'s crime index was so frequently abused, because its figures were suspect, because even those figures showed the crimes of violence lagging far behind, and possibly because they were liberals indulging in wishful thinking, the academicians refused throughout most of the sixties to admit that a serious criminal violence problem had been proved.

The first break in the familiar statistical pattern came when the 1967 crime reports from across the country were tabulated by the F.B.I. The usual pattern of relatively low violent crime rates and high property offenses was shattered by a 16 percent overall increase, composed of a 16 percent rise in violent crimes and a 17 percent increase in property offenses.

But most startling to crime experts was the 28 percent jump in the crime of robbery, which many criminologists consider the bellwether offense in the crime index. Since robbery always involves a threat of force, if not its use, it gives an indication of the public's proclivity toward violence. And since the offender and the victim are usually strangers, the family-quarrel element does not distort the picture. For that reason, criminologists were shocked to see robbery suddenly increasing as rapidly as the property crimes. When the figures for 1968 were released, even those who had taken the most jaundiced view of the F.B.I.'s statistical dexterity began to say that the crime rise was real. Violent crimes had increased by 19 percent over the previous year, and robberies were up by 30 percent.

Meanwhile, new studies showed what Professor Ohlin termed "a pronounced increase in the readiness in people to resort to armed attack." In Philadelphia, where the volume of robberies fluctuated up and down after 1960, the rate of persons injured in robberies began to rise in 1962 and climbed steadily. "Perhaps it is because the robbers tend to be younger, and the young are more likely to use violence," concluded criminologist Marvin E. Wolfgang; "but there has been a considerable increase in the level of violence in robberies."

As remote as the statistical chances were that the average person would become a victim of violent crime in the course of a year, the figures showed that the likelihood had risen alarmingly in the 1960s. By 1968 the average person stood one chance in 14,706 of being killed, one in 3,226—if a woman—of being raped, one in 763 of being robbed, and one chance in 709 of being assaulted seriously. A decade before, the chances had been one in 21,739 of being killed, one in 5,376 of being raped, one in 1,822 of being robbed and 1 in 1,270 of being seriously assaulted. Behind these figures was the further reality that it was not "average" people who were being murdered, raped and robbed—it was, for the most part, people who lived in cities, and their chances of becoming victims were much higher than the figures showed. A grisly pattern began to emerge in some cities, where murder was no longer a "family affair" that happened usually between relatives and acquaintances. As late as 1965 in the District of Columbia, about eight out of ten murder victims and offenders were acquainted or related. By 1969 the wave of homicides in muggings and robberies had reversed this picture to the point that in seven cases out of ten the killer was not known by the victim. By that time the old saw about being safer in a dark alley than in one's automobile no longer rang true; 293 people were murdered in the capital city that year, but only 127 died in car wrecks.

Ronald H. Beattie, chief of California's Bureau of Criminal Statistics, who had declared as late as 1966 that the available crime statistics "indicate no substantial increase in aggressive crimes during recent years," took another look in 1968 and said that violent crime was growing even faster than crimes against property. An example of how grimly familiar crime inflation had become came when the F.B.I. disclosed that its crime index had risen only 11 percent in 1969. That would have been considered a cause for alarm in most prior periods, but after three successive years in which the increase had been above 15 percent, the Nixon administration began to argue that its anticrime program was already proving a success. Most experts now believe that the rise in crime of the 1960s, with its heavy component of crimes of violence, will continue at least through the decade of the 1970s. The reason is that the types of people who, as one observer put it, are "untamed in the ways of society," and are thus inclined to commit crimes, are increasing in proportion to the population as a whole.

By far the most crime-prone of this "untamed" class are young men. More fifteen-year-olds are arrested for serious crimes than any other group. Yet thanks to the postwar baby boom, there are proportionally more of them around to commit crimes than ever before, and their numbers are growing. Each year since 1961 an additional 1,000,000 youths have reached the age of fifteen than did the year before, and already almost one-half of the population is under twenty-five. According to crime experts, almost half of the total increase in arrests in the first half of the 1960s was simply because there were more younger people around.

Another complicating factor is urbanization. Study after study shows that the violent crime rate of Negroes who have moved from the South into the large urban cities is far higher than the national crime rate for Negroes. The same is true, but with less emphasis, for cities as a whole; crime rates invariably rise in proportion to the proximity to an urban center. Concomitant with the anonymity of urban life—where everybody is a stranger to everyone else and the fear of detection and shame of arrest are diminished—a familiar pattern of bold, casual criminality has developed.

There are other indices, all of them pointing upward. Statistics show that communities with large transient populations experience high crime rates, and demographers predict increasing population mobility in the coming years. High crime and narcotics addiction go together, and the narcotics arrest rate (although heavily weighed with many marijuana cases of questionable seriousness) more than trebled during the 1960s. Some scientists believe that overcrowding alone can cause antisocial behavior, and the decrease in living space is obvious. It is sad but not surprising that Professor Wilson concludes: "We shall be fortunate if we can even slow the rate of increase in crime; we shall be impossibly blessed if we can actually reduce the level of crime."

Without more, the simple mathematics of crime would add up to powerful pressures against the Supreme Court's declaration of more rights for individuals in their dealings with the police. But there is more to the crime issue than mere increasing numbers. "Crime" in America is not only a quantitative count of antisocial acts; it has an emotional facet that greatly complicates the prospect that the Court can weather the coming decades with its newly announced doctrines of individual rights intact. For while the public and the Supreme Court have tended to look at crime from different perspectives, both have looked through colored glasses. To a large extent the future of crime and the Supreme Court depends on color—that is, upon the future course of the Negro.

V

Negro Crime

and the Supreme Court

*If ever America undergoes great revolutions, they
will be brought about by the presence of the
black race on the soil of the United States; that is
to say, they will owe their origin, not to the
equality, but to the inequality, of condition.*

ALEXIS DE TOCQUEVILLE

Every nation has its equivalent of the mythical emperor who
wore no clothes. In the fable, nobody could bring himself to believe what he saw until a child blurted out the truth, and then
everyone had a laugh at the emperor's expense. In the United
States the naked emperor was for years the high Negro crime
rate; the boy who broke the spell was George Wallace, and nobody laughed.

In his campaign for President, Governor Wallace did not shout
that the emperor had no clothes; a politician with his segrega-
tionist credentials could make his point without calling a spade

a spade. Instead, he preached incessantly about rising crime. Everyone knew that it was Negro crime that was being deplored.

Wallace's early strength forced his rivals to talk tough about crime, too. Soon so many politicians had vowed that they weren't necessarily criticizing Negroes when they demanded "law and order," that everybody understood that the term really was a racial slur of sorts.

Once established, this issue provided a nice vehicle for those candidates who wished to purify their liberal credentials; several pledged solemnly to call for "order with justice" instead. Vice President Humphrey did this, but he also mentioned Negro crime, stressing that most of the victims were Negroes. Richard Nixon tried "law and order with justice" in his speeches as a compromise, but the phrase did not sing; the "with justice" got lost in the final weeks of his winning campaign.

In mid-September of 1968, when the law-and-order flapdoodle was at its height, Attorney General Ramsey Clark testified before the National Commission on Causes and Prevention of Violence. After a few introductory remarks, Clark made this statement:

"Negroes, 12 percent of the total population, were involved in 59 percent of the arrests for murder: 54 percent of the victims were Negro. Nearly one-half of all persons arrested for aggravated assault were Negro and the Negro was the primary victim of assault. Forty-seven percent of those arrested for rape were Negro and again studies show the Negro is the primary victim. Sixty-one percent of all arrested for robbery were Negro. Less than one-third of the persons arrested for property crime are Negroes."

This paragraph was dropped into the statement without elaboration or recommendations, and since Clark also locked horns that day with J. Edgar Hoover over the issue of police violence (which Clark deplored and Hoover excused), the racial reference passed unnoticed by the news media. But the spell was broken; a high Government official had, apparently for the first time, talked publicly and in some detail about high Negro crime.

The long-standing national myopia about Negro crime has been a remarkable public exercise in whistling past a graveyard. It involved the Federal Bureau of Investigation, which buried the shocking statistics of Negro crime in its annual publications and said nothing; the press, which ignored Negro crime in its reports of the F.B.I.'s crime statistics; the Negro community, which suffered most but feared to be tarred by the lawlessness of the few; the professional criminologists, who saw what was happening but failed to make themselves heard outside academia; and officialdom, which operated under the premise that if nothing were said perhaps the problem would go away.

Rather than going away, it got worse—and while the national tendency continued to be to whistle and not look back, George Wallace saw to it that the phenomenon of Negro crime could never again be simply ignored. Events have shown that Wallace was a symptom and not the disease. His innuendos rang bells because many listeners had begun to suspect, through newspaper and word-of-mouth reports, that Negro street crime was indeed getting worse.

Since then, evidence has come to light to show that they were right. A spate of recent statistical studies by criminologists had suggested that the already high Negro crime rate had begun to accelerate; this phenomenon has now been confirmed by a national statistical survey that bears the imprimatur of the Federal Bureau of Investigation and the National Commission on the Causes and Prevention of Violence. The Violence Commission obtained from the F.B.I. the most complete figures ever assembled on race and crime—figures that show Negro arrest rates for violent crimes in the cities to be twelve times that of whites across the board, as much as eighteen times that of whites for some offenses, and still climbing—especially among young people. The ultimate result of this realization can be constructive or corrosive, depending upon how the public reacts—but it seems inevitable that race and crime will become firmly linked in the public mind, and that the Supreme Court and other institutions that are caught up in the crime crisis will be affected by it.

Of those who had a clear view of the Negro crime situation all along but said nothing, Hoover's F.B.I. has been the most oblivious. Its annual statistical roundup of crime, a tall volume entitled *Crime in the United States*, contains neat tables supported by detailed discussions of the figures. These discussions range from tedious flyspecking about trivia to disapproving comments on such subjects as the high recidivism rate among probationers and parolees, but there has never been an analysis of the lopsided arrest figures for Negroes that the tables show.

For instance, the F.B.I. tabulations for 1967 disclosed—to those determined few who penetrated the columns of fine print —that more Negroes than whites were arrested for murder, robbery, carrying concealed weapons, prostitution and gambling. Only the total number of arrests for each racial group is given for each offense, but since Negroes made up 12 percent of the population, simple arithmetic would show that for the F.B.I.'s "index" crimes, the national arrest rate for Negroes was five times the arrest rate for whites, and for some violent crimes it was more than ten times as high. (When the F.B.I. refined these data for the Violence Commission, it showed that Negro arrest rates in the cities were about double the national ratios. Sociologists despair because the F.B.I.'s failure to routinely refine its published racial data obscures facts such as this.)

Race has never been mentioned in the publicity releases that the Bureau issues with its figures, and because the 1967 racial statistics were dished out cold turkey in the F.B.I.'s tables, the disparity was not mentioned by the wire services' reports of the year's crime. As far as anyone can remember, neither the Associated Press nor the United Press International has ever reported the Negro arrest rates, although the wire services report the F.B.I.'s figures each time they are released.

Negro spokesmen were equally silent until the rhetoric of the 1968 political campaign broke the spell. "The fact that George Wallace said it doesn't mean it isn't true," said a leader of the National Association for the Advancement of Colored People's influential New York chapter, as his group came out, a few weeks after the election, for a tough policy against crime. The NAACP chapter declared that "the reign of criminal terror (in Harlem) must be stopped now." Its demands were almost foursquare with the long-standing suggestions of J. Edgar Hoover— more police protection and tighter bail and probation restrictions.

The most curious lapse was the failure of the academicians to communicate with anyone but each other about the worsening situation. Since the 1920s sociologists have been writing in their scholarly journals about the high Negro arrest rates. If anybody on the outside noticed, for the most part they felt it best not to pass the information along. This was of little importance until the late 1960s, when Negro crime began to accelerate in an alarming pattern—there was a tendency toward more violence, by younger Negroes, more often directed at whites. The academicians called attention to the danger signs, but the accurate word of what is happening has never reached the public beyond the readers of their own academic journals.

The motives behind the Negro crime taboo were obvious. Virtually every sociologist who has studied the subject agrees that the crime rate among blacks is far higher than that of the rest of the population, even after allowing for the blacks' generally low economic status. This is the ultimate product, most experts feel, of the economic and cultural ravages of a segregated system that has been presided over by whites. Thus to dissect the problem would expose flaws in the performances of both races. Moreover, as high as the Negro crime rate has gone, it still represents only a small minority of black people. In a recent year there were 2,923 arrests for "index" crimes for each 100,-000 Negroes in the population, and although that is much higher than the white rate of 607, nobody wanted to tar the law-abiding majority of Negroes with a lawless image they did not deserve.

Yet with the racial disparities as wide as they are, the subject has been unpleasant enough to remind government officials and scholars of the ancient tradition that the messenger who brought bad news forfeited his head. That is apparently why nobody brought the statistics to the public's attention and into perspective when Negro arrest rates began to rise sharply in the mid-1960s—a silence that created a climate favorable for the likes of George Wallace. Under the assumption that nobody has suffered for exposing the crime statistics of the Federal Bureau of Investigation, the Violence Commission's staff decided to break the spell by asking the F.B.I. to compile the most comprehensive report ever made of relative Negro and white arrest statistics and trends. What the F.B.I. did was to take the urban arrest data for 1964 through 1967, relate them to the ages and racial characteristics of the arrestees, and arrive at the first reliable statistics of racial crime trends across the country.

The results showed that Negroes' arrest rates for violent crime were far higher than whites' rates—higher than most experts had guessed in their gloomiest moments. The gap was widening for murder, rape and robbery, where the already high rates for blacks were climbing faster than the whites' rates. Most ominous of all, soaring rates among young blacks promised more of the same for the future.

Robbery presented the gloomiest picture: Where Negroes had been arrested five times more often than whites in the country as a whole in 1950, the F.B.I.'s figures showed the Negro urban robbery rate to be sixteen times greater in 1967, and for the coming generation—those from ages 10 to 17—the Negro rate was twenty times the white rate. In terms of arrest rates (the number per 100,000 persons per year), the national robbery rates in 1950 were 12.6 for whites and 68.8 for Negroes. By 1967 this had risen in the cities to 22.8 for whites and 368.9 for Negroes. Among the younger group, it was 27 for whites and 549.7 for young Negroes. It is this skyrocketing robbery rate among young Negroes that worries the experts most.

The F.B.I.'s study was only slightly less bleak for violent crimes other than robbery. For murder, the Negro arrest rate was eighteen times that of whites for persons of all ages. The rape rate among Negroes was eleven times that of whites of all ages, and twelve times the white rate in the younger group. For aggravated assault, the overall Negro rate was ten times that of whites, but unlike the other three types of violent crime, the whites' assault rate was rising faster. Surprisingly, the F.B.I. found overall violent crime rates for young whites to have risen very little over that period, indicating that the much-discussed rising crime rate among young people could be largely a reflection of soaring crime among young blacks.

The Violence Commission experts knew that these figures tended to underscore black criminality, because only crimes of violence were included, and these have always been prevalent among nonwhites. If white-collar offenses and other middle-class crimes had been cranked in, the picture would not have been so stark. The experts were aware that the President's National Crime Commission had concluded that the Negro rates for burglary, larceny and auto theft (the three property crimes in the F.B.I.'s crime index) increased by 33 percent, while the white rate rose almost as fast, by 24 percent. White Americans were also known to be narrowing the gap in a few crimes other than assaults, notably in the area of narcotics offenses.

But what struck the Violence Commission with such force was that urban violence was much more a Negro phenomenon than people had known (or at least, had been able to prove), and that these trends were so pronounced among young blacks that the situation was almost certain to grow much worse in the future. The final blow was that all of this bore the imprimatur of the Federal Bureau of Investigation, which assured that it would strike public opinion with the force of holy writ.

The impact of this was such that the two Negro members of the Commission, Patricia Harris and Judge A. Leon Higginbotham, at first insisted that the study not be made public. Mrs. Harris, particularly, saw no reason to give ammunition to segregationists. Others on the Commission balked at suppressing the study, but they were torn, as others have been, between the desire to keep racists from exploiting such information and the need to inform society and encourage efforts to correct the conditions that breed crime.

They compromised by disclosing in the final Commission report that violent crime arrest rates for blacks of all ages were far higher than for whites. But no mention was made of the even higher rates of criminal violence found among the upcoming generation of young blacks, and there was no hint that disturbing new information about crime and race had been produced by the revered crime statistics machinery of the Federal Bureau of Investigation. The staff also agreed to strike from its task force report its conclusion that violent crime levels probably are much higher for blacks than for whites, and to substitute the statement that the arrest figures that suggest this are probably reliable.

The Commission disbanded, having published all of its task force reports except one—the one on individual acts of violence that contained the F.B.I.'s racial data. The indications were that a dearth of funds was probably responsible for the delay and that at some future time the data would be published in a form that would enlighten scholars but would probably not reach the general public. The outcome was one that all concerned could accept, and it had the virtue of not adding a new public controversy to an already grim situation. But that did not change the fact that the findings themselves indicate that severe strains will probably come to bear on the Supreme Court, as "street crime" comes to be increasingly associated with one group— young blacks.

Criminologists find it particularly ominous that robbery is becoming so rampant among young Negroes. Robbery includes all thefts carried out by the use or threat of force—which generally means muggings and armed stickups. Thus it is considered a bellwether crime, the one that most accurately indicates peoples' willingness to use force against strangers. Apparently young Negroes are becoming more ready to use force, and against whites; a recent study in Philadelphia revealed a growing tendency among Negroes to rob whites and an increase in the use of violence by Negroes against whites in the course of these crimes.

A straw in the wind came in a 1968 robbery in Washington, D.C. A police radio alert, broadcast at 4:12 P.M. on November 9, after a holdup at a movie theater just three blocks from the White House, alerted all police units to be on the lookout for two Negro males, each four feet tall and weighing about 80 pounds. The cashier at the theater estimated their ages at ten or eleven. Both carried guns. They took $80. One shouted "I'll kill you" as they ran away.

Criminology studies abound with explanations for the traditionally high Negro crime rate, but the experts are mystified by the further recent jump in Negro crime. The long-term picture and the recent rise are almost inconsistent; most experts feel that the Negroes' low economic status is an important factor behind their history of criminality—yet the recent crime spurt came at a time of economic gain among black people.

One possible explanation is that the recent statistical rise in Negro crime is more apparent than real, that the lawlessness was there all along and that society is only now realizing it. Criminologist Marvin Wolfgang sees this as partially responsible for the current crime scare. The unprecedented exposure of traditional slum crime to white society is largely to blame, Wolfgang believes: "Throughout history—on the Left Bank of Paris, in the slums of London and in the worst neighborhoods of every city—there were murders and violence and crime, and society pushed it into the background and ignored it. Now the Negro is pushing out of his old boundaries and moving about in areas where some whites are still living. They are committing more crimes, and more crimes against white people—and, for the first time, society is aware of it. I think we're bound to go through a period of transition, in which the Negro crime rate will go higher."

A more psychological explanation for the recent upsurge is given by Professor Walter B. Miller of the Joint Center for Urban Studies at Cambridge. Dr. Miller is known for his belief in economic class as the predominant factor in determining criminality, a theory that underwent severe strains in the late 1960s, when Negro crime rose during a time of economic upswing for many Negroes. His studies in the 1950s of juvenile crime in low-income Boston neighborhoods showed that when black and white families of similar incomes and job status were compared, the arrest rates of their children were about the same. He concluded that white youngsters even turned up in court slightly more often than did black children on the same socioeconomic level.

But in 1967, Professor Miller returned to the same neighborhoods and found that in that year the black youngsters' rates of arrest almost doubled that of whites—a rise that he blamed on civil rights militancy and the current climate of defiance of authority among young blacks. "Young Negroes were provided incentives to violate the law by civil rights militancy and the riots," he concluded. "Suddenly there was an ideological justification for crime—to compensate for injustice, to punish white society. Because you have been deprived for so many centuries, you have a right to take back what is yours. You help your race when you oppose the police 'pigs.' "

This will pass, Miller believes, just as the riot phase seems to have peaked. He notes that Negro migration from the South into the cities also seems to have begun to decline, and he feels that the current public anxiety about Negro crime will soon be remembered as a passing concern, like the excitement about youth gangs in the 1950s.

In the meantime, the evidence is mounting that crime by ghetto Negroes has reached levels that explained the public's receptivity to the law-and-order appeals during the 1968 campaign. Studies of robbery in Philadelphia and Chicago at about that time showed that blacks' arrest rates were about eighteen times that of white people in those cities—approximately double the disparity between Negroes and whites for the whole country. In Philadelphia, Negroes were charged with rape at twelve times the rate of white men, while the national Negro/white rate was much lower. In Stamford, Connecticut, the same pattern—to a less pronounced degree—was found in a racial analysis of all criminal offenses.

Finally, a study detailing 10,000 Philadelphia juveniles by Wolfgang and Thorsten Sellin corroborated the national urban figures produced by the F.B.I.'s study, which showed that city Negroes' arrest rates are about double the national Negro rates, and far and away higher than the whites'. They believe that the currently booming Negro crime rate may be a product of the shift of the Negro population from the rural South to the city slums but this does not resolve the uncertainty that exists over the root causes of the historically higher Negro criminality.

No respectable sociologist believes that crime is a racial trait of Negroes. "That the serious criminality of the Negro American is greater than that of the white American is an established fact," says Professor Sellin; "but sociological studies have shown that this is due to no inborn racial trait but to the economic, educational and social conditions of the Negro."

The catch comes when sociologists try to establish which conditions of the Negro contribute most to his high crime rate—his generally low economic status, or the cultural isolation and resentment that come from being trapped in a black slum in a white man's world.

"What the high figures for Negro arrests really show is that low-status people commit more crimes," Professor Miller says. "Eighty percent of the Negroes in the country are in what we would call the lowest class. Only 30 percent of the whites are. That's the difference."

Most sociologists believe that there is much more to it than poverty. The unwholesome mix of circumstances that more often than not accompany criminality is likely to be the lot of anyone who is born poor, but these circumstances seem to weigh heaviest on those who are also black. As Marvin Wolfgang puts it:

> Thrust any child, white or colored, from the womb to a world that offers the rewards of status and success. With a moat of discrimination, cut him off from the mainland so that there are few or no opportunities to achieve those rewards. Let him continue to wish for the same things the mainlanders desire, but make him move around much more, lose a father to death or desertion and a mother to work and dependency. Give him less knowledge to absorb, less money than the mainlander receives for the same tasks. Surround him with examples of unlawful achievers, and make him fight to protect the mainland without fully participating in the rules to govern it. Shorten his length of life, expose him to disease, treat him as if he were biologically inferior and call him nasty names to convince him of it. Even if the mainlanders value the service he gives them and the feeling of importance his contrast offers, he is lost.

The question of causation is far more than academic; if Negroes commit proportionately more crimes because poor people tend to break the law and most Negroes are poor, then there is hope in antipoverty programs and other economic measures. But if segregated urban living breeds increasing crime, despite better wages and education for the people who have to live that way, then the prospects for future tranquility are bleak. According to the President's Commission on Urban Problems, the Negro population of the big-city slums will almost double by 1985 (the national nonwhite population is expected to rise from 12 to 16 percent by then), which could create a situation resembling the "apartheid society" that the National Advisory Commission on Civil Disorders warned about.

One of the first good comparative studies of crime by Negroes and white persons of similar economic status was conducted by Prof. Earl R. Moses of Johns Hopkins University in Baltimore in 1940. It produced a bleak conclusion that is still accepted, widely but reluctantly, by most criminologists—that if Negroes and whites of the same socioeconomic levels are compared, the Negro crime rates are still higher.

More recently, Morris A. Forslund, gathering material for his

Ph.D. dissertation at Yale, found that the overall crime rate among Negroes in Stamford, Connecticut, was about six times that of the city's whites. By comparing the frequency of crime among various age and income groups of both races, he concluded that the Negro crime rate was inflated by about 15 percent because so many Negroes were young and thus statistically more likely to get into trouble. Further comparisons showed that another 30 percent of the Negro crime total was due to the fact that so many were poor, and like all poor people, more likely to run afoul of the law. His conclusion: If age and poverty factors could be eliminated, Negroes would still commit three times more crime than whites. This he attributed to resentment by Negroes at white society, plus a ghetto culture that encourages criminal behavior.

The most impressive evidence that money and job status are not the overriding factors was turned up by Professors Wolfgang and Sellin in their study in Philadelphia. When they sorted the white and Negro boys into groups according to their families' earnings and job levels, they found the Negroes' delinquency rates higher for every income bracket. The boys from high-income Negro families, who had the lowest Negro arrest rates, had higher rates than the white boys in the highest-crime, lowest-income bracket. The professors concluded that psychological and cultural influences outweighed economic ones in fostering criminality.

This theory gained further credence when Negro crime was found to have accelerated between 1964 and 1967, while the economic lot of Negroes was improving. The number of non-whites who lived below the government's statistical "poverty line" dropped from 10.9 million to 8.3 million during that time. The inevitable conclusion is that "wars on poverty" even if wildly successful (and some of the increase in Negro income must be credited to the job stimulus of the war in Vietnam) will not greatly sap the growth of Negro crime.

Because these impressions about high criminality among blacks are based upon arrest rates—conviction statistics are almost nonexistent—the argument has been made that they reflect police discrimination, a tendency to haul in Negroes more readily than whites. There are hints in the F.B.I.'s statistics that this is partially so. For years the police have arrested far more Negroes than whites for gambling and prostitution, consentual offenses that involve so much selectivity on the part of arresting officers that some experts have urged that they should not even be published by the F.B.I. In general, arrests across the country have declined for these consentual crimes, indicating that the police are tending to live and let live. But the prostitution arrests of Negro women have continued to climb while arrests of white women have declined. Negroes also constitute the bulk of those arrested for carrying concealed weapons, a statistic that could be partially attributable to the police's reputed readiness to "stop and frisk" Negroes when whites would be let alone.

One development that runs counter to this argument is the change in narcotics arrests over the past two decades. In the early 1950s there were always more narcotics arrests of Negroes each year than whites. This changed. Middle-class whites started smoking marijuana, and the police started arresting them for it. The narcotics arrest rate of Negroes is still high, but for the past few years more whites than Negroes have been arrested on narcotics charges and there is no evidence that race ever affected the situation, either way. Negroes also have extremely high arrest rates for murder (murder is so frequent among both male and female Negroes fifteen to twenty-five years old that it is their second-ranking cause of death), robbery and felonious assault. Murder, and to a lesser extent, robbery, do not lend themselves to selective enforcement by the police because the body or the empty cash register cannot be winked at, regardless of the color of the people involved. If anything, the police have traditionally been lax in arresting Negroes for aggravated assault because the victims are usually black.

Most experts believe that selective arresting probably does inflate the Negro crime rate in certain categories, especially when juveniles are the offenders. But they agree almost unanimously that the crime disparity between the races is real and would still be wide, even if the police always applied evenhanded enforcement.

As the Negro crime problem has begun to come out from under wraps, some whites have sought to blunt the blacklash with a "don't worry, the victims are only Negroes" approach. The assertion is true, but the argument has not been very reassuring to Negroes. The vast majority of people who get murdered, assaulted or raped are attacked by someone they know—relatives, acquaintances or spouses. Even the great bugaboo of interracial crime—the Negro raping a white woman—is relatively rare. One study in Philadelphia showed that interracial rape is more likely to involve a white man and a black victim. Relatively few violent crimes cut across racial lines, with the exception of robbery. There a slim—but apparently growing—majority of the victims of Negro robbers are white. Murder, rape, aggravated assault—the offenses that tend to symbolize "crime" to the average man—involve people of the same race about nine times out of ten.

Whatever consolation it is to the suburbanite to be assured that if he is murdered or his wife is raped, it will be done by a white person, to hear white leaders stress the point makes Negro leaders uneasy. Sterling Tucker, an Urban League official who has a reputation for weighing his words with care, complained that Vice President Humphrey was doing the Negroes no favor by trying to take the edge off the "law and order" issue in this way. In a speech at the 1968 convention of the American Bar Association Convention in Philadelphia, Tucker charged that this psychology could eventually give the white "keepers to the keys of the cities" an excuse to resort to apartheid to contain crime. Ultimately, he said, whites could decide "to seal ghettos off and keep the blacks in enslavement . . . instead of coming to grips with this in all of its ugliness."

It is this danger—that white society will come to see Negro crime as a thing apart, to be contained only through extraordinary measures—that poses the most serious threat to rule of law. An example has already been seen in Wilmington, Delaware, where heavily-armed National Guard troops were sent into the Negro neighborhoods to control the rioting and looting that broke out in April of 1968, following the assassination of Dr. Martin Luther King, Jr. Negro resentment ran so deep that officials were afraid to remove the troops, and almost a year passed before they were withdrawn. A somewhat similar incident took place in Miami, where the Chief of Police sent officers

equipped with shotguns and dogs into the Negro district to deal
with "young hoodlums" who, he said, had taken advantage of
the civil rights campaign. "We don't mind being accused of police brutality," he said; "they haven't seen anything yet." There
were echoes of this in the campaign promises of George Wallace
and Richard Nixon to use all the police presence necessary to
stanch the crime rise in the capital city.

Thus the phenomenon of unusually high Negro crime has its
mirror image in extraordinary police response; with Negro robbery rates already sixteen times that of whites in the cities and
still rising, there is every possibility that efforts to contend with
Negro crime will increasingly be viewed as exercises in urban
pacification. (After the New York NAACP issued its demand
for harsher measures against criminals, a *New York Times* reporter found Harlem merchants urging the removal of young
junkies to camps upstate—a proposal similar to South Vietnam's
indoctrination camps for young Vietcong.) The most notable
example so far is the new law that permits pretrial "preventive
detention" in the District of Columbia of what President Nixon
has called dangerous hard-core criminals. Other signs have
been the increased use of curfews to cool ghetto unrest and
occasional broad-scale searches for weapons in Negro areas.
The ultimate direction of events may well have been foreshad-
owed when a high police official of the Washington, D.C., area's
whitest and wealthiest Maryland suburb, distraught over the
spillover of crimes committed in his community by criminals
from the predominantly black city, felt free to suggest to Senator Joseph D. Tydings that "if you want to help us you should
build a 40-foot chain link fence along the District line and put
barbed wire on top."

For the Supreme Court, this trend creates special pressures that
run counter to its recent rulings on criminal law. "Tension between the police and the judiciary has always been fundamental
to our constitutional system," Nicholas deB. Katzenbach has
said. "It is intentional and healthy and constitutes the real difference between a free society and a police state." Yet there are
aspects to the Supreme Court's recent doctrines toward police
power that make the Court as well as its new doctrines especially
vulnerable to the tensions created by rising crime and racism.

Back when the Court read the Constitution to tolerate conduct by police that conformed with the flexible principle of "fundamental fairness," judges had discretion to limit their intervention in police affairs to those circumstances that they could expect to control. The Warren Court changed that when it laid down procedural rules that are supposed to be followed by police in all instances. Yet the temptation for the police to break the rules, and for the majority of whites to approve of their actions, may be on the rise—at a time when the flexibility of the courts has been reduced. And so a coincidence of events has heightened the traditional tensions between the forces of enforcement and of justice, and has greatly increased the likelihood of a constitutional crisis somewhere down the line.

VI

Re-Trying the Convicted

In most matters it is more important that the applicable rule . . . be settled than it be settled right.

Louis D. Brandeis, 1932

Sam Bongiorno, fourteen years old, did not believe that his father was guilty of murder, despite what the jury had said. So on October 15, 1942, he sat down in the Chicago flat that he shared with his mother and wrote a letter to John P. Barnes, Chief Judge of the United States District Court for the Northern District of Illinois, which has jurisdiction over the Chicago area.

"My father (John Bongiorno) is an inmate of the Illinois State Penitentiary at Joliet, Ill.," Sam wrote. "He has a petition for a writ of habeas corpus which he has been trying to send to you for the past two years, but the authorities will not let it out. If there is any way in which you can obtain, or aid us in obtaining the release of this petition, it will be very much appreciated."

The reasons why John Bongiorno's petition for habeas corpus had been bottled up within Joliet Prison were quite logical to the officials there; the same freeze on petitions existed at virtually every other state penitentiary in the country. For centuries, the crowning feature of Anglo-American law had been finality. The Latin word for it was *res judicata*—a final decision in a case resolves all questions that were or should have been raised during the proceedings.

In criminal law, the result was that if a person was tried and found guilty, he was entitled to only one appeal to test the validity of his conviction. That appeal went from the trial court through an intermediate appellate court if there was one, and then usually to the state supreme court. From there the convicted man could petition the Supreme Court of the United States for a writ of certiorari, the procedure for requesting the Court to review his conviction for violations of his rights under the Federal Constitution. But the Supreme Court rarely granted more than a half-dozen criminal law petitions each year and thus the appellant's odds were long; the chances were that his petition for certiorari would be denied.

That is what had happened to John Bongiorno. It had all begun on July 8, 1933, when Bongiorno and Ross King decided (they later claimed it was because of the Depression and unemployment; their families needed money, they said) to rob a magazine distributor's office. A policeman caught them in the act and Bongiorno put down their pistol and surrendered. King snatched up the weapon and fled. But a few minutes later King, having doubled back, appeared behind the policeman and shot him in the back.

Bongiorno claimed that the murder was none of his doing; he had surrendered, his hands were raised, and his crime was over when King pulled the fatal trigger. But with the Chicago press howling for stern justice, the trial amounted to little more than the ritual of conviction. (The Chicago *Herald-American*'s report of the conviction began: "Another smashing victory in the war against crime was achieved last night.") King was sentenced to death and was quickly executed. For Bongiorno, the jury reserved a sentence that had long been fashionable in Chicago, but is almost unknown elsewhere—a 199-year prison term. Bongiorno was then twenty-six years old. Since a convict is not eligible for parole until he has served one-third of his term, Bongiorno would have gone before the parole board for the first time when he was ninety-two years old. He appealed to the Supreme Court of Illinois and lost, and the Supreme Court of the United States denied certiorari.

Most lawyers would have said at that point that the system had thrown away the key on John Bongiorno. Illinois law followed the pattern that existed in virtually every state—once a person's direct appeal had been decided against him, his conviction could never again be challenged, except under two ancient procedures that applied only to the most exotic circumstances.

Habeas corpus proceedings could be used only by prisoners who could show that the court that convicted them lacked jurisdiction over them or over the case. So habeas corpus was reserved for the colossal judicial blunder, not the run-of-the-mill trial error. It would apply if a convict could show that he was a minor when he was convicted in an adult court, or that the crime occurred across the state line. This was cold comfort to the convict who could not challenge the trial judge's jurisdiction, but felt that the judge abused it to reach an illegal result in his case.

Coram Nobis was an even more esoteric remedy, available only to the convict who discovered some fact which, if known at the time of the trial, would have precluded the judge from entering the sentence. An example is the man convicted of murder who later learns that the victim isn't dead—which explains why most lawyers know this procedure only as something a law teacher mentioned once in the first semester of a criminal law course. What this meant in practice was that individuals could be convicted by patently unconstitutional means, yet there would be no way to get the matter before a court to obtain relief.

At first blush it appears that criminal convictions could be adequately reviewed by direct appeals; civil trials have been reviewed that way for better than a century and there has never been a clamor for alternate methods of review. But for years criminal appeals were treated with disfavor in the law, as if they were no more than the last recourse of scoundrels. Until the 1950s, appeals were rare. Before a defendant could appeal without paying heavy appellate costs, he had to prove—not just declare, as now—abject poverty. Anyone who could prove it, was too poor to pay for a lawyer or a trial transcript (neither of which were furnished then), and if he did, the appellate courts had a way of throwing appeals out as frivolous without answering the complaints of those who were facing prison.

There were many reasons why a defendant's conviction could become final without valid objections to his prosecution ever having been reviewed on appeal. Timid or inept counsel could fail to raise or properly pursue objections to the proceedings. Even when all legal questions were thoroughly reviewed at the time of the trial, it often happened that a later Supreme Court ruling would raise new ones. But most important, for the eight or nine defendants out of ten who pleaded guilty and thus did not appeal, there was no way to get complaints about their cases into court at a later date. Some of these defendants were so frightened, ashamed or intimidated that they pleaded guilty despite defenses that might have been crucial in full-scale trials. Some were victims of lawyers who were lazy, incompetent or overworked. Yet once they had entered guilty pleas and had gone to prison, it was too late to point out such flaws in the guilty pleas as the allegation that a defendant had pleaded guilty under duress, or without being told his rights, or when he was insane. Whatever the circumstances of the convictions, in most cases state courts simply refused to hear the convicts' subsequent complaints.

In 1965 the Supreme Court seemed to come within an eyelash of deciding that this use of *res judicata* to foreclose effective review of criminal convictions violates the Constitution. The Justices granted the appeal of a Nebraska convict who had tried to assert the claim that he had been coerced into pleading guilty without counsel. The Nebraska courts answered simply that there was no way to raise such a claim in Nebraska. After the Justices agreed to hear the case, Nebraska quickly—and prudently—passed a law establishing a procedure for hearing such claims. The Supreme Court sent the case back for a hearing under the new procedure, leaving unanswered the very pregnant question of whether such niggardly state post-conviction review systems deny convicts due process of law.

But in 1942 things were not much different in Federal courts, where most judges felt that there was something unsavory or even undermining about reconsidering final state judgments. Thus many penitentiaries had for years rationalized their enforcement of no-writ rules similar to the one that had kept John Bongiorno's petition bottled up in Joliet—it would have been futile to forward petitions that could not possibly result in judicial relief. But a process of legal dynamics was already under way, generated as much by the force of prisoners' demands for justice (or at least, for freedom) as by any doctrinal shift among the judiciary. As it happened, Sam Bongiorno's letter for his father was the key to the logjam which, when released, set off one of the most significant legal movements in American history.

Judge Barnes ordered Warden Joseph E. Ragen of Joliet to appear in court on December 7, 1942, to explain why Bongiorno had not been allowed to petition the Court. When the morning of the 7th arrived and no representative of the prison appeared, Judge Barnes issued a writ of habeas corpus, ordering the release of John Bongiorno. It was not the end of Bongiorno's courtroom activity, but that one dramatic display of the Federal judiciary's power to reach into state penitentiaries and affect the freedom of men whose fates had supposedly been sealed touched off immense excitement among the 150,000 men in the country's penitentiaries. (Strangely, it stirred no discernible yen for freedom among women inmates—to this day, it is rare for a female prisoner to ask a court to let her out.)

In 1942 a total of 130 petitions for habeas corpus had been filed by prisoners in the entire United States court system—none, of course, from Joliet. The next year, after Judge Barnes' reaction to Sam Bongiorno's letter, there were 125 from Joliet alone, and the word was spreading to other penitentiaries. A decade later, in 1952, 541 petitions were filed by convicts, and the snowball was just beginning to move; by 1969 the number was 10,971—sixteen percent of the entire caseload on the civil dockets of the United States trial courts.

The result has been a remarkable change in the ancient principle that an accused person is given one, and only one, trial of the facts of his case. He still gets only one trial of the facts of the crime itself (Who fired the first shot? What was the holdup man wearing? Did the supposed rape victim have an unsavory past?), but now he can demand and get another hearing (or possibly, even successive hearings) to test various crucial facts that affect the constitutionality of the trial (How long was the accused questioned before he confessed? Did the prosecutor conceal information favorable to the defendant? Did newspaper publicity prejudice the jury?).

The seed of this transformation was planted not by the Supreme Court but by Congress. Like most of the radical changes in American criminal procedure, it was made in hopes of safeguarding the rights of Negroes. In 1867 the Reconstruction Congress, realizing that emancipation would be hollow if Negroes were left completely at the mercy of Southern justice, passed a law that allowed Federal district judges to use the writ of habeas corpus to reopen "all cases where any person may be restrained of his or her liberty in violation of the Constitution, or of any treaty or law of the United States."

Before the Federal trial courts had an opportunity to start using this power, the Supreme Court reduced it to a shadow by ruling, in *The Slaughter House Cases* of 1873, that the Constitution's list of procedural safeguards did not apply to the states. So Federal habeas corpus remained a remedy with few rights to vindicate. Moreover, the Supreme Court continued to accept the classic view that the writ could be used only when the court which had committed the prisoner lacked jurisdiction to do so. The break came in 1923, when the Supreme Court was confronted with a case that epitomized every evil that the Reconstruction Congress had intended to counteract back in 1867.

In *Moore* v. *Dempsey* the Court was faced with the death sentences of five Arkansas Negroes who had been convicted of murder in a courtroom dominated by a mob. Justice Holmes' decision for the majority compared the proceedings to "a mask" that served to deprive the court of jurisdiction, with "counsel, jury and judge . . . swept to the fatal end by an irresistible wave of public passion." The Court declared that if the Negroes could prove their charges in a habeas corpus hearing before a Federal District judge, then their treatment amounted to a denial of due process and they should be given a new trial. (The case was sent back to Arkansas for such a hearing, and the sentences were eventually commuted.)

From that time on, the Justices were quick to find that unfair actions stripped state courts of jurisdiction, so that each time the Supreme Court swept a new right within the scope of "due process," it created another ground for Federal court reversal of state decisions. At present, this list is so full that it is difficult to imagine a trial that would not raise questions concerning at least one of them. Was a confession coerced? Was the defendant sane? Did he have effective counsel? Did the prosecutor fail to disclose exculpatory evidence? Was a search illegal? Was the publicity prejudicial? Was the defendant properly warned of his rights by the police? Were Negroes excluded from the jury?

There are more, but these questions, each of constitutional dimension, suggest the variety of issues that convicts can raise from their prison cells in handwritten petitions (jailhouse lawyering is more sophisticated in litigious Joliet, where 400 inmates have equipped themselves with typewriters), years after their convictions have become "final." Not only did the Court rapidly expand this list, it swept away state and Federal rules that tended to prevent prisoners from reaching the U.S. courts with their claims and which relegated them to cursory consideration of the claims if they got there.

In 1953 the Court struck down the states' contention that a prisoner's claims should be considered settled—*res judicata*—if he had been given an adverse ruling on them from the courts of the state and had failed in an effort to have the Supreme Court review them on certiorari. Justice Frankfurter's opinion emphasized that so many appeals come to the Court on certiorari that a denial by the Court cannot be considered a ruling on any issue presented by the appeal. This meant that years after a defendant had exhausted his appeals and had been consigned to prison, he could have a brainstorm in his cell, discover a flaw in his trial, and win his release in the nearest Federal District Court. One major stumbling block remained: The convict had to first apply to the state courts and give them a chance to correct their error before taking the matter into Federal court.

But when a petition arrived there, it often got brusque treatment from a busy judge. The petitions were often rambling and
opaque, and the judges frequently found it difficult to tell what
constitutional right, if any, the prisoner was attempting to raise.
(One prisoner claimed that trial by battle had not been abandoned by the courts of his state; another sent a petition consisting entirely of caricatures of the judges and prosecutors in his
case; many quoted liberally from the Bible.) Most inmate petitions were dismissed with a quick order declaring either that
they raised no substantial question or that state remedies had not
been exhausted.

The Supreme Court acted to further open the U.S. courts to
state prisoners in two 1963 decisions designed to assure "a full
and fair hearing" on every constitutional claim. In one case, *Fay*
v. *Noia*, the Court swept away the states' rules that held objections to be waived if they had not been claimed at the trial. Federal judges were required to consider most constitutional claims,
even if the prisoner had slept on his rights at the time of his trial
and appeal. On the same day the Justices ruled in *Townsend* v.
Sain that Federal judges must give each prisoner's petition a full
hearing, unless the record of the state trial showed that the issues had been thoroughly thrashed out and fairly decided. The
justices also abandoned the fiction that the Federal courts would
intervene only when the convicting court had lacked jurisdiction. As a result the last barriers between state convicts and Federal courts were thrown down; if a prisoner had a constitutional
complaint, he was assured of a full hearing.

This has brought America's prisons to a writ-writing binge
that is unique in the history of penology. "The State court first
tries a defendant, and then the defendant tries the State court
in the post-conviction procedure. He can now, under some recent decisions of the Federal Courts, go into court a third time
and try his lawyer," complains Senator Sam J. Ervin, Jr., of
North Carolina; "There is no longer any finality to a criminal
trial so long as the defendant is concerned." John J. Parker,
one of the country's most distinguished—and conservative—
judges, was more aghast: "It is hard for a lawyer to really
think," he once exclaimed, "that this is the law in this country
now—but it is!"

Most aggrieved of all were the justices of the state supreme courts, who were offended to see convictions that had been upheld by the highest court of a state overturned by a single Federal District judge. Beginning in 1952 and continuing to the present, the state chief justices convene annually and complain about this. As they put it in 1952: "Orderly procedure under our dual system of government should require that a final judgment of a state's highest court be subject to review or reversal only by the Supreme Court of the United States." "Every conscientious state court judge is irked," grumbled Charles S. Desmond, former Chief Judge of the State of New York, "by the covert suggestion that he needs to be watched closely lest he deviously steal away the citizen's rights." Also irked by the development were the states' Attorneys General, who have the job of defending the states against the flood of petitions (one prisoner is known to have filed fifty petitions in five years) from the state penitentiaries, and who resent having to devote increasing amounts of time and effort just to keep convicted men in jail.

Despite all this organized indignation, the great American writ-writing binge has developed into a curious episode in institutional non-problem solving. Whether or not the do-it-yourself system of perpetual appeals is an evil, there can be no question that the flood of petitions is a growing problem. Yet in recent years, as the number of petitions has grown, the concern voiced over it in legal and judicial circles has dwindled. With the flow of petitions having reached a volume that even the most pessimistic lawyers would not have predicted five years ago, the controversy over the situation has virtually died.

In the early 1950s, with the state judges and attorneys general gnashing their teeth over the five hundred-odd petitions that were being filed each year, a bill was introduced in Congress that would have virtually eliminated the Federal District judges' jurisdiction to consider state prisoners' petitions. Except in extreme cases, a defendant's only route of review would have been to raise his objections in the state courts and hope that the Supreme Court would grant certiorari. Liberal senators threatened to filibuster and the bill was dropped.

A decade later the number of petitions filed each year had doubled, and the anguish of the state judiciary had become so pronounced that the Judicial Conference of the United States, the official policy-making body of the Federal judiciary, pitched in to help work out a solution. The Judicial Conference activated a committee to study the problem, and for a brief time the Federal judges supported a bill in Congress that would have salved the state supreme courts' feelings by requiring the judgment of a three-judge Federal court to set a state prisoner free. But then the Federal judges saw how rapidly the number of petitions were increasing, calculated the amount of judge-hours that three-judge courts would consume, and balked. The measure failed again in Congress and it was clear that the problem was outstripping the possibility of solution so rapidly that the passage of time was making a remedy less likely, instead of more so.

When the habeas corpus law was finally modified in 1966, the annual volume of petitions from state prisoners alone had risen to 5,339, and Congress did little more than confirm the rule that prisoners can bring successive petitions, so long as they raise different points in each one. Congress threw a sop to the Federal judiciary by permitting harassed judges who sit near state prisons to transfer habeas corpus cases to the Federal district where the original trial had occurred. But for the state judges, who had been most aggrieved, there was nothing.

Curiously, the state officials have reacted with mounting apathy. Perhaps this is because, despite the Supreme Court decisions in 1963 that told the Federal judges to give the petitions closer consideration, the percentage that result in hearings has remained miniscule, and the number of convicts who actually get out has stayed low. So the burden has fallen on the Federal judges to plow through the reams of hand-lettered paper, and the state officials have lapsed into a righteous silence; as the flow of petitioners has risen, there has been a steady decline in the number of angry resolutions, indignant speeches and concerned law review articles. The Federal judiciary, having savored the satisfaction of righting a few spectacular state wrongs, has now been left to cope with the Good Samaritan's burdens.

At the heart of the matter is a condition that underlies many of the actions by the Supreme Court that have led to charges that the Justices are coddling criminals and tilting the scales of justice too far toward defendants. That is that criminal penalties are too harsh in the United States, and American prisons seem to be among the least rehabilitative in the world. "There is general agreement among most who have recently studied the pattern of sentencing in this country that the average sentence to prison is for a term in excess of what can reasonably be justified and that there are far too many long-term commitments," concluded a special study group of the American Bar Association in 1967. More than one-half of the prisoners in state penitentiaries in the U.S. serve maximum terms as high as ten years; at last count in Sweden, out of 11,227 prisoners, 8 were serving terms of longer than ten years. A similar pattern is evident wherever statistics are available—prison terms in the United States are longer.

Moreover, a long stretch in the average American prison almost appears to be the measure least likely to rehabilitate an offender. Roughly one-third of all offenders released from prison are back behind bars within five years, often for committing more serious crimes. This has prompted many criminologists to speculate that both society and the offenders might be better off if, after a short period of incarceration, all inmates were released and sent back into the community. Something like this happened in Florida in 1963 with intriguing results.

In the spring of 1963, when the Supreme Court overturned the conviction of Clarence Earl Gideon because he had been tried without a lawyer, the decision fell like a thunderbolt on the penal institutions of Florida. For years, felons had been routinely tried in noncapital cases there without the benefit of counsel. After *Gideon* v. *Wainwright*, more than 1,000 convicts were quickly freed. Later, a research team checked the records of 110 former inmates who had been arbitrarily freed by the *Gideon* case and 110 men of similar backgrounds who had served out their terms and had been released in the usual way. Within two years, 13 percent of the *Gideon* beneficiaries had committed another crime. Twenty-five percent of those who had been kept in prison had become repeaters. An experiment with juvenile delinquents in California produced similar results; offenders selected by lot and released under intensive probationary supervision, without any incarceration, have had approximately one-half the recidivism rate of others who were institutionalized in the normal way. Such studies do not purport to show that the same result would happen in every case, and they cannot account for the dangerous criminals who must be locked up to protect society. But taken to their logical conclusion, they suggest, in the ABA committee's words, "that if we, today, turned loose all of the inmates of our prisons without regard to the length of their sentences and, with only some exceptions, without regard to their previous offenses, we might *reduce* the recidivism rate over what it would be if we kept each prisoner incarcerated until his sentence expired." This combination of overly-long sentences and debilitating incarceration has placed great pressure on the Federal judiciary to liberalize prisoners' constitutional remedies —pressures that have outweighed the fears that prisoners will abuse the Great Writ, or that the valuable time of judges and prosecutors will be wasted, or that the judiciary will be accused of coddling criminals.

These pressures have been brought into their sharpest focus in the cases of men sentenced to die, and it is no coincidence that capital punishment has dwindled to the vanishing point as Federal habeas corpus blossomed. Executions reached their peak of 199 deaths in 1935, just seven years before John Bongiorno filed his writ from Joliet. In the succeeding years only seven states have abolished capital punishment (joining six states that had previously done so), yet 1968 became the first year on record in which no person was put to death in the United States and some lawyers believe it will be years before executions resume, if they ever do.

The reason: Condemned men have seized on the liberalized habeas corpus rules to file chains of petitions, a ploy that has proved capable of keeping prisoners alive and litigating indefinitely, whether they have any legitimate constitutional complaints or not. If a petition raises a point that could possibly be valid, the courts usually stay the prisoner's execution pending a final decision. Since the average petition takes two years to reach the Supreme Court, a Death Row inmate is given adequate time to think up a new constitutional challenge to file after his pending writ fails. This prompted the State Chief Justices to complain that habeas corpus was creating "inordinate delays in the enforcement of criminal justice." The "enforcement" they had in mind was death—prison terms have not been affected because time-servers litigate while they put in their time.

By 1968, about 500 inmates were stalled on Death Rows across the country, spinning out their years in life-preserving litigation. For them a series of failures was success enough, although there was always a chance for freedom; the all-time record holders for fending off the executioner litigated for seventeen years after their conviction and finally went free. They are Edgar Labat and Clifton Poret, two New Orleans men who were sentenced to death for rape in 1953. The Supreme Court heard their case once and affirmed the sentence, and on two later occasions refused to review habeas corpus appeals. But they persisted, and when a lower Federal court finally ordered a new trial the Louisiana authorities found that they could no longer muster the witnesses to make out a case against them. They finally walked free in 1970.

A more familiar figure is the "antihero" of Death Row who never manages to raise any substantial doubt about his guilt or even to make out a colorable constitutional case, but who gains renown and some admiration for his tenacity and ingenuity in fighting off the executioner. Caryl Chessman, the "Red Light Bandit" who was condemned for a series of sex crimes in California, set the style when he avoided the gas chamber for twelve years, writing four books in the process and arguing his early cases himself. His misfortune was to be before his time; the Supreme Court was just beginning to open up fertile possibilities for delay when he was executed in 1960.

In his wake came a succession of more-or-less villainous characters who have won unanticipated longevity and some fame by cashing in on the Supreme Court's habeas corpus rulings and a rising public distaste for executions. The current record-holder, Jimmie Snyder, Jr., of Virginia's Death Row, was convicted of statutory rape in 1956 and has long since given up contending that his trial was unfair. In recent years he has insisted in his petitions that he is too insane to be executed—a contention that has met with no courtroom success at all, other than to keep him alive, and to suggest that perhaps he may be crazy in the manner of a fox. Another long-term Death Row antihero is Edgar H. Smith, Jr., who since his conviction for murder in New Jersey in 1957 has taken his case to the Supreme Court four times, has won the friendship and aid of columnist William F. Buckley, Jr., and has raised money for his defense by writing a book, *Brief*

Against Death. One of the oddest cases concerns John Brady, a Maryland convict who won a Supreme Court ruling in 1963 to the effect that he must be given a new trial, solely to reconsider his sentence. Since Maryland law does not allow for such a trial he has simply been kept in prison, where he will probably stay.

Most of these jailhouse antiheroes began as did William C. Witherspoon of Illinois' Death Row, by concocting their own challenges and filing their own papers until they interested outsiders in their causes. Witherspoon wrote a book—predictably, about Death Row—and drafted his early petitions, until finally his case was taken by Albert E. Jenner, Jr., a leading Chicago trial lawyer. Jenner took the case to the Supreme Court, where he won the important ruling, in *Witherspoon* v. *Illinois*, that death sentences are unconstitutional if all persons with conscientious scruples against capital punishment have been excluded from the jury.

Prison officials have not been overly hostile to the habeas corpus trend. As Professor Paul Freund of Harvard has pointed out, it is better to have a freedom-hungry convict flailing away at a typewriter than with a pick and shovel. In some penitentiaries law books clutter the cells and pile up in the corridors, and wardens' efforts to crack down on their use have a way of coming to grief—several court rulings have held that prisoners cannot constitutionally be separated from their books and briefs. The ultimate ruling of this genre came in 1968 when the Supreme Court upheld the constitutional right of William Joe Johnson of the Tennessee State Penitentiary to act as a jailhouse lawyer and to draw up writs for other prisoners. Johnson has no legal training, but his court-appointed attorney convinced the Justices that he and other jailhouse lawyers like him are the only "counsel" that most of his penurious fellow-convicts are ever likely to have.

Critics of the Supreme Court's generous habeas corpus policy object that the writ was never intended to be a substitute for orthodox appeals and that the idea of perpetual review of state judgments in Federal courts violates sound principles of federalism as well as law. Professor Paul M. Bator of Harvard argues that there are psychological as well as legal benefits to finality; a prisoner will never make the decision to rehabilitate himself, he says, so long as "society itself continuously tells the convict that he may not be justly subject to re-education and treatment in the first place." Indeed, the critics charge that the system tends to reward the convicts with the most flexible concept of the truth. Since convicts can raise almost any point at any time, they can benefit by recalling past injustices that the state is least in a position to refute. The result is often a swearing contest between a prisoner with a vivid recollection of past wrongs and officials whose memories are dim and whose corroborating witnesses are unavailable, presided over by a Federal District judge who may have a jaundiced view of state criminal justice.

It is this second-guessing of the judge who saw the evidence first-hand that most galls state officials. To avoid rulings based on stone-cold evidence, Chief Judge Desmond contends that at least a five-year statute of limitations should be placed on these swearing contests. "The fact that a prisoner, believed by some Federal District court, says that his conviction in 1922 was obtained by a state prosecutor long dead having gotten perjured evidence from some witness long dead in the presence of a state court judge long dead does not make it so," he insists.

Some lawyers who approve of the Supreme Court's liberality are disturbed by the system because it tempts convicts to lie and holds no sanctions against those who do. The inmate who swears to a whopper in his petition and receives a hearing is rewarded by a trip away from the boredom of the prison routine to a courthouse where he usually has an opportunity to visit with his friends and family, plus the long-shot chance that the judge will believe him and not the State. If he is made out to be a liar, nothing has been lost. Ernest C. Friesen, Jr., the young and compassionate former director of the Administrative Office of the United States Courts, believes that a good many of the abuses of Federal habeas corpus would vanish if a prisoner could be given, say, an extra thirty days to serve for each sworn petition found to be a blatant lie.

Judging from past experience, this could produce either a habeas corpus famine or many months of extra jailhouse time. In the past, a staggering percentage of inmates' petitions have been found to be spurious. Out of every ten petitions filed during the 1950s, more than one was withdrawn by the petitioners without any action, eight more were dismissed without hearings because the convicts hadn't first asked the states for relief, or had failed to raise a legal issue, and less than one—6 percent—resulted in court hearings to determine the facts. The end result was that 1.4 percent resulted in some relief, and less than one petition out of 100 was actually granted. Since some of these petitioners were being held in local jails and mental institutions prior to trial, the effect was that a tiny fraction of convicted penitentiary inmates were winning their freedom in Federal court: Out of 5,570 convicts who filed petitions during one nine-year period, only 24 actually went free. This confetti of worthless writs has worked to the disadvantage of prisoners with legitimate complaints; as the paper avalanche has grown, the percentage of those that receive serious consideration has declined. The best explanation is that some Federal judges have been discounting the petitions in advance, bearing out Justice Robert H. Jackson's warning that "one who must search a haystack for a needle is likely to end up with the attitude that the needle is not worth the search."

Yet enough needles have been found to indicate that the tedious process mandated by the Supreme Court is worth the trouble. Some examples, taken from the Federal case reports of a single recent year, show why:

—John (Snooks) Jackson, a Philadelphia man without enough education to realize immediately what was happening, pleaded guilty to involvement in a series of robberies and received a twenty- to forty-year jail sentence. After the state courts twice refused to hear his complaint, a Federal judge did, and learned that Jackson had pleaded guilty only because the police had a fabricated confession which he had been tricked into signing without a reading. In overturning what he called "a nightmare of justice," the judge observed that "aside from his misconceived guilty plea, he (Jackson) has been convicted on a fraudulent confession, material misstatements of fact by the District Attorney, a confession of a mentally ill co-defendant and the lack of effective representation by his own counsel."

—James Byrnes of Ouachita, Louisiana, was arrested without a warrant and held incommunicado for almost four months, in violation of a state law requiring speedy arraignment, until he finally gave a statement and was charged with burglary. He was persuaded to plead guilty and was given a six-year sentence, all without any notification that he had a right to counsel. After state officials explained that he was treated this way because he could not have afforded to make bond or hire a lawyer anyway, a Federal District judge threw the conviction out in disgust.

—Fay Ward, Jr., was convicted of rape in a Utah trial, in which a physician testified that the alleged rape victim had indeed been raped. Later, the doctor confessed to a Federal judge that he had told the District Attorney that the woman had not been raped and that the prosecutor had persuaded him to swear that she had. The judge ordered a new trial.

As satisfying as Federal judges might find it to do justice in such extreme cases, the Federal judiciary, from the Supreme Court down, has given every indication that it would far prefer to have the states purge their own errors. The problem has not been so much that state judges fail to give prisoners a fair review, but that archaic state procedures either prevent a full hearing or fail to produce a record that shows clearly whether or not a fair review took place.

When the Supreme Court backed away from an ultimate ruling on the subject in the 1965 Nebraska case, Justice William J. Brennan, Jr., insisted in his opinion that the Court would be delighted to "remove the irritant of participation by the Federal District Courts in state criminal procedure." He spelled out in detail what the states should do to bring this about. What is needed, he said, is a procedure in each state that would give convicts a simple way to raise any Federal constitutional question, obtain a full hearing to resolve any factual disputes, and get a ruling on the claim. If the states would preserve the record of these hearings, he said, and if the state judges would include in their decisions their specific rulings on each dispute of fact or law, then Federal judges could later review the cases on the written record and everyone would be spared the irksome retrials of state actions in United States courts.

With the blizzard of writs from Joliet driving home the point,

Illinois got the message first and adopted such a procedure. At this writing about one-half of the states have done the same, with mixed results. In some states the number of Federal habeas corpus hearings have declined, but in others the Federal judges, unconvinced, have continued to hear convicts' claims.

The results show that a state's good intentions clearly do not pave the way to independence from Federal habeas corpus action. The Southern states, for all their reputation for chain-gang justice, have never had to put up with more than a trickle of prisoner petitions to Federal court. Yet California, Illinois and New York, with their enlightened court procedures, have been smothered with charges that their trials were unfair. Writ-writing, it seems, reflects prisoners' sophistication more than their sense of outrage. Yet despite the growth of a court-wise prison population and the consequent habeas corpus craze, it is still well within manageable limits; less than 4 of every 100 convicts now file petitions each year. Considering the explosion in due process, this has to be considered surprisingly low, and the states have managed to cope with it.

As it happened, it was state action and not Federal intervention that decided the fate of the prisoner who triggered it all, John Bongiorno. Within hours after Judge Barnes issued the writ of habeas corpus on December 7, 1942, Joliet officials rushed to the courthouse and declared that of course Bongiorno could file his petition. A long hearing resulted. Judge Barnes was deeply impressed by his main contention—that the 199-year sentence was "cruel and unusual" punishment, which is prohibited by the Eighth Amendment. His decision left no doubt that he found the sentence vindictive and unwarranted, but at that time no court had ever found a prison term so long as to be unconstitutional and he explained that it was not his place to be the first to do so.

Bongiorno returned to Joliet, expecting to be there for the rest of his life. He had already persuaded his wife to divorce him, and he turned his interests inward, to the prison library. Bongiorno studied biology, mathematics and philosophy, he mastered shorthand, and he learned to read and write eight languages. In 1960 Governor William G. Stratton accepted the parole board's conclusion that Bongiorno was no longer a threat to society. His sentence was commuted and he went free on July 1, 1960. Bongiorno died in Chicago in July of 1967, having spent twenty-seven years of his adult life inside Joliet Prison and twelve adult years outside.

For the Supreme Court, the deflation of the habeas corpus controversy in the early 1960s was an important symbolic development. It had been the petition binge that prompted the Conference of State Chief Justices in 1952 to first accuse the Supreme Court of overstepping its bounds to help criminals. By 1958 the State Justices' pique had reached the point that they issued a broadside blast at the Court, using the habeas corpus issue as a springboard to accuse the Justices of a growing lack of self-restraint in criminal matters. At that time such blunt talk about the Court was so rare that it touched off an incident that furnished one of the first public signs as to how deep the feelings were beginning to run. At the 1958 annual convention of the American Bar Association in Los Angeles, Chief Justice John R. Dethmers of the Michigan Supreme Court, who was head of the conference of chief justices, delivered a banquet speech with Chief Justice Warren and other Supreme Court members present as honored guests at the speakers' table. Dethmers took the occasion to elaborate on his group's recent criticism of the Supreme Court. Warren's annoyance was obvious to all, and he promptly resigned from the Bar Association. It was ten years later—after he announced his intention to retire from the court—before Warren appeared at another ABA meeting.

This was one of the rare public manifestations of a mini-controversy over the Supreme Court and crime, focused on habeas corpus, that was acted out virtually in the privacy of the legal establishment a full decade before cries of "criminal-coddling" became commonplace in public discourse. It had the major ingredients of the present controversy: the charges that the Supreme Court had ignored precedents and had violated states' rights; the complaints that it was unduly stressing individual rights at the expense of the system; the claims that eventually the legal system, if not law and order itself, would be undermined. There was one major difference—the habeas corpus furor soon ended, leaving the Supreme Court unbloodied, if not vindicated. In the teeth of ancient legal tradition and the conventional wisdom of the bench and bar, the Justices had insisted on radical changes in the name of individual rights. Despite the darkest warnings of havoc, the legal system adjusted nicely to the change. By the early 1960s, when the criminal-coddling charges began to be repeated by persons outside the legal world, it was widely felt in legal circles that in the similar intramural controversy that had already occurred, the Supreme Court had been proven to have been right.

There was a feeling in influential circles—perhaps including some members of the Court—that the criminal justice system would adjust equally smoothly to further reforms. At least it seemed likely that the public, after a period of unrest, would get used to the new order and would cease to complain. Thus it came as a stunning surprise to some in 1968 when the Supreme Court was rapped sharply across the knuckles in the anti-Court sections of the Omnibus Crime Control Act, the Senate rejection of Abe Fortas' nomination as Chief Justice and the enormous public vote for George Wallace and Richard Nixon. Obviously, the early, semiprivate controversy and the later public one were not completely analogous—not only because the volume of reported crime had risen in the meantime, but also because the Court had shifted its legal reform efforts from the courts to the more sensitive and difficult world of the police.

VII

Policing the Police

*The criminal is to go free because the constable
has blundered.*

BENJAMIN N. CARDOZO

Within hours after the police clashed with the antiwar demonstrators in Chicago, it could be seen that the incident was to become an important, divisive national controversy. It was not just that television cameras were there to film the 1968 Democratic National Convention and caught the police in a wild, club-swinging assault on fleeing demonstrators. Enough police riot action had been seen on TV that the viewing of Chicago itself would not have generated the heat that followed. The immediate national anger, the side-taking, the political fence-straddling, the recriminations revealed that more than an unpleasant vicarious experience was at work. At first, it seemed incredible that a thing could have been so widely seen and yet so bitterly disputed. A study group of the National Commission on Causes and Prevention of Violence canvassed 3,437 eyewitnesses and termed it a "police riot," and a sensitive observer concluded that "these were our children in the streets, and the Chicago police beat them up"; yet more than one-half of the Americans questioned by the Gallup Poll applauded the way Mayor Richard Daley's police had performed. Later, the division over Chicago came into sharper focus. What had happened was that millions saw for the first time their police smashing unprotected skulls in the name of the law, and they were forced to weigh conflicting values that until then most people had managed to ignore: How much control over the police can the community risk; how much lawlessness can it hazard, as the price of protection from police abuse?

In view of the public trauma that followed the exposure of this dilemma in Chicago, it is not surprising that the same issue has brought down such bitterness on the Supreme Court. For despite the fundamental importance of the haunting question once posed by Ramsey Clark—"Who will protect the people when the police violate the law?"—it has been left almost entirely to judges to find ways of controlling the police without paralyzing law enforcement. In theory, the law seems to have developed legal forms adequate to deter the police from violating the law, or at least to punish the offenders and compensate the victims for their trouble. Yet in practice, society has proved more fearful of police impotence than of police brutality. In a variety of effective ways, these sanctions against police misconduct have been disarmed, and the Supreme Court has been left to make do with what remains. To a large extent, the present charge that the Supreme Court is "handcuffing the police" results from the fact that it has been left almost alone to police the police.

To understand why this risky task has gravitated to the Supreme Court, it is instructive to examine why, in a specific instance, the police were not deterred from acting illegally and were not punished for it later. Take the case of Webster Bivens —ex-convict, narcotics pusher, Negro:

"At approximately 6:30 A.M. on the morning of November 25, 1965, the six defendants, acting as agents of the Federal Bureau of Narcotics, forced their way into Bivens' home in the Bronx with drawn firearms and proceeded to search the premises. In the presence of his wife and children, the agents forcibly hand-cuffed Bivens, placing him under arrest for violation of the nar-cotics laws. They threatened to arrest his entire family, and searched and restrained his brother who was at the time visiting as a guest in the home. The agents then took Bivens away to be questioned, fingerprinted, photographed and booked, as well as subjected to a thorough search of his person. At all perti-nent times the agents acted without the authority of a search warrant or a warrant for Bivens' arrest."

As far as anyone has been able to learn from the tangled cir-cumstances of his case, the agents dispensed with the procedural niceties when they picked Bivens up, partially because narcotics arrests are notoriously dangerous and they were taking no chances, and also because Bivens is a disreputable character who would not be likely to catch the ear of any important person with his complaint. It happened, though, that Bivens was an experienced do-it-yourself lawyer, and he was determined to have legal satisfaction. (The paragraph quoted above is from an ap-peal drafted later by a court-appointed Wall Street lawyer, Stephen A. Grant.) His legal efforts eventually taught him a bitter lesson about the law and the police: United States law is resplendent with layers of protective provisions against law-less police conduct; the most effective rarely work, and some never work at all.

There is a Federal law for all to see printed in Title 18 of the United States Code, Section 2236, which says that it is a crime for a U.S. official to take part in an illegal search. It has been on the books since 1921, and so far as anyone knows, it has never been used. Most other types of heavy-handed police ac-tion are likewise criminal offenses. Unlawful arrests usually violate the laws against false imprisonment. Third-degree meth-ods often involve unlawful assaults. Illegal searches usually vio-late the laws against criminal trespass. Yet as a practical matter, the threat of criminal prosecution is so remote that it is not a deterrent to police lawlessness. The law-enforcement machinery is in the hands of the police, and as one observer has put it, "policemen and prosecutors do not punish themselves."

One exception is the occasional willingness of the Justice Department to crack down on local police under an 1866 Reconstruction statute that makes it a crime for the police to use their official powers to violate citizens' rights. It was this law that was invoked against eight Chicago policemen after the Democratic Convention. They were acquitted, which only served to underscore an inadequacy in the law that the Supreme Court itself had unintentionally demonstrated, years before.

In 1954 the Court was committed to the doctrine, since discarded, that while state officers were bound by the Fourth Amendment's rule against unreasonable searches, evidence obtained in violation of the rule could still be used in court. That required the Court to uphold a gambling conviction that year in *Irvine* v. *California*, even though the police had thoroughly breached the search rule. They had burgled the defendants' house at night to plant a hidden microphone, and had later made arrests and searched the house without a warrant. Justice Robert H. Jackson and Chief Justice Earl Warren, evidently worried that their ruling could encourage the police to cheat, joined in an opinion that noted pointedly that the officers might have committed a Federal crime by violating the gamblers' civil rights when they bugged the house. The opinion suggested that the Clerk of the Supreme Court should send a copy of the opinion to the Attorney General for appropriate action. Justices Hugo L. Black and William O. Douglas objected in a dissent that this would be an improper judicial step, and the Clerk did not send the opinion. Nevertheless, Warren Olney, the Assistant Attorney General in charge of the Criminal Division of the Justice Department and an old friend of Warren's, decided to prosecute the state officers if possible. Soon after, a disgruntled Olney informed Warren that despite the Justice Department's best investigative efforts, there was no chance of a successful prosecution. The detectives had been acting under orders from superiors when they planted the listening devices, and Olney felt that none of them could be convicted under the 1866 law. So even though two members of the Supreme Court had gone out on a limb to say that the men probably should be prosecuted, the matter was dropped.

When Warren Burger was a frustrated dissenter on the liberal Court of Appeals for the District of Columbia he used to speak wistfully of how much more sense it would be to punish errant policemen than to punish society by suppressing evidence. But the obstacles to punishment are so imposing that nobody really expected him to lay his prestige as Chief Justice behind the idea that the Supreme Court should rely in its decision-making on the expectation that law enforcement will punish those of its own who violate citizens' rights.

Another possibility for police control is a civilian review board with power to investigate and punish police misconduct. Again, an idea that makes sense on paper has proved toothless. "Police Review Board" has been associated with "Negroes" in the public mind—and, more significantly, in the minds of the police—and the concept has become a political pariah. It began bravely in Philadelphia in 1958, and for a time the idea picked up momentum. Boards were established in York, Philadelphia, Minneapolis, Detroit, Rochester, New York and Washington, D.C. Then the police and their supporters mounted courtroom counterattack, claiming that the boards violated policemen's rights. At one time or another all but the Washington panel were closed down by court orders, and the concept was backlashed into oblivion in 1966 when it went on the New York City ballot with the enthusiastic support of Mayor John V. Lindsay—and was voted down by a margin of almost 2 to 1. Since then there has been scattered talk about the Swedish Ombudsmen, the official who has power to review a broad range of governmental actions and to vindicate the rights of those who have been wronged by public officers. But a police review board by any other name would be odious to the police, who apparently have the political muscle to defeat it in most communities. In any event, the Federal Government has never had such a board, so Bivens could not seriously consider this course.

Instead, he tried a third course. Most illegal police acts are also civil wrongs, or torts. This means that the victim himself can initiate a suit for civil damages, which the law permits under the theory that a money judgment will salve the victim's sense of injury and will deter the police from repeating the offense. Bivens hand-lettered his own court papers, suing each of the agents for $15,000 in damages for violating the Fourth Amendment's prohibition against unreasonable searches and seizures.

Again, he encountered a gap between what the lawbooks say and what the law allows. In theory, police misconduct would be discouraged if the victim could sue the government, which would have to control its police or risk a run on the treasury. This danger has been largely vitiated in the United States by the ancient English doctrine of sovereign immunity, "The King can do no wrong." The idea that a subject cannot sue the sovereign arrived from England with the common law, and the various governments have generally been pleased to see it remain in effect. It has proved to be a durable legal concept, despite the logic of Justice Holmes' observation that "it is revolting to have no better reason for a rule of law than that it was laid down in the time of Henry IV. It is still more revolting if the grounds upon which it was laid down have vanished long since, and the rule simply persists from blind imitation of the past." Eight state Supreme Courts have abandoned the doctrine and opened their governments to suits, but this leaves most of the jurisdictions with their sovereign immunity intact, including the United States. The Federal Government has relaxed the doctrine to permit negligence suits and in a few other types of cases, none of which applied in Webster Bivens' situation.

The alternative to suing the government is to sue the policemen, and there the obstacles may be as imposing in fact, if not in appearance. Tort law is laced with exceptions and restrictions that limit the amount of damages that an aggrieved person can recover for police misconduct, but the most important limitation is one that is not written in the books—the traditional reluctance of juries to render verdicts against policemen. Police officers make uninviting defendants; they are usually short in the purse, and they tend to have more rapport with jurors than the sort of people who sue them. A study in Los Angeles showed how niggardly juries can be in these cases—91 percent of those suing policemen lost, and those who "won" were awarded, on the average, one-twentieth of 1 percent of their claimed damages. If Bivens had sued the agents for trespassing on his property, he would have been limited in any event to the actual damage to his apartment, plus punitive damages if he could prove that their search was motivated by personal malice toward him.

In the case of Federal agents, the Supreme Court has added a wrinkle that complicates the plaintiff's situation even more. It arose in 1959 out of a libel suit against the acting director of the Office of Rent Stabilization for statements made in a press release. In *Barr* v. *Matteo*, the Supreme Court granted Federal officials an absolute privilege against suits that "might appreciably inhibit the fearless, vigorous and effective administration of policies of government." There were suggestions in the prevailing opinion by Justice John M. Harlan that the Justices might have intended to limit the privilege to high policy-making officials and to suits for libel, but the lower courts have been generous in enlarging it to protect law-enforcement officers from such routine cases as trespass actions and false arrest suits.

The travails of Anthony J. Scherer, Jr., a Chicago weapons dealer and gun buff, show how pervasive this protection can be. When Scherer returned home from work on the evening of October 7, 1964, he was met by two Federal agents who notified him that President Johnson planned to spend the night at nearby O'Hare Inn. They observed that Scherer kept a cannon in his garage and machine guns in his house and that O'Hare Inn was well within range of both. Scherer had no known political beliefs, but the agents were taking no chances. They invited themselves inside in order to keep Scherer under constant surveillance throughout the night. When he demurred, they offered to make him their guest at a motel in another part of town. He rejected this suggestion too, so they refused to let him in his house.

When he subsequently sued them, he ran headlong into *Barr* v. *Matteo*. The trial court quickly dismissed his suit, relying on the Supreme Court's rationale that government agents must feel free to do their duty without fear of damage suits. Scherer appealed up the line to the Supreme Court, losing at every step.

A sequel occurred when, a year later, a Secret Service official was lecturing trainees of the Chicago Police Department and was asked about the Scherer incident. The agent dismissed the matter by calling Scherer "a nut." Scherer returned to court, this time with a suit for slander. Again the trial judge threw out his suit, again citing *Barr* v. *Matteo*, and again the Supreme Court let the judgment stand.

In Bivens' case, the Federal District court in New York followed almost the opposite reasoning, but arrived at the same conclusion—in favor of the police. Since the Supreme Court has not yet decided whether a Federal official can be sued for violating a citizen's constitutional rights, the lower courts, including Bivens' court, have been left to answer the questions themselves. All have said no. Their reason is so circuitous as to boggle the brain: the Fourth Amendment forbids unreasonable searches by the Government, not private individuals. When the agents searched without a warrant they went beyond their authority and did not act for the Government. Thus, the agents could not be liable for a violation of the Fourth Amendment.

The Court of Appeals for the Second Circuit affirmed, although it conceded that in Bivens' situation this left him with no remedy at all against the agents. And so a question came to the Supreme Court that was, in view of the composition of the Burger Court, almost irresistible. The liberal holdovers from the Warren majority were confirmed policers of the police, whatever the method. Burger had railed against the exclusionary rule, insisting that other, more rational deterrents should be developed. On June 22, 1970, the Supreme Court agreed to hear Webster Bivens' case, setting the stage for what could become a major Supreme Court decision of 1971.

To the victims of bullying by Federal officials, the cases of Scherer and Bivens represent you're-damned-if-they-do and you're-damned-if-they-don't, back to back. If an officer mistreats a person in the line of duty, *Barr* v. *Matteo* forbids a suit. If the agent steps out of line to be abusive, the Constitution will not support a suit.

When the law is this consistent, it is telling the litigant something—that strong policy pressures are at work against effective control of the police by judges or anyone else. But law abhors a vacuum, and the search for an effective judicial deterrent has continued. Much of the Supreme Court's recent grief has resulted from the fact that in default of all other remedies, lawyers have pressed the Justices to act, and they have tried to fill the void with a device known as the "exclusionary rule."

Only a nation that reveres its judges would permit them to bar illegally obtained evidence from use, regardless of its probity, or the enormity of the crime, or the degree of police malfeasance. The United States does, and the exclusionary rule in this absolute form is a unique American device. Its uniqueness is all the more surprising because the Constitution does not say that evidence obtained in violation of the Bill of Rights cannot be used. But the Bill of Rights does declare flatly that certain things are not to be done by the police, and this prompted the Justice of a half-century ago to recoil from the use of improperly obtained items, more as a matter of propriety than of police control. The result was a decision in 1914, called *Weeks* v. *United States*, which has proved to be one of the most significant decisions of American law—and certainly the most disarming.

Weeks established the principle that evidence seized in violation of the Fourth Amendment could not be used in Federal court against the victim of the search. Two generations of judges since then have expanded the use of the exclusionary rule announced in *Weeks*, lulled by the feeling that no doctrine that received the unanimous blessing of the Supreme Court of 1914 could be dangerously generous to defendants. The fallacy of that assumption was that the Court in *Weeks* fully appreciated what it was undertaking; for while its ruling was deceptively clear-cut, the Court's reason for making it was doctrinaire and unsupported by an analysis of where it would eventually lead. Justice William R. Day's rambling opinion seemed to conclude that as a matter of judicial practice the Court did not wish to give even tacit approval to official defiance of the Constitution.

Since then a number of arguments have been advanced to support the rule, but all are versions of one of two rationales—one rooted deeply in constitutional theory and the other intensely pragmatic. The theoretical rationale is that it mocks the concept of a Constitution which limits governmental powers to have citizens go to prison on the strength of officials' violations of the Bill of Rights. If this had been the sole reason for the rule, then the courts might well have worked out a more flexible approach to it. Inadvertent or technical violation of the Bill of

Rights might have been overlooked, and suppression of "fruit
of the poisonous tree" evidence might not have been considered
necessary. But the pragmatic rationale—the use of exclusion of
evidence to deter the police from lawless conduct—prompted
the courts to continually close loopholes and to forgive nothing,
for fear that the police might be encouraged to believe that other
missteps would also be overlooked.

The Constitution does not expressly give the judiciary the
power to try to police the police, so the judiciary tended to
justify the exclusionary rule under the first rationale, even though
the Supreme Court was increasingly motivated by the second
one. The result was that for decades the courts were to fumble
forward, citing *Weeks* and expanding the use of the exclusionary
rule, without ever analyzing whether it was in fact deterring
the police, and if so whether it was worth the price.

Instead, the Supreme Court began suppressing evidence for
doctrinaire reasons that precluded the courts from experimenting
with a flexible, ad hoc rule that could be invoked only when
the police needed to have their knuckles rapped. Justices Holmes
and Brandeis declared in 1928 that it should be used in wiretap cases, not to chastise the police who wiretapped, but "to
preserve the judicial process from contamination." As recently
as 1948 four members of the Court insisted in an opinion that
its purpose was to purify the Federal courts and not to discipline the police. But as the failure of other deterrents became
clear and the shadow of police power became more ominous,
the liberal Justices began to justify the expanding exclusionary
rule purely in terms of the need to control the police. By 1948,
when the Court shied away in *Wolf* v. *Colorado* from imposing
the exclusionary rule on the states, Justice Frank Murphy argued
bluntly in his dissent that other measures had failed and that the
Supreme Court should step in to deter the police from violating
the Constitution. He ticked off the reasons why the police
did not fear criminal prosecution or civil damages, and concluded: "The conclusion is inescapable that but one remedy exists to deter violations of the search and seizure clause. That is
the rule which excludes illegally obtained evidence. Only by exclusion can we impress upon the zealous prosecutor that violation
of the Constitution will do him no good. And only when that

point is driven home can the prosecutor be expected to empha-
size the importance of observing constitutional demands in his
instructions to the police."

Once the exclusionary idea surfaced as a police control
measure, it proved exceedingly contagious. It was extended to
the "seizure" aspect of the Fourth Amendment, ruling out confessions and fingerprints obtained after improper arrests. It was
applied to confessions obtained by coercion or in violation of
the *Miranda* rule, and to lineups conducted without a right of
counsel. It was also extended to evidence obtained in violation
of Federal statutes, including the antiwiretap law and a law that
required the prompt arraignment of arrested suspects. Moreover, it was extended laterally, under the "fruit of the poisonous
tree" theory, to suppress evidence obtained from leads gar-
nered by illegal means. Finally, most of this exclusionary law has
been made binding on the states.

The result is a pervasive system of calculated non-use of evidence that astounds the lawyers of other countries. Among the
major nations, England's "Judges' Rules" governing police interrogation are the nearest thing to the American exclusionary
rule. But if an English judge finds that a policeman has failed
to give the full warnings or has otherwise acted improperly, the
judge considers the seriousness of the breach and suppresses the
confession only if it serves the interest of justice. Lord Justice
Kenneth Diplock of the Royal Courts of Justice in London estimates that of the approximately 1,000 criminal cases that he has
tried, probably less than one-half of 1 percent have involved a
"trial within a trial"—a test of the propriety of the police's actions. In only one did he exclude the defendant's confession.
(There is no exclusionary rule in England for illegal searches:
an aggrieved person may sue the transgressing constable, but
the evidence is used against the aggrieved person if he is prosecuted.) If trial evidence indicates that the police are getting out
of line, "I have a chat with the Queen's constable," Lord Diplock says, and an effort is made to set things right without sac-
rificing convictions of guilty defendants.

The American rule contains no such flexibility. If a procedure
has been violated, the evidence cannot be used. There have
been suggestions that the exclusionary rule should be relaxed

along the lines of the English Judges' rules, and Title II of the Omnibus Crime Control Act of 1968 purports to make the *Miranda* warnings discretionary. But such a move would run counter to the absolutist theory that bottoms the entire criminal justice revolution (and, incidentally, to the Justices' apparent distrust of many state judges), and the Supreme Court has never publicly discussed the possibility.

The effect is that crucial evidence can be suppressed and important cases lost because of what most people would consider insignificant lapses in police procedures. This has fueled the charges that criminals are being released on technicalities, while providing some memorable abortions of justice that have helped to create the impression that the criminal law is seriously off the track:

—Tom E. Alston, Jr., was arrested for murder by the District of Columbia police and taken to police headquarters. After he was questioned in private for about five minutes he was permitted to talk to his wife, who persuaded him to confess. His conviction was overturned by the Court of Appeals for the District of Columbia because he confessed during a five-minute "unnecessary" delay between arrest and arraignment before a magistrate. He was never tried again, and is still free.

—Donald M. Painten and George Ash were visited at their Boston apartment one night by police officers who strongly suspected them of a string of armed robberies. When the officers knocked, the two men tossed a bag containing their guns onto the fire escape and then invited the policemen in. A detective on watch outside saw the maneuver, retrieved the guns, and arrested them. Painten's conviction was overturned by the United States Court of Appeals for the First Circuit on the ground that the guns were illegally obtained. The court's reasoning was that the officers intended to conduct an illegal search when they knocked on the door, and this illegal intent caused the robbers to toss their guns out the window and into view.

—Robert N. Paille was one of three policemen implicated in the killing of three Negroes in a Detroit motel during the riots of 1967. Shortly after the shootings Paille answered a general call for all policemen who knew about the incident to make a statement to their superiors. He wrote out an exculpatory statement and, when it appeared that his story might be contradicted by another officer, he suddenly blurted out to one of his superiors that "I shot one of the men." A state trial judge held that Paille should have first been warned of his rights, and threw out the murder charge against him.

Members of the legal profession understand that cases such as these are aberrations that the Supreme Court probably never intended to occur, but that they are an inevitable by-product of a rigid exclusionary system that is designed to be a strong deterrent against police misconduct. Over the years many judges have enforced the rule and have borne the "criminal coddling" complaints with good grace because they felt that the protection of individual rights was worth it. It has only been in recent years that evidence has accumulated to indicate that despite its occasional wallop, the exclusionary rule has a limited effect on police conduct, and that in many situations it has none at all.

The classic judicial thinking behind the exclusionary rule has been stated by Chief Justice Roger J. Traynor of California, who reasoned that "Police officers and prosecuting officials are primarily interested in convicting criminals. Given the exclusionary rule and a choice between securing evidence by legal rather than illegal means, officers will be impelled to obey the law themselves since not to do so will jeopardize their objectives." As the Supreme Court has put it in an opinion by Justice Potter Stewart, "the rule is calculated to prevent, not to repair. Its purpose is to deter—to compel respect for the constitutional guaranty in the only effectively available way—by removing the incentive to disregard it."

The trouble with this rationale is that in practice both of its major premises frequently prove to be wrong. According to empirical studies of police conduct, officers are not so much concerned with convicting criminals as with "ferreting out crime," an important distinction that makes successful court action secondary to effective police action. And while the police are undoubtedly encouraged to follow the rules, they are not impelled to do so; the indications are that they manage to cut corners and still do very nicely in the conviction column.

The most serious flaw in the exclusionary rule is the assumption that police are motivated primarily by the desire to convict wrongdoers. Criminologists who have studied police methods conclude that this is not necessarily so. The average policeman believes his job is to fight crime—and when he is faced with a situation that calls for one response if crime is to be suppressed and another if a conviction is to be preserved, he will usually choose the first. Arthur Train, the lawyer and author, pointed out years ago that policemen are constantly in a tug-of-war between what their superiors expect and what the courts will permit. Assuming that a policeman saw a seedy-looking character sneaking down a dark street with his pockets bulging with jewelry and silver, he noted that "the rules of the New York police department require him to arrest all persons carrying bags in the small hours who cannot give a satisfactory account of themselves. Yet there is no such thing under the laws of the state as a right 'to arrest on suspicion.' No citizen may be arrested under the statutes unless a crime has actually been committed. Thus, the police regulations deliberately compel every officer either to violate the law or to be made the object of charges for dereliction of duty."

The average officer is unlikely to let the suspicious-looking character pass and explain later to his superior that he held back for bear of violating a Supreme Court decision. One reason why not is that he may well get a conviction anyway. In many urban areas more than 90 percent of those charged with crimes plead guilty. A suspect is less likely to plead if there is a question about the legality of the police's conduct, and the prosecuting attorney is more likely to reduce the charge in order to get a guilty plea in such cases, but for various reasons the vast majority of defendants do plead guilty, despite the legal questions that can be raised in almost any complicated case. A crushing combination of pressures can bear down upon a defendant, pressing him to plead guilty—from his own lawyer's reluctance to spend long hours in court to the statistical proof that he who puts the state to the trouble of a trial often gets a whopping sentence if convicted. An example of the pressures for guilty plea bargaining all along the line was seen in 1967, when New York's highest court affirmed a conviction in which the defendant had been permitted to plead guilty to a nonexistent crime—attempted manslaughter. Even if the accused goes to trial, the police often manage to remember facts about the case that bring it within the four corners of the Constitution. The most celebrated method of accomplishing this is called "dropsy" testimony, in which the police explain to an understanding judge that when the suspect saw the police closing in, he pulled the packet of narcotics from his pocket (where the police could not have legally reached it) and threw it on the ground, where it became legal evidence.

If ever there were grounds to fear that law enforcement would follow the dinosaur into extinction because it couldn't turn around fast enough to deal with the due process revolution, this was dispelled by the evolution of policemen's dropsy testimony after *Mapp* v. *Ohio*. Before *Mapp*, when police could frisk suspicious-looking characters and use the results for evidence, many dope pushers and numbers runners believed that they could not be convicted if they could drop the incriminating evidence so that the arresting officer couldn't say that he actually saw the item fall. This resulted in a dropsy scenario that was repeated daily in courtrooms across the land. The defendant would deny dropping anything. The officer would swear that he saw the drop, or saw the item in the defendant's hand before it was found on the ground. The judge would usually believe the policeman.

After the *Mapp* decision, the suspects had every reason never to drop evidence, since the police supposedly couldn't search them for it without a warrant. But in the teeth of the reduced likelihood of dropsies, the police continued to tell the same stories, only more often.

Some idea of the versatility of dropsy testimony was learned when a team of researchers from Columbia University checked narcotics arrests in New York for comparable periods before and after the *Mapp* decision was announced in 1961. During a six-month period preceding *Mapp*, when evidence could be used even if it were taken in an illegal search, the narcotics bureau agents stated that in more than one-third of its arrests, the narcotics were found by searching the suspects' pockets— in most cases in violation of the Fourth Amendment. In that period prior to *Mapp* only 16.8 percent of the evidence was said to have been obtained by dropsies. In the six-month period following *Mapp*, when illegally-obtained evidence could no longer be used, the agents' version of how they got their evidence did a dramatic turnabout. Searches of the person accounted for only 3 percent of the evidence, they said, and dropsies doubled, to 43.2 percent. New York's uniformed police did even better. Prior to *Mapp*, when evidence fished out of suspects' pockets could be used, they claimed in only 27.5 percent of their narcotics cases that their evidence was either seen in the suspect's hand or obtained by dropsy. In the six months shortly after *Mapp* this rose to 39.6 percent, and by 1964 they were claiming to have found their evidence on the ground or in the defendant's visible possession in 72.7 percent of their cases. The explanation, according to the researchers, was unpleasant but simple: "Police allegations as to how evidence was obtained changed after the *Mapp* decision. There is some indication, however, that police practices in the field have not changed substantially, and that police officers often merely fabricate testimony to avoid the effects of *Mapp*-based motions to suppress illegally seized evidence."

Many trial judges are impatient with what they consider to be unduly strict Supreme Court procedures, and their credulity in the face of unlikely police testimony can be remarkable. This facility was demonstrated in communities across the country in the wake of the *Miranda* decision. Only the most prophetic policeman would have had the vision, before the Court announced its detailed, four-point warning, to recite exactly that warning before questioning a suspect. Yet a number of confessions that had already been obtained by the police were admitted into evidence in post-*Miranda* trials, based on the officers' statements that a complete *Miranda*-type warning had been given. A situation in Nashville, Tennessee, demonstrated the capacity of the police and the courts to proceed smoothly along with the usual conviction rate despite a yearlong delay in fully implementing the *Miranda* decision.

Immediately after the *Miranda* ruling was announced in June of 1966, many police departments printed up "Miranda Cards" bearing the prescribed warnings. The purpose was to give each policeman a handy copy of the exact warning, for under the *Miranda* opinion if any of the four elements were omitted or not accurately stated, then any resulting confession was supposed to be suppressed. A typical Miranda Card is the one used by the San Francisco police department, which reads:

1. You have the right to remain silent.
2. Anything you say can and will be used against you in a court of law.
3. You have the right to talk to a lawyer and have him present with you while you are being questioned.
4. If you cannot afford to hire a lawyer one will be appointed to represent you before any questioning, if you wish one.

Before the officer proceeds with the interrogation, he is also required to ask:

1. Do you understand each of these rights I have explained to you?
2. Having these rights in mind, do you wish to talk to us now?

If possible, the policeman obtains the suspect's signature on the card before he asks any questions.

This suggests the complexity of the formalities that must be observed before a confession satisfies the rigid *Miranda* test. With this in mind, Thomas A. Shriver, Nashville's District Attorney, acted immediately after the ruling came down to prepare a similar warning for use by the city's police. But a snag developed. First he and police officials haggled for several months over the wording. After that was settled and the Miranda Cards were printed, sixteen months passed before the police department got around to distributing them to the police. Yet despite the many months in which the police had to rely upon memory to deliver the complicated warning, a subsequent check showed that only one confession had been thrown out in Nashville's criminal courts in the two years following *Miranda*. (The defendant was convicted anyway.) When the irked District Attorney was asked later how the police managed to persuade the judges in so many cases that the full warning had been properly remembered and given, Shriver snapped: "I think they just lied."

Even when a judge excludes evidence, the police will not necessarily be deterred from repeating the infraction. Most judges see their role as merely to decide legal questions; it rarely occurs to one to find out if his ruling contradicts some standing police policy that must be changed if the same breach is not to be repeated again and again. The President's Crime Commission even found that some judges felt that if they communicated their rulings to police policy-makers they would be guilty of "coaching" the police, to the detriment of defendants' rights.

Two law professors who have studied the operation of the exclusionary rule, Wayne R. LaFave of the University of Illinois and Frank J. Remington of the University of Wisconsin, have concluded that the police rarely get a clear picture of the court rulings that are supposed to guide their actions:

> The trial judge seldom explains his decision in a way likely to be understood by the police officer, and the prosecutor assigned to the case rarely assumes it to be his duty to inform the police department of the meaning of the decision or of its intended impact upon current police practice. The individual officer whose case has been lost is not now expected to report the reason for the decision to his superiors. Some decisions, usually those the officer believes to be particularly outrageous, may be passed on to other officers by word of mouth, but they often become distorted in the retelling. If a "court officer" is assigned to the court by the police department, his responsibilities do not include reporting the judge's rulings on police conduct. Obviously, police cannot be affirmatively influenced to change their methods of law enforcement by the exclusion of evidence when there is no communication to them of why the decision was made.

The confusion is compounded, they found, because different trial judges sometimes enforce different rules. Many individual judges also use the exclusionary rule erratically—they will enforce it to the hilt to knock down petty gambling cases or other prosecutions which they consider to be unworthy of police attention, and then look the other way to let a narcotics arrest stand in the face of a police infraction. Thus the best-informed thinking is that while the exclusionary rule does affect police conduct to some extent, it probably doesn't have as much influence as police customs and rules. "A moment's reflection," Thurman Arnold once said, "would indicate that the temper of the police commissioner is of much more significance on governmental interference with rights of respectable citizens than appellate-court utterances." Some doubts have even been raised as to whether the threat that a judge may suppress evidence is the strongest inducement for proper police conduct. Several years ago a research team commissioned by the American Bar Foundation found that the police in a state that had no exclusionary rule used search warrants as frequently as the police did in nearby states where the exclusionary rule was in effect. The studies were made in communities in Kansas, where prior to the *Mapp* decision the fruits of illegal searches could be used in court, and in Michigan and Wisconsin, where they could not. Prosecutory prudence explained why search warrants were used as often in Kansas—juries often reacted unfavorably to illegal police raids, so wise prosecutors protected their important cases by going by the book. Such doubts about the effectiveness of the exclusionary rule have reinforced the resentment that it has caused in those unavoidable instances when it frustrates justice. All this raises grave questions in view of its adverse effects on the law and the public's opinion of the courts, as to whether the exclusionary rule has been worth it all.

John Henry Wigmore, the authority on the law of evidence, pointed out years ago that in those cases in which the exclusionary rule fails to deter the police and thus has to be enforced, a contradictory logic comes into play which is difficult to justify. He used this parable:

Titus, you have been found guilty of conducting a lottery; Flavius, you have confessedly violated the Constitution. Titus ought to suffer imprisonment for crime, and Flavius for contempt. But no! We shall let you *both* go free. We shall not punish Flavius directly, but shall do so by reversing Titus' conviction. This is our way of teaching people like Flavius to behave, and of teaching people like Titus to behave, and incidentally of securing respect for the Constitution. Our way of upholding the Constitution is not to strike at the man who breaks it, but to let off somebody else who broke something else.

Whether or not the criminal law has indeed become this perverse, the rationale behind the exclusionary rule seems to have been undercut by the feeling among many police that it has. There has been a tendency among some big-city police forces in recent years to stress police tactics that are not aimed primarily at obtaining convictions, but rather at preventing crime. At least part of the reason for the trend is the belief by police that the prosecution of criminals is too time-consuming and unpredictable, and that the prospect of punishment is too weak a deterrent, for the police to focus their efforts primarily at obtaining convictions. The result has been a growing use of a tactic called "aggressive patrol." It was first used on a large scale in Chicago, where in the early 1960s squads of police began to saturate high-crime areas, questioning suspicious-looking persons, frisking some for weapons, and making a show of force. The strategy paid off in lower crime rates and other cities have adopted it. One important objective of aggressive patrol action is to disarm the ghetto population—an aim that is difficult to fault, since a study of one city showed that one out of five persons frisked was packing either a gun or a knife. But searches "on suspicion" are unconstitutional, and before the Supreme Court surprised nearly everybody in 1968 by declining to apply the exclusionary rule to the routine "stop and frisk" situation, the police were usually content to collect the hardware and eschew prosecutions. An observer for the American Bar Foundation who watched the Chicago police operate prior to the "stop and frisk" decision concluded that the threat of exclusion did not affect them. "Since there is no particular police concern with prosecution," he said, "evidentiary standards enforced by the threat to exclude the evidence illegally obtained do not deter the police from engaging in these practices."

Burton B. Roberts, who as District Attorney of Bronx County has been plagued with crime by narcotics addicts, has stated that the police there routinely make illegal searches of known narcotics offenders as a way of slowing down the dope traffic. "If a cop sees a guy on the street and knows he's a pusher, he'll grab him and search him, to harass him—he's not going to let him go on his way," Roberts says. "Of course," he adds, "he's not going to do this to a stranger."

A combination of these factors explains the rough handling of Webster Bivens, despite the exclusionary rule. The narcotics agents felt that they already had an airtight case before they arrested him and searched his home without a warrant. Illegally arrested *people* are not excluded under the rule, and since the agents needed no more evidence to convict him, they had nothing to lose. His home was apparently ransacked in hopes of obtaining evidence of illegal drug suppliers. Since only Bivens' Fourth Amendment rights had been violated, his suppliers would not have had "standing" to complain about the violation. Evidence of their guilt, if any had been found, could have been used in court against them. Bivens would undoubtedly have been convicted despite it all, except that the informer who had been counted on to testify about a transaction with Bivens skipped out on the prosecution and was not available for trial. The charges were dropped and Bivens brought his fateful lawsuit.

The Justices were aware of some of the serpentine workings of the exclusionary rule long before the Court became deeply committed to it. Justice Jackson frequently questioned why police abuse was no less apparent in jurisdictions that enforced the exclusionary rule than in those that did not. He concluded that "there are many unlawful searches of homes and automobiles of innocent people which turn up nothing incriminating, in which no arrest is made, about which courts do nothing, and about which we never hear."

Yet two factors propelled the Court toward a more aggressive use of the rule. One was the absolutist view of the Bill of Rights that provided the doctrinal underpinning for the Court's activism in criminal law. At a time when the Supreme Court was replacing the "fairness" view of due process with the theory that the states are strictly bound to the strictures of the Bill of Rights, it would have been incongruous for the Court to agree to an ad hoc method of enforcing the new rights, patterned after the English Judges' Rules. Moreover, the Justices had seen the erratic results of the ad hoc approach to the admissibility of confessions, and they were not convinced that a "fairness" exclusionary rule would be either very fair or very exclusionary.

The second reason was that the *Weeks* exclusionary rule, limited to the Fourth Amendment and Federal officers, had worked fairly well. When the Justices insisted on the suppression of evidence in Federal trials, they were sending signals to an unusually well-educated corps of law-enforcement agents who usually dealt with a relatively civilized brand of crime. The Court spoke and the word filtered down through channels to agents who were instructed by their superiors to mend their ways. Even if it had cramped their style, the public would not have risen up in protest over an increase in embezzling, tax cheating and transporting of immoral females across state lines.

The contradictions began to surface after 1961 as local police came under the same curbs. There the faulty communications, the more rough-hewn constabulary, the hostility to the rules and the pressure of rising street crime, brought out the faults in the exclusionary rule. Soon the Supreme Court began to cut and fill.

In *Miranda* it cracked down on the use of incriminating statements, but then it immediately began to make it easier for the police to prove probable cause to search, while enlarging the types of evidence that could be seized once probable cause was established. It held that confessions and fingerprints must be excluded if they are obtained after illegal arrests, but it kept tight limits on those who had standing to challenge the use of illegally seized evidence. Finally, in the stop-and-frisk decision the Court conceded for the first time that under certain circumstances police could search without probable cause and the fruits of their searches could be used against those whose rights had been infringed. Furthermore, the decision reflected a pragmatism that was uncharacteristic of the Court's earlier rulings. What had happened was that the Fourth Amendment had been seriously compromised by the easy availability of firearms and the disposition of many Americans to use them. Under the Fourth Amendment the police are forbidden to search a person without a search warrant, unless there is probable cause to arrest the individual, who can then be searched as an incident to the arrest. The mere fact that a tough-looking subject lives in a neighborhood where a high percentage of the residents are stick-up men does not establish probable cause. Yet the police often stopped and searched such individuals anyway, even if they could do no more than confiscate weapons. The result was that the exclusionary rule was deterring the police from prosecuting gun-toters, but was not deterring the police from searching "on suspicion."

In the Court's stop-and-frisk ruling, *Terry* v. *Ohio*, Chief Justice Earl Warren capitulated so decisively to these practical arguments against the exclusionary rule that he erased in one stroke the long-standing assumption that evidence seized without probable cause can never be used. "A ruling admitting evidence in a criminal trial, we recognize, has the necessary effect of legitimizing the conduct which produced the evidence, while an application of the exclusionary rule withholds the constitutional imprimatur," he said. "The exclusionary rule has its limitations, however, as a tool of judicial control. . . . In some contexts the rule is ineffective as a deterrent. . . . Doubtless some police 'field interrogation' conduct violates the Fourth Amendment. But a stern refusal by this Court to condone such activity does not necessarily render it responsive to the exclusionary rule. Regardless of how effective the rule may be where obtaining convictions is an important objective of the police, it is powerless to deter invasions of constitutionally guaranteed rights where the police either have no interest in prosecuting or are willing to forego successful prosecution in the interest of serving some other goal. . . . The wholesale harassment by certain elements of the police community, of which minority groups, particularly Negroes, frequently complain, will not be stopped by the exclusion of any evidence from any criminal trial. Yet a rigid unthinking application of the exclusionary rule, in futile protest against practices which it can never be used effectively to control, may exact a high toll in human injury and frustration of efforts to prevent crime. No judicial opinion can comprehend the protean variety of the street encounter, and we can only judge the facts of the case before us. . . ." The Court held, 8 to 1, that so long as an officer is in reasonable apprehension of danger when he frisks a suspect for weapons, any weapons that are found may be used in evidence. Left open was a crucial question that the Court must resolve in the future—whether incriminating items other than weapons can be used in evidence if they are found in a "frisk" of a dangerous-looking suspect.

Not long after, a little-noticed incident occurred in Philadelphia that summed up the ironies of the Supreme Court's effort to police the police through the exclusionary rule: Three young men sued the Chief of Police for damages, charging that they had been picked up without reason and held in police custody for six hours because they were needed to stand in a lineup—which the police were dutifully holding in compliance with a Supreme Court decision. At about that time Justice William J. Brennan declared in a speech that the exclusionary rule had never been intended to police the police anyway. "It is a mistake often made that deterrence of unlawful police action is the underlying basis of this rule," Brennan said; "The true reason is that exclusion is necessary to vindicate the right itself, whether or not that vindication also operates to deter."

With the imperfections in the exclusionary rule now conceded by the Supreme Court, there are already indications that the pressures for controls over the police are shifting to other legal ground. Tort litigation against police and governments has increased, and some courts have responded with a greater willingness to penetrate governmental immunity or to hold officers liable. In 1968 Congress also beefed up the criminal penalties that can be imposed against policemen who violate citizens' civil rights.

But the most significant pressures are those growing out of minority groups' efforts to persuade Federal judges to intervene directly in police-community relations by enjoining local police from violating individuals' rights. Chief Justice Warren gave oblique encouragement to this in his stop-and-frisk opinion when he declared that the Court's backpedalling on the exclusionary rule "should in no way discourage the employment of other remedies than the exclusionary rule to curtail abuses for which that sanction may prove inappropriate." Warren apparently had in mind a procedure authorized by the Civil Rights Act of 1871, a measure enacted by the Reconstruction Congress to protect the newly freed slaves from abuse by Southern officials. One section gives Federal judges power to use court orders to stop local officials from violating individuals' rights. This poses an obvious threat of state-Federal friction, and the power was rarely used until racial tensions increased in recent years.

It has come before the Supreme Court only once, when the Congress for Industrial Organizations used it during the Depression to fight off the efforts of "Boss" Frank Hague of Jersey City to run the CIO's organizers out of town. Hague announced his intention to rid Jersey City of the CIO "Communists," and his police embarked on a campaign of harassing arrests, deportation of union officials and suppression of union circulars and public meetings. A Federal District judge ordered Hague and his underlings to halt their "deliberate policy" of violating the unionists' rights, and the Supreme Court agreed by a 5 to 2 vote. Justice James C. McReynolds protested in a dissent that "the court should have respected the essential rights of the municipality to control its own parks and streets. Wise management of such intimate local affairs, generally at least, is beyond the competency of Federal courts." Even during that time of economic trouble the Federal courts were not brought under pressure to intervene between the police and the people of other communities, so McReynolds' warning was quickly forgotten.

Several developments—both legal and social—have meshed in the past few years to bring the issue forward again, but this time with more serious overtones. One is the specificity that the Supreme Court has given to Federal constitutional rights. In 1939 only the First Amendment was considered binding on Boss Hague and his police, and if they had been content to use billysticks, warrantless searches and unlawful arrests against the CIO, the Federal courts might have felt themselves without jurisdiction to intervene. But when Hague denied the unionists the right to distribute literature and to meet in public he gave the Supreme Court the First Amendment handle it needed to take jurisdiction over the case. Since then the Supreme Court has made most of the prohibitions of the Bill of Rights binding on state officers, and in a number of instances it has defined in great detail what the officers must do to comply with the Constitution. As Judge Henry Friendly has pointed out, for better or for worse, much of the "play in the joints" of law enforcement has been eliminated. Now, a wide range of routine police activity, including arrests, searches, interrogation and lineups, can be measured against objective constitutional standards. If the police tactics do not pass muster then the Federal judiciary may have little alternative but to intervene.

Until recently, U.S. trial judges could have fallen back gracefully on a handy legal principle called "abstention." This is a judicial invention, which Congress thought well of and wrote into Federal law, that instructs Federal judges to abstain from intervening in local criminal justice matters, since any unconstitutional actions can be cured later upon appeal or by habeas corpus. While this was a sound doctrine from the standpoint of federalism, it was taken as a license to bully by some Southern lawmen who customarily used the badge to keep Negroes in their place. The abstention doctrine began to pinch during the early 1960s, as civil rights activity spread across the South and local police officials retaliated with illegal arrests and groundless prosecutions. Eventually these actions would have been struck down in Federal courts, but meanwhile the law was being used to frustrate the Negroes' legitimate civil rights efforts.

The Supreme Court gave the lower U.S. judges the green light to intervene in these situations in a murky but important 1965 decision, *Dombrowski* v. *Pfister*. It came to the Supreme Court after Louisiana law-enforcement officials teamed up with the state legislature's Joint Committee on Un-American Activities to harass a civil rights group called the Southern Conference Educational Fund.

The Louisiana antisubversive laws that were invoked against SCEF's officers were palpably unconstitutional, so the local officials were in no hurry to obtain convictions that could be appealed. Instead, they used them as the basis for arrests, searches, and other harassing tactics, without prosecuting the civil rights' activists. In the *Dombrowski* decision the Supreme Court neatly finessed the statutory abstention rule and ordered the Federal District Court in New Orleans to enjoin the state officers from invoking those laws to stifle the activities of the civil rights activists. Justice William J. Brennan's opinion stressed "the chilling effect on free expression" that resulted from the prosecutions, but the decision has been taken by some lawyers to constitute more than a procedure for protecting speech and assembly. Traditionally the Supreme Court has used the First Amendment as the opening wedge to establish broader Federal jurisdiction over state justice, and many lawyers see the *Dombrowski* decision as a signal to the Federal judiciary to intervene when local officers use the law to harass unpopular elements in a community.

A final legal development has been the increasing availability of well-financed, able teams of attorneys to represent clients who are long on rights but short of funds. The American Civil Liberties Union, the NAACP Legal Defense and Educational Fund, Inc., the Legal Services Units of the Office of Economic Opportunity and a host of smaller, more militant libertarian legal organizations have ended the long-standing capability of John Law to fall back on muscle as a last resort in dealing with troublesome elements in the population. For years it had been a tenet of American folklore that the sheriff could clean up the town by warning the thugs at the saloon that he'd gun them down if they weren't out of town by sundown. If he were to do that today, the ACLU would get a temporary restraining order from the Federal District Court before high noon.

With the Federal courts inclining toward the role of protectors as well as arbiters of constitutional rights, rising militancy— among the ranks of the police as well as among the policed— has raised the likelihood that the judges will have to step in. As "Blue Power" becomes an established political force in the big cities, the police have been inclined to draw support from anti-Negro, "law and order" elements. If the police did not previously see their role as protecting certain elements of society against others, this drawing of political lines has increased their tendency to do so now. "There were worrisome indications in the past year," reported the Urban Coalition and Urban America, Inc., in 1969, "that the police were moving further toward an 'our side, their side' mentality." Robert L. Carter, the former general counsel for the National Association for the Advancement of Colored People, agreed: "Police too often regard their function as protecting white people from Negroes—their function has to be to protect all citizens." But with crime and disorder increasingly associated with Negroes and with white students and radicals, the police often have felt that they could dispense with the usual safeguards in dealing with these types.

So far these factors have coalesced in one notable incident

that demonstrates how the Federal courts can be drawn into the middle of emotional local conflicts. It began with a 1964 Christmas-eve liquor store holdup in Baltimore, in which a police sergeant was murdered and a lieutenant wounded. The police quickly learned that two Negro brothers, Samuel and Earl Veney, had done the shooting. There followed a nineteen-day manhunt that included more than 300 searches of Negroes' homes, all without warrants and most based on anonymous tips. Since the police knew that they had enough proof to convict the Veneys they were not concerned that their methods of capturing the fugitives would, probably, result in the exclusion of any additional evidence that might be found. Squads of men wielding shotguns and clad in bulletproof vests prowled the Negro neighborhoods, ransacking homes at the slightest tip that the Veneys might be inside. One of the searches was later described in an opinion by Judge Simon E. Sobeloff of the U S. Court of Appeals for the Fourth Circuit:

A few minutes before 2:00 A.M., Lieutenant Hewes and his search party converged upon Parkwood Avenue. Upon their arrival in the neighborhood they met on the street a Negro man, described by the lieutenant as "respectable looking," who identified himself as the person that had called the communications center. He told Lieutenant Hewes that he had been told by a newspaper boy that two men resembling the Veneys had entered a house on Parkwood Avenue. At 2:00 A.M. a search party led by the lieutenant knocked on the door, and Mrs. Lankford, awakened by the knock, opened the door. The officers entered the house and began their search while the lieutenant talked with the woman. She told him that her name was not Garrett. At the trial she denied that the officers had asked for or were given permission to search, and Lieutenant Hewes acknowledged that his men had already gone to the second floor while he was talking to her. The husband was awakened in his second floor bedroom by two flashlights shining in his face and found four men with shotguns in his room. They questioned him, while other officers searched the remaining rooms, including the children's bedrooms, and left.

In his opinion Judge Sobeloff made much of three factors: that the Baltimore police had customarily searched on the basis of anonymous tips and without search warrants when they felt that the circumstances justified it; that Baltimore's Negroes, realizing that these tactics were not used in white neighborhoods, bitterly resented it; and that the threat of civil suits or the exclusionary rule were not effective deterrents under these circumstances. The court placed the Baltimore police under a permanent injunction against searching residences without warrants on the basis of anonymous tips. The order is still in effect.

This action was not lost on the legal profession when the ghetto riots of the next three summers were followed by systematic police abuse of Negroes in some of the riot areas. Actions were quickly filed in Newark and Plainfield, New Jersey, and in New York, Philadelphia, and St. Louis, asking the Federal courts to issue permanent injunctions barring the police from using unconstitutional tactics in their dealings with ghetto residents. In each instance the situation that prompted the suit has cooled and the Negroes have not pressed for decisions on the injunctions. As a result, there has not yet been a test of the Federal judiciary's willingness to step into an open-ended conflict between a city's police and its Negro population and order the police to stop using certain tactics, under pain of contempt (the Veneys had been caught and the Baltimore searches had ended when that injunction was issued). Both the police and the civil libertarians appear to have shied away from a showdown; the police seem to have been sobered by the threat of Federal court intervention, and the Negroes have been pleased with the fact that the mere pendency of court suits gives them the power to hale any policeman accused of abuse into a deposition hearing, where he can be grilled under oath about his conduct. "In effect, we created our own civilian review boards," one civil liberties lawyer said of the Newark suit.

The idea has also spread beyond the racial scene. Hippies at the Aspen, Colorado, ski area sued to stop the police from delivering get-out-of-town edicts to shaggy ski enthusiasts. Antiwar activists won a decree preventing policemen from interfering with their pamphleteering inside the world's largest bus terminal in New York. A Manhattan bookseller obtained a court order barring the police department from stationing a uniformed officer inside a shop that the police suspected of selling dirty books to children. Some lawyers feel that if the trend continues, some local police officials will be placed under mandatory injunctions requiring them to come up with plans to protect citizens' rights from police abuse, much as school officials have had to present desegregation plans.

The trouble with Federal court intervention may well prove to be that it *is* an effective way for the judiciary to police the police. This could bring into sharp focus conflicts between the Supreme Court's version of proper police conduct and methods deemed necessary by the police to maintain public order—conflicts which have been blurred by the slippage in the enforcement of the Court's decisions. The result could be a constitutional crisis of major proportions.

In view of the wide dissatisfaction with the Supreme Court's role in policing the police, it is remarkable that so little thought and effort has gone into devising other methods of controlling police conduct. Police review boards seem politically beyond the pale, but this leaves ample room for experimentation with other techniques that have not been stigmatized. It has been suggested that police pay raises, which are much in vogue these days, could be channeled partially into "good conduct" funds for each officer. This would be a bonus nest-egg when a policeman leaves the force—unless he has abused some individual who has been paid damages out of the fund. The theory is that this carrot might achieve far more than the stick of the police review board, without creating the same concern about police "handcuffing."

Arbitration works in the emotion-charged world of labor relations, and its use has been suggested in the field of citizen-police complaints as well. Because arbitrators are selected by lot, or by agreement, the police's fear of militant-dominated police review boards might be eased. Legislatures have been urged to try waiving governmental immunity for certain types of police abuse, or to provide state-financed liability insurance for policemen, or at least to modernize the rickety tort remedies that now confront aggrieved citizens. Some lawyers feel that police forces should be placed under the control of the prosecutors' offices, which have the job of trying to make arrests stick and would be inclined to see that the police make them in a constitutional way.

For all of the frustrations over the Supreme Court's efforts to police the police, there can be no question that the level of police conduct is higher now than it was ten or twenty years ago. In this the Supreme Court surely played an important part. Its exclusionary rules set a meaningful standard that police and courts were called upon to observe, and many did.

The question that remained is whether the Warren Court accomplished this with the least possible injury to the Court and to the public temper. Its rulings were most effective when they inspired broad changes in public and official thinking as to what fair treatment should be. In some instances, the shock effect of strong judicial measures may have helped to do this, but there is some reason to feel that the Warren Court relied too much on pulling its rank. The public interest in equal justice that followed the *Gideon* ruling showed that the Supreme Court was most effective when it acted as a constitutional teacher and not as a constitutional cop. The "or else" flavor of some of its exclusionary rule pronouncements had a way of generating self-defeating resentment among police and the public. Since nine men would not be enough under the best of circumstances to police the police of the entire nation, the point of diminishing returns on the use of the exclusionary rule tended to move closer with each turn of the screw by the Supreme Court. This was especially so when the Court applied restrictions on the police that struck many people as too strict. All of these factors converged on the Warren Court when it set out to limit interrogation by the police.

VIII

Miranda: Self-Inflicted Wound

Do Judges make law? Course they do. Made some myself.

JEREMIAH SMITH, Supreme Court of New Hampshire, 1867–1874

Habits change slowly, when at all, in the Supreme Court. Knickers were worn by the pages there until 1963. It was only two years before that that the Court abandoned its nineteenth-century noontime gavel in favor of a daily beginning at 10 A.M. In arguments before the Court the Federal Government's attorneys still wear a style of formal morning attire that is otherwise seen only at weddings and inaugurations. So when the Supreme Court met in conference on Monday, November 22, 1965, rather than on the traditional conference day—Friday—and when the results of that meeting were released to the press in the dark of that evening rather than at a regular morning session, it was obvious to the most casual observers that the Supreme Court was preparing to do something rare.

On the surface, the Court's release—a supplement to the long list of court orders that had been issued in the courtroom that morning—was noncommittal. It began: "Certiorari Granted—419 Misc. Miranda v. Arizona."

The order went on to say that Ernesto Miranda's request to be allowed to appeal in *forma pauperis*—without paying the usual costs—had been granted (the Miscellaneous Docket number is the Supreme Court's way of signifying that the appellant is a pauper), and that his petition for review had been granted. One hour was allocated for argument. The order then listed three other appeals that had also been granted and that would be argued in succession after the *Miranda* argument: *Vignera* v. *New York, Westover* v. *United States* and *Johnson* v. *New Jersey*. Nothing about the order gave a hint as to the reasons for the Court's irregular conduct that day. But to those who had access to the copies of the Justices' weekly conference lists that were kept in the office of John F. Davis, the Clerk of the Supreme Court, the significance was immediately clear. For more than a year, Davis had been marking certain appeals with the initials "E.C.," to indicate that they were to be held until some future time. By November 22, 1965, approximately 140 appeals had been marked "E.C." and held—including *Miranda* v. *Arizona* and the three other petitions for certiorari that were granted that evening. The code "E.C." meant that they were "Escobedo Cases," and the Court's announcement that it would hear them meant that it would finally deal with the criminal justice problem that had haunted the Supreme Court for decades —confessions.

Voluntariness had been the standard for judging the admissibility of confessions for so long that the idea of throwing out a voluntary admission rated among lawyers as the rankest heresy. Then in its enigmatic 1964 decision, *Escobedo* v. *Illinois*, the Supreme Court had discarded a confession, not because it was coerced, but because the suspect had been denied access to his lawyer during his interrogation. This happened during a heady time at the Supreme Court, when the criminal law was being revamped by a rapid-fire series of constitutional rulings on the rights of suspects. *Escobedo* had been an obscure case until the Court reached its decision in such a novel way; then it was quickly recognized as an important, if inconclusive, step. The Court had turned a corner in *Escobedo*, but the opinion did not say where the new course would lead. It said only that "when the (criminal justice) process shifts from investigatory to accusatory—when its focus is on the accused and its purpose is to elicit a confession—our adversary system begins to operate, and, under the circumstances here, the accused must be permitted to consult with his lawyer." *Escobedo* posed more questions than it answered, because it was an unusual fact situation, used as a vehicle to launch an absolute right to counsel that would apply during all interrogation. If a person had a constitutional right to his lawyer's counsel during interrogation, then didn't he have to be informed of that fact before any questioning? If he asked to see his lawyer, didn't all questioning have to cease until the lawyer arrived? If he wanted a lawyer but could not afford one, didn't the state have to provide counsel?

The Supreme Court had been expected to let these and other questions simmer for years in the lower courts, where various solutions could be tested and modified, with the Supreme Court ruling on an occasional narrow issue to keep the process moving in the proper direction. But events forced another course. Appeals flooded the lower courts. Most of them stood pat on *Escobedo* and passed the cases up to the Supreme Court for further amplification. By the autumn of 1965 the Court had decided to answer all of the questions at once, to undertake a broad rule-making hearing unlike anything that had ever occurred before in a court in the United States. Prior to *Mapp v. Ohio*, no single governmental body had jurisdiction to set police procedure for the entire country. But once the Supreme Court assumed the authority to do so with regard to searches, unanswered questions could be expected to collect so rapidly that at some point the Court would have to convene in a rule-making session, not for the primary purpose of deciding an individual appeal, but to frame broad legislative codes to cover future police conduct.

That was the purpose of *Miranda*. The four appeals chosen by the Court (a fifth, *California* v. *Stewart*, was granted later and argued and decided with *Miranda*) were as representative of police interrogation situations as *Escobedo* had been unique. Ernesto Miranda, who gave the case its name, was a twenty-three-year-old emotionally disturbed Arizona truck driver who had been given a 25- to 30-year prison sentence for robbing, kidnapping and raping an eighteen-year-old girl. After the girl identified him in a lineup he talked freely to the police, giving a full statement after less than two hours' interrogation. There was no evidence in his case or in any of the others that the police used physical brutality or torture or any of the psychological techniques suggested in the police interrogation manuals that the Court stressed so heavily in justifying its decision. But taken as a whole, the five cases included most of the abuses of the interrogation system that bothered critics of the system—prolonged questioning (Roy Stewart, the California defendant, had been grilled nine times over a period of five days), failure to inform defendants of their rights, failure to obey state laws requiring prompt arraignment of suspects and taking advantage of suspects' isolation from co-defendants and friends. Yet taken individually, none of the cases, with the possible exception of the *Stewart* case, included enough of these abuses to have been considered involuntary under the old "totality of the circumstances" test. Again excepting the *Stewart* case, there was no serious question but that the confessions were noncoerced and true.

This was the core of the Supreme Court's difficulties over *Miranda*—in order to abolish the abuses that cropped up in some but by no means all police investigations, it would have to condemn the "voluntariness" approach, which the Court itself had always approved before and which the police saw as a reasonable way to do their job. If the Court were to frame a prophylactic procedure rigid enough to rule out all of the abuses that the voluntariness approach could permit, it would also outlaw many instances of reasonable, noncoercive police inquiry about crime. It could be argued that the time for the rigid procedure had nevertheless come—that all other courses had failed; that the price in law enforcement was worth the protection of individuals' rights; that the police would develop other investigative methods or would at least learn to live with the new confessions restrictions—but regardless of the validity of these arguments, a rigid interrogation code would appear to many people to be unreasonable.

As it turned out, *Miranda* was the high-water mark of the due process revolution, the ultimate expression of the judicial philosophy and technique that had characterized the Warren Court on crime. It reflected the highest ideals of that philosophy, and the most serious flaws of that technique. The guiding ideal had been that bold and idealistic advances by judges can inspire the nation to purify its civilization. The flaws were inherent in the Court's assumption that broad gains in human rights can be enforced from the top by means of rigid, objective procedures backed up by the automatic exclusionary rule. It was an exercise in benevolent authoritarianism by the judiciary at a moment in history when there was great faith in Washington in the capacity of Federal power to do good—and an abiding suspicion that local people, given leeway to express parochial interests and emotions, would likely do the opposite.

Miranda reflected a conflict basically of means, but also of ends. The Supreme Court had concluded that the subjective voluntariness test was too flabby; that the law could protect individuals from oppressive interrogation only by means of objective interrogation rules that would be required in every case. Law-enforcement officials argued that criminal investigation was too complex to be conducted according to procedures laid down in advance by judges in Washington; that by taking away local officials' flexibility, the Court was "handcuffing the police." The Supreme Court itself was soon to have second thoughts about the technique of controlling the procedures of criminal investigation through objective constitutional rules. As effective as rigid requirements had been in upgrading the well-rehearsed rituals of the nation's courtrooms, they proved to be forbidding in the complex world of police investigation. Two years after *Miranda* the Justices avoided laying down objective procedures for the stop-and-frisk, with evident relief, citing "the limitations of the judicial function in controlling the myriad daily situations in which policemen and citizens confront each other on the street." Police questioning also occurred under varied circumstances. (Later, the Supreme Court was to throw out a murder conviction because the suspect, apprehended in bed by the police, had groggily responded to a few quick questions. The Court's decision would require the officers to rattle off the full *Miranda* warning to the supine suspect first.) Thus there were equal reasons for questioning the wisdom of attempting to deal with it by means of an inflexible constitutional rule.

But *Miranda* also presented a conflict of ultimate values. The Supreme Court approached the case from the assumption—already expressed in *Escobedo*—that even noncoercive questioning was constitutionally suspect and perhaps should be phased out as an investigative tool. Whether such broad value judgments are for Supreme Court Justices to make is a serious constitutional question, one that was doubly serious from the Supreme Court's point of view because a large percentage of the public apparently did not share its aversion to confessions.

With the Court riding the crest of its faith in the bold stroke and in the objective exclusionary rule, *Miranda* was destined to be an outsized example of both. Where its predecessors had been bold, *Miranda* was to be brazen—*Gideon* v. *Wainwright* had created a constitutional right to counsel in felony cases at a time when all but five states already provided it; *Mapp* v. *Ohio* had extended the exclusionary rule to illegal searches after roughly one-half of the states had adopted the same rule; *Miranda* was to impose limits on police interrogation that no state had even approached prior to the *Escobedo* decision. Also, where the previous landmark decisions had imposed rigid but narrow restrictions on state officials' conduct, *Miranda* was to lay down a statutelike code of procedure consisting of four commandments, some of which included sub-commandments.

When Senator Sam J. Ervin later used *Miranda* as the cutting edge of his attack against Chief Justice nominee Abe Fortas during the Senate confirmation hearings of 1968, he repeated over and over that the decision had changed the law as it had been for more than 180 years, "without support in any prior decision." Nobody called him on this statement, but many legal scholars would have disagreed with it. There was precedent for *Miranda*, but it took the form of a long trial-and-error search for workable constitutional restrictions on police interrogation

methods, and not the usual orderly chain of judicial precedents. This process was so erratic that even the Court's most
faithful adherents guessed wrong as to how the Justices would
justify their decision in *Miranda*. After the *Escobedo* decision
was announced in 1964, most lower courts marked time in confusion or dismay, but four appellate courts—the highest courts
of California, Oregon and Rhode Island, and the U.S. Court of
Appeals for the Third Circuit in Philadelphia—announced man-
fully that the Supreme Court had obviously meant in *Escobedo*
that the Sixth Amendment's guarantee of counsel requires that
suspects be warned of their rights and offered legal advice before interrogation begins. They were wrong. In *Miranda* the
court later reached this result, but based it on the Fifth Amendment's privilege against self-incrimination, which had not been
held to apply to the states until two years before, and which had
rarely been mentioned in prior confessions decisions. Despite the
Court's zigzag course, its trend was clear; it would continue to
cast about for an objective standard by which police questioning
could be regulated—and if the standard proved so rigid that the
police could not interrogate effectively at all, that would be a
tolerable outcome in the Warren Court's eyes.

Confessions, and the third-degree methods that have sometimes been used to obtain them, are only the most notorious
aspect of an approach toward law enforcement that had bedeviled the Supreme Court for years. Although the term is not
used in the Constitution, the Court reads the Bill of Rights as
having constructed an "accusatorial" system of justice, in which
law enforcement officials who charge an individual with a
crime must bear the burden of proving the case without relying
on the accused to provide the evidence of guilt. This is con-
trasted with the Continental "inquisitorial" system, in which
prosecutors may question accused persons under oath prior to
the trial as a means of making out the state's case.

The problem is that the American system, while accusatorial
in approach, has always depended in part on the defendant for
evidence of guilt. Police officials can rarely make a case without
reference to its most important figure, the man suspected of having committed the crime. At some point, the police usually must
have the suspect's fingerprints, his blood type, the sound of

his voice, his physical presence in a lineup, or his version of what happened, before they can decide if he should be prosecuted. On one extreme, the police have used mass arrests-for-investigation known as "dragnet arrests," in which police officers without enough evidence to justify arresting any specific suspect simply seize a number of likely suspects and rely upon interrogation, fingerprints or other methods to identify the guilty one. This is obviously "inquisitorial" and the Supreme Court has declared it unconstitutional. On the other extreme is the volunteered confession of the suspect who strides into the police station and announces his guilt. Its use is considered within proper accusatorial bounds, even under *Miranda* v. *Arizona*.

The problem is that the multitude of circumstances between these extremes cannot be sorted into constitutional and unconstitutional categories simply by the pejorative process of labeling some inquisitorial. "Ours is the accusatorial as opposed to the inquisitorial system," Felix Frankfurter once declared in a case in which he disapproved of the interrogating policemen's method. "Society carries the burden of proving its charge against the accused not out of his own mouth," he said, "but by evidence independently secured through skillful investigation." Yet in another case, when the officers' conduct struck him as reasonable, he noted that "Offenses frequently occur [in which] nothing remains—if police investigation is not to be balked before it has fairly begun—but to seek out possibly guilty witnesses and ask them questions." He concluced that "such questioning is often indispensable to crime detection."

For years the Court's course between the Scylla of the third degree and the Charybdis of a complete interrogation ban was the concept of "voluntariness." When the Court first applied the standard to the states in *Brown* v. *Mississippi*, its meaning was clear enough; physical torture with metal-studded belts is beyond the pale of constitutional interrogation. Later, it became a constitutional word of art that represented a complex mixture of subjective elements reflecting the suspect's freedom to speak or remain silent, plus a number of objective factors keyed to the propriety of the police's tactics. In some instances a confession would be thrown out because it appeared from the suspect's age, intelligence, education and race that his will had been overborne by his interrogators. Other decisions concentrated on the objective facts of what the police did, holding that statements obtained under circumstances of physical abuse, threats, promises, tricks and long detention were not fairly given.

In thirty-six opinions the Supreme Court sifted through these factors and decided, on the basis of the "totality of the circumstances," that some confessions had been "the offspring of a reasoned choice," and that others had been products of "a will overborne." The result was that a trial judge could pick through the Court's opinions and find authority for admitting almost any confession. It would have been difficult enough for the Supreme Court to examine the facts behind each of these confessions, assuming that all convicted persons appealed. But because more than eight out of ten defendants consistently pleaded guilty and did not appeal, the voluntariness test reduced the Federal courts to fishing with a hopelessly wide net. As this became apparent, the Justices began to grope for an objective standard that could be policed from the top.

The first moves came in the Federal system, where the Supreme Court's supervisory status gave it the flexibility to act without tampering with the Constitution. In 1943, it ruled that confessions could be excluded on the ground that defendant's interrogation had violated Rule 5(a) of the Federal Rules of Criminal Procedure, which requires Federal officers to take arrested persons before a committing magistrate "without unnecessary delay." But the lower courts read this as a statutory voluntariness test. They continued to exclude confessions only when the delays included coercive questioning. Finally, in the 1957 case of *Mallory* v. *United States* the Supreme Court declared that any confession obtained during an unnecessary delay in arraignment is inadmissible.

In *Mallory* the Supreme Court finally had a totally objective procedure for determining the validity of confessions—with results that were just short of ruinous for the Court. Logically, the only way to preserve the objectivity of the rule was to hold that "without unnecessary delay" meant without *any* delay solely for the purpose of interrogation, and that was the way the Court of Appeals for the District of Columbia interpreted the rule. The effect was to throw out the baby with the bath-water; the courts had put an end to coercive questioning, but at the cost of outlawing noncoercive questioning too. The most surprising outcome of the entire episode was the ability of the police either to cheat on the rule or to win convictions with-out interrogation—only eleven cases were reported to have been lost in the District of Columbia because of the rule in its first five years. But these were highly publicized, and the police claimed that due to the restrictions many other crimes were simply never solved. This was sufficient to convince Congress that the *Mallory* rule had been a donnybrook, and in the 1968 Crime Control Act the law was changed to state that no confession would be thrown out merely because of a delay in arraignment, so long as the delay wasn't more than six hours.

Meanwhile, the Supreme Court was turning back to the prin-ciple underlying its most successful exercise in objective rule-making, *Gideon* v. *Wainwright*. Prior to the *Gideon* decision, the Court had said that the right to counsel applied at an arraign-ment and a preliminary hearing, on the ground that each step was a "critical stage" in the prosecution. However, the impact of those rulings had been blunted because the Supreme Court still adhered to the position, set out in the 1942 *Betts* v. *Brady* de-cision, that even where the general right to counsel applied, an attorney was required in any given situation only when the "special circumstances" of the case warranted it. When the Supreme Court eliminated the special circumstances approach in the *Gideon* decision, it proved a happy event from all points of view. State prosecutors and judges were spared tiresome liti-gation over whether or not a particular suspect really needed a lawyer. No more convictions were lost when lawyerless suspects later convinced the Federal courts that the state offi-cials had guessed wrong. The Supreme Court was spared the tedious job of second-guessing the state judges' evaluation of each case. Criminal justice was spared the sorry spectacle of penniless and therefore lawyerless defendants in inept court-room combat against state prosecutors. The happy demise of the special circumstances rule regarding counsel at trial encouraged wishful thinking that the ad hoc approach to confessions could be as painlessly replaced by an absolute rule. What this missed was that the certainty achieved by requiring counsel at all trials was "free"—it cost nothing in terms of the efficiency of criminal justice. But an effective objective rule for police interrogation would almost certainly rule out most police questioning—a price that society might be unwilling to pay to be rid of the imperfections of case-by-case review of confessions.

In 1964, the year after *Gideon*, the Court made its first move to label certain police investigative activities "critical stages" of prosecutions. The test was neatly objective: Just as guilty pleas without counsel were void, so were statements taken without benefit of counsel where the right of counsel applies, whether the statements were voluntary or not. The old saw that hard cases make bad law does not necessarily have to apply to the Supreme Court, which is virtually free to review only the appeals it wishes to decide. Almost the opposite occurred in the events leading up to *Miranda*. Free to pick and choose its cases, the Court selected two off-beat appeals and decided them in far-reaching terms that forced an upheaval in the law of confessions.

The first case involved an accused narcotics peddler named Winston Massiah. After he had been arraigned, released on bail and had retained a lawyer, he was tricked by a Government informer into making incriminating statements about the crime. Nothing goes quite as abrasively against the grain of lawyers' thinking than efforts by one side of a controversy to go behind the opposing attorney's back to weaken his case through direct contacts with his client. In civil litigation it can lead to settlements that threaten the wronged attorneys' fees as well as the strength of their cases, and judges, having been lawyers themselves, consider it impropriety of the highest order. In Massiah's case the Supreme Court found it no less than a breach of the Sixth Amendment's declaration that "in all criminal prosecutions, the accused shall enjoy the right . . . to have the assistance of counsel for his defense." Potter Stewart, who had once indicated his philosophical leanings by referring to himself as "a lawyer," wrote the majority opinion that overturned the conviction and declared the statements inadmissible under the Sixth Amendment. The ruling was a narrow one in that the situation was unlikely to recur. But the holding established the precedent that fully voluntary admissions can be ruled out for failure of the police to respect a suspect's right of counsel prior to trial.

Still, the Court did not move *Gideon* from the court house to the station house until it encountered the equally unusual case of Danny Escobedo. Escobedo, a trouble-prone, scrawny little Chicago laborer, was a rare breed of criminal suspect— he was shrewd enough to have a lawyer on call when the police pulled him in for questioning, and simple enough to be tricked into confessing when his lawyer was not present to protect him. Prior to his case it was unusual for lawyers to appear at police stations when their clients were being questioned. Few people other than experienced criminals could anticipate that they would be arrested and could arrange to have someone summon a lawyer. When the lawyer arrived the police often stopped questioning these suspects, who were usually close-mouthed types anyway. But Escobedo had been accused of a family murder (his brother-in-law had been gunned down from ambush) and he was new enough to interrogation rooms that the detectives thought it worth their time to keep the lawyer outside while they tried an old police trick. They told Escobedo that an accomplice had blamed the whole thing on him—and then suddenly confronted Escobedo with the supposed stool-pigeon. It worked. Escobedo accused the accomplice of having been the trigger man, and with that as a lever the detectives got a full statement out of Escobedo. It was crucial in bringing about his conviction.

In the past the Supreme Court had found confessions to be "involuntary" under less odious circumstances than this, and Escobedo's lawyer had asked for such a ruling in this case. But he also asked the Court to declare the confession inadmissible under the Sixth Amendment without regard to its voluntariness, a move that constitutional lawyers knew would place all police questioning in doubt. In 1958 the Supreme Court had faced the same issue in two appeals and had held, in two 5 to 4 decisions, that the impact of such a holding on law enforcement would be too great.

One of the cases posed the legal dilemma in its most painful form: a vicious murder solved because the killer, confronted with evidence he could not explain, admitted his guilt—yet the police deliberately refused to let him see a lawyer, who would have prevented the confession. The defendant was a thirty-one-year-old college graduate and former law student, John Russell Crooker, Jr., who had immediately become the prime suspect when his mistress was found strangled and stabbed to death in the bedroom of her Los Angeles home. When the police asked Crooker about the scratches on his hands and face he blamed careless shaving and an automobile accident. When he could not furnish details of the car wreck, the police took him to the station house for questioning. There, he asked for permission to telephone an attorney whom he knew, but the police said no—not until the investigation was completed. The scratches alone would not have been enough to convict Crooker, but they were enough to make his denials untenable, and a team of five detectives got a detailed written confession out of him after three hours of grilling. The Supreme Court majority could take no pride in the method used to convict Crooker, but it was swayed by the strong proof that he admitted the killing, not because his will was overborne by the questioning, but because he could not reasonably deny it. As for Crooker's claim that the questioning infringed his right to counsel, the majority concluded that to accept this view would have a "devastating effect on enforcement of criminal law, for it would effectively preclude police questioning—*fair as well as unfair*—until the accused was afforded opportunity to call his attorney."

Justice Arthur J. Goldberg was fully aware of this dilemma when he wrote the Court's opinion in the *Escobedo* case. He grasped the nettle of the Sixth Amendment, throwing out Danny Escobedo's conviction without regard to voluntariness, because he had been denied his right to have his attorney's assistance during his interrogation. If a defendant has a constitutional right to a lawyer at his arraignment and preliminary hearing, Goldberg reasoned that he should likewise be entitled to counsel during his interrogation—which could, he said, be a far more critical stage of the criminal process. A trial became "no more than an appeal from the interrogation" if police were allowed to make an ironclad case through methods of station-house questioning that mocked the elaborate safeguards of the subsequent trial.

"A system of criminal law enforcement which comes to depend on the 'confession' will, in the long run, be less reliable and more subject to abuses than a system which depends on extrinsic evidence independently secured through skillful investigation," Goldberg asserted. But after making it clear that confessions in general were being questioned, the Court reversed Escobedo's conviction on the narrowest possible grounds. "We hold," Goldberg wrote, "that where, as here, the investigation is no longer a general inquiry into an unsolved crime but has begun to focus on a particular suspect, the suspect has been taken into police custody, the police carry out a process of interrogations that lends itself to eliciting incriminating statements, the suspect has requested and been denied an opportunity to consult with his lawyer, and the police have not effectively warned him of his absolute constitutional right to remain silent, the accused has been denied 'the assistance of Counsel' in violation of the Sixth Amendment to the Constitution."

Few non-lawyers would have imagined that two atypical cases such as *Massiah* and *Escobedo* could make it necessary to abandon the traditional assumption that voluntary confessions are valid evidence; but to lawyers it meant exactly that. The Supreme Court, with lawyerlike logic, had placed itself in a position in which it would feel compelled to make a far-reaching change in the law. The logic went like this:

—Once it is established that a person in Escobedo's situation is in a critical stage of a criminal proceeding and has a constitutional right to counsel if he asks for it, then it follows that the police must warn all suspects at this stage that they have a right to a lawyer's presence during the interrogation. Otherwise, the sophisticated and well-informed suspect will have superior Sixth Amendment rights to the rights of the ignorant and naive.

—If police interrogation is at a sufficiently critical stage to bring the Sixth Amendment's right to counsel into play, the Fifth Amendment's declaration that no person "shall be compelled in any criminal case to be a witness against himself" also applies at that point. So unless the privilege is to assist only those who know about it before they run afoul of the law, all suspects must be warned that they have a right to silence and that anything they say may be used against them.

—If all suspects must be informed that they have a right to the aid of counsel during interrogation, lawyers must be provided for those who are too poor to pay for legal counsel. This follows from a line of cases in which the Supreme Court held that where the affluent have a right to the assistance of their retained counsel, the state must provide lawyers for the poor.

The conclusion had to be that all suspects must be offered the opportunity to consult a lawyer before the police could begin their interrogation. Since Justice Robert Jackson was probably right in concluding that "any lawyer worth his salt will tell the suspect in no uncertain terms to make no statement to police under any circumstances," the result would probably be a substantial restriction on police questioning. Goldberg put his finger on the reason for the dilemma when he declared in *Escobedo* that "no system of criminal justice can, or should, survive if it comes to depend for its continued effectiveness on the citizens' abdication through unawareness of their constitutional rights. No system worth preserving should have to *fear* that if an accused is permitted to consult with a lawyer, he will become aware of, and exercise, these rights." The trouble with the American system was precisely that; it had evolved in such a way that if every suspect were given counsel prior to any interrogation, there would be every reason to fear that many crimes would go unsolved.

Every Western democracy has faced the same dilemma over how to give the police enough freedom to investigate crimes without abandoning their citizens to coercive police interrogation. While none can claim to have resolved it, all have managed to create more rational systems than has the United States. Most European countries have a rule that requires the police to produce all accused persons before a magistrate within twenty-four hours after their arrests. This is similar to the prompt-arraignment laws that exist in many American states and in the Federal Rules of Criminal Procedure. But the American states have tended to ignore these laws, and the Federal courts created a furor when they attempted in *Mallory* v. *United States* to enforce the Federal rule. The difference is that the European systems work. One reason for this is that European police departments tend to be more professional and controlled than American police, but also because the production of the defendant before a Continental magistrate does not mean the automatic end of interrogation. The questioning continues, with the suspect entitled to counsel and to remain silent, but prompted to answer by the knowledge that his silence will be made much of at his subsequent trial. England operates on the opposite reasoning; the police are granted much leeway to interrogate suspects, the exclusionary rule is used sparingly to chastise them when they overreach, and production of the defendant before a magistrate means the end of questioning.

The American system has developed in a way that lacks the rationality of the procedures used in England and on the Continent. This is partly because of the hypocrisy that has always been an assumption of the American system. Because it was known that the privilege against compulsory self-incrimination was often flagrantly abused in the station house, it was given an exaggerated status in court. Over the years a majority of the states developed rules that forbade prosecutors to comment in court on the defendant's failure to explain himself, and in 1965 the Supreme Court handed down a decision that imposed that rule on all the states. Moreover, committing magistrates in the United States do not question suspects. Instead, they end the interrogation by formally charging the accused and setting the amount of his bail. As a result, to make lawyers actually available to suspects at the time of arrest in the United States would mean that no further information could be obtained from the accused, and no comment could be made of his refusal to cooperate—a prospect that is indeed more fearsome than it would be under the systems operating in other major countries.

It was the prospect of this result that inspired most of the public criticism that descended upon the Supreme Court after *Miranda*. But the process by which the Court reached it had also drawn criticism from within the legal profession, and some lawyers questioned whether the Supreme Court was equipped to deal with the problem at all. Unless Justice Jackson's prophecy was to come true and all questioning was to cease, it seemed to many criminal law specialists that some new legal concept would have to be worked out. Some lawyers suggested adopting a version of the Continental system of questioning by magistrates. Others thought suspects could be brought immediately before a magistrate, who would warn them of their rights and would then remand them back to the police for limited periods of interrogation without counsel. Officials in the District of Columbia experimented with a three-hour limit on questioning. All of these proposals had one element in common: They could not be worked out conveniently by the Supreme Court in the form of a constitutional interpretation.

In September of 1965, just two months before the Supreme Court granted certiorari in *Miranda* v. *Arizona*, Paul M. Bator and James Vorenberg, two Harvard law professors who had been working on the American Law Institute's model statute on post-arrest procedures, explained at an international legal conference at Ditchley Park, England, why the ALI had undertaken to work out a solution to the interrogation dilemma. Their reasoning was prophetic of some of the criticism that was later to come down on the Supreme Court over *Miranda*. Judicial decisions, they wrote, "can be only partially effective in establishing procedures which respect both the legitimate interests of the individual and the needs of law enforcement."

Unlike a court, a legislature enacting a comprehensive code can evaluate and adjust the various interrelated portions of an interrelated process. A court may be considering, for instance, a case in which an accused has been held in police custody for a period during which he has been subjected to questioning and has given a confession. Although the court may find that the defendant was not under any misconception as to his obligation to cooperate with the police and was not subject to abuse or harassment, it may nevertheless be troubled by the possibility that, in the absence of a coherent system of protective provisions, the detention might not be so benign in another case. Furthermore, in a case where the court finds some impropriety, it can only deal with what it thought was wrong, rather than setting out other steps which the police might have taken and which would have made the procedure as a whole fair. In each case, any response will necessarily treat part of the problem as if it were the whole problem. In the context of a particular case the court cannot tell the police exactly what they should have done from the moment when they first established contact with a man until the time he was brought to court. A legislature, however, can do just that.

A legislature may also frankly engage in a process of line-drawing which in a court decision must seem arbitrary. For example, what period of detention is too long? A court is bound to decide such an issue in the light of the circumstances of a particular case. If a court says a particular period of minutes or hours is reasonable and any time longer is not, the court acts in a way which one generally expects of a legislature; and yet, if the law is to speak to law enforcement officers, it must provide a rule which is clear and sharp.

As ominous as this caveat was, it at least assumed that the Court would be free to respond rationally to the problems involved, as a legislature would. But in approaching *Miranda* the Supreme Court did not possess a legislature's flexibility. Where legislators might have sensed trouble ahead and would have considered it honorable and proper to trim their sails, the oral arguments were to show that the Justices in the majority felt committed by their decision in *Escobedo* to move on to a broader rule. A constitutional dialectic had been set in motion that called for the *Miranda* decision, yet at no place along the line did the Justices have an unfettered opportunity to take into consideration empirical proof as to whether the reform was needed or what its impact might be. The *Escobedo* case had been treated as a narrow appeal that applied only to those rare persons who demanded to see their attorney, who were rebuffed, and who then confessed to the police. The litigants' briefs and arguments concentrated on that narrow point. The American Civil Liberties Union filed the only friend-of-the-court statement, and its brief in support of *Escobedo* devoted only a page and a half to the possible impact of the ruling.

After *Miranda* was granted, the National District Attorney's Association and the Attorney General of New York, supported by the attorneys general of twenty-six other states, submitted *amicus curiae* briefs in an attempt to show what the proposed decision might do to law enforcement. One of the aspects of the *Miranda* decision that most upset its critics was that the Supreme Court majority, apparently satisfied to find itself locked into its course of action by the dialectic of *Escobedo* and its precursors, gave every impression that it was not interested in this line of argument. It was true that little empirical data were known about the need for such a rule and its probable effect, but the Justices showed no interest in the scraps of evidence that were available. The National District Attorney's Association had submitted scattered statistics from various members, showing that confessions had been a helpful tool of their trade. Since much had been made of the fact that warnings were already required in England in the form of the Judges' Rules, they compared the reported crime rates to point out such revealing contrasts as England's robbery rate of 6.5 per 100,000 people, as against Chicago's rate of 273.9 per 100,000—which to them suggested caution in saddling U.S. law enforcement with tighter interrogation limits than those in effect in England. (Soon after, a move began in England to relax the restrictions on police interrogation on the ground that the crime rate was alarmingly high.) But the Supreme Court had been confronted with scare statistics before and had found them less reliable than its own instincts for reform, and some of the Justices made it clear during the *Miranda* arguments that *Escobedo* had made these arguments irrelevant.

The Supreme Court has always faced some uncertainties in making criminal law because of the inherent difficulties of anticipating what impact a given decision would have when applied to police officers across the country. To reduce the risk as far as possible, it developed an approach that permitted the Court to move cautiously in the direction that the majority deemed proper, while the state served as proving-grounds for its unfolding legal doctrines. The Court would typically approach a new issue warily, issuing first a narrowly limited decision which contained a hint of the result that might finally be required. A few criminal lawyers would get that hint, cases would develop, and lower court decisions would result. These decisions would usually not be consistent with each other, which could be a boon to the Supreme Court; it could deny petitions for certiorari in all of these appeals, leaving the lower court rulings in effect without indicating whether it approved or disapproved of the results. Over the years experience would develop in the lower courts as to the best way to proceed with the problem, and any warning signs would be detected before the Supreme Court had to take its position. Thus twenty-one years lapsed between *Betts* v. *Brady*'s holding that attorneys need not be furnished for poor defendants in all felony trials and *Gideon*'s decision that they must. By that time so many states were requiring counsel anyway that *Gideon* was known to be feasible before it was announced. The Court waited thirteen years after it hinted in *Wolf* v. *Colorado* that the states should exclude illegally obtained evidence before it required them to do so in *Mapp*. Half of them were doing it by then, and no difference could be detected between the crime rates in those states that enforced the exclusionary rule and in those that did not.

The same cautious process seemed to have been in prospect when the Court issued the narrow *Escobedo* ruling. California's Supreme Court quickly caught on and handed down a *Miranda*-like decision, and a few other state Supreme Courts held that suspects need not be advised of their rights. The Supreme Court denied certiorari, and the waiting period seemed to have begun.

Then, within the span of six months in the spring and summer of 1965, events suddenly began to move with such speed that it became clear that the wait-and-see process was no longer valid. In prior years the Supreme Court's leisurely pace had been made possible by the slow reflexes of the criminal bar. Many criminal lawyers paid little attention to the United States Supreme Court, and only an observant few capitalized on the Court's hints. As a result, the Justices could float a constitutional trial balloon and watch its performance in the lower courts for a number of years, without coming under heavy pressure to resolve the questions it raised. An illustration of the legal profession's capacity for obtuseness came in the *Mapp* case, where Miss Mapp's attorney, who had failed to cite the *Wolf* decision in his brief, was asked during the oral argument if he thought it was time to reverse *Wolf* and make the exclusionary rule mandatory on the states. He stammered that he was not too familiar with that case and finally suggested that it probably would not be a good idea to reverse it. But the legal profession's response to *Escobedo* was so rousing that the Court's usual timetable became untenable. A new breed of perceptive young lawyers was moving into public defender offices and private criminal practice, and they followed the hints of the Supreme Court with great interest. Almost every confessions case became an "Escobedo case," and as the appeals flooded into the Supreme Court, the Clerk was instructed to begin holding them for a landmark decision that would have to come soon.

At the same time, a related but more controversial chain of events was taking place in other legal circles, where the prospect of an expanded *Escobedo* doctrine was viewed with apprehension. In prior years the erratic efforts on behalf of defendants had been marked by an equal dearth of cohesive resistance to the liberal criminal law developments. Some local prosecutors and police chiefs had protested, but they had no national voice. The Justice Department, which until then could take satisfaction in seeing state law-enforcement standards raised more nearly up to its own level, kept an approving silence. But the same ferment that was bringing some of the brightest graduates of the best law schools into public defender offices was also having its effects on the law-enforcement side. Young, promising legal scholars were becoming interested in the problems of law enforcement, and suddenly their weight began to be felt.

The most visible example of this was James Vorenberg. To the liberals who were cheering the Supreme Court on in the early 1960s, Vorenberg came to represent the epitome of the conservative establishment that they believed had allowed the criminal law to become careless of the rights of the poor and the ignorant. A tall, rangy, dark-haired young man with the confident air of one who had always done well, Vorenberg had come to Washington in 1964 as Director of the Justice Department's Office of Criminal Justice. Before that he had been a professor specializing in corporate law at the Harvard Law School, which the liberals tended to see as a breeding ground for conservative, law-enforcement-minded attorneys. Most suspect of all in the eyes of the liberals, he had been a law clerk to Felix Frankfurter.

Once in Washington, Vorenberg quickly became the keystone of an interlocking directorate of criminal law institutions with a decided Harvard flavor and a plan to preserve the police's authority to interrogate. As Director of the Office of Criminal Justice, he was called upon to help work out a solution to the District of Columbia's interrogation difficulties under the *Mallory* decision. His solution: A six-hour (it later shrank to three) period of permissible police questioning without counsel. Vorenberg's proposal caught on with Congress and was passed the next year, but vetoed by President Johnson. It was pat-

terned after the procedure that Vorenberg was then helping
to develop as one of the two primary draftsmen of the American Law Institute's Model Code of Pre-Arraignment Procedure. His associate in that venture, Professor Bator, was also a
Harvard law graduate and a former clerk to Justice Harlan,
Felix Frankfurter's philosophical heir. In the spring of 1965,
Judge J. Edward Lumbard (LL.B., Harvard, Class of 1925),
the Chairman of the American Bar Association's massive Project on Minimum Standards for Criminal Justice, announced that
his group would not attempt a separate study of the confessions
problem, but would instead contribute additional members
to the advisory committee that was assisting in the preparation of
the ALI code. This meant that the ALI proposals would eventually become the ABA's position also. By the autumn of 1965,
it appeared that the Supreme Court could soon find the nation's
two most prestigious legal organizations on record in support of
a proposed interrogation law that allowed some police questioning without counsel. The only other institution that might have
had the prestige and the inclination to bolster the Court's position was the new President's Commission on Law Enforcement
and Administration of Justice. Vorenberg became director of
this also, and the Commission decided to leave the confessions
issue to the ALI. Thus in the autumn of 1965, a more-than-
coincidental concert of views on police interrogation began to
take shape between the most powerful nonjudicial legal institutions in the United States. Congress, the Justice Department, the
American Law Institute and the American Bar Association
were gravitating toward the theory of police interrogation
espoused by James Vorenberg. It was a theory that many
lawyers found reasonable, but it represented the views of the conservative element of the legal profession and the law-enforcement establishment. Most important, it was inconsistent with the
confessions doctrine that had been taking shape through the
recent decisions of the Warren Court, because it would have
permitted some interrogation without counsel.

The first vote by the ALI's membership on the tentative proposal was scheduled for mid-May, 1966. Since the group of attorneys, law scholars and judges that made up the ALI could be
expected to give the proposal its overwhelming approval, the

Court could soon find its freedom of action on confessions sorely compromised. The ALI draftsmen had decided that police interrogation was necessary and had tentatively approved a plan for four hours of questioning without counsel, provided that warnings of rights were given beforehand and some measures such as tape-recording were used to discourage coercion. The interrogation proposal, ninety-three printed pages of detailed statute language and explanatory text that had been hammered out by a forty-four-member committee of criminal law specialists, stood as a monument to the complexity of the problem that the Supreme Court would have to resolve on the basis of a few hours of legal arguments and emanations from the *Escobedo* decision. If the ALI were to approve its plan before the Supreme Court made its confessions decision, the slim Warren majority could find itself declaring a new constitutional right that the nation's legal establishment had only recently rejected.

When the Court granted certiorari in *Miranda* v. *Arizona* in November of 1965, this threat began to melt away. By the time the ALI met in Washington in May, the Court had already heard arguments and there were rumors that the opinion had been written. Chief Justice Warren deviated from his usual custom of addressing the group in its first session, and waited until the second day, when the pre-arraignment code was to be acted upon. After his routine speech, Warren surprised everyone by staying on to sit in on the debate. To the acute discomfort of those who had come to argue for an immediate, strong stand by the ALI in favor of giving the police at least four hours to interrogate, Warren remained at the dais, as smiling and genial as always. This seemed to have an unsettling effect on the conservatives, and the effort to crowd the Supreme Court on confessions turned into a shambles. The discussion degenerated into a series of impassioned speeches that produced little more than a consensus not to vote on the proposed interrogation code.

Once the Supreme Court had decided to hear *Miranda*, there would have been little doubt about the outcome, but for the departure of Arthur Goldberg from the Court in 1965 and his replacement by Abe Fortas. When Fortas had been asked about the confessions issue at his Senate confirmation hearing, he had struck a fairly conservative note. It was "absolutely essential to law enforcement," he said, that there be "an adequate opportunity in the hands of the police to interrogate persons who are accused of crime." Yet it is difficult to imagine another attorney who could have come to the Supreme Court as personally inclined toward a future ruling as Abe Fortas was to the principle of *Miranda*. Fortas personified free counsel for the poor; his role as court-appointed attorney for Clarence Earl Gideon had brought many Americans to see the attorney and not the judge as the foundation of justice for the accused. He also had a solid track record as a civil libertarian. Finally, Fortas had spent much of his professional life in the service of the New Deal; he had seen government serve as a pump-primer to revive a stagnant economy, and it would soon become evident that he had a profound faith in the ability of the Supreme Court to accomplish the same feat in the field of criminal suspects' rights.

The few doubts about Fortas' position vanished as soon as the arguments began on Monday, February 28. Justices frequently tip their hands on a case by the friendly or hostile way in which they treat the opposing arguments. The *Miranda* arguments brought out such combative instincts that every Justice on the bench—with the exception of William J. Brennan, Jr., who spoke only one sentence during the three days of arguments—made it perfectly clear where he stood. Fortas was the first to begin punching holes in the prosecution's arguments. When Telford Taylor, the courtly law professor who argued as *amicus curiae* for the Attorneys General of twenty-seven states, suggested that the problem of confessions was so complex that the Court should stand pat and let state legislatures deal with the details of police procedure, Fortas asked impatiently "whether it is not too late in the day" to confine *Escobedo* to a request for counsel.

Then Fortas suggested that the *Miranda* case should be viewed "in terms of the great human adventure towards some kind of truly civilized order." "What we are dealing with here is not just the criminal in society," he added, "but it is the problem of the relationship of the state and the individual, in the large and total philosophical sense, viewed in the light of the total history of mankind, part of that being the Magna Charta and the Bill of Rights." With the one uncommitted Justice discussing the suspects' side of the case in the same breath with the Magna Charta, it was clear that the Supreme Court had made up its mind.

Facing a decision which should have turned on delicate questions of public order and individual rights, the Justices revealed during the arguments that they were frozen in by legal syllogisms and emotional commitments. When an attorney for one of the convicted men began to waffle over the prospect of extending a full-blown right of counsel to all arrested persons, Justice Douglas cut him off by asking "Which part of the Escobedo case represents the law?" The lawyer agreed that the majority opinion did and changed the subject.

Justice Black saw the problem as one of defining terms. The Fifth Amendment proscribes compelling a person to incriminate himself: If a person under arrest is compelled to stay in the station house and he confesses to the police while there, isn't the confession "compelled"?

Chief Justice Earl Warren, who had been a prosecutor and knew about station-house "squealrooms," made it clear that he was committed emotionally to increasing the rights of persons under interrogation—and over the years it had been well established that the cause that was blessed with Warren's emotional commitment would usually have his vote and his influence. Warren often saw great constitutional issues in intensely personal terms. A decade before, he had been outraged by press reports of a "dragnet arrest" incident in Washington, in which policemen in search of three "stocky" Negro robbery suspects rounded up ninety youths who seemed to match the description —and ultimately charged someone not among the ninety. In criminal cases that came to the Supreme Court after that, states' attorneys learned to dread the Dragnet Story, for if Warren told it during the oral arguments, he was certain to vote for the accused. Early in the *Miranda* arguments he related the Dragnet Story in vivid detail, telling how "the police went out to a certain area of the city and gathered up 90—not 9 but 90— people who might answer that description, knocked them out of bed, and threw them into jail and didn't process them by morning." With four of the necessary five Justices openly committed to the proposed confessions limitations and the fifth, Justice Brennan, already committed to the principle of *Escobedo*, there was little left for the states' attorneys to say.

Their only chance seemed to lie in some thoughts that Brennan had expressed in some speeches he had made, back when the first protests were being heard against the Court's criminal decisions. He had pointed out that the Court had been forced to act because of the default of everyone else. This was no longer true; interest was high across the country on the subject of suspects' rights and police authority, and the state legislatures could be expected to act as soon as the American Law Institute completed its work on the Pre-Arraignment Code. The lawyers urged the Court to wait a while longer. Brennan maintained his silence, but Hugo Black, speaking in soft, Southern tones that carried to the rear of the hushed courtroom, dismissed the subject with two questions: "What is that Model Code? Is it in the Constitution?"

There proved to be considerable irony to this remark, for when the *Miranda* decision was handed down on June 13, one of the features that first drew critics' attack was that it was so like a statutory code. Ever since 1962, when the press failed to grasp the modest reach of the Supreme Court's invalidation of an officially-prescribed prayer for New York public school children—some newspapers implied that the Court had undertaken to declare God unconstitutional—the Justices had taken pains in controversial opinions to state early and in simple language precisely what the Court was doing, shorn of its legalistic reasons for doing it. When Chief Justice Earl Warren did this in the opening paragraphs of his *Miranda* decision, however, the result was a case decision that read revealingly like a statute. He said:

Our holding will be spelled out with some specificity in the pages which follow but briefly stated it is this: the prosecution may not use statements, whether exculpatory or inculpatory, stemming from custodial interrogation of the defendant unless it demonstrates the use of procedural safeguards effective to secure the privilege against self-incrimination. By custodial interrogation, we mean questioning initiated by law enforcement officers after a person has been taken into custody or otherwise deprived of his freedom of action in any significant way. As for the procedural safeguards to be employed, unless other fully effective means are devised to inform accused persons of their right of silence and to assure a continuous opportunity to exercise it, the following measures are required. Prior to any questioning, the person must be warned that he has a right to remain silent, that any statement he does make may be used as evidence against him, and that he has a right to the presence of an attorney, either retained or appointed. The defendant may waive effectuation of these rights, provided the waiver is made voluntarily, knowingly and intelligently. If, however, he indicates in any manner and at any stage of the process that he wishes to consult with an attorney before speaking there can be no questioning. Likewise, if the individual is alone and indicates in any manner that he does not wish to be interrogated, the police may not question him. The mere fact that he may have answered some questions or volunteered some statement on his own does not deprive him of the right to refrain from answering any further inquiries until he has consulted with an attorney and thereafter consents to be questioned.

Most lawyers had expected the Supreme Court to begin with a much smaller bite; the conventional wisdom among judges had been to decide only those issues in each case that had to be resolved to dispose of the case. But the flood of appeals in the wake of *Escobedo* apparently convinced the Court that many answers would be demanded of it in time, so it delivered in the eighty-six–page *Miranda* opinion a complete interrogation procedure. It was, less than a decade after the false start of *Mallory* v. *United States*, a second, more sophisticated attempt to solve the troublesome confession problem by creating a rigid procedure that could be easily policed by the lower judiciary, hopefully without case-by-case review by the Supreme Court.

It was also an innovative departure from the constitutional development of the past, for even though *Escobedo* made the adoption of an objective standard inevitable, the *Miranda* opinion proved to be a result in search of a constitutional reason. Where *Escobedo* had been based on the premise that the Sixth Amendment right to counsel should be extended to the "critical" interrogation stage, *Miranda* was bottomed on the principle that suspects' Fifth Amendment privilege against self-incrimination must be protected in the police station.

This required two conclusions, which Warren's opinion reached in two hefty jumps. First, he held that police interrogation of persons in custody was "inherently compelling." He reeled off some recent examples—and some not so recent—of brutal "third degree" interrogation, but he conceded that these incidents "are undoubtedly the exception now." However, he found incommunicado interrogation odious by nature because its purpose was to get suspects to admit something they do not want to tell. This had often been done by means of psychological persuasion and trickery (Warren quoted from police training manuals that were self-incriminating in the extreme—they taught how to play on suspects' ignorance, conscience and sense of isolation to get them to confess), and Warren held that by submitting a suspect to it against his will, the police were compelling him to incriminate himself even if his disclosures were "voluntary."

Second, he held that the Fifth Amendment's declaration that no person "shall be compelled in any criminal case to be a witness against himself" applied to station-house interrogation as well as to actual courtroom testimony. This brought the privilege against self-incrimination a long way from its origins in seventeenth-century England. It had begun as a reaction against the procedures in the Courts of Star Chamber and High Commission, where defendants were required to take an oath and to answer all questions asked by the prosecution. There first developed a defendant's right to sit silent, and later a right not to take the stand at all. In the United States the self-incrimination privilege came to be viewed essentially as a right to be invoked in court. It blocked the Government from using individuals' private documents against their wishes, and it shielded them from being forced to testify against themselves under oath. In recent Red-hunting eras individuals were permitted to "take the Fifth" in legislative hearings to protect them from bullying questioning about their beliefs and associations. But other than that, the Fifth Amendment privilege to remain silent had been given little effect outside the courtroom, and had not been thought to regulate the informal contacts between individuals and investigating officials.

In reaching the contrary conclusion in *Miranda* the Court was the beneficiary of one of the curious episodes in Supreme Court history. Seventy years before, a far more conservative Supreme Court had declared, in a case called *Bram* v. *United States*, that a confession's validity depends upon whether or not it was obtained in compliance with the Fifth Amendment. Nobody seemed to notice it at the time, but the Court was toying with Pandora's box when it dealt with confessions in terms of the privilege against self-incrimination, instead of the right to due process. In *Bram* the accused had been stripped and bullied into confessing, so the Supreme Court simply concluded that his Fifth Amendment rights had been violated, without focusing on the array of knotty questions that a case without obvious physical coercion would have raised. If a person being questioned has a constitutional right not to be compelled to talk, does he have to be told that the Constitution gives him that right? Does he also have to be warned that anything he says may be used against him? Does he have to be told that he is entitled to counsel to explain his rights and help him assert them? Does it have to be shown that he understood these rights, and waived them, before he talked? The *Bram* opinion slid over these issues, and for almost three-quarters of a century voluntariness was the litmus of confessions. But Chief Justice Earl Warren was eager to practice in 1966 what the Supreme Court had preached in 1897; he asked the questions overlooked in *Bram* and answered them all—in favor of the accused.

The similarities between the questions posed by the *Escobedo* case—a Sixth Amendment decision—and the *Bram* case—a Fifth Amendment ruling—demonstrated how the Supreme Court's efforts to protect individuals from the Government's power by extending both amendments had been drifting toward the same result. Despite the different origins of the two amendments, the rights converged in the *Miranda* opinion, which insisted on the right to counsel during interrogation to protect the right against compulsory self-incrimination. If both rights were truly to be enforced, there could be little room left for police interrogation.

Warren attempted to soften the blow by saying that the *Miranda* rules were similar to procedures followed by the Federal Bureau of Investigation and to rules in effect in England, India, Ceylon and Scotland. He closed his eyes to important differences that made the *Miranda* rule far more generous to the suspected criminal than any of these. The F.B.I. agents had not been required to obtain a waiver before they started asking questions, and they weren't required to stop asking questions if the suspect began to balk. They also didn't offer to furnish poor suspects with counsel during interrogation—only when they appeared before a judge. The English judges' rules did require warnings, but they also permitted each judge to ignore failures to give the warnings and to admit voluntary confessions anyway. India and Ceylon likewise permit the use of confessions obtained in violation of the interrogation restrictions. Only Scotland enforces its restrictions with an automatic exclusionary rule, but it hedges on the right to silence by allowing its prosecutors to point out to the jury the possible implications of a suspect's refusal to answer questions—a tactic that the Supreme Court does not permit.

The *Miranda* rule was indeed too good to suspects to be true. It contained a loophole, which subsequent events were quick to expose and which the majority Justices well understood. Abe Fortas, in a conversation in his chambers a few months later, characterized it as a "conservative decision." "The police can still get confessions," he said; "many people will waive their rights." In fact, the opinion's wording opened the way for the same type of subjective considerations that the Court had sought to escape when it abandoned the "totality of the circumstances" test. In *Miranda* the Court had placed "a heavy burden" on the prosecution in every case to show that a defendant who was questioned outside of his attorney's presence "knowingly and intelligently" waived his rights. In theory this created a presumption that every confession was invalid until proved otherwise; in practice, the test was still a subjective one. Moreover, the subjective question that the trial courts must first answer in ruling on the admissibility of a confession—whether the accused acted intelligently when he waived his right to counsel and agreed to talk—is far more difficult for a judge to ascertain than the question of voluntariness. "Hell, if he waives his right to a lawyer, what's intelligent about that?" asks Alfred G. Arnaud, a lawyer and assistant deputy chief of police of San Francisco, who reports that nevertheless many of the suspects questioned by his officers sign away their *Miranda* rights. James Vorenberg predicted on the day after *Miranda* was announced that the waiver provision "just moves the battleground from the voluntariness of the confession to the voluntariness of the waiver." So the validity of confessions was still to turn on trial judges' choice between the defendants' versions of the circumstances or the polices'. "The police," Vorenberg added, "have done pretty well with these swearing contests over the years."

Much of the energy behind the drive to clamp down on confessions had been generated by distaste for the hypocrisy of the old system. People were bothered by a legal arrangement that surrounded defendants with the trappings of due process at their trials, after airtight cases had been made against them in interrogation rooms where the law granted them few rights. *Miranda* did not eliminate that hypocrisy, but only gave it a reverse twist. It appeared to insulate suspects during interrogation with the same right of counsel that obtains at trials, but in fact it created a situation in which those safeguards would usually be waived. The issue in *Miranda*, Warren's opinion declared, "is not whether (a suspect) is allowed to talk to the police without the benefit of warnings and counsel, but whether he can be interrogated. There is no requirement that police stop a person who enters a police station and states that he wishes to confess to a crime."

The impression was that in-custody interrogation was being virtually eliminated. Warren could have abolished it by taking Justice Jackson's hint that any lawyer worth his salt will tell a client not to talk to the police, and by requiring an attorney's advice before any suspect could waive his rights—by requiring a lawyer to waive a lawyer. This wasn't done, so the Justices apparently realized and intended that the local trial judges would still have a great deal of elbow room in dealing with confessions. The Supreme Court had deliberately given the impression that it had dealt police interrogation a grievous blow, when the Justices had to know that it had really only dealt a tap on the wrist. The motive for this can only be assumed. The Justices may have felt that constitutional rights are always watered down in practice, and that the only proper course for the Court is to insist on the ideal and hope for the best. They may have thought that by attacking all police interrogation, they might at least eliminate some of its worst abuses. They might have planned to eliminate interrogation by degrees, tightening the loopholes in future decisions until no suspect could be questioned outside the presence of his lawyer.

But whatever the intention, it was clear that the Court had not succeeded in achieving the main result that *Miranda* seemed designed to accomplish—the creation of an objective test for the validity of confessions. Realizing this, the Court could have taken much of the sting out of its decision by declaring that all suspects should be warned of their rights, but that trial judges would be permitted to admit otherwise untainted confessions in the interest of justice when the failure to give the correct warnings was inadvertent, or could otherwise be explained. Instead, it chose to hazard the wounds that could be inflicted by those who felt that the decision was more stringent than it was. The resulting furor seems to have had the beneficial effect of spreading the understanding among the public—and to a certain extent, among the police—that people do not have to explain their conduct to the Government. Many observers of police activities also believe that since *Miranda*, the frequency of dragnet arrests, prolonged incommunicado interrogation and physical brutality has greatly diminished. If the Supreme Court deliberately painted with a broad brush to achieve dramatic effect in *Miranda*, that effort had been a success.

It is entirely possible that the Supreme Court could have gained these results and could have avoided the injuries inflicted in the Fortas hearings in 1968 and by the Omnibus Crime Control Act, but for a blunder that gave the impression that *Miranda* had affected police interrogation far more than it actually had. Within weeks after the *Miranda* case was announced, a deeply unsettling phenomenon began to occur across the country; self-confessed criminals began to walk free. There had been a small-scale preview of this after *Escobedo* when California's Supreme Court anticipated *Miranda* and seven confessed killers were released because they could not be convicted without their confessions. But when it began to happen across the country, the public outrage assumed a snowball effect, with each incident recalling the celebrated cases that had happened elsewhere, adding to the impression that the jail-house doors had been flung open. The most widely publicized was the case of Jose Suarez, who had walked free from a Brooklyn courtroom after admitting he had seized a butcher knife in a fit of rage and had killed his wife and five small children. "This is a very sad thing," the trial judge said as he released Suarez; "It is so repulsive it makes one's blood run cold and any decent human being's stomach turn to let a thing like this out on the street." Suarez' own attorney, embarrassed by the outcome, blurted, "This is terrible, I agree, but what can you do under the circumstances?" No one knows how many of these cases have occurred, but whenever they have found their way into print, they have made striking headlines: "Bronx Man Who Admitted Rape Set Free Under Miranda Ruling"; "Confessed Slayer of Wife and 5 Children Freed"; "Two Who Confessed Go Free in Slaying"; "Illegal Confession Frees Mother Here in Slaying of Boy, 4"; and "Miranda Rule Voided 72 Maryland Confessions." Editorial writers began increasingly to recall the complaint by a member of the District of Columbia Court of Appeals in the heyday of its crackdown on confessions: "Nice people have some rights, too."

What was too rarely made clear to the public was that these confessions that were being thrown out were only a relatively tiny, special group that were reached retroactively by the *Miranda* decision. Under the decision the new rules were applied in all trials occurring after June 13, 1966. Virtually every confession ever taken prior to the announcement of the *Miranda* case would have failed to meet the new test, which was so novel and so detailed that no policeman could have known in advance to go through precisely the right rituals in conducting an interrogation. Since the Court's purpose was to deter the police from violating individuals' rights during questioning, the new rule logically should have been applied to any *interrogation* taking place after it was announced, not *trials* conducted after that date. But because the Court related the rule to future trials, the *Miranda* rule fell with full weight on the narrow slice of evidence that had been gathered by police before the rule was announced and not yet used in court. (Later, impressed by the public fury over *Miranda* and by the failure of exclusionary rules to control the police, the Supreme Court caved in to pressure from the state courts and held that re-trials of cases tried prior to *Miranda*, but subsequently overturned, were not "trials" and that the *Miranda* rule would not be applied.)

This created the impression that killers like Jose Suarez would continue to go free, so long as the *Miranda* case remained on the books. It gave tremendous emotional impact to the argument that voluntary confessions should be usable in court, as they always had been, and it probably did more to put the brakes on the due process revolution than any other single event. It was a colossal blunder on the Supreme Court's part, and it resulted in a serious self-inflicted wound. Yet, although it was needless, it was not wholly accidental—it cannot be dismissed as merely the unlucky product of an unguarded moment, a mistake committed in the final rush of the Court term. A complicated and even bizarre chain of events led up to it, yet these events were in many ways a product of the same unlikely mix of result-oriented decision-making and excessive rationality that had colored the Warren Court's entire approach to criminal suspects' rights. In this instance it led the Court to deal itself a stunning blow.

As the Supreme Court began in the mid-1960s to make wholesale changes in the meaning of due process, it encountered a complication called by lawyers—with some glee—the "Sunburst" problem. The name came from the 1932 Supreme Court decision, *Great Northern Railroad* v. *Sunburst Oil and Refining Company*, which established that the Constitution neither required nor forbade the courts to apply their decisions retroactively when they suddenly changed the law. For the next three decades the retroactivity issue arose primarily in the context of civil cases, and they gave it a deceptively simple cast. But when *Mapp* v. *Ohio* signaled the imminent overturn of many criminal procedures in many states, the retroactivity question became far more than an interesting academic exercise. If the Supreme Court were to give *Mapp* and its successors full retroactive effect, then prison gates would open across the country to thousands of prisoners who had been convicted before the due process revolution occurred.

There were strong reasons for and against giving retroactive effect to criminal rulings such as *Mapp* v. *Ohio*. Logically, it is difficult to justify holding in prison a person who was put there with the aid of a constitutional violation, no matter when the breach occurred. Moreover, some violations—a coerced confession, a lawyerless trial, a rigged lineup—can lead to the conviction of the innocent. Finally, statutes historically have been applied to future events, while constitutional interpretations have been considered theoretically timeless; to apply Supreme Court rulings only to the future would have reinforced the charges that the Court had been legislating. Yet to release convicts en masse because of past police fluffs doesn't deter the police, which is supposed to be the principal purpose of the exclusionary rule.

It was 1965 before the Supreme Court focused on the question for the first time in a criminal law context, when it set out in a case called *Linkletter* v. *Walker* to decide to what extent *Mapp* v. *Ohio* should be applied retroactively. The most reasonable solution, the Justices were told, would be to relate the rule to the official activity that it was designed to regulate. Since the *Mapp* decision was designed to deter illegal searches, it should be applied only to *searches* that took place after the ruling was announced. The problem was that by 1965 the Supreme Court had already applied the *Mapp* decision retroactively by summarily reversing several appeals that had reached the court in the wake of *Mapp* and which involved illegal searches that occurred prior to the *Mapp* decision. There would have been red faces on the Court if it had declared in 1965 that aside from a few appeals that slipped by the Justices before they focused on the problem, only illegal searches that occurred after the *Mapp* decision would be affected by it.

The Court's solution was a triumph of consistency over farsightedness. It held that *Mapp* would be applied retrospectively only to those convictions that were not yet final—in the sense that direct appeal in the state courts and certiorari to the Supreme Court were no longer available. Later it applied the same standard when it held that the rule in *Griffin* v. *California*, which declared that prosecutors and judges could not comment on a defendant's failure to take the stand, would be applied only to convictions that were not yet final when the *Griffin* case was announced.

By the time that *Miranda* came before the Court, the Supreme Court had fallen into the habit of treating the retroactivity question as a heads-or-tails proposition: either a new ruling was to be treated like *Gideon* v. *Wainwright* and applied retroactively to all convictions, no matter how ancient; or it was to be denied retroactive effect, meaning it would not be applied after a conviction became final. Long-established patterns of court procedure bolstered this two-pronged view of the retroactivity question. If a ruling was given retroactive effect, a convict could raise it in a petition for habeas corpus. If retroactive effect was denied, then the new point could be raised only in a direct appeal from a conviction.

As the Supreme Court was to realize soon enough, there were in fact many shades of retroactivity that could come into play with devastating effect on pending or future prosecutions, even if the Court "denied retroactive effect" to a new ruling by not applying it to final judgments. But that had not yet become evident at the time of *Miranda*, and it was natural for the Court to approach the question of that landmark decision's retroactivity as if the main point at issue was whether final convictions involving confessions would be disturbed.

Normally, the things that happen behind the official scenes at the Supreme Court never become public. But occasionally, when the Justices decide in the dying hours of a court term to make a sharp change in direction from their planned course, the sudden shifting of the machinery of the Court creates sufficient signs of friction and strain to be discernible to those who are near the Court but not a part of it. This happened late in the 1964 term, when Justice Tom C. Clark switched sides on the Billie Sol Estes case after the opinions had been drafted and were almost ready to be announced. Initially he had been the crucial fifth vote in favor of affirming the conviction. When he made his eleventh-hour switch, Warren tapped him to write the Court's opinion reversing the conviction of Estes. This left Warren to file a long concurring opinion that had all the earmarks of having been hastily modified from a major dissent, and left Justice Stewart to submit a dissent that read strikingly like a majority opinion.

A similar change of direction took place on Friday, June 10, 1966, in connection with *Miranda* v. *Arizona*. The Court had initially voted to decide in one single opinion by the Chief Justice all five appeals that had been argued as a package during the three-day session the previous winter. The *Miranda* opinion was drafted, disposing not only of the four direct appeals that eventually did appear in the *Miranda* opinion, but also of *Johnson* v. *New Jersey*, which raised the retroactivity question. Sylvester Johnson and Stanley Cassidy, the appellants, had been on New Jersey's Death Row for six years and their convictions were long since final when the Supreme Court granted their appeal along with the *Miranda* case. It was the fourth time they had sought certiorari to the Supreme Court after unsuccessfully challenging the validity of their confessions in habeas corpus actions, and if the Court were to hold in their favor, it would open the cell doors to virtually every convict who had ever been put behind bars with the aid of a confession. The majority had decided instead to apply the same limited rule of retroactivity that it had applied to *Mapp* v. *Ohio* and *Griffin* v. *California*, and Warren included a section in his early drafts of the *Miranda* opinion to that effect. It turned down the claims of Johnson and Cassidy because their conviction was final. His clerks then began sifting through the "Escobedo cases," sorting out those that were not yet final—and thus would be reversed—from the habeas corpus appeals, which would all be dismissed, leaving the convictions intact.

When the Justices met in conference on June 10 to put the final touches on the massive *Miranda* opinion for release on June 13, the enormous complexity of the retroactivity problem began to surface. With *Miranda* and its four companion cases to be disposed of in Warren's long opinion, there remained 144 pending "Escobedo cases" that had to be decided in accordance with the majority decision. But when the Justices placed on one side of the ledger the appeals of those who had initially brought the issue into court in habeas corpus petitions and thus were to stay in prison, and those who were appealing convictions and thus were to get new trials, some troubling contradictions came to light.

The basic problem was that constitutional rights and criminal responsibility were to become secondary to accidents of timing. Some defendants were to benefit because they had avoided capture for a long time after their crimes and thus their convictions were not yet final. Others were fortunate because they were convicted in states with slow justice and their convictions had taken years to reach the Supreme Court. All this was complicated further by differences in various states' procedures, but the result was clear enough—some of the 144 appellants had been caught up in the machinery of justice relatively recently, but the police's failure to warn them of their rights could never be raised because their convictions were final. Other appellants on the list, who had been interrogated months or even years earlier, would get to challenge their interrogation in new trials.

Beyond the anomalies of timing was the fact that the proposed retroactivity formula would have denied relief to some appellants who had been treated rather shabbily by the police, while capriciously overturning the convictions of a few individuals who did not seem to deserve it. One appeal in particular fell into this category.

It grew out of a grisly incident that occurred on the night of April 21, 1965, when two men sprang from ambush upon a young couple in a lovers' lane area near Longview, Texas. One of the intruders, later identified as Johnny Lee Clemons, shot the girl's escort in the head and chest and dumped him into a stream. Clemons and his companion then raped the girl. Then, apparently determined to leave no witnesses, Clemons shot the girl four times in the head and neck. Miraculously, both victims lived, although Clemons' purpose had succeeded in shooting the man; his brain was so damaged that he could not testify. But the girl could, and Clemons was convicted and sentenced to death on the strength of her testimony, plus his bloody clothing and his pistol with the barrel removed—and his confession. Clemons had confessed so readily that his lawyer did not dispute the voluntariness of the statement. But although he had been warned of his right to counsel, there was no proof that he had waived his right to consult legal counsel before he confessed, and his attorney challenged the confession on the authority of *Escobedo*.

In his petition for certiorari to the Supreme Court his attorney attempted what has to be one of the most ill-advised bits of advocacy in the Court's history. He argued that the girl, who was white, lied when she claimed to have been raped by Negro men (Clemons was a Negro). Furthermore, the lawyer declared that the lovers' lane area where the crime occurred is so notorious for petting parties that the young couple forfeited "their claim for the protection of the law when they went there at night."

Chief Justice Earl Warren was a deeply moral man, whose passion for fair play was rivalled only by his respect for womanhood. More than once he had flabbergasted casual acquaintances by remarking in his genial, casual way that he would personally throttle any smut-peddler who tried to pander pornography to one of his daughters. He was also a tough, unyielding judge who tended to rely on his instincts to help him reach proper solutions to difficult questions. With the Clemons appeal as an illustration of the aberrations that would flow from the proposed retroactivity ruling, Warren was persuaded at the June 10 meeting to abandon it in favor of a rule that would deny all convicted persons the benefit of the *Miranda* rule.

It was impossible to unscramble the situation by Monday morning, so the appeal of Johnson and Cassidy was deleted from the *Miranda* opinion and Warren wrote a separate opinion for announcement on June 20, *Johnson* v. *New Jersey*. It was a change of plans that could have saved the Supreme Court the embarrassment of Jose Suarez and his ilk, if the Court had gone all the way and had made *Miranda* applicable only to confessions taken after June 13, 1966. But while the Court's opinion in *Johnson* v. *New Jersey* said that *Miranda* and *Escobedo* "should not be applied retroactively," it did provide for limited retroactive effect by setting the date of the trial as the cutoff point. Johnny Lee Clemons' petition for certiorari was denied, and he began the long process of fighting off his execution through habeas corpus proceedings.

As it turned out, the Supreme Court's new constitutional doctrine was applied to only four trials that took place before June 13, 1966. Those, of course, were the trials of the four appellants whose cases were selected to be discussed at the confessions hearing—Miranda, Vignera, Westover and Stewart. All but Stewart were quickly re-tried and convicted. Meanwhile, the Supreme Court was realizing—too late—its retroactivity error. The next year, when the Court extended the right of counsel to identification lineups in *United States* v. *Wade*, the

Justices ruled that the new doctrine would apply only to identifications made after the date of the *Wade* decision.

Once decided, it was inevitable that the controversy over crime
and the Supreme Court would center around *Miranda* v. *Arizona*.
With the decision made and the lines drawn, it was difficult to
fault the Warren Court for declaring that suspects should be
warned of their constitutional rights. But that assumed that
Miranda was really necessary, and that the mechanical formula
produced by the Warren Court was required by the Constitution. In fact, the Court had raised the point artlessly, in *Escobedo*
v. *Illinois*, when it did not have to be raised. It had rushed into
a decision, when it could have been delayed. It had chosen an
artificially mechanical solution, when human judgment was inevitable. And finally, it gave the ruling partially retroactive
effect, to the benefit of none but a few confessed criminals and
the most ruthless of the court's enemies. And so the ultimate
judgment of the Warren Court's involvement in the question
of confessions is likely to be not whether suspects should be
warned of their rights, but whether *Miranda* v. *Arizona* was
worth the price.

Supreme Court Justices are professional men, and for the
most part they go about their decision-making as detached
professionals. But *Miranda* v. *Arizona* touched emotions on the
Court as well as in the country at large. Earl Warren's opinion
was long, but he did not summarize it when he delivered it
from the bench on the morning of June 13. He read almost
all of it, savoring the unexpected Fifth Amendment rationale
and dwelling on the allegations of heavy-handedness against the
police. Tom Clark, the soft-spoken, low-keyed Texan, began
with an unaccustomed edge on his voice when his turn to
dissent came. He had written a brief dissent, easily the mild-
est filed in that acerbic case. Clark was a former Attorney
General who had frequently expressed in his opinions sympathy
for the lot of the police, but he had not made a point of
dissenting vigorously against the Court's use of the exclusionary
rule to police them—perhaps because he had begun the process
with *Mapp.* v. *Ohio*. But as he spoke that day he began to
elaborate on his written dissent, and it was clear that he did
not appreciate some of Warren's assumptions of systematic

wrongdoing by the police. It wasn't fair, he grumbled, to pillory the police over interrogation manuals written by law professors and perhaps rarely used by the police.

When the Justices left the bench Clark returned to his desk and took out his written dissent. For reasons of custom and practicality it was too late to change it, for it had been issued to the press and had been released for publication. One legal reporting service, *United States Law Week*, had already printed the opinion and had mailed it to its subscribers. Still, Clark could not resist adding some bite to his dissent. He got out the copy of the dissent that would be sent to the United States Government Printing Office for official publication in the *United States Reports*, and slipped in these words, which appear in the official version:

"The police agencies—all the way from municipal and state forces to the Federal bureau—are responsible for law enforcement and public safety in this country. I am proud of their efforts, which in my view are not fairly characterized by the Court's opinion."

IX

Searches: From Confusion
Toward a Rule of Reason

*The course of true law pertaining to searches
and seizures . . . has not—to put it mildly—run
smooth.* FELIX FRANKFURTER

Justice Abe Fortas, a man normally about as inclined toward
unplanned responses as a blackjack dealer, sounded off at length
to his questioners on one notable occasion during the Senate
Judiciary Committee's hearings on his ill-starred nomination as
Chief Justice. Toward the end of his second day in the witness
chair, the Southern senators who were out to block his nomination began to draw blood. They had not made much headway
with their complaints about the Supreme Court's desegregation
decisions and its proclivity for overruling old precedents, but as
the questioning progressed it became clear that Fortas, as a mem-

ber of the liberal wing of the Court, was vulnerable on the issue
of criminal law. Fortas had said from the start that he could not
answer questions about current judicial issues. So for hours he
was forced to sit as an unresponsive sounding board for the
senators' indignation over recent rulings on habeas corpus,
confessions and lineups. Finally, with a trace of forgive-them-
for-they-know-not-what-they-do in his voice, Fortas began to
reply:

"There are opinions that I think are significant in addition to
those that Senator Ervin has talked about. For example—may
I mention one, I wonder, without breaching my constitutional
responsibility as I see it—just one.

"For example, I think that one of the most important decisions
that we made in my three years on the Court in the field of
criminal law is a case that has received no notice, a case called
Warden v. *Hayden*. In that case we did overrule a precedent.
We overruled the case of *Gouled* v. *United States*, decided in
1921 by a unanimous Court. Holmes and Brandeis were on that
Court and if I correctly recall, Justice Clarke—not the present
Justice Clark—C-l-a-r-k-e—wrote the opinion. We overruled that
case, and established for the first time that the Fourth Amendment did not prohibit the police when they were making a
valid and authorized search from seizing evidence, evidentiary
materials. . . . There are other cases—stop and frisk, and so
on. . . . It is kind of rough when all that is visible on the Court,
Senator, are the hard cases."

Fortas had reason to be piqued at the senators' blind spot toward
the Supreme Court's ruling on searches and seizures. *Warden*
v. *Hayden* had gone too far, he thought, in enlarging the power
of the police to search and seize—so far that he had charged
in an opinion that the decision "needlessly destroys, root and
branch, a basic part of liberty's heritage." This was a recent
instance in which the Court had added substantially to the
state's ability to obtain incriminatory evidence, at the expense
of long-standing prerogatives of criminal defendants. It was
the type of ruling that the complaining senators would have been
expected to approve, and Fortas thought that the Court should
at least be given the benefit of what he saw as its own bad
judgment.

Fortas' antagonists were proceeding from the assumption that all decisions that limited the police were "bad" decisions—a position that proved to be sound politics, if dubious constitutional theory. But even by those lights, the Supreme Court's performance had not been all "bad." (Although by that scale, less could be said for Fortas himself.) It was not true, as Senator Strom Thurmond had implied, that all of the Court's decisions "shackle the police and courts and make it terribly difficult to protect society from crime and criminals." In the area of searches and seizures by police, several important recent decisions had cut the other way. Limitations on the police that had stood for decades had been washed away, and dissenting Justices had protested that the Court was favoring the police and was tipping the scales of justice too far toward the prosecution.

Thus by 1968, only seven years after *Mapp* v. *Ohio* had laid the groundwork for the "criminal coddling" controversy by making the Fourth Amendment effectively binding on the states, the Senators who were snapping at the Court's heels over crime took pains to avoid the subject of police searches. It was not that searches are less important than confessions and eyewitness identifications to law enforcement. In the prosecution of such consentual crimes as narcotics, liquor and gambling offenses, which produce no victim to testify against the offenders, searches are critical. Rather, it was that those who wished to fault the Court for "handcuffing the police" could not make their case over searches.

Historically, search and seizure has been the one area of police activity where the courts could crack down and find the public instinctively on their side. To the nonlawyer, the Fourth Amendment is the apple pie and the Fourth of July of constitutional law, the Constitution's way of expressing the deeply rooted American conviction that a man's home is his castle. The Fifth Amendment's privilege against compulsory self-incrimination may conjure up grisly images of torture racks and thumbscrews in medieval England, but physical coercion is now a remote threat, and the self-incrimination privilege is rooted in an alien experience. When the courts enforce it to rule out noncoercive questioning in routine criminal investigations, the public has tended to feel uncomfortable with the results. But the Fourth Amendment was inspired by searches of homes on these shores by British tax collectors, and there is a feeling that it can and does still happen here. Even when the courts enforce the Fourth Amendment to the hilt, politicians do not demand more power for the police to enter and search.

Furthermore, the law of searches is so incredibly complex that it defies sloganeering, and all but precludes informed public debate. Most people don't even realize that the same search warrant requirements that protect a man's castle also bar the police from searching the pockets of the seamy-looking character suspected of selling marijuana to the man's school-age children. The Fourth Amendment applies equally to individuals' "persons, houses, papers, and effects," which means that the police can't search the suspected pot-pusher unless they either have enough evidence to legally arrest him, or if they have obtained a search warrant, based upon sworn affidavits indicating that the search will probably turn up evidence of a crime. This is strong protection for the individual, and few thoughtful Americans would want to tamper with it in any substantial way. But it is probably also true that few Americans understand the extent to which the Fourth Amendment, as interpreted by the Supreme Court and enforced by the exlusionary rule, seeks to immobilize American policemen in situations in which any reasonable person would suspect that the law was being broken before his very eyes.

Lawyers have a game in which they try to outdo one another in dreaming up hypothetical situations in which no legal search could be made because probable cause to search would not exist, yet the appearance of wrongdoing clearly would. Several years before he became a Justice, Thurgood Marshall sat in on one of these sessions and came up with this one:

"A man dressed as a longshoreman walks through the lobby of the Mayflower Hotel, carrying a new coat over his arm. It is a woman's coat.

"And get this—it's summertime!"

Since Marshall thought that one up, the Supreme Court has taken some of the sting out of such situations by ruling (with Justice Marshall in agreement) that an officer could stop the longshoreman and ask about the coat. But it is still the law that if the longshoreman's pockets were bulging with lumps that looked suspiciously like loot, yet his answers to the policeman's inquiries were satisfactory and the policeman knew of no burglary, the officer would have to let him go on his way without a search. No other major nation attempts to restrict police searches so severely; the idea of suppressing improperly obtained evidence is almost unknown in other countries. Yet Americans have paid the law-enforcement price of their stricter system with pride—bolstered, perhaps, by their ignorance of the rules' effects and the fact that the rules did not apply nationally until 1961.

Despite all of this, Fortas had probably been spared a Senatorial attack over *Mapp* v. *Ohio* primarily because, as he suggested, the Court had handed down a trio of important decisions in the previous eighteen months that had eased the Fourth Amendment's restrictions on police searches. This was largely fortuitous, but not completely so.

It was true that some repairs on the intricate law of searches had been long overdue. The Supreme Court's first exclusion of evidence under the Fourth Amendment dated back to 1886, and by the time the Court made it effectively binding upon all of the states in 1961, the body of law that had been put together to enforce the amendment contained some features of a Rube Goldberg nightmare. Its quirks cut both ways—some needlessly limited the police too much, and others failed to extend the reach of the Fourth Amendment far enough. Throughout, the law of search and seizure was freckled with musty common law concepts which had a way either of frustrating rational police procedures on the one hand or of permitting unnecessary personal indignities on the other. So long as only the tiny percentage of criminal cases that were handled in Federal courts were affected by it, nobody but legal purists objected. Then *Mapp* v. *Ohio* made it all binding on the states and thereby magnified the impact of its flaws by fifty. With the entire American legal system suddenly faced with the consequences of abiding by this body of law, the Supreme Court had turned in the mid-1960s to the business of ironing out some kinks that had been visible but neglected for years, as well as others that were brought to the surface by the chemistry of *Mapp*.

By the time of Fortas' interrogation in the summer of 1968, this process had produced three important cases that measurably aided the police—*McCray* v. *Illinois*, *Warden* v. *Hayden* and *Terry* v. *Ohio*. Not all of the patchwork performed on the Fourth Amendment was to favor the police: *Spinelli* v. *United States* would be announced the following January and would make it more difficult for the police to obtain search warrants, and *Chimel* v. *California*, to be issued on the day of Warren's retirement in 1969, would tighten the screw again by requiring search warrants in many situations where searches "as an incident to an arrest" had previously been allowed. But out of these reforms by the Warren Court came an impression, expressed most clearly in the "stop and frisk" case, *Terry* v. *Ohio*, that the Court was beginning to draw a distinction between searches of premises and of persons. Where searches of private quarters or immobilized vehicles were concerned, situations that usually allow time for the structured procedures of search warrant law, the Court was prepared to stick doggedly to its technique of requiring the police to comply with objective procedures, on pain of automatic suppression of evidence. But where on-the-street police investigation was involved, because the Court had begun to learn by bitter experience that rigid constitutional rules could be made only to be broken, it began to drift away from its exclusive reliance upon the objective exclusionary rule. In the stop-and-frisk situation it frankly abandoned any attempt to lay down a procedure to be followed in all cases, and adopted instead a rule of reason that could not be effectively policed from the top. As a result, the law of searches, which had always been one of the most confused and complex areas of constitutional law, emerged from the Warren era in a more stable condition than the law governing confessions and eyewitness identifications.

Few people other than a handful of criminal lawyers realized in 1961, when all of the nation's courts and police became bound by the Fourth Amendment, how irrational the law of searches actually was and how different it was from the popular view of it. The wording was familiar enough:

The right of the people to be secure in their persons, houses, papers, and effects, against unreasonable searches and seizures, shall not be violated, and no warrants shall issue, but upon probable cause, supported by oath or affirmation, and particularly describing the place to be searched, and the persons or things to be seized.

The prevailing Dick Tracy–Perry Mason impression of how it worked was something like this:

The District Attorney, having been tipped off about foul play by a conscience-stricken member of the mob, gets a search warrant from a thoughtful, gray-haired judge and swoops down on the nightclub where the Boss has his luxurious suite of offices. On the way in, the police frisk and disarm every man with a five-o'clock shadow in the house, and in a wall safe they find a bloody shirt worn by the Boss during the recent gangland-style farewell to a rival hoodlum. They also find the victim's valuables, bearing the blood-smeared fingerprints of a hired killer from Chicago. The Boss and the hired killer are swiftly convicted. Reason and justice triumph.

Actually, as the law stood after *Mapp* standardized it in 1961, the scene would more likely have occurred as follows: (1) The raid would have been made without a search warrant, as an "incident" to the arrest of the Boss. The District Attorney would have realized that while many judges are quite casual about issuing search warrants, at the trial and upon appeal many otherwise-reasonable judges examine all search warrants through a constitutional magnifying glass, and that the search would more likely be upheld if it was done without than with a search warrant. (2) At the trial the D.A. would have had to muster some evidence to make it appear that he had valid proof to justify making the arrests and search without mentioning the informer. Under the Federal precedents he would have been required to have the informer testify in court if he admitted relying on his tip and if the defendant demanded his presence, and that could prove fatal to the informer. (3) The Boss' bloody shirt would not be admissible as evidence, so he might be acquitted. Under *Gouled* v. *United States*, the decision mentioned by Justice Fortas, the shirt could not be legally seized, for the astonishing reason that it was only evidence of guilt. (4)

The hired killer from Chicago would be convicted, even if the search was palpably unconstitutional. Because the office was not his property, his Fourth Amendment rights were not violated by the search and he would have no legal standing to object to the use of the items bearing his fingerprints. (5) The men who were frisked "on suspicion" would have been disarmed and booked on petty charges and allowed to forfeit their bail. The District Attorney would not have known whether evidence obtained under such circumstances could be used and it would have been best not to make waves.

The first legal problem exposed by the mythical District Attorney's raid and the most persistent difficulty raised by the Fourth Amendment—its tendency to encourage warrantless searches while ostensibly stressing the importance of search warrants—had been a thorn in the Supreme Court's side for decades before 1961. This schizophrenia seems basic to the law of searches; it was written into the Fourth Amendment by the Founding Fathers, and it has bedeviled the Supreme Court for decades.

The Fourth Amendment is divided into neat, divergent halves. The first lays down the general principle that the people shall be secure from unreasonable searches and seizures. The second says that all search warrants must be supported by sworn evidence of probable cause, and must particularly describe the places to be searched and the items to be seized. If this meant that any search is constitutional so long as it is reasonable under all of the circumstances, one of the circumstances being the requirement that when search warrants are deemed necessary they must meet the standards of probable cause and specificity, then there would be no internal tension. Until the stop-and-frisk decision of 1968, however, the Supreme Court always gave the amendment a much stricter interpretation. A general "reasonableness" test can be riddled by hindsight; judges can be convinced after the fact that the police had subjective reasons for almost any intrusion— especially if proof of guilt was found. So the Supreme Court rejected this view from the outset and read the reasonableness clause of the Fourth Amendment into the search warrant clause. It equated reasonableness with the requirements of probable cause and specificity, and assumed that a reasonable search would have to comply with the search warrant clause of the Fourth Amendment.

The problem is that for all of the Fourth Amendment's stiff requirements for a valid search warrant, it cannot be read to require that all searches be made with search warrants. There are two rather typical law-enforcement situations in which searches without search warrants are considered necessary and proper. It has been well established in both English and American law (and by bitter experience) that when persons are arrested, their clothing and their immediate surroundings should be searched, if for no other reason than to remove all weapons from the suspects' reach. This is not as inconsistent with the search warrant clause of the Fourth Amendment as it might seem. Because the Fourth Amendment mentions seizures of persons as well as effects, it has been held to govern arrests as well as searches. Thus police may make arrests only if they have "probable cause"—sufficient evidence to persuade an ordinary person that an offense has been committed and that the arrested person probably committed it. To obtain a search warrant, they must show that a specific crime has been committed and that certain incriminating evidence will probably be found in the place to be searched. Because these two standards of probability are virtually identical, an officer who has probable cause to make an arrest could usually obtain a search warrant on the same facts.

Warrantless searches are also permitted under certain "exigent circumstances," when the opportunity to make a search would be lost if an officer hesitates. These circumstances often involve vehicles. If a policeman has probable cause to search a car (but not to make an arrest), it is usually apparent that if he goes for a warrant the car will go for the county line. So warrantless searches of cars that are likely to move on are routinely upheld, so long as there was probable cause for the search. Another frequent exigent circumstance is the "hot pursuit" situation, in which a suspected felon is on the run and is thought to have ducked into a building. Pursuing officers can legally go in after him.

Finally, policemen manage to make many searches without search warrants merely by asking permission to look around, as if they have the right to do so. If a person consents, the search is valid. This raises some of the same questions about voluntariness and intimidation that have plagued the law of confessions, and the Supreme Court will probably have to crack down on the heavy-handed "consent" search in due time.

Because arrests and exigent circumstances are the meat and potatoes of law enforcement, search warrants tend to become the soufflé. They are much admired, but they are too much trouble to be attractive to the police. There is the paper work, perhaps a check with the District Attorney's office on legality, the trip to the courthouse for the magistrate's signature, the possibility that a courthouse "leak" will alert the suspect before the officer arrives, and above all the likelihood that the search warrant will be scrutinized more critically later in court than the search would be if it had been made without a search warrant. So the practical pressures are strong for searches to be conducted without search warrants.

These pressures would have posed no problem if the Supreme Court had read the Fourth Amendment as no more than a caveat to the police that their cases would not stand up in court if they searched on mere suspicion and without probable cause. If this were all that it were held to mean, then there would be no need to require a warrant in advance. Each search and arrest would be followed by a hearing on the defendant's motion to suppress the evidence, and a judge would decide then if the search had been based upon probable cause and had been otherwise reasonable. Instead, the Court has insisted that it is important to make the policeman persuade a judicial officer *in advance* that there are legal grounds to conduct a search. This would spare individuals from injudicious searches and would also spare trial judges the temptation to justify searches of borderline legality after the fact, when incriminating evidence had been found. The present-day Supreme Court likes to hark back to Justice Jackson's explanation:

The point of the Fourth Amendment, which often is not grasped by zealous officers, is not that it denies law enforcement the support of the usual inferences which reasonable men draw from evidence. Its protection consists in requiring that those inferences be drawn by a neutral and detached magistrate instead of being judged by the officer engaged in the often competitive enterprise of ferreting out crime. Any assumption that evidence sufficient to support a magistrate's disinterested determination to issue a search will justify the officers in making a search without a warrant would reduce the Amendment to a nullity and leave the people's homes secure only in the discretion of police officers.

To this end the Court has pursued two policies. It has declared that when the police apply for search warrants their affidavits must present enough evidence to permit the magistrate to make an independent judgment as to whether the search should be allowed; and it has required search warrants in as many situations as possible, under the theory that warrantless searches should occur only in a few narrow circumstances. This dual policy has tended to be contradictory: As the standards for search warrants have been raised, policemen have been encouraged to search without them.

Nobody knows how many search warrants are actually used in the United States; statistics on the subject range from inadequate to nonexistent. But the few figures that do exist show that the ratio of searches with warrants to searches without them is tiny. In San Francisco, a city of three-quarters of a million people and about 30,000 reported major crimes per year, the police obtained 20 search warrants in 1968. In the city of Los Angeles, an area with a population of about 3 million people, only 1,897 search warrants were issued from 1930, when court officials began keeping a count, through 1968. In 1968, a record year, 197 were issued. A study of three cities in the Midwest disclosed the same pattern: search warrants were the exception, not the rule. In a one-year period 29 search warrants were issued in Detroit, 17 in Wichita, Kansas, and approximately 30 in Milwaukee. The glaring exception is New York City, where search warrants were almost unknown before *Mapp* v. *Ohio* was announced in 1961, but by 1963, 5,132 were used in that one year. When experts are pressed to estimate how many police searches are made without warrants, they say about 90 percent, and they could probably make a case for 95 percent.

If this record seemed inconsistent with the Supreme Court's position that "exceptions to the requirement that searches and seizures be undertaken only after obtaining a warrant are limited," it was not because the Court was oblivious to reality. For many years prior to *Mapp* it was an open secret in legal circles that Federal agents were outflanking the Fourth Amendment's search warrant requirements by arresting suspects at strategic places, which were then searched as "incidents" to the arrests. At its worst, this technique was used as a dodge to permit a search when officers had enough evidence to arrest a suspect, but had no more than suspicions as to where further evidence of the crime might be found. The trick was to wait for the suspect at the spot where the evidence would most likely be—typically at his home, office or moonshine still—and by arresting him there and making a search in the course of the arrest, gain access to a place that no judge would have issued a search warrant to enter. In some instances, the officers could make a wider, more intensive search in this way than would have been allowed in any search warrant, which must "particularly describe the place to be searched" and the things to be seized. The courts always struck these searches down when it was shown that the agents deliberately used the arrest ploy to search because they knew that no search warrant could have been obtained, but such motives were rarely proved, and the "search as an incident to arrest" flourished.

The argument usually made for it by prosecutors was persuasively practical: Granted that a suspect's clothing and immediate surroundings must be searched in the course of a warrantless arrest, there was no point in requiring the police to go for a search warrant to complete the search of the suspect's premises. The arrested person's family or friends would surely squirrel the evidence away while the police were going for the search warrant, which at that point had become a formality because the police probably had seen or learned enough in the course of the arrest to provide ample probable cause for a search. What the prosecutors didn't say in court, but was widely known anyway, was that many judges already treated such warrants as formalities. Many of them signed almost any application for a search warrant that was thrust before them, and some even let their clerks approve and sign search warrants for them. One court clerk in North Carolina, when asked about the care with which he considered the applications for search warrants before authorizing the searches, replied; "All I can say is they come in and ask if I will witness their signatures, and I witness it." In a given case, it could be made to appear almost ludicrous to make a busy policeman trek from the scene of an arrest to the courthouse for such a piece of paper, and try to make it back to the arrest scene before the evidence disappeared. But as a matter of policy, the Supreme Court could see that unless there was a rigid rule that "arrest" searches could not range beyond the arrested person's immediate surroundings, search warrants would continue to be almost as rare as the whooping crane.

Confronted with this dilemma, the Supreme Court zigzagged between the two unsatisfactory alternatives, careening from one side of the issue to the other as the competing sides alternately won and lost the Justices' favor. As far back as 1914, when the Supreme Court first excluded illegally obtained evidence in *Weeks* v. *United States*, it noted that officers could search without search warrants for items "within the control" of the accused at the time of his arrest. This exception had developed out of a desire to thwart suspects from laying their hands on weapons or evidence, but the Supreme Court switched the meaning of "control" from the original practical definition to a legal one that gave the police a longer reach when they were not armed with a search warrant than when they were. There is an ancient common law doctrine that says that a person who has ownership or possession of premises has constructive control of the entire premises. This definition of "control" allowed wide-range searches of arrested suspects' premises, and the courts tended to give it that meaning in the post-World War I era.

Then during Prohibition, when revenue officers often cut corners, lawbreaking smacked of public service and enforcement could create a thirst, the Supreme Court reversed its field, ruling in two decisions that Prohibition agents could not legally range so far without search warrants.

Law enforcement took on a more serious character during World War II, and in 1947 the pendulum swung back in *Harris* v.

United States, which involved such a broad search that the Supreme Court's blessing of it gave the police almost carte blanche authority to search while arresting. The F.B.I. had arrested a man named George Harris at his apartment on two warrants charging fraud and forgery. They handcuffed him, and as an "incident" to his arrest, spent the next five hours combing through the apartment. They finally found forged Selective Service certificates, and Harris was eventually convicted of possessing these. In an opinion by Chief Justice Fred M. Vinson, the Supreme Court ruled, 6 to 3, that the search was legally conducted as an incident to the arrest and that the conviction could stand.

Just one year later, in another moonshine case, the Court took the opposite view in *Trupiano* v. *United States*, where it said that if an officer has time to go for a search warrant and doesn't, the subsequent search of premises as an incident to an arrest is invalid. Two years later, in 1950, the Court zigged again in *United States* v. *Rabinowitz*. It rejected the *Trupiano* reasoning and held that so long as the search incident to an arrest was reasonable under all of the circumstances, it made no difference that the officers had time to get a search warrant and failed to do so.

By this time the Supreme Court had performed one of the most remarkable displays of vacillation in its history, yet the outcome relied heavily on practical arguments. In terms of sound legal theory, there was little reason to allow a search of an arrested person's entire premises on the strength of the feudal principle that it was all within his control. Furthermore, searches of this type tended to degenerate into general searches for unspecified evidence, which the Fourth Amendment had been specifically adopted to preclude.

So there was little comment in 1969 when the Court zagged again in *Chimel* v. *California* and held that officers cannot search beyond the immediate area of an arrested suspect on the theory that the premises are in his legal "control." The opinion written by Potter Stewart, for a 6 to 2 Court, had an aura of durability about it that suggested that the Supreme Court had finally taken its stand. Stewart dissected the historic reasons for permitting warrantless searches in the course of arrests, and declared that the *Harris* and *Rabinowitz* decisions could not stand up under that reasoning. In the *Chimel* situation three police officers had arrested a Santa Ana, California, coin collector at his home on an arrest warrant charging him with having burglarized a coin shop. As an incident to the arrest they made an hour-long search of his entire three-bedroom house, including the attic, garage and a small workshop, and found enough stolen coins to convict him of two burglaries. The search "went far beyond the petitioner's person and the area from within which he might have obtained either a weapon or something that could have been used as evidence against him," the Court said. It concluded that "there was no constitutional justification, in the absence of a search warrant, for extending the search beyond that area."

Under the best of circumstances, this ruling could be expected to run headlong into resistance in many states where search warrants have been oddities. The situation is likely to result in a vast stretching of the concept of "exigent circumstances," as sympathetic judges find that police were forced to make arrests and broad searches without warrants in order to prevent the destruction of evidence. One reason why resistance of this nature is to be expected is the second legal quirk encountered in the hypothetical raid—the fact that in past years search warrants could have been obtained by the police with considerable ease and with scanty proof of probable cause, but that the Warren Court escalated the proof required of police who apply for search warrants.

Appellate Courts are forever reminding themselves in their opinions that an extra presumption of legality should be accorded to any search made with a search warrant, in order to encourage police to use them. Unfortunately, this statement is frequently a prelude to a finding that in *this* case, however, the search warrant cannot stand. Policemen and prosecutors know from painful experience that despite the judiciary's best intentions, the legal mind tends to shift into reverse when it sees a printed page. Judges who would breezily approve evidence seized as an incident to an arrest will comb search warrants for error and will frequently demonstrate their legal acumen by finding it. In the lower courts this has been reinforced by a regrettable disinclination on some judges' part to expose themselves to possible reversal by high tribunals. Because the state cannot appeal in most jurisdictions but the defendant can, some lower-level judges have avoided reversals by resolving most doubts in favor of the accused.

At the Supreme Court level an opposite psychology comes into play, but it has the same result of exposing the police's actions to microscopic scrutiny. Because they are the last word, the Justices are under pressure not to overlook anything. The Court's Fourth Amendment opinions occasionally have a this-may-seem-silly-but flavor, yet the Court has in general hewed to the position that if it didn't insist on the dotting of i's and the crossing of t's, nobody else would and the rule against unreasonable searches and seizures would soon be riddled with loopholes. The result has been to dampen any easygoing toleration of minor fluffs by the police, and to steadily escalate the requisites for a valid search warrant.

The first step came in 1933, when the Court rejected an officer's sworn statement that he had "cause to suspect and does believe" that stolen merchandise was in a specific location. The Court held that the bald recitation of belief, without a "statement of adequate supporting facts," was insufficient to support a search warrant. Next the question came back before the Justices in the form of an affidavit in which the policeman had provided "supporting facts" by swearing that the person to be searched "did receive, conceal, etc., narcotic drugs." The Court rejected this because "it does not indicate any sources for the complaining belief." This message apparently registered, and the Court was next confronted with a search warrant application that explained that the officers "have received reliable information from a credible person and do believe" that narcotics were being kept at a suspect's home. The Court rejected this formula and added two new criteria: (a) a valid search warrant affidavit should have given some "underlying circumstances" that led the informer to conclude that the narcotics were where they were said to be, plus (b) some of the facts that led the officer to believe that the informant was reliable.

In the most recent episode, the Court was confronted in 1969 with an F.B.I. search warrant affidavit which stated that the Bureau had "been informed by a confidential reliable informant" that a St. Louis man was operating a bookie establishment in a residential apartment. This did not give the underlying facts about the informer's source of information and his asserted reliability, but the F.B.I. did add an impressive array of facts to indicate that the apartment was being used for bookmaking. This included the circumstances that the suspect, one William Spinelli, was a veteran bookie, that the apartment was equipped with two telephones with two different numbers, and that the woman who had leased the apartment was never there. The Court found the additional circumstances insufficient to make up for the lack of more "underlying" information about the informer, and the search warrant was declared invalid.

The *Spinelli* decision is a classic illustration of the hazards that the Supreme Court encounters when it sets constitutional policy for the entire nation in a specific case. There is a heavy hint in the concurring opinion by Justice Byron R. White that the Court believed that the F.B.I.'s "confidential reliable informant" might well have been a tap on those two suspicious telephone lines (a belief that was widely shared by officials within the Justice Department itself). So the Court laid down the new constitutional rule that the police's failure to give specific facts about their informer cannot be overcome by other evidence that serves to establish probable cause. This rule was not necessary to prevent wiretap abuses, because the Supreme Court held shortly thereafter that the Government must disclose all of its illegal eavesdropping activities to the defendant before the trial. Yet the *Spinelli* rule stands as another tightening of the screw on search warrants, a process that has tended to counteract the Supreme Court's policy of encouraging the widest possible use of search warrants.

Of the five major Fourth Amendment problem areas dealt with by the Warren Court, the first one suggested by the hypothetical nightclub raid—the matter of how stringent the requirements for search warrants should be and in what situations the police should be required to obtain them—has been the one issue that the Supreme Court has clearly resolved in a way that substantially narrowed the police's authority to search. Its decisions on the other four points have struck a balance since 1961 that is definitely in the favor of the police.

In the second matter raised by the hypothetical raid the District Attorney could have lost his case because he could not afford to disclose the identity of his informer, yet Federal law required the state to do so if it relied upon his tip as the basis for the arrest and search. So long as the Fourth Amendment had been applicable only to Federal officers, the Court had carefully blocked all loopholes that might allow the police to make arrests and searches without probable cause and then prove their cases with the fruits of the searches. However, after the *Mapp* decision it soon became apparent that this policy would play havoc with the informer systems that were the mainstay of urban police departments' law-enforcement efforts. In 1957, the Court had handed down in *Rovario* v. *United States* what virtually amounted to a one-informer, one-conviction rule for Federal cases; if Federal agents had relied upon an informer's information in making a case and the defendant's lawyer demanded the right to cross-examine the informer at the trial, the judge could make the Government produce its stool pigeon or forfeit the case. The Government well knew that once the informer appeared in court that would be the end of his usefulness as an informer, and the informer often believed that it would be the end of him, period. So cases were usually not brought until they could be proved by evidence other than an informer's testimony.

Many state courts, however, had dealt kindlier with the stool pigeon system. They had let the police get by with testifying that they acted on an anonymous informer's tips. The prosecution could refuse to give the tipster's names. This preserved the informer system, but it also gave the police, if they were so inclined, an opportunity to cover up unwarranted actions by claiming that they had acted on information from informers whose identities would have to remain secret. When the Supreme Court encountered the issue in the case of *McCray* v. *Illinois*, it was apparent that if the Court was to preserve the stool pigeon system intact it would have to open up a large loophole in the Fourth Amendment that the *Rovario* decision had appeared to have closed. George McCray had been stopped and searched on a Chicago street by two policemen who did not have a warrant for the arrest or the search. They found heroin

in his pocket and charged him with unlawful possession of narcotics. Under the law the on-the-spot arrest and search would
have been lawful only if the officers had probable cause to believe that McCray was in the act of committing the crime of unlawful possession. When McCray's lawyer asserted that they
could not possibly have known that because he had been at a
friend's apartment until shortly before the arrest, the police replied that they knew McCray had been selling narcotics because
an informer had told them, only moments before the arrest.
They testified at a pretrial hearing on the legality of the search
that the informer was a reliable one who had contributed to
many successful arrests in the past, but they refused to give his
name.

The Supreme Court upheld this procedure by a margin of 5 to
4, ruling that it does not violate the Sixth Amendment's guarantee of the defendant's right to confront his accusers. The
decision was obviously an accommodation to the important informer system, but, technically, at least, there was justification
for Justice Douglas' dissenting statement that it had entrusted
the Fourth Amendment "to the tender mercies of the police."
If the police were willing to lie (and sociologist Paul Chevigny,
after a close study of police methods, concluded that police lies
could be expected "whenever there was a criminal trial"), the
Supreme Court had opened a loophole through the nice safeguards of the Fourth Amendment.

The third issue encountered by the hypothetical District Attorney—the inadmissibility of the bloody shirt—was also resolved to the advantage of the police in the aftermath of the
Mapp case. It concerned the so-called mere evidence rule mentioned by Justice Fortas in his Senate testimony. The police had
been on the short end of that matter ever since the authors of
the Bill of Rights, who were avid letter-writers, diary-keepers
and pamphleteers, stressed "papers" among the items to be safe-
guarded by the Fourth Amendment. It was abhorrent to them
that the Government could seize written documents and thereby
use an individual's most private thoughts against him. From this
concept of the sanctity of private papers, police searching of
private homes came to be constitutionally twice-cursed—the
seizure of individuals' written thoughts without their permission

was held to be a violation of the Fifth Amendment's privilege against self-incrimination, and the searches themselves were subjected to formidable Fourth Amendment limitations.

Thus from the first, searching for documents was unthinkable. In the first Fourth Amendment ruling ever made by the Supreme Court in 1886, the case did not even involve a search. Federal officers had subpoenaed an invoice from two New York businessmen in an effort to prove that they had imported some glass without paying customs duties. In holding that the businessmen's rights had been violated, the Supreme Court ruled that the subpoena had violated the spirit of the Fourth as well as the Fifth Amendment. Because there had actually been no search, the Supreme Court in the opinion by Justice Joseph P. Bradley explained that where a citizen's Fourth Amendment rights are concerned "it is not the breaking of his doors and the rummaging of his drawers that constitutes the essence of the offense; but it is the invasion of his indefeasible right of personal security, personal liberty and private property."

In those days lawyers tended to think of rights more in terms of private property than the personal security and liberty that Justice Bradley also mentioned. So over the years the lower courts focused their attention on the fact that the businessmen's invoice had been protected by the Fourth Amendment because it was their property. The idea came to be accepted that searches were unreasonable—and thus unconstitutional under the Fourth Amendment—unless the police had some right to possess the property that they seized. Thus the ancient common law remedy known as replevin became the keystone of the law of searches and seizures. If an individual had a right to possess an article so that he could replevy it (regain it in a court action) under the ancient rules of possession, then the police could not seize it during a search, even if they had a warrant and the search was otherwise legal. The courts' theory was that if the defendant could regain an item from the police by civil court action prior to his criminal trial, then it was not reasonable to seize it in the first place.

There was no rational explanation why this major personal safeguard of the Bill of Rights should be dominated by antiquated rules of property, but it did serve the purpose of severely restricting the police's power to search and seize. In this sense it was in harmony with the Fourth Amendment's purpose of shielding private premises from police intrusion. Thus this strange mixture of property and criminal law came to be accepted by liberals and traditionalists alike—but for different reasons. When the Supreme Court finally considered the matter in 1921, the liberals and conservatives joined in the unanimous decision mentioned later by Justice Fortas, which made a constitutional requirement of the so-called mere evidence rule.

The question was raised by a man named Felix Gouled, who had been convicted of defrauding the Government on war contracts during World War II. In the course of its investigation the Justice Department obtained valid search warrants and had made two legal searches of Gouled's office. These searches turned up contracts, letters and other papers that supported the Government's charge that Gouled had managed to cheat on his contracts by bribing a Federal official. The Supreme Court held that since these items were "of evidential value only," they could not be seized by the Government, even in a legal search. Although the non-lawyer might assume that the police would have no purpose to conduct a search other than to get evidence, the Supreme Court laid down a rule that any search for "mere evidence" is unconstitutional. Its reasoning was that the police can take only that property which they have a right to possess and which the victim of the search has no right to keep. This meant that the police could take only three types of items: stolen property, because the thief had no right to keep it; contraband such as narcotics and moonshine whiskey, because the law made its possession illegal; and instrumentalities of a crime, such as weapons and burglar tools, because they were a danger to the police and the community. The Court explained its reversal of Gouled's conviction with a straightforward simplicity that makes the nonlegal brain reel. Referring to the seized evidence, it held that "the government could desire its possession only to use it as evidence against the defendant, and to search for and seize it for such purpose was unlawful."

So long as the *Gouled* rule was confined to the relatively few prosecutions tried in Federal courts its contradictions amounted to little more than an irritant. But when it became binding on the states, its potential for mischief multiplied. In the 1967 case of *Warden* v. *Hayden*, the Court had a perfect vehicle to use in abandoning the rule. Bennie Joe Hayden had robbed the Diamond Cab Company in Baltimore at gunpoint one morning. He had dashed home, peeled off his clothes, piled into bed, and jerked the covers up to his chin. Radio cabs that had followed him home summoned the police, who swarmed inside in what was later held to be a legal search in hot pursuit. There they found the prostrate Hayden, plus the guns used in the holdup and the clothing that had been described over the taxi radio net as those worn by the bandit. All of this was used against Hayden at his trial, but after his conviction he filed for a writ of habeas corpus in Federal Court. The Court of Appeals for the Fourth Circuit held that he should be released. Although the guns were admissible as instrumentalities of the crime, the clothing was said to be inadmissible because it had "evidential value only."

When the Hayden case reached the Supreme Court the *Gouled* rule had been in effect for almost a half-century. An air of relief hovered about the opinion of Justice William J. Brennan, Jr., as he finally laid it to rest. "We have recognized that the principal object of the Fourth Amendment is the protection of privacy rather than property, and have increasingly discarded fictional and procedural barriers rested on property concepts," he wrote. The Court found that there was no valid reason to admit the weapons and exclude the clothes that were found in the same search. It discarded the mere evidence rule, but left open the question of whether incriminating writings and other personal items may be seized solely for use as evidence, even in lawful searches.

The fourth hypothetical issue, which resulted in the use of the incriminating fingerprints against the hired killer from Chicago, even if they were obtained by means of unlawful police actions, concerned the question of "standing" to raise the Fourth Amendment as a defense. This was a legal question that would have seemed esoteric to a layman unless he was a defendant and found himself going to jail because he lacked legal standing to object to an unconstitutional raid by the police. It arose out of the theory that the Fourth Amendment was designed to protect people in the enjoyment of their private premises and property, and thus a defendant could not object to the prosecution's use of evidence seized illegally from another's premises, because the defendant's Fourth Amendment rights had not been violated. If, for instance, the police were to force their way illegally into the home of a suspected "fence" of stolen goods, he would be safe from prosecution because the exclusionary rule would prevent the use of any of the stolen items against him in court. But the items could be used to convict the thief who happened to be there disposing of stolen goods, since no property right of his had been violated by the illegal entry into the house.

The irrationality of this was too much for the Warren Court, which rejected the property rationale in a 1960 decision, *Jones* v. *United States*, and ruled that any person who has been a victim of a search and whose own personal privacy has been violated may object to the use of illegally obtained evidence. This meant that the thief who was lucky enough to be present during the raid at the "fence's" house could suppress any evidence against him, but his fellow thieves who were not there still could not object to the use in court of stolen goods bearing their fingerprints. If the exclusionary rule were viewed essentially as a means of deterring governmental lawlessness, this was still an irrational result because it allowed the Government to use the fruits of its own wrongdoing. But in practice the matter rarely came up until the F.B.I. began "bugging" racketeers on a large scale in 1961. Then, the "standing" rules established by the *Jones* decision meant that when Federal agents broke into a racketeer's establishment to plant a hidden microphone and thus violated the Fourth Amendment, the gambler and any person overheard on his premises would have standing to challenge the use of any overheard conversations on Fourth Amendment grounds. But if the men in the "bugged" room discussed other racketeers' affairs, and this led to the oth-

ers' arrests, they would not have standing to object to the use
of the leads that had been obtained by unconstitutional bugging.

In 1969, two Cosa Nostra figures who had been convicted
of extortion—with an assist, they thought, from illegal F.B.I.
"bugging" of other Mafia figures' conversations—asked the
Supreme Court to rule that any person aggrieved by the use of
illegally obtained evidence should be permitted to complain
about it. Here the Court was faced with a conflict between its
desire to rationalize the law of searches and its movement away
from reliance on the exclusionary rule. As a rational matter,
police lawlessness would be deterred more effectively by a rule
that excluded all of the fruits of their illegality. Furthermore,
there seemed to be little reason to allow the owner of the
"bugged" premises, who was not present when an incriminating
conversation took place, to suppress the use of the information,
when no other person except those who were actually overheard
would have standing to object. But the Court by 1969 was
showing signs of concern over the inexorable tendency of exclusionary rules to expand. With Justices Fortas and Douglas
protesting that the Court was twisting reason to avoid further
suppression of evidence, the Court decided in *Alderman* v.
United States that it had already been generous enough. "We are
not convinced," Byron R. White wrote for the Court, "that the
additional benefits of extending the exclusionary rule to other
defendants would justify further encroachment upon the public
interest in prosecuting those accused of crime and having them
acquitted or convicted on the basis of all the evidence which
exposes the truth." Faced with lingering irrationality in the
law and a further spread of the exclusionary rule, the Court
decided, 6 to 2, to stand pat.

The Supreme Court's reservations about the automatic extension of the exclusionary rule to protect all safeguards in the
Bill of Rights had already surfaced, of course, in the stop-and-
frisk decision of the previous June. There was some astonish-
ment, in retrospect, that the Supreme Court had taken so long to
come to grips with these issues, and that the outcome could
have been so vigorously contested. Yet it was 1968, almost two
hundred years after the Fourth Amendment was written and

seven years after it had been made binding on the states, before the Supreme Court ruled on the authority, if any, of the police to detain, question and search suspicious-looking persons without complying with the probable cause requirements of the Fourth Amendment. It was particularly astounding because this is the most typical of all encounters between the police and the public; an officer's suspicions are aroused and he stops a person whom he could not legally arrest and demands that he give an account of himself. Is the citizen required to answer? If the officer does not have probable cause to make an arrest, can the individual refuse to identify himself and just walk away? Can the officer take the person's refusal to cooperate as evidence that he has something to hide? Even if he can't legally arrest a suspicious person, can a policeman frisk him for dangerous weapons?

The complexities of these encounters and the numerous possible variations that they could take struck a sobering note, for until that time the Court had always managed to lay down objective rules for the enforcement of all constitutional rights. If street encounters were so unpredictable that it would be impossible to declare in advance what the Fourth Amendment allowed, then the Court would have no choice but to fall back on broad principles of reasonableness and to trust to local police officials and judges to see that they were observed. This was a particularly bitter dose to swallow, because it had been suspicion of the good faith of local police and judges that had given the due process revolution its momentum in the first instance. Moreover, local officials' bad faith had tended to be taken out on Negroes, who were the most frequent victims of the stop-and-frisk.

The ironies of the situation could not have been lost upon the Supreme Court, where Thurgood Marshall, the first Negro member, knew the problem first-hand. He occasionally told friends of having been stopped and questioned twice by policemen in his younger days. The first time was in Harlem; Marshall had just been walking along—not, he thought, acting suspiciously. So when he was asked to identify himself he told the policeman to mind his own business. There was a tense moment as the policeman told Marshall that he could run him in, and Marshall said yes and he could take the officer's badge number. Then Marshall walked away and that was that. Several years later, Marshall, then Chief Counsel for the National Association for the Advancement of Colored People, was stopped again by a policeman, this time in the affluent surroundings of downtown Manhattan. He readily gave his name to the officer and went his way. In later years he used to wonder why he acted differently under the two circumstances, but he never suggested that he might have been wrong that day in Harlem when he walked away from the law.

Yet Marshall joined with the Court when it ruled, with only Justice Douglas dissenting, that the police do have the authority to stop and question suspicious-looking persons and to frisk the dangerous-looking ones for weapons. The Court adopted an approach that was almost the opposite of *Miranda*. Instead of adopting broad, legislative standards designed to cover all situations, it dealt only with the narrow circumstance in which a policeman, having stopped a suspicious person for questioning, reasonably feared for his own safety. In that situation the officer could pat down the suspect's clothing for weapons, and if weapons were found, they could be used in court. The touchstone was the reasonableness of the policeman's apprehension in view of the circumstances, without regard to probable cause.

Barring such a result, a pattern seems to have been set which leads toward stricter enforcement of rigid search warrant standards where the privacy of premises is concerned, but a reluctance to invoke the exclusionary rule to deal with fluid, on-the-street law enforcement. If the hypothetical 1961 nightclub search had occurred at the end of the Warren era in 1969, the outcome would have been revealingly different. The search would have been made with a search warrant, based on an officer's sworn statement as to the informer's disclosures about the crime and the reasons why the informer was felt to be reliable. The informer's anonymity would have been protected. All of the evidence would have been admissible—the bloody shirt, the victim's valuables and the weapons obtained by stop-and-frisk—and all of the defendants presumably would have been convicted. Thus the Warren Court, chided for excessive idealism and belabored for coddling criminals, had embarked on an idealistic venture to reform the law of searches and had arrived at a position that disarmed senators indignant over courts and crime. The Supreme Court had purged the major anachronisms from the Fourth Amendment and had substituted rules that admit more evidence—yet require the police to cut squarer corners—than before.

X

Identification: Lawyers
and Lineups

*What is the worth of identification testimony
even when uncontradicted? The identification of
strangers is inherently untrustworthy.*

FELIX FRANKFURTER

Warren E. Burger, a judge who was known for views that
were strong and occasionally crochety, sat down one day in
the winter of 1965, took his pen in hand, and embellished his
reputation for both. His Midwestern-Presbyterian-Republican
nature had rebelled at much that had been done by the liberal
Court of Appeals for the District of Columbia during the
decade in which he had sat as one of its members. But two
matters rankled above all. One was the expansive view of criminal suspects' rights taken by that Court's liberal majority, whose
hospitality toward the defense had inspired the Washington Bar

to earn a reputation as perhaps the most ingenious in the nation at dreaming up—and frequently winning—exotic legal arguments on behalf of accused persons. The second was what he saw as growing excesses in the adversary system of justice that encouraged attorneys to engage in overly aggressive or even rude conduct or to press legal points that he believed could play no constructive part in a rational system of justice.

As he turned his attention to the case of Anthony Williams, Judge Burger saw the worst of both failings. By conventional standards, Williams' arrest and conviction demonstrated police ingenuity rather than police misconduct. The two bandits who had robbed a real estate rental office had fled, but the police had found a loan payment book near their escape route. They traced it to a woman who said she had given it to her grandson, Anthony Williams. He was arrested and placed in a lineup, where three employees of the rental office identified him as one of the robbers. Williams took the stand and swore it was a case of mistaken identity, that he did not even know the person who was being tried with him as the other bandit. He was not believed, and received a four- to twelve-year prison sentence.

Because Williams was without funds, an attorney was appointed to argue his appeal without fee, a chore that is rotated in the District of Columbia among all the members of the Bar. Thus, Bruce E. Clubb, an attorney who specialized in the law of trade and finance, was appointed to brief and argue *Williams* v. *United States* before the Court of Appeals.

The old saw that legal advice is worth what you pay for it often proves true when attorneys are appointed to handle cases for accused criminals without fee. Some of the most disgraceful miscarriages of justice in legal folklore have been attributable to the inept services rendered by attorneys in these circumstances. Lately, though, this shortcoming of the Bar seems to have been going out of style, as lawyers have become more sensitive to the problems of criminal justice, and also as experienced defendants have learned how to keep their court-appointed counsel on their toes. By 1965, it was not unusual for a convicted person in the District of Columbia to charge in post-conviction habeas corpus actions that he had been denied his constitutional right to the effective assistance of counsel because his court-appointed lawyer was inept. This did the attorney's reputation no good, so court-appointed counsel were disposed to protect their flanks by dutifully raising every conceivable defense for their penurious criminal clients.

Williams' case was different. Clubb, a sober, conscientious lawyer, who was soon to be named to the United States Tariff Commission by President Lyndon Johnson, marshaled the talents of his ten-man corporate law firm to study his new client's case. After long self-education in criminal law and a heated dispute within the firm over the possible detrimental public consequences if he won his point, Clubb filed his appeal: He contended that Williams' Sixth Amendment right to the assistance of counsel had been violated when he was identified in a lineup at which he was not represented by a lawyer. Even for the D.C. Circuit this was a bit rich; the three-judge panel that considered the case voted unanimously to dismiss the appeal in a two-paragraph, unsigned opinion. But as a member of the panel, Judge Burger could not let this double-barreled example of two of his pet peeves pass. He added a concurring opinion:

> Such "Disneyland" contentions as that absence of counsel at the police line-up voids a conviction are becoming commonplace. Some arise from the hard experience of court appointed lawyers who, having served diligently without compensation, later find themselves subjected to vicious and unwarranted attacks by their ex-clients for failing to raise some bizarre point conceived by the "legal experts" in prison. Having found that the indigent client's sense of gratitude is readily dulled by incarceration, some court appointed counsel find it expedient to protect themselves by raising every point, however absurd, which indigent appellants suggest.

Williams went to prison. Two years later the Supreme Court handed down a landmark case entitled *United States* v. *Wade*. The ruling: that suspects *are* entitled to counsel at lineups.

Even for an era of revolution in criminal due process, this transformation of a legal claim in two years from a "Disneyland" contention in the view of a promising appellate judge to a constitutional ruling by the Supreme Court was a remarkable event. How it came to be attests to the pressing need for reform of the methods of identifying suspects, the momentum of the due process revolution, and the lockstep thinking that permeated some of the decisions of the Warren Court.

From a standing start on June 12, 1967, the Supreme Court fashioned a body of constitutional law in *United States v. Wade* and two companion eyewitness cases, *Gilbert v. California* and *Stovall v. Denno*, that brought the United States in one day from the status of a country with almost no national law on the subject of eyewitness identification, to the position of the nation with the perhaps most rigid standards in the world for the eyewitness identification of suspects. It is hands-down the oddest performance of the due process revolution, riddled with inconsistencies and easily debunked. But in some respects it is the Supreme Court's most successful excursion into the criminal law. For the Justices wisely gave the decisions no retroactive effect, thereby avoiding the unnecessary miscarriages of justice that followed *Miranda v. Arizona*. The new rules have cost almost nothing in terms of law-enforcement efficiency, yet they could eventually generate a long-overdue review of the faulty methods of identification that are in common use in the United States. This could become one of the most successful examples of the Supreme Court as Teacher, for it could encourage the law-enforcement establishment and the legal profession to reduce avoidable errors that contribute to that most tragic of all malfunctions of justice—the conviction of innocent men.

The Supreme Court was first moved to reform criminal justice because the prevailing procedures were unjust, not because they were unreliable. The brutal early confessions cases did sometimes raise suspicions that innocent men were being convicted, but the Court was concerned more with the police-state methods that these cases exposed than the occasional false convictions that must have resulted. When the Justices finally began to crack down on state law-enforcement procedures in *Mapp v. Ohio*, the purpose was to stop police searches without probable cause—an abuse that rarely produced false evidence of guilt.

When it finally turned to the question of eyewitness identification of suspects, the Supreme Court dealt with an area of police investigation that had rarely stirred criticism in this country, but which was probably responsible for more miscarriages of justice than any other single aspect of criminal law. Many people are completely nondescript in appearance. Others have poor eyesight, or dismal powers of observation. Yet even when the latter identify the former in a criminal trial, there is a special impact that sways jurors beyond almost anything else. Of necessity, most of what goes on in a trial is word-painting—re-creations of past events. So when a witness points at a defendant and identifies him as a criminal before the jury's very eyes— and especially when that witness recalls having picked the same suspect out of a lineup shortly after the crime—an impression is made that is difficult to overcome.

In the Federal Bureau of Investigation's section of the Justice Department building in Washington is a large poster bearing photographs of two men in prison attire who appear to be twins. They are Negroes, and their chocolate skin, dark eyes, thin lips and straight noses are so similar that visitors are constantly drawn to the poster, searching for a clue to show that the pictures are really two shots of the same man. The poster explains that the top man is Will West, who was committed to Leavenworth Penitentiary in 1903 and was found to be a virtual carbon copy of William West, who was already there. So far as anyone could discover, they were not related. At that time American law enforcement relied heavily upon the technique of identification developed by the French anthropologist, Alphonse Bertillon, who taught that each individual could be identified by concise measurements of the head, body and limbs. Will and William West proved to be almost identical in every measurement. When a relatively new technique was tried— fingerprinting—their prints proved to be decidedly different. The Bertillon system was soon abandoned.

Cases of exact look-alikes are rare, but it is not unusual for two people to resemble each other so closely that one can easily be mistaken for the other. Yet there have been many instances of mistaken identification when the physical resemblance between the real culprit and the wrongly identified suspect was not even close. The most famous was that of Adolf Beck, who was twice convicted of defrauding gullible ladies in London at the turn of the last century. A score of irate fraud victims positively identified him as the confidence man who had identified himself as a man of noble birth, had borrowed money and jewelry from them, and had disappeared. When it was later proved conclusively that another man—who did not even closely resemble Beck—had swindled the ladies, the public indignation was such that Parliament created the Court of Criminal Appeal, with jurisdiction to review the facts of criminal cases. The treacherous nature of eyewitness identification was documented several decades ago by a Yale law professor, Edwin M. Borchard, in a book entitled, *Convicting the Innocent*. Of the sixty-five cases he found of persons who had been wrongfully convicted of crimes, twenty-nine were victims of mistaken identifications. In one case, seventeen witnesses identified a defendant as a forger, although he bore no resemblance at all to the man who was later found to have been the guilty person.

Despite the hazards of eyewitness identification, juries seem inevitably impressed when a defendent is pointed out, even if the circumstances of the identification verge on the incredible. A Florida jury once meted out a death sentence for rape based almost exclusively on the victim's testimony that the suspect fired a pistol in her darkened bedroom and that she saw his features in the flash of the gun. In Memphis, Tennessee, after a number of women were raped by a masked figure who came to be known in the press as "The Foul-Smelling Rapist," a burglary suspect named Clayton Dawson became the prime suspect because of his extraordinary body odor. He was convicted and sentenced to death after ten women identified him as the masked, odoriferous intruder. Such incredible identifications are not reserved only for obscure prosecutions. In the Sacco and Vanzetti trial, the prosecutor introduced some incredible identification testimony, including a woman's point-by-point physical description of one of the criminals—whom she identified as Sacco—based upon a glimpse of the occupants of a passing car. In the trial of Bruno Hauptmann for the murder of the Lindbergh baby, witnesses identified Hauptmann as the man they had seen years before—in various activities that later proved criminal, but could not then have aroused anyone's suspicion.

Human psychology being what it is, it is not as surprising that eyewitness identification is so subject to error as it is astounding that its shortcomings have caused so little concern about police methods of obtaining identifications. Often these procedures magnify the opportunities for error, rather than narrowing them. Yet, until the Supreme Court decided *United States* v. *Wade*, very little effort had been made in this country to devise identification procedures designed to protect innocent people from being identified as criminals. In that sense alone, the *Wade* case stands out in the Supreme Court's experience. Before the Court came to grips with the confessions problem in *Escobedo* and *Miranda*, it had heard and decided thirty-six confessions cases under the "totality of the circumstances" standard. Any observant attorney could have predicted that drastic developments in the law of interrogation were likely. *Mapp* v. *Ohio* came almost a half-century after the Supreme Court first suppressed illegally seized evidence in a Federal prosecution, and the cases leading up to *Mapp* made it clear that the Supreme Court would soon apply the same rule to state trials. But *United States* v. *Wade* and the two appeals that were decided with it, *Gilbert* v. *California* and *Stovall* v. *Denno*, were the first appeals that turned on witness identification ever to be decided by the Supreme Court, and the Court's decision caught the bulk of the legal community completely by surprise.

Americans being the enthusiastic reformers that they are, it is curious that there had been no agitation for reform in identification procedures in the United States. Many people are susceptible to suggestion as to identifications, and once having singled out a person as a criminal, they are unlikely to admit, when the state has gone to the trouble of bringing the identified suspect to trial, that they might have been wrong. Yet the usual technique used by the police to present a suspect for identification has traditionally been the "show-up," in which the police simply confront a witness with a suspect and ask if he is the offender. Sometimes, the suspect is in handcuffs, or behind bars, and almost always the circumstances strongly suggest that he is the guilty party. Caryl Chessman was once thrust before a robbery victim, who was told by a policeman: "Well, here's your bandit. Here's the man that held you up." This witness refused to make an identification, but Chessman was identified by another witness, a young girl who had been a victim of a brutal sexual attack. He was placed in handcuffs on the sidewalk in front of her house, where the girl looked at him at a distance of about 50 feet through eyes that were swollen almost shut, and identified him as her assailant. In another case, the police brought a suspect before an assault victim, who positively identified him as his assailant. Because the suspect did not exactly match the description initially given by the victim, the police asked how he could be positive. His reply: "You certainly would not have brought him here if he were not the right man."

Incidents such as these have led the courts of England, Canada, Australia and other countries with legal systems similar to the United States' to reject the show-up as a permissible method of obtaining identifications. If there is not solid evidence of guilt other than a show-up identification, convictions in these countries will not be upheld. Under this pressure from the courts, the British police developed the lineup. In a lineup, the suspect and others stand in a row, and the witnesses must pick the suspect out of the group. If all those in the line reasonably resemble the suspect, and if the witnesses view the lineup individually and nothing is done to single out the suspect, this offers an opportunity for an identification that is about as reliable as human fallibility will allow.

In the United States, at least until the *Wade* decision, there was no movement toward disapproval of the show-up, and lineups remained rare. Even when they were used, there were no standards for sifting out suggestive features. This meant that suspects could face the double hazard of being unfairly identified, yet in a procedure that would seem clean to a jury. Sometimes shortcomings in lineups are obvious—such as one instance, in which a suspect, an Oriental, was picked out of a lineup, composed otherwise of Caucasians; another where a black-haired suspect was lined up with a group of fair-haired men; others that grouped tall suspects with short nonsuspects; and one that placed a teen-age suspect in a line with five other men, all of whom were forty or over. Some lineup gimmicks can be much more subtle. In lineups in which all the participants but the suspects were detectives, the officers have been known to cut their eyes toward the suspect, to guide the witnesses' attention to the right man. Sometimes the police tip

the witnesses off in advance by showing a picture of the suspect, or describing his clothing, or telling where he will stand.
One ploy is so well-known that it has been given a name in
police jargon: the "Oklahoma Show-up." This involves arrang-
ing to have the witnesses "accidentally" see the suspect in police
custody before the lineup.

Despite the inherent hazards of identifications and the tricks
of the police trade that have made the situation worse, the
problem had been ignored in American law prior to the *Wade*
decision. The general rule was that all identifications were admissible in court, subject to the defense lawyer's right to try to
point out any flaws by cross-examining the witnesses. If any
were exposed, this would be taken into consideration by the
jury in assessing the reliability of the identification, but no exclusionary rule was applied to defective identification procedures.

This placed little pressure on police departments to improve
their identification procedures, and few did. When the Supreme
Court belatedly turned its attention to the matter in the *Wade-
Gilbert-Stovall* rulings, it was almost as an afterthought of the
due process revolution. Thus, the philosophy behind the earlier
criminal decisions heavily influenced the Supreme Court's approach to identification, and produced a result that was predictable but odd.

By the time the *Wade* case reached the Supreme Court, the
American judiciary had developed the habit of dealing with
various forms of injustice by requiring the presence of a lawyer,
much as physicians used to treat assorted physical ills by pre-
scribing an enema. *Gideon* v. *Wainwright* was a natural, sensi-
ble manifestation of this. The absence of a defense lawyer put
a poor man at a critical disadvantage in court; the obvious
remedy was to require lawyers for the poor. This led to the
establishment of a right to counsel at pretrial stages, then to post-
conviction appeals, and eventually to probation revocation
hearings. When the confessions problem failed to respond to the
fairness approach, the Supreme Court fell back on the right to
counsel again. By finding interrogation a "critical stage" of a
criminal prosecution, it opened the interrogation rooms to defense lawyers in order to bolster the suspects' defenses against
self-incrimination. Thus it was not surprising that the Court was

receptive to the suggestion that it should deal with the eyewitness problem by requiring the presence of counsel at lineups.

This approach occurred to Weldon Holcomb, a Tyler, Texas, lawyer, after he was appointed in the spring of 1965 to defend an accused bank robber named Billy Joe Wade. Six months earlier a man with a small strip of tape on each side of his face had entered a bank in Eustace, Texas, brandishing a pistol and demanding money. He took it in a pillow case from the cashier and a bank officer (the only two people there) and made his getaway in a waiting car. After Wade was accused in an indictment of having been the gunman and after Holcomb had been appointed to defend him, an F.B.I. agent took Wade from his cell and placed him in a lineup with five or six other prisoners. All of the men wore strips of tape on their faces and all were required to repeat the bandit's words: "Put the money in the bag." The cashier and bank official picked Wade out as the bandit. Attorney Holcomb didn't learn about this crucial turn in his case until later.

The cross-examination at the trial made it embarrassingly likely that Wade had been a victim of an "Oklahoma Show-up." Both bank employees admitted that a door had been left open as they waited in the lineup room, and that they saw Wade alone with the F.B.I. agents before the other prisoners appeared. Holcomb moved to strike their testimony, raising objections that had been heard in very few courts before: that Wade's Fifth Amendment self-incrimination privilege had been violated when he was required to speak the bandit's words, and that his Sixth Amendment right to counsel was violated because he did not have the assistance of counsel at the lineup. These were quickly brushed aside by the trial judge and Wade was convicted.

The appeal went to the Court of Appeals for the Fifth Circuit, a court that had devoted most of its attention in the previous decade to desegregation cases brought by the Negroes of the Deep South. It was a court peculiarly attuned to the legal pleas of the underdog, and it decided that Billy Joe Wade's lawyer was right. Billy Joe's lawyer should have been present at the lineup, the Fifth Circuit ruled—and since he wasn't even told it would be held, not only the lineup identification must be excluded from evidence, but also the courtroom identification of Billy Joe by the bank employees who had familiarized themselves with his face at the tainted lineup.

The Government appealed to the Supreme Court, where the case was heard with the appeals of a convicted bank robber-murderer named Jesse James Gilbert, and a man convicted of murder, Theodore Stovall. Gilbert had been identified at a lineup at which more than 100 witnesses of various armed robberies were assembled. This resulted in a wholesale selection of Gilbert as the gunman in a series of crimes, with each identification being made in full view of the other witnesses. Stovall had been brought alone in handcuffs to a hospital to be identified at the bedside of a murder victim's wife. She was in critical condition because of her own wounds, but later survived to identify him again at the trial as the man who had broken into their home and had attacked her husband and her with a knife. Lower courts had held that neither man's rights had been violated by the use of the identification testimony against them.

With the identification issue finally before the Supreme Court in those three appeals, there were two approaches that the Justices could have taken to deal with the problem. One possibility was the "fairness" approach that had been used to deal with confessions prior to *Miranda* v. *Arizona.* The Court could have undertaken a case-by-case analysis of various identification situations (as the English courts had done a half-century before), throwing out convictions where the identification methods used seemed unfair or unreliable, and thereby building a body of precedents to guide the police in handling suspect identifications. The Justices' freshest memories of this technique were negative, for it had been only one year since the Court had given up on this approach in *Miranda.* This suggested a second approach; that the Court might just as well leapfrog the "fairness" stage and extend the right of counsel to lineups, as Billy Joe Wade's lawyer had urged.

After almost a decade of stirring the pot in criminal law, the Warren Court was equal to the situation. It did both. In the *Wade* and *Gilbert* cases it held that after suspects have been indicted and have obtained counsel, they cannot be placed in a lineup for identification without notice and opportunity for their counsel to be present. If the rule is broken, no witness may testify that he identified the suspect in the lineup. The witness also cannot point out the suspect in the courtroom, unless the state can show by clear and convincing evidence that the in-court identification has been made with no reliance on the view of the suspect at the unconstitutional lineup. In the *Stovall* opinion the Court held that the *Wade* decision would not be applied retroactively to affect any identification made prior to June 12, 1967, the day when the triumvirate was announced. However, the *Stovall* decision added that no identification may be used in evidence if the "totality of the circumstances" shows that the situation was "so unnecessarily suggestive and conducive to irreparable mistaken identification that the suspect was denied due process of law." Since in the *Stovall* case the lone eyewitness was thought to be at death's door, the Court concluded that the hospital show-up was not unreasonable, and his petition for habeas corpus was denied.

In one day's decisions on identification the Supreme Court had spanned the same legal ground that had been covered in three decades of decision-making on confessions. It was an impressive display of the momentum of the due process revolution, but it did raise questions as to whether constructive reform could penetrate much farther into the complex world of criminal justice by the process of extending the reach of the Bill of Rights.

There was a compelling logical argument for extending the right of counsel to lineups. In *Massiah* v. *United States*, *Escobedo* v. *Illinois* and *Miranda* v. *Arizona* the Supreme Court had extended the right of counsel to pretrial interrogation, on the ground that this was a "critical stage" of the prosecution, where the defendant's rights could be affected as vitally as at any stage of the actual trial. In view of the many miscarriages of justice that have resulted from faulty identifications, if there was ever another stage that was also "critical," the lineup was it. (Borchard had found that twenty-nine out of sixty-five wrongly convicted innocent people were victims of mistaken identity, but false confessions figured in only six of the cases.) The logic was so compelling that Justice Tom C. Clark found himself joining the five Justices with whom he had differed so bitterly in *Miranda*, to make the vote 6 to 3 in favor of lawyers at line-ups. He filed a one-paragraph concurring statement that revealed his own amazement at his position: "I cannot, for the life of me, see why a lineup is not a critical stage of the prosecution. Identification of the suspect—a prerequisite to establishment of guilt—occurs at this stage, and with *Miranda* v. *Arizona* on the books, the requirement of the presence of counsel arises, unless waived by the suspect. I dissented in *Miranda* but I am bound by it now, as we all are."

As compelling as Justice Clark found the logic behind the extension of the *Miranda* principle to lineups, Justice William J. Brennan, Jr.'s, majority opinion revealed a fundamental difference: the appearance of a defense lawyer at an interrogation puts an immediate end to all questioning, while a lawyer at a lineup has almost nothing to do. The reason is that a suspect has a constitutional right under the Fifth Amendment to remain silent, a right that his lawyer can invoke by telling the suspect to stand mute. But a suspect has no constitutional right not to appear in a lineup. Only the previous year, in the critical *Schmerber* v. *California* decision, the Supreme Court had drawn the distinction between the power of the law to force a suspect to make his person available as evidence against himself, and the Fifth Amendment privilege against "testimonial" self-incrimination. In the *Schmerber* case the Court held that a suspect could be required to let the state take a sample of his blood to determine its alcohol content, because that did not require him to give oral testimony against himself. Justice Brennan's opinion in *Schmerber* made it clear that this limitation of the self-incrimination privilege to "testimonial" or "communicative" self-incrimination would be crucial to law enforcement. The privilege against compulsory self-incrimination, he declared, "offers no protection against compulsion to submit to fingerprinting, photography, or measurements, to write or speak for identification, to appear in court, to stand, to assume a stance, to walk, or to make a particular gesture." This meant that Billy Joe Wade had no valid constitutional objection to being required to wear the strips of tape and to repeat the bandit's words. The four Justices who dissented from the *Schmerber* decision—Warren, Black, Douglas and

Fortas—also dissented from that part of Brennan's opinion that held that Wade could constitutionally be required to speak the gunman's words (Black even insisted that he could not be required to stand in a lineup), but all four agreed with Brennan and Clark that he did have a right to a lawyer.

The result was a curious but perhaps predictable outgrowth of the *Gideon* syndrome—a decision upholding the right of a suspect to have a lawyer, even when there is no lawyer's work to be done. Brennan's opinion was understandably vague on this point. It stated hopefully that "the presence of counsel itself can often avert prejudice and assure a meaningful confrontation at trial." Otherwise, the Court seemed to expect little more of the lawyer than a watchful eye to spot cute police tactics— which could put the attorney in the position (frowned upon by the legal profession's Canons of Ethics) of testifying at the trial for his own client. The result was less than an unblemished triumph for suspects' rights. The police could still secretly take witnesses aside prior to lineups and nudge them toward the desired identification. Defense lawyers were powerless to change the lineup if they didn't like some of its features. Finally, if the lawyer later testified as to some irregularity, the jury might discount his testimony as excessive advocacy.

At the same time, the *Wade* decision lacked that element of intrusion of rigid constitutional rules into in-the-field police work that had made the interrogation and search rulings so unpopular with the police. Barring a future expansion of the *Wade* doctrine by the Supreme Court, it operates in practice much as did the *Gideon* decision's requirement of counsel at trials. Both applied to controlled law-enforcement rituals that could be planned in advance to include the participation of counsel, with little or no drag on law enforcement. So although Brennan spoke of creating an exclusionary rule to suppress lineup identifications made outside the presence of counsel, there has been no more reason for the police to omit counsel at lineups than there was to deny lawyers at trials, once the Supreme Court laid down the rule. The decision permits lineup suspects to waive their right to counsel, and some do; but lawyers at lineups are of little concern to the police, and waivers have not become routine, as they have in interrogation. To prevent defense lawyers from frustrating any valid identification by being perpetually unavailable to attend lineups, the Supreme Court said that "substitute counsel" could act for absent attorneys. This has become routine in some cities. Public defenders supervise most lineups, take notes, and pass them along to private counsel.

If this were the extent of the *Wade-Gilbert-Stovall* doctrine, it would stand as a constructive but innocuous development in criminal justice. The presence of lawyers at station-house lineups, as required by the *Wade* and *Gilbert* decisions, would make lineups fairer but no less efficient than before. The police could still carry out certain informal identification proceedings outside the presence of defense counsel when necessary (the hospital identification of Theodore Stovall is an example), but under the *Stovall* decision the identification testimony would be ruled out as a violation of due process only if the circumstances of any given case were so suggestive that the witnesses seemed likely to have identified the wrong man. But while each alternative was innocuous by itself, together they confronted the police with a familiar constitutional problem: how to know, in the fluid and unpredictable world of criminal investigation, when the absolute rule comes into play.

Justice Brennan wrote a notably elastic opinion in the *Wade* case, using expansive terms that seemed to anticipate further extensions of the right to counsel beyond lineups to other identification situations. The opinion spoke of the principle that "the accused is guaranteed that he need not stand alone against the State at any stage of the prosecution, formal or informal, in court or out, where counsel's absence might derogate the accused's right to a fair trial." Tracing this right all the way back to the first right-of-counsel ruling in the Scottsboro Boys' case, Justice Brennan concluded that "In sum, the principle of *Powell* v. *Alabama* and succeeding cases requires that we scrutinize *any* pretrial confrontation of the accused to determine whether the presence of counsel is necessary to preserve the defendant's basic right to a fair trial as affected by his right meaningfully to cross-examine the witnesses against him and to have effective assistance of counsel at the trial itself." The Court seemed to be serving notice that it would not tolerate a repeat of its search-and-seizure experience, where the Justices had made search warrants difficult to obtain and the police simply searched without them, as "incidents" to arrests. Brennan was keeping the Court's opinions open to extend the right of counsel further if the police attempted to avoid the *Wade* ruling by having most identifications take place by means of photographs or informal show-ups, rather than at lineups.

Experiences in the lower courts since then have shown, however, that when the right to counsel is extended beyond the controlled lineup stage into the informal world of in-the-field police investigation, trouble develops. In the case of searches and interrogation, the Supreme Court itself extended absolute constitutional rules to cover the cop on the beat, so the Justices have had to struggle with the resulting strains and complications. But so far the Supreme Court has not specifically extended the right to counsel at identifications beyond formal lineups, and the unhappy experiences of those judges who have done so may well persuade the Justices that lawyers at lineups are enough.

The hazards of extending *Wade* into the streets surface most convincingly in the typical situation where, late at night and far from the pat surroundings of a lineup room, a witness sees an offender commit a crime and run away. The police are notified, and soon they pick up someone who answers the criminal's description. He protests innocence, so they take him to the scene, where the witness either confirms that they have the right man or tells them that they have made a mistake. Unquestionably, this is a critical confrontation for the suspect, and it is loaded with suggestive elements that could lead to a false identification. But if a lawyer must be summoned and a full scale lineup held before the suspect can be showed to the witness, complications arise. The innocent suspect can't be quickly cleared and permitted to go on his way. The witness doesn't see the suspect with a fresh memory of the event. The grumpy presence of attorneys roused from their sleep at late hours still doesn't add measurably to the suspect's rights.

Shortly after the *Wade* decision was announced, these complications were brought to the attention of candidate Richard Nixon in the form of *United States* v. *Beasley*, the first known case in which the *Wade* principle was relied upon to rule out an on-the-street identification. He branded this "an almost ridiculous, if logical" extension of *United States* v. *Wade,* and absorbed it into his campaign arsenal. "In the Beasley case," Nixon explained, "police observed three men beating and robbing an elderly man on the streets of Washington, D.C. When they approached, the assailants fled leaving their victim behind. Police gave chase and apprehended one man, and returned with him to the scene to aid the victim and radio for help. There was thus an inevitable confrontation between the suspect and the victim, and the former was positively identified by the latter as one of his assailants. The identification made on the spot was ruled as inadmissible evidence because the alleged assailant did not have an attorney present when he confronted the victim on the street, immediately following the crime."

Before long the criminal justice system in the District of Columbia was jolted again by a repeat of this situation. A few minutes after the midnight hold-up of a sandwich shop in March of 1968, the police stopped an automobile that matched the description of the getaway car. Inside they found Darnell R. Kinnard, Jr., in possession of a large sum of money and a petty cash slip from the shop that had just been robbed. The police hustled Kinnard back to the shop, where two of the waitresses identified him as the bandit. When Kinnard's attorney objected to their testimony, an anguished trial judge concluded "most reluctantly" that the identification "must be attempted only after the defendant has counsel and a lineup can be arranged."

By then identification procedures in the District of Columbia were in total confusion and it fell to the liberal Court of Appeals there, and specifically to its guiding spirit, Chief Judge David L. Bazelon, to announce the first Federal appellate decision on the subject. This time, it was Judge Bazelon who ruled "with some hesitation." For he was a libertarian whose legal opinions through the years had reflected a distrust of police power, yet he found no reason to disapprove the way it was used to obtain the eyewitness testimony of one George McCann.

McCann had been awakened at dawn on a June night in 1967 by the blaring of a radio and the crashing of glass. He looked across the street at a shoe shine shop, where a portable radio sat on the sidewalk in front of the open door, pumping out rock music as the tinkling of more glass inside attested to the larcenous activities of the radio's owner. Soon a man emerged, stepped into the light where McCann could see his face, retrieved his radio and blared off down the street. McCann dialed the police, told what he had seen and waited.

Soon they arrived with Bobby Russell in tow. He seemed a likely suspect, as he had run when the police approached, had been caught carrying coins and cigarettes apparently rifled from a vending machine, and, in mid-summer, had been wearing gloves. McCann identified him as the thief, and Russell was subsequently convicted of housebreaking and petty larceny.

Prison bars were soon to attest to the "critical" nature of the early morning confrontation between McCann and Russell, yet Judge Bazelon could not bring himself to say that a lawyer should have been there. To avoid saying so, he had to fall back on a technical distinction that had been the refuge of the foot-dragging conservatives who refused to extend the *Massiah* and *Escobedo* decisions to require counsel at station-house interrogation, until *Miranda* v. *Arizona* spelled it out for them. Bazelon noted that he was not necessarily bound by the *Wade* and *Gilbert* rulings, since both lineups involved prisoners who had been indicted and had lawyers. His case, he noted, involved "an immediate on-the-scene confrontation at five o'clock in the morning when there would necessarily be a long delay in summoning appellant's counsel, or a substitute counsel, to observe a formal lineup. Such delay may not only cause the detention of an innocent suspect, it may also diminish the reliability of any identification obtained, thus defeating a principal purpose of the counsel requirement." So far, no other appellate court has reached contrary conclusion, so that unless the Supreme Court insists on the presence of counsel at in-the-field show-ups—a move its new Chief Justice is unlikely to encourage—the *Wade* ruling is likely to remain a greater annoyance to the legal profession than to the police.

Defense lawyers were also quick to contend that a "critical stage" of a case occurred when police showed photographs of defendants to witnesses for identification. There was little doubt that these occasions are crucial to many prosecutions and that the technique places suggestive pressures on witnesses to make identifications. Any seasoned defense lawyer can tell horror stories of innocent individuals with bad records who have been singled out for prosecution because someone picked their photos out of a pile at the police station. The frequency of this rarely becomes a matter of public record, because the instances are buried, one-by-one, either in the files of those questioned and released, or those found guilty and sent away. One discussion of it was spread on the record of the Senate Judiciary Committee in 1969 when the Senate was considering if accused persons who were thought likely to commit crimes should be held in preventive detention instead of being freed on bail. Bruce Beaudin, director of the District of Columbia bail agency and a former defense attorney, was asked if it would make sense to lock up, pending trial, people with bad records who had been arrested again. "I can think of three cases," he replied, "where I represented men charged with armed robberies, who were picked up because they were identified out of a number of photos that the police had on file, and, of course, they don't have your photo on file or mine. They have got the photos of prior violators. These men were picked out by the photo, and in two out of three of the cases the alibi was so good that the U.S. Attorney's office dismissed the charge. In the third case, we went to trial and it resulted in a 'not guilty' verdict within 15 minutes." But here again, it was unclear what a defense lawyer could do to aid his client while the witnesses shuffled through mug shots, and there was something faintly ludicrous in the contention that a lawyer should be present.

When the photograph question first reached the Supreme Court, in a 1968 case known as *Simmons* v. *United States*, the appellant's counsel did not even claim that he should have been present when the witnesses examined the photographs although that claim had been made in lower courts. Simmons contended that it was inherently unfair to show witnesses of a bank robbery his picture and ask if he were the bandit. In Simmons' case, they all agreed that he was the man, and he was promptly arrested and later convicted. The Supreme Court affirmed his conviction without dissent, brushing the photograph claim aside with the observation that "this procedure has been used widely and effectively in criminal law enforcement." The only crumb for the defense was the Court's statement that if the defendant's lawyer could prove by cross-examination that the manner of showing the photos was so suggestive that the witnesses' identifications were probably mistaken, then the judge should suppress the witnesses' testimony. Since no jury would be impressed with identifications under these circumstances anyway, this was a modest milestone in criminal law.

Of the four exclusionary rules fashioned by the Supreme Court to police the police—the first one governing searches, the one pegged to illegal arrests, the interrogation rules, and finally the lineup cases—the only one that the courts have not patched up to meet shifting police tactics is the lineup cases. A major reason for this seems to be the growing realization that the peculiar nature of identification testimony makes it almost impossible to suppress anyway.

If an object is seized by police in an illegal search, that object can be excluded from evidence. If a confession is obtained by coercion, the jury will never hear that the defendant confessed. But if a witness has refreshed his memory of a suspect's face through an illegal lineup, show-up, or display of mug-shots, the witness' recognition of the defendant's features cannot be kept from the courtroom if the witness takes the stand. The defendant's lawyer may have won a pretrial ruling that a witness cannot tell a jury that he identified the defendant as the criminal shortly after the offense. But according to the *Wade* opinion the witness can still point the defendant out in court and say that he recognizes him, if there is "clear and convincing evidence" that his courtroom recognition is independent of anything he learned or saw at the illegal lineup.

Before it was tested in trial courts, this requirement seemed roughly comparable to requiring clear and convincing proof that the witness did not covet his neighbor's wife; only the witness would know, and his denial would not necessarily be clear and convincing. "How is a witness capable of probing the recesses of his mind to draw a sharp line between a courtroom confrontation due exclusively to an earlier line-up and a courtroom identification due to memory not based on the line-up?" asked Hugo Black in his dissent to the *Wade* ruling. "What kind of 'clear and convincing evidence' can the prosecution offer to prove upon what particular events memories resulting in an in-court identification rest? How long will trials be delayed while judges turn psychologists to probe the subconscious minds of witnesses?" The prosecution's burden is "probably an impossible one," Byron White concluded in his dissent: "To all intents and purposes, courtroom identifications are barred if pre-trial identifications have occurred without counsel being present."

It quickly developed that the dissenting Justices had taken the Supreme Court's powers too seriously. Suspects continued to be identified, about as before. Trial judges, faced with a well-coached witness' insistence that he had an "independent recollection" of the defendant's face because he watched him closely during the hold-up and that the subsequent view of the suspect at an illegal show-up has been wiped from his mind, invariably held that the in-court identification could stand. Ronald Webster, a bespectacled young District Attorney from Knoxville, Tennessee, who could easily pass as one of the town's promising young preachers, explains why it works out this way. "You put a man on and he says he remembers the defendant from the crime and that's him sitting over there between those two defense lawyers. Who can say he doesn't remember?"

Apparently judges and juries can't, for even those defendants who have won landmark identification rulings haven't gained their freedom. When Jesse James Gilbert went to trial for the second time, armed with the Supreme Court's decree that the lineup identifications could not be mentioned in the courtroom, he was convicted and sentenced to the gas chamber again. By then the witnesses had seen him at the first trial as well as at the tainted lineup, and they had no difficulty in mustering "independent recollections" of him as the triggerman in the fatal stickup. Billy Joe Wade was wise enough in the ways of courts and juries to jump bail and fail to appear for his second trial. The witnesses in his case may indeed have been able honestly to remember him as the bandit; he has since been locked up in Arizona on three concurrent life sentences for armed robbery.

At first, prosecutors complained that they had lost the ability to identify suspects on the sly. "There's been a robbery and the police think a fellow who works at a service station did it," explained one of the attorneys who represented the Government in the *Wade* case; "The police don't have enough evidence to make an arrest and hold a line-up, so they used to drive the witness by the station. If the witness could identify the fellow, then they'd arrest him. Can they still do that? I don't know." The question has not been answered in court, possibly because identifications of that type are not being mentioned by witnesses, and it never comes to light that the confrontation took place. Sheriff Ray Bridges of Mobile County, Alabama, an old-fashioned lawman with a rumpled, beagle-with-a-hangover style, explained once that with so much uncertainty about the legality of identifications, he doesn't attempt lineups. "If we have a suspect in a rape case or something like that, we just bring him down from his cell like we was going to ask him some questions," Sheriff Bridges explains. "Then we have the lady just walk past, where she can see him. You might say we do it off the record."

In some instances, *Wade* seems even to have worked to the advantage of the prosecution. Police department officials in San Francisco take great glee in photographing defense attorneys in the audience at lineups. When those are shown to the juries, it lends an authenticity that lineups used to lack. In the District of Columbia the judges routinely order suspects to appear for lineups scheduled several days in advance, to make certain that defense lawyers can be present. This gives the police an opportunity they seldom had before to put prime suspects on display before virtually every person in town who has been a victim of a crime that the suspect might have committed. Prior to the *Wade* decision, any defendant who could make bond could avoid such a hazard, and now so many suspects are being identified for crimes other than the ones for which they were initially arrested that the Legal Aid Society has threatened to bring suit to end the procedure. One Washington lawyer proved that even with an experienced attorney on the scene, the hazards of faulty identifications remain. To pass the time he agreed to stand in one lineup to supplement the number of "suspects"—whereupon an outraged lady picked him out as an accused rapist and refused to back down until he proved that he was trying a case at the time of the rape.

In a few instances, the presence of counsel has posed difficult questions of legal ethics and law-enforcement effectiveness. Chief Justice Burger used to tell in his speeches of an incident in which a lawyer attended a lineup and advised his client to lie face down. As Burger told it, the police had the other participants in the lineup flatten out too, and the witnesses stepped gingerly among the prostrate bodies, peering down at what Burger called "the lie-down lineup." In another instance, a female impersonator was arrested in his feminine disguise. The lineup was delayed for several days to give him time to retain an attorney, after which the suspect showed up for the lineup neatly turned out in a business suit and tie.

In most large cities lineups are arranged so that one-way mirrors or screens or bright lights in the eyes of the suspects prevent them from seeing witnesses in the audience. This is important to many witnesses, who fear—apparently with some justification—that trouble will come their way if they are known to be cooperating with the police. There have been instances in which attorneys apparently identified prosecution witnesses at lineups and passed the word along to the suspects. When the suspects got out on bail, the witnesses were made to believe that testifying for the state was dangerous, and the prosecution's case melted away.

Felix Frankfurter would have shaken his head at some of the bizarre results of the Supreme Court's attempt to compensate for the fallible memory of eyewitnesses by extending the Sixth Amendment's right to counsel. For he had warned that not all of the problems of law enforcement and individual rights could be solved by reference to the Bill of Rights. "It leads inevitably to a warped construction of specific provisions of the Bill of Rights," he predicted, "to bring within their scope conduct clearly condemned by due process but not easily fitting into the pigeon-holes of the specific provisions." He could well have had in mind—if his imagination had been so rich—the Supreme Court's subsequent attempt to deal with the problem of faulty eyewitness identification by invoking the Constitution's command that "in all criminal prosecutions, the accused shall . . . have the assistance of counsel for his defense."

There were hints in the *Wade* opinion that Justice Brennan had qualms about this himself. These hints were so elaborate that they suggest an attempt by the Court to develop a technique for dealing with law-enforcement situations that don't actually fit within any of the safeguards of the Bill of Rights. The technique: to require a lawyer's presence, but as an incentive to further reform, suggest that the need for counsel could be erased if legislators and police officials perfect rules and procedures that would protect suspects' rights equally as well.

The Supreme Court had toyed with this approach in the *Miranda* decision, when it invited Congress and the states to "develop their own safeguards" as substitutes for the *Miranda* procedures. But since these had to be "fully as effective" as *Miranda*, the suggestion struck most police officials as an offer of hemlock—in theory, *Miranda* should have done away with most questioning, and the police had no enthusiasm for concocting effective substitutes.

This may have dulled the law-enforcement establishment's sensitivity to a similar suggestion in the *Wade* opinion that should have been appealing to the police and to the legal profession. In the lineup situation, it was clearly possible for law-enforcement officials to devise rules and procedures that would make identifications more reliable, with less fuss, than the mandatory presence of lawyers. Brennan invited them to do so. If Congress, state legislatures or local police departments would adopt and follow rules to "eliminate the risks of abuse and unintentional suggestion at lineup proceedings" and also to "eliminate impediments to meaningful confrontation at trial," Brennan said in the *Wade* opinion, this could "remove the basis for regarding the [lineup] stage as 'critical.'" Procedures have since been suggested that could presumably eliminate the need for attorneys' presence—as, for instance, a rule that all lineups be composed of at least five persons of similar age, size, sex and complexion; that witnesses submit written descriptions of the suspect in advance; and that the entire procedure be recorded on videotape or color film.

It was a pregnant moment for such a suggestion from the Supreme Court. Senate hearings were nearing their conclusion on a bill that was to become the most comprehensive crime bill in history. Much of the steam behind it had come from the public heat over the Supreme Court's decisions. If a cooperative approach was to develop between the two branches of government toward law enforcement and individual rights, that was the time for it to begin.

Four weeks after the *Wade* decision was announced, the final three days of Senate hearings on the crime bill were held, and Congress and the Supreme Court passed like trains in the night. There was the familiar grousing about *Miranda* by Southern senators, but the hearings closed with only one brief discussion of the *Wade* decision. Senator Sam J. Ervin, Jr., who had read more Supreme Court decisions and had agreed with less than any other member of the Senate, mentioned that the decision had been announced, but that he could discern no constitutional basis for it. His analysis was limited to the observation that "the logical extent of these cases would be for the Court to hold next that you cannot prosecute a man unless you have a lawyer present . . . at the time he allegedly committed the crime."

With that predicate (there were no House hearings), Congress responded to the *Wade* decision by passing a law that ordered Federal judges to admit identification testimony by witnesses to crimes, regardless of the circumstances. It was a legislative absurdity that did no credit to Congress, and visited a curious indignity on the Supreme Court. When the Warren Court risked self-inflicted wounds in its pursuit of constitutional protection for the accused, there was at least the prospect that its setbacks would be moral victories, on behalf of principles that would endure and eventually carry the day. In that context, the lineup decisions were a disappointment. The Supreme Court's solution was better than the status quo, but there was a contrived quality to it. When the Justices signaled for help and Congress responded with an awkward rebuke, it cast a shadow over the future role of the Supreme Court on crime. If the Warren Court in baring its breast on crime had become such an inviting political target that even the easy issues produced conflict, then the Supreme Court's prospects for dealing successfully with the future problems of crime and race were far from happy.

XI

Police Eavesdropping:
Law-Enforcement Revolution

A standard which would forbid the reception of evidence if obtained by other than nice ethical conduct by government officials would make society suffer and give criminals greater immunity than has been known before.

WILLIAM HOWARD TAFT

Any one of a number of incidents might legitimately be singled out as the one that did most to trigger the remarkable change that took place in the law of electronic eavesdropping in the final years of the Warren Court. But in restrospect, it appears that Al Kee moved the pebble that loosed the avalanche when he shoved Edward Levinson's desk from its accustomed spot in the Fremont Hotel and gambling casino on Saturday morning, April 27, 1963.

The official story that has since been told in court proceedings and to the press is that it all happened by accident, that it was just an unlucky day for the Federal Bureau of Investigation. According to the official version, Al Kee, an employee of the Central Telephone Company of Las Vegas who knew all about the workings of telephones, happened to be moonlighting that day to pick up some extra cash and as a personal favor to Levinson. Levinson was president and major stockholder of the Fremont Hotel, and the story has it that his office there was beginning to bore him. He called in his friend Kee to do some rearranging, to move the furniture around and jazz things up. To move the desk, Kee had to adjust the telephone cord, which revealed a puzzling thing: inside the cord were four wires, not the usual three. Kee traced the fourth wire up into the telephone base. There, tucked into a nook inside the telephone's works, he found a tiny microphone.

By tracing the mysterious fourth wire back to the hotel's telephone room and then by referring to the telephone company's cable diagram, it was learned that the little microphone hidden in the telephone on Ed Levinson's desk had been connected to a line leased by the telephone company to the Henderson Novelty Company. It did not take Levinson long to discover that no such company existed in Las Vegas, and that the leased line led to the Las Vegas office of the Federal Bureau of Investigation.

The unofficial version of the discovery, the one that is believed by many people in top law-enforcement circles in Washington, is less colorful but more credible. It is that Levinson and his Washington attorney, Edward Bennett Williams, were the beneficiaries of a rare "leak" from within the F.B.I.—that they had been told that the "bug" was there and that the remodeling was staged to let Kee find it. In any event, word of his discovery flashed immediately along the green felt grapevine of Las Vegas' gambling casinos, where searches uncovered more "bugs"—first in the Sands Hotel (where the device may have picked up some famous voices, since Frank Sinatra and Dean Martin were shareholders), then in the Dunes, the Stardust, the Desert Inn and, finally, in the home of one casino operator.

To the men who found the tiny devices in their offices, sitting rooms and bedrooms, the meaning was unmistakable. With the election of John F. Kennedy as President in 1960 and the appointment of his brother Robert as Attorney General, the Federal government had developed a strong prosecutorial interest in the activities of the nationwide crime syndicate known as the Mafia, or as it was then coming to be called, "La Cosa Nostra." It was no secret that the F.B.I. believed that the key to the Mafia's secrets might be found in Las Vegas, where some casinos were said to represent the most visible enterprises of La Cosa Nostra.

In the years of litigation that followed, it came to light that the F.B.I. had leased twenty-five lines in Las Vegas, and that a number of them were used to maintain around-the-clock surveillance of certain gambling casinos. Similar eavesdropping was being employed in Kansas City, Chicago, Miami, New York, Providence and perhaps a dozen other cities where the crime syndicate had flourished. As the successive disclosures of governmental eavesdropping were publicized and as the inevitable court challenges worked their way through the courts, the Supreme Court and Congress were forced to come to grips with the reality that police surveillance was widespread and was out of legal control. It had long been apparent that the law of electronic eavesdropping was in a hopeless muddle, but the Government had given the impression that very little of it was going on. The discovery that it was in wide use, and that it was so effective that pressures for its further use would inevitably increase, preceded one of the odd phenomena of the Warren Court. At a time when the Court tended to take a critical view of many police investigative techniques and was actively expanding the constitutional protections of individuals to speak boldly without fear of reprisal, the Warren Court enlarged the legal power of the Government to spy on its citizens by means of the new electronic technology.

The story of how this electronic anomaly came into being affords a revealing insight into how factors other than briefs, arguments and precedents go into making of law in the Supreme Court. For in retrospect it appears that two separate developments outside the Court and one within it converged in the mid-1960s to change the Supreme Court's course. One was the F.B.I.'s intensive use of electronic bugging, which produced proof of the scope of organized crime and of the capacity of electronic surveillance to penetrate it, as well as a public flap over the disclosures. Another was the efforts of a small but strategically placed group of lawyers on the staff of the National Crime Commission and in other law-enforcement positions, who became alarmed about organized crime and began to advocate electronic eavesdropping as a weapon to use against it. The third was a movement within the Court, begun by Justice William J. Brennan, Jr., to re-examine an eavesdrop doctrine which he considered dangerously inadequate to the task of regulating the sophisticated new electronic devices.

When the microphone and the telephone were invented in the late 1800s, the law was unprepared to deal with the new threats to privacy, and it has been scrambling to catch up ever since. People had barely ceased to marvel over Alexander Graham Bell's first public demonstration of telephones in 1876 before the police department in New York began to tap them. In no time the police established a cozy working relationship with the New York Telephone Company to permit ease in tapping phones. By 1895, New York's finest had been caught for the first time using wiretaps. In time, earphones became such a mainstay of law and order that New York wrote into its Constitution as well as its statute books the authority of the police to tap wires with court consent.

Only the fact that the police in most communities were undereducated, unimaginative and ill-equipped prevented a parade of eavesdrop scandals, and in the few large cities where the police were in better shape, scandals abounded. Many states passed laws against wiretapping, but the police rarely felt that the laws applied to them. The lawmakers at the Federal level—Congress and the Supreme Court—proved their ineptitude in this area early and often, so that for the most part police eavesdropping was limited primarily by law-enforcement officials' lack of imagination, sense of propriety or fear of public outrage.

This condition of laissez-faire was threatened in 1928 when the Supreme Court finally considered the constitutionality of wiretapping by Federal agents. Law and order usually meant parched palates in those days of Prohibition, and the issue predictably came before the Court in the form of the convictions of a group of bootleggers. Wiretaps on the home and office telephones of the ringleaders of a Canada-to-Seattle bootleg operation had proved so productive that eighty-one individuals in the liquor trade in and around Seattle were indicted, and many went to jail. In an effort to avoid this, the boss of the operation, Roy Olmstead, and a handful of his lieutenants, brought a landmark appeal to the Supreme Court. They argued that wiretapping was unconstitutional because it violated the Fifth Amendment's privilege against compulsory self-incrimination, and that it invaded a zone of privacy that is protected by the Fourth Amendment's prohibition against unreasonable search and seizures.

The Fifth Amendment argument struck the Court as far-fetched, since they voluntarily conducted their illicit business over the telephone. But the Fourth Amendment has been designed to insulate private premises from unreasonable government intrusion, and four of the nine Justices concluded that the wiretap evidence was illegally obtained. The majority, however, took the Fourth Amendment at its face value. There had been no "search" because the Prohibition agents had carefully avoided entering private premises, and there had been no "seizures" because words are not things with handles that police may grasp. There had, indeed, been a state statute that made wiretapping a crime, but the Supreme Court felt that U.S. courts could not vary their rules of evidence according to each state's law. The decision was an occasion for one of Brandeis' eloquent dissents, protesting that the Fourth Amendment applied to "any unjustifiable intrusion by the Government upon the privacy of the individual." Holmes added his unforgettable remark that illegal police wiretapping is "dirty business."

However logical it was to conclude that the Founding Fathers did not intend to strike at a then-unimagined form of electrical surveillance when they drafted the Fourth Amendment, the *Olmstead* decision had the eventual effect of creating a labyrinthian maze of laws governing electronic eavesdropping. By 1963, when Al Kee found the bug in Ed Levinson's telephone, a few of the legal possibilities were these:

If the device picked up both ends of conversations over the bugged telephone, then it would have been a wiretap forbidden by Federal law but occasionally authorized by the Attorney General in national security investigations. No information or leads gained by a wiretap would have been admissible in Federal court if the tap had been the work of Federal or state agents, but evidence from a wiretap installed without a trespass by state or local police would have been admissible under Federal law in state but not Federal courts.

If the device was a "bug"—a microphone that picked up conversations in the room but not both ends of calls over the telephone—then there would have been no Federal law specifically forbidding its use. But since it was placed in private premises by stealth, no information obtained by it could have been admitted in court, and under the law of Nevada, whoever planted it committed a crime.

All of which was of scant consolation to the gambler-businessmen who had been bugged, because they knew that however the legalities sorted out, such elaborate surveillance would not have been carried out unless it was distinctly to their disadvantage. The fact that they had been victimized by pervasive F.B.I. eavesdropping attested to the legal deterioration that was in an advanced stage by the early 1960s. Some of the devices had been in operation for more than two years; the F.B.I. had become so blasé that its agents planted a final bug in another casino several weeks after F.B.I. eavesdroppers heard Al Kee find the Levinson bug. Almost a quarter-century had passed since *Olmstead* v. *United States* and police eavesdropping was virtually outside the law.

It all began with the unstated assumption by the Justices in the *Olmstead* case that if police wiretapping were covered by the Fourth Amendment, then all wiretapping must necessarily be forbidden.

To make this assumption virtually decided the case, for police eavesdropping seemed too valuable a law-enforcement tool to be strangled in its cradle by the Supreme Court. Yet, in 1928, it was quite logical to assume that if police wiretapping were controlled by the Fourth Amendment then it would have to be prohibited as an inherently unreasonable form of search and seizure. The Court found itself paying a price for its own zeal in shrinking the area of legal searches. As a practical matter, it had lost the option to bring wiretapping within the Fourth Amendment, because the rules for warrants were so strict that they seemed to preclude a valid warrant to wiretap.

In the first place, the Fourth Amendment requires that all warrants state the particular things to be seized. But a wiretap is inherently indiscriminate, seizing all the words that flow on the tapped lines. Inevitably, a warrant to overhear certain conversations would pick up others as well, amounting to a warrant to conduct a "general search." Another stumbling block was the "mere evidence" rule which forbade the seizure of items other than the fruits or instrumentalities of crime. Words could never be anything but evidence, so under the Supreme Court's rules, they could not legally be taken by the police for use in court. Finally, a valid search always requires notice to the subject of the search. Prior notice of a wiretap would be like asking permission to administer a hotfoot.

So torn between absolute prohibition and complete toleration of police eavesdropping, the law wobbled, contorted, stretched. In 1934, Congress passed the Federal Communications Act, which carried over from the earlier act a prohibition against the interception of any communication and the divulgence or use of such communication. The Supreme Court, apparently relieved to have a statutory basis for approaching the problem without freezing its solutions into the Constitution, ruled that this made wiretapping a crime, even when done by the police. Nothing had been said in the statute about excluding evidence by wiretap, but the Supreme Court nevertheless tagged an exclusionary rule onto the law, making it the first act of Congress to be thus reinforced by the Court.

An awkward double standard quickly developed, because the Supreme Court, having dealt imaginatively with the statute to ban wiretapping by Federal officers, concluded that it would be unseemly to encroach on states' rights by applying the exclusionary rule to state and local police. The Court did say that these police would commit a crime whenever they testified in court about their interceptions. But because the Justice Department was quietly fudging on the antiwiretap law itself, it was in no position to prosecute local police for the same failing, and no local officer was ever prosecuted. Eventually, the laws of five states came to authorize police wiretapping with court approval—yet each time a policeman testified in court as to what he overheard with a state judge's approval, he committed a Federal crime.

While the law was foundering over wiretapping, it was also being outflanked by technological developments in the science that came to be known as "bugging." The invention of transistors made possible the construction of tiny microphones and radio transmitters—"bugs"—that could do their work at unlikely times and places. The bugged olive in the martini that captured the public's imagination was probably never used (it was suggested by a Senate investigating committee to illustrate the possibilities), but other equally ingenious devices were. The Russians bugged the Great Seal of the United States that hung in the Ambassador's study at the American Embassy in Moscow. An inventor in New York devised a bug that can be placed in a telephone and activated from anywhere in the world. The eavesdropper simply dials the number of the bugged telephone and quickly blows a harmonica tone into his own telephone. This silently activates the bug in the other telephone, which monitors all conversations in the room until the eavesdropper hangs up or the bugged telephone is lifted from its cradle.

Other instruments even removed the necessity for illegal entry to plant bugs. A device called a "detectaphone" looks and operates much like a physician's stethoscope. When pressed against the outside wall of a room it overhears the conversations within. The sill mike is designed to rest on the floor outside a closed door, where it can overhear conversations inside without a physical intrusion into the room.

For outside surveillance, the type of directional microphones used by television sports announcers to pick up sounds on the playing field can also overhear private discussions in parks and streets. To further complicate the trespass question, eavesdroppers can bug a victim without his knowledge, turning him into a walking eavesdropping device to enter private premises for the eavesdropper. An intriguing illustration of the potentialities of this technique surfaced in Washington several years ago when rumors spread that the Central Intelligence Agency had bribed a local cobbler to plant bugs in the heels of foreign diplomats' shoes.

Although these techniques posed a greater threat to privacy than wiretaps because they tended to operate when speakers were least on their guard, as late as 1963 they were largely outside the reach of the law. There was no Federal statute against bugging (although theoretically, Federal agents might have been punished under a statute that forbade them to conduct illegal searches), and since the *Olmstead* case had held that the Fourth Amendment did not apply to seizures of words, evidence obtained by police bugging was admissible in court unless the police committed a physical trespass to plant the bug. This led to legal results that verged on the ridiculous. In a leading case, *Goldman* v. *United States*, the Supreme Court demonstrated how capricious its rules could be in practice. Federal agents had entered a suspect's office at night to plant a microphone, which failed to work. So they pressed a detecta-phone against the outside wall and overheard conversations, including those of a suspect within speaking into a telephone. Because the device planted by trespass wasn't used, and because only one end of the telephone conversations were overheard, no legal rule was violated, and the conviction was upheld. Yet in a subsequent case, when a police "spike mike" penetrated the common wall between a room being used by eavesdropping police officers and an adjoining suspect's room, the Supreme Court found a physical trespass and excluded all that the eavesdroppers had overheard. The Court reached the ultimate refinement of this theory in 1964 when it reversed a conviction because the police used a listening device that penetrated the outside wall the depth of a thumb tack—exposing the Court to the jibe that under its doctrines a thumb-tack's length could separate an individual from the protection of the Bill of Rights.

These legal quirks inevitably shaped the Government's eavesdrop policy. Because wiretapping was a Federal crime, most of the official attention centered on it, while bugging was developing into a greater threat to privacy. Even after the Supreme Court ruled that the 1934 law applied to law-enforcement officers, the Justice Department insisted that it could still tap wires without violating the law, so long as it did not divulge the wiretap information outside of the Government. This resulted in enough wiretapping to produce an unseemly succession of public disclosures of Governmental snooping, and in March of 1940, Attorney General Robert H. Jackson announced that the Justice Department had "completely abandoned the practice" of wiretapping. This self-denial quickly gave in to an important exception. The impending war brought a threat of espionage and sabotage and President Roosevelt decided that the Government should use wiretapping in self-defense.

Roosevelt took great care, in these instructions to Jackson, to create only a narrow exception to the general ban on Governmental wiretapping. The President began by expressing his agreement with the Supreme Court's restrictions on wiretapping by the police. "The Court is undoubtedly sound in regard to the use of evidence secured over tapped wires in the prosecution of citizens in criminal cases," he said, "and is also right in its opinion that under ordinary and normal circumstances wiretapping by Government agents should not be carried on for the excellent reason that it is almost bound to lead to abuse of civil rights." But he felt that the Court did not intend to preclude wiretapping regarding "grave matters involving the defense of the nation," so he authorized Jackson to use it, limited "to a minimum," and "insofar as possible, to aliens."

About a year after Roosevelt's death, a future member of the Warren Court played a key role in prying open this narrow exception to permit wiretapping beyond cases involving foreign intrigue. Tom C. Clark, the new Attorney General, wrote a letter to President Harry S Truman on July 17, 1946, quoting one passage of Roosevelt's wiretap instructions, but leaving out Roosevelt's statement that wiretapping in criminal cases would threaten civil liberties and his orders to confine it as much as possible to investigations of foreign-born spy suspects. Clark observed that "the country is threatened by a very substantial increase in crime," and that while he was reluctant to use such measures in domestic cases, "it seems imperative to use them in cases vitally affecting the domestic security, or where human life is in jeopardy." His letter left no doubt that he was requesting an expansion of the Roosevelt policy, but it downplayed the significance of the change.

Truman granted the new authority to use wiretapping in domestic cases. Clark lost no time in using it. He encouraged J. Edgar Hoover to crank up the F.B.I.'s "Top Hood" gang-busting program and he is said personally to have approved the wiretapping of such rackets figures as Mafia playgirl Virginia Hill, and Ralph Capone, brother of the notorious Al.

A measure of the shifts in legal thinking that occurred within the Warren Court came twenty years later, when Justice Tom Clark wrote the Supreme Court's opinion in *Berger* v. *New York*. He declared unconstitutional New York's permissive police eavesdropping law, with the warning that "few threats to liberty exist which are greater than that posed by the use of eavesdropping devices."

As fascinating as the national leaders' contortions over wire-tapping proved to be, they obscured the true conditions of police violations of privacy, rather than illuminating it. For the word "wiretapping" came to be equated in the public mind with electronic eavesdropping in the broad sense. If high public officials eschewed all wiretapping, or reeled off careful statistics to show how little wiretapping was going on, then people assumed that their private words were fairly safe from Government ears. This was totally misleading, for the strictures on wiretapping had encouraged other types of governmental eavesdropping that were far more destructive of privacy than the tapping of telephone lines.

One of the rituals of public deception was the annual appearance of J. Edgar Hoover before the House Appropriations Committee. Until the lid blew off the F.B.I.'s surveillance activities in the late 1960s, Hoover unfailingly gave careful statistics as to the limited amount of wiretapping that was going on and omitted any public reference to the mushrooming use of bugging by the F.B.I. Several weeks before Al Kee found the F.B.I. bug in Las Vegas, Hoover appeared before an appropriations subcommittee and explained that as of that day the F.B.I. had a total of ninety-five wiretaps in operation, all in "security cases." "In accordance with the policy of many years standing," he added, "telephone taps are utilized only in cases where the internal security of the country is involved, or where kidnapping and extortion may bring about the jeopardy of human life. The F.B.I. does not have authority to authorize a wiretap. Each one must be authorized in advance and in writing by the Attorney General."

This was, of course, only an artful half-truth. While the F.B.I. was keeping a careful public tally of its national security wiretaps, it was planting bugs across the country in domestic criminal cases as well as in security investigations. That was why the devices hidden in the telephones in Las Vegas were wired so that they would not intercept calls on the bugged phones, although apparently they could easily have been installed so that they would have done so. By picking up only words spoken in the room where the bugged telephone sat, they did not qualify as "wiretaps," and thus could be omitted from Hoover's report.

The F.B.I.'s wiretap total eventually took on such psychological importance that the Bureau went to extreme exertions to keep the figure below 100. One ex-agent has told of an instance when the number of taps was pushing 100 and an instruction came down to disconnect a wiretap in order to free a tap for a more important case. He did so. Then, under orders, he picked the lock of the home where the tapped telephone had been and planted a bug in its place. By 1965, when acting Attorney General Nicholas deB. Katzenbach insisted on seeing a list of the F.B.I.'s anti-Mafia bugs, he was stunned to find 98 then in use —meaning that the Bureau's eavesdropping was roughly double what the public had been led to believe.

Officially, the impression was given that F.B.I. electronic surveillance was being kept under the watchful eye of the Attorney General and was limited to internal security investigations. Even many sophisticated journalists missed the distinction between wiretapping and bugging. This led them to ask the wrong questions of public officials, and allowed the officials to perpetuate the false impression of limited governmental eavesdropping. Three years after the Las Vegas disclosures, when Robert Kennedy and Hoover were feuding over who was ultimately to blame for the violations of privacy, a reporter on a television interview show asked Senator Kennedy: "Did you authorize the F.B.I. wiretaps of gamblers' telephones in Las Vegas in '62 and '63?"

"No, I did not," Kennedy solemnly replied, knowing that the devices had been bugs—not taps. He then vowed that he had never authorized any wiretaps except in national security cases. Later, Hoover released documents that left little doubt that Kennedy had given the F.B.I. a virtual blank check to bug suspected Mafia chieftains.

It also came to light toward the end of the Warren era that the Government's concept of "national security" wiretapping was far more elastic than the public generally realized. Because the Government had inherited its wiretap policy from Roosevelt's 1940 directive, most people assumed that wiretapping was being used basically to thwart espionage and sabotage efforts by foreign powers. But when a series of court challenges by defendants who had been overheard exposed the nature of some of the F.B.I.'s national security wiretapping, it became clear that the Government considered it in the interest of national security to keep taps on home-grown radicals as well.

Two subjects of sustained wiretap surveillance were revealed to have been Dr. Martin Luther King, Jr., civil rights leader and Nobel Prize winner, and Elijah Muhammad, leader of the Black Muslims. In Dr. King's case, the surveillance had been started well before he became an international celebrity, and it had its benevolent aspects. President Kennedy had become closely identified with Dr. King as early as 1960, when a telephone call from candidate Kennedy to the then imprisoned civil rights leader's wife assured Kennedy the lion's share of the Negro vote. Later, when Attorney General Robert Kennedy came to believe that Dr. King was in some danger of becoming a cat's-paw for Communists, he felt that it was a good idea for both President Kennedy and Dr. King if the Government were to keep the civil rights leader under protective surveillance. In Elijah Muhammad's case, also, the wiretapping was said to have been partially prompted by reasons other than keeping tabs on black militants. But whatever the reasons, this use of constant electronic surveillance to keep the Government informed of the activities of dissident elements was reminiscent enough of George Orwell's *1984* to bring a sense of urgency to legislative and judicial efforts to bring governmental surveillance within legal bounds.

In the Supreme Court, the first public move came in May of

1963—before the news of the F.B.I.'s anti-Mafia bugging had spread beyond Las Vegas—in the form of a dissenting opinion issued by William J. Brennan, Jr. One mark of an influential Justice is the capacity to single out deficiencies in the law and to articulate persuasive reasons why the law should be changed. That is why Holmes, Brandeis and Black have been so widely admired for their numerous dissents that later became majority rulings. Justice Brennan wrote such a dissent when he took stock of the eavesdrop situation and proposed a fundamental constitutional change.

The case, *Lopez* v. *United States*, was an unfortunate one for this purpose, because it involved a hybrid form of electronic listening that could logically be said not to constitute eavesdropping at all. It grew out of a situation in which a government agent who had been offered a bribe had tucked a transmitter into his clothing and had gone to talk money with the briber, with other agents listening in. The Court had already held, in a 1952 case, that there is nothing improper about this surreptitious use of electronics. The Justices reasoned that the person who speaks under these circumstances is not betrayed by the hidden transmitter but by his decision to converse with a second person, who could testify to the conversation in court, even without the electronically provided corroborations.

Brennan argued that a person engaged in private conversation should at least be assured that third persons could not throw the words back at him in court. Brennan's point was that this use of electronics need not be precluded, but only controlled, if brought within the Fourth Amendment. He felt that the Supreme Court had shied away from overturning *Olmstead*, even though it had been eroded by subsequent events, because the Justices had assumed that no wiretap warrant could be drawn that would satisfy the standards of the Fourth Amendment. The difficulties, he felt, had been exaggerated by the analogy with search warrants. Wiretapping is a distinct form of searching, so he argued that the Fourth Amendment might well tolerate differences between wiretap warrants and search warrants. Brennan attempted to make the point that it was an open question as to whether bringing eavesdropping within the Fourth Amendment would curtail its usefulness to the police, but his invitation to the more conservative Justices to re-open the question smacked of the spider speaking to the fly; as the Fourth Amendment precedents stood, it seemed unlikely that they would permit much eavesdropping. His dissent was joined by only Douglas and Goldberg—two Justices who rarely saw things the police's way. In any event, Brennan warned that an attempt should be made to bring electronic surveillance within constitutional controls, before surveillance became so widespread that the people's rights of political anonymity and free speech were undermined.

From this equivocal initiative in 1963, the constitutional atmosphere surrounding eavesdropping changed so rapidly that by 1969 police wiretapping was being authorized by Federal judges and the fruits were being used as evidence in United States courts. Moreover, this did not come in spite of the Supreme Court; it was encouraged by it. Within three years after *Lopez*, the Supreme Court majority began to take steps that in retrospect can be seen as preparation for a reversal of the *Olmstead* decision, without automatically eliminating police eavesdropping. In 1968 the Court pointedly nudged Congress toward enactment of a permissive eavesdrop law.

For the Supreme Court, this was blinding speed—and there were developments on the outside that helped account for it. The Las Vegas disclosures and the others that followed soured many people on lawless police snooping, and defense lawyers were learning to ferret it out where formerly it would have gone unnoticed. The prospect was that years of tiresome litigation would be required to determine which convictions had been tainted and which had not. Unless some way were found to legitimate reasonable police eavesdropping and eliminate the rest, this would become a chronic judicial headache.

However, the litigation of this type that did take place proved very educational to the Federal judiciary and to the American public. The first logs of F.B.I. surveillances were revealed secretly to a few Federal judges in 1966 in the course of routine criminal trials. This began to happen with increasing frequency as defense lawyers, realizing that their clients may have been overheard by F.B.I. bugs in Las Vegas or elsewhere, began to demand that trial judges require the F.B.I. to produce the transcripts and logs of all surveillances that arguably could have related to the charges against the defendants. The Justice Department cooperated by systematically reviewing the transcripts of surveillances to determine if anyone being prosecuted by the Government had ever been a victim of illegal eavesdropping.

In order to satisfy themselves that none of this illegally obtained information contributed in any way to the Government's case, trial judges found it necessary to comb through huge volumes of transcripts and digests of the unguarded conversations of crime syndicate bosses. Later, a few such logs became public in the course of litigation, disclosing that the F.B.I. learned almost daily of extortion, blackmail, narcotics smuggling and other crimes, and that the agents even prevented some murders and learned of others through these conversations. It may have been that when word of the scope of the F.B.I.'s eavesdropping and the value of its findings became known within the Federal judiciary, that the Justices became impressed with the urgency of curbing the practice without eliminating it.

In any event, it now seems clear that by 1966 a majority of the Court had been won over to Brennan's view that something had to be done about eavesdropping, although there probably was not then a consensus of the Court as to what it should be. The situation raised a novel problem of Supreme Court methodology. For all of the activism of the Warren Court, it had operated within the traditional appellate framework, resolving points brought for decision by opposing advocates. Here, Brennan was asking the Court to change its course, when change was not being vigorously urged upon the Court by either side in the police wiretap controversy. Both sides were essentially satisfied with the status quo on wiretapping, since both stood to lose if changes were made. Law enforcement had been denied the authority in most situations to use electronic eavesdropping to gather evidence for courtroom use, but the Las Vegas disclosures demonstrated that eavesdropping was still well worth the Government's trouble in terms of providing criminal intelligence (plus, many defense lawyers suspected, some well-disguised leads to evidence). In view of the Warren Court's tendency to rule on defendants' behalf, the police could not be enthusiastic over the prospect of closer judicial attention to police wiretapping. Civil libertarians, on the other hand, realized that under the prevailing law-and-order mood in the country, any ferment would probably bring changes that they would not like.

The result was that neither side was pressing the Supreme Court to do what it was suddenly prepared to consider— sweeping electronic surveillance within the ambit of the Fourth Amendment, while relaxing the rules so that some form of eavesdropping could be employed with proper court approval. Even if the Justice Department had wished to test the idea, there was no convenient way to do so; Federal statutes did not provide for court-approved wiretapping. Then in 1966 a unique chain of circumstances combined to bring before the Supreme Court an unprecedented instance of eavesdropping that had been approved by a Federal court.

It had begun two years before, when a prominent Tennessee lawyer set out to use bribery to hang a jury in the prosecution of Teamster President James R. Hoffa. Two factors were responsible for the extraordinary steps that had been taken by the Justice Department in investigating this very special bribery case: Z. T. "Tommy" Osborn was one of Nashville's most popular lawyers, and Jimmy Hoffa was one of the country's most consistently successful defendants. Until the bribery scandal broke in 1963, Osborn was the Cinderella lawyer of the Nashville legal community; the poor boy from across the tracks who had gone to night law school, had become a crack trial lawyer, had argued for the city voters before the Supreme Court in the historic reapportionment case, *Baker* v. *Carr*, and who was slated to be the next president of the city bar association. Hoffa had been prosecuted so often that he claimed more courtroom experience than some of his lawyers. Yet the Justice Department had never been able to convict him; his legal tactics were known to be wily, to say the least. So when Robert Vick, a Nashville policeman with a cloudy reputation, brought a story of attempted bribery to the Federal prosecutors who were preparing to try Hoffa in Nashville for tampering with a jury in an earlier case, the Government lawyers were understandably wary.

Vick's story was that Osborn had hired him to help run background investigations on prospective jurors, but that when the lawyer learned that one of the veniremen on the panel was Vick's cousin, Osborn suggested that Vick offer the cousin $10,000 to vote for acquittal and hang the jury. The routine procedure in such cases would have called for U.S. agents to confirm the bribery charge by equipping Vick with a hidden recorder for his future conversations with Osborn. But the Government's lawyers suspected that the incident might have been a Hoffa ruse to mousetrap the prosecution into eavesdropping on Osborn. This could give the Teamster chief grounds to accuse the Justice Department of violating the confidentiality of his attorney-client relationship. The prosecutors were also painfully aware that the Federal government was then in bad odor with many citizens of that Southern city and that Federal electronic surveillance of one of its leading lawyers would be a major scandal unless it were clearly justified.

With matters in such a delicate state, the Government lawyers had Vick put his report in the form of a sworn affidavit, which they presented in chambers to the court's two Federal District judges. The judges authorized the use of the hidden recording device by Vick, thus setting up the first known instance of court-approved eavesdropping by Federal judges, done for a narrowly limited purpose that the Supreme Court could later warmly approve. Wired for sound, Vick returned to Osborn's office and obtained a vivid recording of the lawyer's offer to pay the juror $10,000 to hang the case, plus Osborn's further promise that the bribed juror could be assured that "there will be at least two others with him."

When the Supreme Court accepted Osborn's appeal of his jury-tampering conviction, close observers anticipated that the Justices were preparing to make an important statement about eavesdropping. Osborn's situation was almost identical to the surveillance that the Court had approved in the *Lopez* case, except for the prior judicial approval of the Osborn surveillance. Thus it seemed that the petition for certiorari had most likely been granted to give the Justices an occasion to applaud this approach to law-enforcement eavesdropping. This proved to be the case. The opinion by Potter Stewart pointed out that even without the two District judges' approval, the use of the recorder was permissible under the *Lopez* rationale. Nevertheless, the Court approved the surreptitious recording of Osborn's words on the broader ground that the procedure that had been used complied with the warrant requirements of the Fourth Amendment. Quoting Justice Brennan's assertion in his *Lopez* dissent that "the procedure of antecedent justification before a magistrate that is central to the Fourth Amendment" is "a precondition of lawful electronic surveillance," the Stewart opinion dwelt at length on the benefits that the prosecution had gained in terms of credibility and legitimacy because of the compliance with the Fourth Amendment standards. Without actually reversing *Olmstead*, the Court had applied Fourth Amendment standards to an eavesdropping situation, and had given a sign that some electronic surveillance could still survive.

Only Douglas dissented in the *Osborn* case. He felt that the use of the recorder was a "search" for "mere evidence," and he reminded the majority that the lawbooks were sprinkled with decisions that said such evidence was barred by the Fourth Amendment. But that obstacle to a warrant system of eavesdropping was about to be swept away, too. A few months later the Supreme Court jettisoned the mere evidence rule in the landmark *Warden* v. *Hayden* decision. The opinion by Justice Brennan did reserve judgment as to whether "there are items of evidential value whose very nature precludes them from being the object of a reasonable search and seizure." Technically, this preserved a rationale for a subsequent invalidation of eavesdropping. But psychologically, it eliminated an old (and therefore, to lawyers, a substantial) barrier against legitimation of eavesdropping.

Two weeks later sweet reason suffered a jolt in the form of the parting shot of retiring Justice Tom C. Clark. Supreme Court decisions are frequently a mixed product of reason, indignation, egotism and horse-trading, yet it is a process that permits a surprising flow of continuity in the law. Each Justice constantly feels the tug of his own past record and the realization that tomorrow's decision must be squared with the positions taken today. For Tom Clark in June of 1967, though, the usual forces of equilibrium had gone awry. He had decided to retire from the bench to clear the way for his son, Ramsey, who had been appointed Attorney General by Clark's old friend and fellow Texan, Lyndon Johnson. The elder Clark had agreed to step down because it was felt that his son's position as the Government's chief legal officer might give an appearance of legal logrolling from son to father. Justice Clark's final decision showed that those fears were well founded.

As Acting Attorney General, Ramsey Clark had become strongly identified as a partisan on one public issue; he abhorred police eavesdropping. Clark considered it unconstitutional, distasteful, and not an efficient law-enforcement tool. On the final day of the Supreme Court term, Justice Clark, who as Attorney General had once used fancy footwork to maneuver Harry Truman into expanding the Justice Department's wiretap authority, and who had often chastised the Court's liberals for dealing too sternly with the police, delivered an opinion that seemed to all but preclude constitutional eavesdropping by the police. At issue in *Berger* v. *New York* was the conviction of an enterprising entrepreneur who had arranged to obtain a liquor license for a new Playboy bunny club in Manhattan by bribing officials of the State Liquor Authority. The District Attorney's office got wind of the plot and obtained court orders authorizing the bugging of the offices of two men believed to be serving as middlemen for the payoff. The bug picked up and recorded conversations that later proved persuasive to a jury, which found Berger guilty on two counts of conspiracy to bribe. When the case reached the Supreme Court it presented a mixed bag of constitutional issues, but the four-man liberal core of the Warren Court—Chief Justice Warren, and Justices Brennan, Douglas and Fortas—with Justice Clark unexpectedly on their side, seized the opportunity to declare New York's eavesdrop law unconstitutional under the Fourth Amendment.

On the face of it, *Berger* v. *New York* should have been a turning point in the law, but Clark's opinion and the circumstances surrounding it were so enigmatic that the legal profession did not know quite what to make of it. Berger's conviction could have been painlessly overturned without a pronouncement one way or the other on the constitutionality of the eavesdrop statute (the bugging warrant was apparently defective), but the Supreme Court seemed determined to render what amounted to an advisory opinion. Yet the advice was mostly negative; it seemed to imply that no eavesdrop law could be drafted with enough built-in safeguards to square with the Fourth Amendment.

The Clark opinion held the New York law invalid on its face, primarily on the ground that the court-approved surveillance technique permitted "general searches," in which conversations other than the one being sought by the police were also likely to be overheard. It also found fault with the fact that the "bug" was not to be removed as soon as the desired conversations were obtained. In a final, devastatingly understated observation, the Clark opinion noted that the law didn't require prior notice to the suspect of the intended eavesdropping—or proof of exigent circumstances to justify waiving the notice. As an additional hint that the outcome of the decision was to preclude and not to control police eavesdropping, Justice Clark included an argument—reminiscent of the sentiments of Ramsey Clark —that police bugging is an inefficient way to combat crime anyway, and that "techniques and practices may well be developed that will operate just as speedily and certainly."

After the decision, almost nothing changed except that Clark left the Court, thus dissolving the five-member majority that had issued the ruling. New York's highest court upheld subsequent convictions obtained under the same bugging statute, simply by re-interpreting the law in a way that the state court said cured the deficiencies cited in the *Berger* decision. New York's prosecutors let it be known that they were continuing to wiretap under a companion statute to the supposedly defunct bugging law. On the national political scene, Richard Nixon and the House Republicans competed with Democratic Senator John L. McClellan in pushing for a Federal wiretapping and bugging law.

This effort encountered slow going in the muddy constitutional terrain surrounding eavesdropping, until the Supreme Court firmed things up six months later in *Katz* v. *United States*. There, Government agents had convicted a bookie by attaching a microphone to the outside of the telephone booth where he habitually conducted his business. Under all of the classic tests, the Government had steered clear of the Bill of Rights

and the wiretap law with this surveillance; the job had been
done without a physical intrusion into private premises; no interception of telephone calls had occurred; and the agents had
even disconnected the microphone when the suspect wasn't
using the telephone booth. But the court declared the lack of
physical intrusion into the booth irrelevant, and held that "the
Fourth Amendment protects people, not places." Since the
gambler had every reason to believe that his conversations were
confidential, then even in his favorite telephone booth, the
Fourth Amendment protected him from unreasonable eavesdropping by the Government. The Court declared that after almost
forty years, *Olmstead* v. *United States* had become so eroded
by qualifying decisions that it no longer would be followed.
Only Justice Black dissented.

Having brandished the stick of the Fourth Amendment, the
Court offered the carrot of the wiretap warrant. If the officers
had obtained a warrant to bug the telephone booth, Potter
Stewart wrote for the Court, then the eavesdropping would have
been constitutional, even though it was a clear-cut example of electronic spying by the Government on an unsuspecting person. He
said that the precautions taken to limit the intrusion into private
affairs were careful enough to meet the Fourth Amendment's
standards of particularity, and thus a judicial order "could have
accomplished 'the legitimate needs of law enforcement' by authorizing the carefully limited use of electronic surveillance."
As for the heavy hint in Tom Clark's *Berger* opinion that eavesdropping could never be done constitutionally because the
Fourth Amendment requires prior notice of the search and
seizure, Stewart noted that if officers can constitutionally finesse
formalities and kick a door down to prevent the destruction of
evidence, they could eavesdrop without prior notice.

Six months later, Congress passed the Omnibus Crime Control and Safe Streets Act of 1968, which contained in Title III
the first Federal statute authorizing the police to use court-
approved wiretapping and bugging to gather evidence. This
unaccustomed harmony between Congress and the Supreme
Court on criminal law had many roots, but some of the most
interesting involved a young law professor who played a role
similar to that of James Vorenberg on confessions, only with

considerably more success. G. Robert Blakey had been one of Robert F. Kennedy's young hotshots in the organized crime section of the Justice Department in the days when hardly anyone outside that intense circle knew what La Cosa Nostra meant. He became convinced that organized crime was a cancer, and that it was lunacy not to let the police use electronic surveillance to combat it. Blakey saw electronic eavesdropping as no different from any other police tool; it would be abused if not controlled, but that to him was no reason to bar its use entirely. He moved to the law faculty at Notre Dame, where he developed a complex, detailed model law designed to permit police eavesdropping with court approval, all supposedly within the Byzantine constitutional rules that were then being laid out by the Supreme Court.

Often, the major obstacle to new legislation is getting people to agree on details, not goals. This did not happen when it came time to consider a law to authorize police wiretapping, because the subject was so complicated that the various interested Congressmen and legal groups did not undertake to draft their own bills. Instead, the American Bar Association's Project on Minimum Standards for Criminal Justice, the President's National Crime Commission, and leaders in both houses of Congress decided to call in outside help. In each case, the call went to G. Robert Blakey. Not surprisingly, the various groups' proposals were remarkably alike. The result was Title III, which went through Congress with little quibbling among wiretap proponents as to detail, so they were easily able to subdue those who opposed police eavesdropping on principle. A major step had been taken toward finally bringing governmental eavesdropping within legal control. But it remained to be seen if the Supreme Court, having chosen to ride the tiger of electronic surveillance, might yet end up inside, locked into a permissive position that would encourage police eavesdropping without effectively controlling it.

For having invited the enactment of an eavesdrop statute, the Supreme Court had limited its own freedom to thereafter strike it down. It could still tighten up the law by giving some provisions narrowing interpretations. It could also knock out particularly obnoxious sections. But it appeared barely conceivable

under the political conditions of the 1970s that the Supreme
Court would attempt to make it impossible for the Government
to tap lines and bug premises with court approval and to use
the fruits in court. To do so would provoke political reprisals
that the Court would be in no position to withstand. Attorney
General John N. Mitchell, a staunch advocate of the new
eavesdrop law, took care to use it sparingly, so that he could
boast that his Justice Department was still doing less eavesdropping than his Democratic predecessors did before eavesdropping
was legalized. Now that the Government was in a position to
publicize its use of legalized snoopery to bring criminals to
book, while still concealing its surreptitious "dirty business,"
the courts were likely to find it difficult to cut back on eavesdropping.

Yet doubts have arisen already as to the bargain the Court
struck when it traded legitimacy for controls. Nobody imagined that Congress would spread police eavesdropping around
as generously as Title III eventually did. Under it, Federal
agents can get warrants to eavesdrop in investigations of offenses ranging from planting marijuana in the south forty, to
running off homemade greenbacks, to crossing state lines to
instigate campus riots. The Federal Government has not used it
so widely, but the law authorizes states to do even more if they
pass laws similar to Title III. If they do, then with only the
approval of the local District Attorney and a friendly judge,
local police could, if their statute allowed, eavesdrop on any felony involving a threat to life, limb or property—which in
some states could include such relatively innocuous pursuits as
chicken stealing, snake handling and wife beating.

There have been other second thoughts about potential abuses
of court-approved eavesdropping under Title III, but the most
explosive question to be raised about the new eavesdrop law
came from the Office of Attorney General John Mitchell, and
had nothing to do with judges and warrants. The public understanding behind Title III was the legitimation of governmental
eavesdropping in exchange for control over that same surveillance. The most corrosive aspect of the earlier regime had
been fear. So long as the Government was forced to eavesdrop
in the shadows outside the law, then nobody knew the extent

of that surveillance and anyone could suspect that it had happened to him. The advantage of Title III, as generous as it was, was that court approval had to be obtained, statistics of eavesdropping had to be published each year, and the subjects of governmental eavesdropping had to be told (after each device was disconnected) what had been done. Officialdom had been given a reluctant green light, but at least the public would finally feel that the law had a grasp on the Government's Big Ear.

Then on June 13, 1969, Attorney General Mitchell let it be known that the Government intended to have its cake and eat it too. On that day the Justice Department filed papers in the Federal District Court in Chicago in connection with the Government's prosecution of eight of the activists who had led the peace demonstrations during the Democratic National Convention in 1968. The defendants had demanded to be shown transcripts of any conversations involving them that had been picked up by illegal government listening devices, so that they could be satisfied that no unconstitutionally obtained evidence was being used against them. Mitchell's answer: no disclosure of any such surveillance needed to be made, because they were not "illegal"; the President had the constitutional authority to order electronic surveillance of their activities and those of any other domestic groups "which seek to attack and subvert the government by unlawful means."

With this claim, Mitchell revealed fully for the first time how little the Government intended to concede in the deal to legitimate eavesdropping. Title III of the Crime Control Act, for all its protective procedures and reporting requirements, had expressly left open the question of the legality of eavesdropping aimed at gathering "foreign intelligence information or preventing the overthrow of the Government by force or other unlawful means," or "any other clear and present danger to the structure or existence of the Government." Now the Government was saying that surveillance of radical domestic groups was within that zone of unfettered discretion that the executive branch occupied in matters concerning national security—thus this brand of eavesdropping was unaffected by all of the nice procedures written into the 1968 law. As the Government's position paper filed in the Chicago case put it, the country had experienced urban riots and violence stirred up by dissident groups, and "the question whether it is appropriate to utilize electronic surveillance to gather intelligence information concerning the activities and plans of such organizations in order to protect the nation against the possible danger which they present is one that properly comes within the competence of the executive and not the judicial branch."

This claim of a blank check to wiretap was based upon a facet of eavesdropping that had been dimly understood outside of select Government circles. That is, that for law-enforcement purposes, the use of electronic listening devices to keep tabs on suspect groups is quite distinct from its use to gather evidence of crimes. The procedures set out in Title III work nicely when the police have probable cause to suspect that a specific crime is being committed but lack the evidence to convict the guilty parties. The police can listen until they hear what they want, stop listening, arrest the offenders and bring them to trial.

But electronic surveillance has another use which is a product of its peculiarly insinuating nature. It is an incomparable technique for gathering intelligence of subversive or criminal elements. Electronic surveillance has taught Government officials some surprising truths about human communications—that even revolutionaries and professional criminals feel compelled to talk to each other about their common interests, and that they will do so despite well-founded suspicions that their telephones are tapped. Justice Department officials can recount astounding admissions by shrewd men over suspect telephones, admissions so damaging that the officials can only partially explain why they occur. Often it is inconvenient for the eavesdrop victims to communicate in more secure ways, or they assume that the Government knows the information anyway, or they simply succumb to wishful thinking that nobody is listening.

Moreover, protracted surveillance has shown that by monitoring the conversations of a few forceful leaders, the Government can keep itself informed of the doings of the activist elements of a nation of 200 million people. By eavesdropping on Dr. Martin Luther King, Jr., Elijah Muhammad, and perhaps a dozen other black leaders with whom all dissident blacks were likely to touch base at some time, the Government could be fairly certain that it was not ignorant of any major movement among this large and frequently disgruntled segment of the population. According to persistent rumors in Washington, the same type of surveillance has been directed at leaders of the Ku Klux Klan, the American Nazis, and other right-wing extremist groups. Title III's procedures do not hold the answer to this brand of snoopery; even if the judges who approved such interesting surveillances could be trusted to keep them secret, the Government might find it difficult to show probable cause to listen for years to the sitting room conversations of Nobel Prize winners and religious leaders.

Yet the men who run the Government are supposed to know what is going on in this vast country, and John Mitchell's legal stand in Chicago showed how important unfettered eavesdropping is to them. The problem is that it brings the eavesdrop question full cycle from 1963, minus the ground that was lost in terms of privacy by the warrant technique of Title III. For if the men in the Government can decide in the secrecy of their own councils who may be placed under surveillance as posing a threat to the existing form of government, then despite the best efforts of the custodians of the law, governmental eavesdropping is open-ended. When it comes to taking the measure of an alleged national threat, the past performances of men in high office are not always reassuring. In 1965, when an organization of young Marxists called the DuBois Club (pronounced du-boys, after the Negro civil rights leader, W. E. B. DuBois) became briefly notorious and some patriots mistakenly pilloried the Boys Club of America, Richard Nixon, then a national director of the Boys Clubs, issued a public statement denouncing the name similarities as an example of a deliberate and duplicitous Communist effort to smear the Boys Club. On another occasion, when the F.B.I. was found to have bugged a gangster hangout in Kansas City known as Red's Taco House, an F.B.I. spokesman justified the surveillance on the ground that the Mafia was a threat to the national security.

Such episodes have moved some lawyers to suggest that judges might be better equipped than elected public officials or bureaucrats to decide when domestic groups should be bugged.

This is what is at stake in Attorney General Mitchell's demand for a free hand in such matters, and the Government has demonstrated that it can be stubborn when its autonomy in this area is questioned by the courts.

Solicitor General Erwin N. Griswold, a former Harvard law dean who revered the Supreme Court as one who for years was mentioned as a possible nominee, once reacted so heatedly to a Supreme Court incursion into this field that he handed the Court what amounted to a veiled threat in urging it to change its position. It happened in 1969, after the Court ruled that the Government must let criminal defendants, in all cases, including "national security" cases, see all records of illegal governmental eavesdropping concerning them. Mr. Griswold filed a rare Justice Department petition for a rehearing arguing that this would permit defendants to romp through files of the most sensitive nature—including, he implied, wiretaps on foreign embassies in Washington. Unless the Court saw things the Government's way, Mr. Griswold said, the Justice Department might be forced to deviate from its long tradition of candor with the courts and to stop telling the Justices of the existence of wiretap transcripts that the Government considered none of the judiciary's business. The Court quickly backed away, with Potter Stewart writing an opinion to assure the Government that the Court had not yet decided whether eavesdropping in foreign intelligence investigations is covered by the Fourth Amendment and is thus "illegal." Stewart chided Griswold for becoming prematurely excited about the prospect of disclosure, which will never materialize if the Court eventually holds that national security surveillance is entirely within the President's discretion.

The Potter Stewart–Erwin Griswold spat had enlivened the issue enough to obscure the fact that it had only been pushed into the background. Then Attorney General Mitchell's move in Chicago quickly reminded the Court that it must soon decide if it must go to the mat with the President over who shall supervise and control electronic surveillance of the nation's radical groups. When the Court finally confronts this question, the Justices may have to sacrifice, in the interest of national security, much of William Brennan's vision of tight judicial control of surveillance.

If they conclude that the sacrifice is too great, then the Court may find itself again in conflict with the other branches of the Government, as it has been whenever it has sought to impose tight controls on investigative activities by the police.

XII

Handcuffing the Police

*Justice, though due the accused, is due the accuser
also. The concept of fairness is not to be strained
until it is narrowed to a filament. We are to keep
the balance true.*

BENJAMIN N. CARDOZO

Yale men have been accused of arrogance, pomposity, con-
formity and other vices, but seldom of stupidity or a failure of
self-interest. Yet on Monday, October 23, 1967, a team of
agents for the Federal Bureau of Investigation appeared on the
Yale campus in New Haven, Connecticut, and almost effortlessly began to persuade a group of Yale men to talk themselves
into serious legal trouble. In the process, the agents gave a
classic demonstration of why the Supreme Court's decision in
Miranda v. *Arizona* has not stopped suspects from talking to
the police.

The Yale suspects were twenty-one graduate students, under-graduates and members of the faculty whose draft cards had been dumped, along with hundreds of others, at the Justice Department as a part of a massive anti-Vietnam War protest held in Washington on the previous weekend. The owners of the cards presumably knew that they were supposed to carry them at all times and that violations of the Selective Service Laws can carry a maximum penalty of five years in prison and a $10,000 fine. By Monday, polite investigators for the F.B.I. began to sift through the campus, reading the *Miranda* warning to the draft-cardless Yale men and then asking them to give information that could only serve to complicate their lives greatly, with the least possible exertion by the Government.

On the first day the agents questioned five suspects. Each was told, courtesy of *Miranda* v. *Arizona*, that he could remain silent, that anything he said could be used against him, that he had a right to have counsel present during the questioning and that counsel would be appointed if he could not afford to pay. The men had turned in their cards knowing that the Government might exact its pound of flesh, but none of them were eager to wear stripes, and least of all were they interested in easing the Government's burden in making out its case. Yet each of them gave a written incriminating statement.

The word quickly reached the Yale Law School that the F.B.I. agents were on the campus and that the suspects were giving evidence against themselves. A meeting was hurriedly called for that night. When the law professors met with the protesters, the lawyers were stunned to learn that no advance thought had been given to whether or not the protesters should cooperate with the authorities, and that despite the intelligence and strongmindedness of the suspects, the *Miranda* warning had done nothing to bolster their defenses against the agents' questioning. Because the protesters did not appreciate what they were being asked to give away by their admissions—evidence that otherwise the Government would (if it could) have to dig up for itself—the warnings were little more than a meaningless babble. (The agents tended to recite the warnings as if they were meaningless. At the same time, a waiver-of-rights form was often thrust at a suspect, suggesting that a part of the *Miranda* ritual was the signing of a waiver by the person to be questioned.) That night the law teachers explained in detail what was at stake and offered to remain on call to counsel the remaining sixteen men during their interviews with the agents.

After that night, all sixteen protesters refused to give incriminating statements to the agents. But even though they had made up their minds not to say anything, all of them did make small talk with the agents and some of them let themselves be maneuvered into dropping crumbs of information that might have been used against them. When the law teachers reviewed the incident later they concluded that if the *Miranda* warnings couldn't do more for this intelligent and strong-willed group, they would be almost worthless to the average criminal suspect. Ignorance of the law, a natural desire to justify one's actions, feelings of guilt, and the skill of the investigators combined, they thought, to riddle *Miranda*'s frail barrier against the incrimination of suspects out of their own mouths. If the privilege against self-incrimination includes the right to be shielded from the consequence of one's own conscience, ignorance, gullibility or garrulousness, then the Yale men proved that *Miranda* is a failure. The only effective protection for a right of this dimension, the law professors concluded, would be to require that all suspects have legal counsel before and during interrogation.

The F.B.I.'s easy pickings among the Yale men only served to flesh out for the legal profession what had become widely suspected—that despite the thunder that it had called down upon its own head, the Supreme Court hadn't made confessions obsolete when it decreed *Miranda* v. *Arizona*. In its own refined way, this incident contributed to a growing understanding by scholars and officials of the extent to which the Supreme Court's due process revolution has affected law enforcement. Storm clouds of public displeasure began to gather as early as *Mapp* v. *Ohio* and the contemporaneous crime index rise, but *Miranda* became the lightning rod. It has remained the focal point of the controversy, and the ultimate public verdict as to whether the Supreme Court has handicapped the police is likely to depend largely on the impact of *Miranda*.

However, the case against the Supreme Court has always been broader than the complaint that its decisions have placed unreasonable restrictions on the authority of the police to investigate crime. It has also been claimed that whether or not the police and prosecutors have actually been handicapped, the decisions have contributed crucially to an easy, permissive climate in which responsible elements have been demoralized and criminals have been encouraged to feel that they could "get away with it." Enough time has passed to convince many observers that the direct impact of the Court's rulings upon the police has been slight. But there is a growing feeling among persons close to criminal justice that the Supreme Court's due process revolution may have contributed to a deterioration of the system of justice in an unanticipated way—by making justice more cumbersome and slow—and that this could eventually blemish the record of reforms that the Warren Court achieved.

Miranda v. *Arizona*, with all of its salient qualities, has now been in effect long enough to serve as a proving ground for the charge that the decisions are handcuffing the police. The legal scholars have churned out a series of empirical studies of the effects of *Miranda*, and while the chips have tended to fall on the side of each researcher's bias, there is a striking paucity of convincing evidence that the police have been substantially handicapped, and a strong overall impression that their ability to solve crimes has not been greatly affected.

In Washington, D.C., where volunteer attorneys stood ready on an around-the-clock basis to rush to the station house to give advice, only seven percent of those who were arrested for felonies or serious misdemeanors asked for legal help. A team of researchers from Georgetown University Law School set out to find out why. They found that some policemen didn't give the warnings and others mumbled them into an unintelligible gibberish (*The New York Times* quoted a New York detective's *Miranda* warning as follows: "You mungble bruup stend lawyer"), but basically they found that both the suspects and the lawyers had concluded that summoning lawyers to the station house did no good. The police usually managed to pump the suspects for an hour or so on the way to the station and later while the lawyer was en route to the jail (another study showed that the average interrogation lasts only thirty minutes), and the attorneys usually arrived to find the police quite willing to have the lawyer to step in—having already gotten all they needed from the suspects. The word quickly spread through jailhouse circles in the Capital about the lawyers' ineffectiveness, and after a year the volunteer program died; the suspects had all but stopped accepting the proffered free legal help. One defendant, asked later why he didn't request a lawyer's aid, confessed, "I wanted them [the police] to make a mistake."

Observations of all actual police interrogations in New Haven for an eleven-week period by researchers at the Yale Law School turned up more surprising information: that the detectives got more confessions out of suspects who had been given the *Miranda* warnings then from those who hadn't. The explanation was that the warnings didn't do much to raise suspects' resistance to questioning, and that the police were more punctilious about *Miranda* when they expected to get a confession and thought they might need it. This needn't have occurred too often, for the researchers found that confessions were necessary in less than 15 percent of the cases—far less than the figure of 80 or 90 percent that many law-enforcement officials had tossed around during the immediate post-*Miranda* furor. Researchers from the University of Pittsburgh concluded that confessions in Pittsburgh were necessary in a slightly higher ratio of cases—about 20 percent—and that the number of suspects who confessed declined by 16 percent after *Miranda*. Still, they found that the conviction rate remained stable at about 67 percent, and the percentage of cases "cleared"—declared solved by the police—actually rose slightly after *Miranda*. Despite this statistical good news, the researchers suspected that *Miranda* had pinched the law enforcement slightly by weakening a few cases to the extent that the suspects were never indicted or tried. The extent of the increase, if any, in these cases that wash out for lack of adequate proof is almost impossible to gauge empirically—and it is here that most experts feel that *Miranda* has probably had its most serious impact.

The verdict of the academic researchers has been virtually unanimous—that the impact of *Miranda* has not been great; that the warnings are given in an offhand manner when at all (the New Haven detectives gave the full four-part warning in only one case out of five), and that in any event most suspects go ahead and talk. None of the academicians suggest that *Miranda* has not made the policeman's lot more difficult, but there is a feeling that it has helped to keep law enforcement on its toes, has encouraged policemen to rely less on questioning and to do a more thorough job.

This solid scholarly front has been dented by some studies conducted by prosecutors and police officials, but even in their ranks there are some who say that *Miranda* hasn't changed things much. Two of the country's most respected prosecutors, Frank S. Hogan of New York County and Arlen Specter of Philadelphia, have offered the most convincing arguments that *Miranda* has made it substantially more difficult to enforce the law. Their studies of pre- and post-*Miranda* investigations show that fewer suspects have been willing to talk to the police since *Miranda*. Since certain types of offenses, such as murder and burglary, tend to leave no eyewitnesses, they claim that without questioning the police are often almost powerless to solve these crimes. Prior to *Miranda*, Hogan says, "it was the homicide bureau experience that rarely did a suspect refuse to make any kind of statement, even if it was only to protest his innocence." But in the year after *Miranda* was announced, the homicide bureau obtained confessions from only 35 percent of its suspects and almost one-third refused to say anything. On the other hand, District Attorney Evelle J. Younger of Los Angeles County and Detroit Police Chief Vincent Piersante compared results before and after their officers were required to give warnings, and found that the warnings didn't make much difference and that confessions weren't as important as had been thought.

The one study published by a judge, an analysis by State Supreme Court Justice Nathan R. Sobel of Kings County, New York, produced a questionable but highly publicized claim that confessions were of scant importance in his jurisdiction. He disclosed that the District Attorney's office had filed a "notice of intention" to use a confession in only 86 of the first 1,000 indictments filed in Kings County early in 1965. From this he concluded that confessions may be involved in less than 10 percent of the cases. However, it has since been pointed out that notices of intention were filed only after many cases had been disposed of by guilty pleas and by other procedures, that these cases were the ones most likely to have been bolstered by confessions, and that many cases may have been made with the aid of admissions although the statements were not used in Court.

Despite the evidence that some lips have been sealed by *Miranda* and the initial despair in police circles over several of the major decisions, it soon became evident that law enforcement could still carry on quite well. One of the lessons of the due process revolution of the 1960s was that the struggle between criminals and the police has its own dynamics, governed by social forces far more powerful than court decisions and highly resilient to changes in legal rules. An early demonstration of this came out of the District of Columbia's unhappy experience with the ill-fated *Mallory* decision of 1957. Shortly after the Supreme Court ruled out in that case all confessions obtained during unreasonable delays in arraignments, the percentage of cases cleared by arrest in the District of Columbia began to decline from its pre-*Mallory* level of about 50 percent. This brought charges that the interrogation curb had lowered police effectiveness. The resulting pressures, coupled with shifting lower court decisions, produced a series of changes in the interrogation rules. In the early 1960s some interrogation was permitted, followed by a nine-month period in 1964 and 1965 when all interrogation delays were forbidden, followed by a three-year period in which three hours of questioning were allowed, and a final change in 1968, when Congress set the permissible period of delay for interrogation at six hours for all Federal jurisdictions. Despite this yo-yo effect on the interrogation rules, the clearance rate continued its steady slide, from above 50 percent in 1956 to 22 percent in 1968. Furthermore more crimes were solved during the period when all interrogation was forbidden than in a later period, when three hours of questioning was allowed.

Puzzled, criminal experts in the Capital investigated and concluded that the same number of police, solving roughly the same number of crimes, simply were not keeping pace with the crime rise. Another discovery was that the interrogation restrictions could not have affected a large chunk of the city's crime because the questioning curb did not apply to juveniles, who were responsible for much of the crime rise. This was found to be true across the country. Arrests of persons over eighteen years old for serious crimes rose 20 percent when the due process revolution was getting under way, from 1960 to 1965. None of the decisions then applied to juveniles, but their arrest rate rose much faster—by 52 percent over the same period. It was argued that if liberal court decisions had been fueling the crime rise, then the rise should have been greater among adults, who were the only beneficiaries of the new rules.

Now that the police have had a few years experience in living with the handiwork of the Warren Court, it is becoming clear that local justice is well cushioned from the impact of Supreme Court thunderbolts by the enormous "give" in the criminal justice system. Landmark rulings, which always develop out of litigated cases, are designed to operate through adversary litigation. But the policeman who investigates a crime knows that his conduct will probably never be questioned in court. If his case happens to be the one serious crime in five that is solved, and if an indictment results, the chances can still be as high as nine to one that the defendant will plead guilty. Studies show that in large cities as many as 95 percent of all defendants in nontraffic cases plead guilty, including about 70 percent of the defendants in felony cases. This shrinkage, plus judges' penchant for believing policemen's versions of how evidence was obtained, gives officers elbow room that is not discernible from reading the Supreme Court's opinions.

An idea of how roomy this elbow space can be, can be seen from the experience of a medium-sized city, Nashville, Tennessee, in a recent year. Out of the 21,274 serious crimes reported to the F.B.I., 6,325 were said by the police to have been cleared, and 1,325 felony indictments resulted. After many defendants pleaded guilty and some cases were dropped, 150 felony trials were held. So assuming that the Nashville Police Department investigated all 21,274 of the reported felonies, an officer on a case could assume that the chances were about 1 in 140 that his investigation would ever be scrutinized in an adversary felony trial.

So great is the slippage in the criminal justice system that former Attorney General Nicholas deB. Katzenbach claims that *Miranda* probably affects "less than one percent of the serious crimes in the United States." He reasons that many crimes are not reported, that arrests are made in less than one-quarter of those that are, and that confessions are crucial to only a fraction of the prosecutions that result.

Still, the impression persists that the society does not cope with crime as well as it did before the days of the Warren Court. Richard Nixon, who always had a good feel for public attitudes, claimed during his 1968 campaign that the effect of *Miranda* "has been to very nearly rule out the 'confession' as an effective major tool in prosecution and law enforcement"—and while the jails are now full of people who could challenge his facts, he proved that you don't have to be right to be President if your conclusions seem correct. Clearly, Nixon was right in saying that the police weren't doing as well as they did before the Warren Court began transforming the criminal law. Statistics support this impression, particularly where cities are concerned. But a glance at the F.B.I.'s crime figures, which are said to understate actual crime by a wide margin, shows that from 1961 through 1969, crime simply outpaced the capacity of the police to enforce the law. The ratio of police to civilians climbed slightly. The rise in crime trebled the increase in arrests. The clearance rate plummeted. Of those prosecuted, the conviction rate dropped slightly. Overall, the picture was this:

	1961	1969
Crime Index Offenses—up 139%	2,082,400	4,983,600
Arrests—Up 64%	667,700	1,422,800
Police—Up 39.5%	311,535	415,000
Police Per 1,000 Population—Up 16%	1.9	2.2
Clearance Rate—Down 31%	30.5%	20%
Convictions Rate—Down 6%	76.5%	72%

If Katzenbach's estimate of *Miranda*'s impact on crime is even close, then this makes it clear that what shocked the American public in the 1960s was the rumble of the crime glacier and not the rattle of the pebbles that the Supreme Court spread in its path. The tides of crime, demography and urbanization were broad and strong, but they were never as visible or dramatic as were the landmark decisions of the Supreme Court. So as the model of law and order that had existed prior to 1961 began to creak and crumble, people blamed the Supreme Court.

When the panorama of crime and punishment of the later Warren years is parsed, it is evident that the uneasy feelings among the public were justified, if for the wrong reasons. The criminal justice system *was* eroding. Crime was increasing, and there was a decline in the system's capacity to deal with each crime. For each 100 serious crimes reported at the end of the Warren era, fewer were solved by the police than had been the case in 1961. Thus there were fewer arrests, fewer convictions. For law-abiding citizens, the chances of becoming crime victims had increased; for criminals, the prospects of punishment had declined. The F.B.I.'s Uniform Crime Reports show the extent of this erosion during the period when the Supreme Court's activism was at its height:

DISPOSITIONS PER 100 CRIME INDEX OFFENSES REPORTED

1961		1969
26	Cleared	20
23	Persons arrested	19
22	Persons charged	17
9	Adults found guilty	6
3	Acquitted	2
8	Referred to juvenile court	7

Now that hindsight has exposed the factors that muffled the effects of the Court's decisions, as well as the relatively massive outside forces that were at work during the 1960s, it seems safe to speculate that the ultimate verdict will be that the direct effect of the Court's rulings on law enforcement was relatively slight. Yet the second, more subtle question remains—whether Supreme Court's actions contributed substantially to the deterioration in public order that took place. One of the most frequent arguments made against the Court is psychological—that the decisions demoralized society and encouraged criminals. Crime has always been prevalent in America, and people have claimed—and denied—for so many years that it is encouraged by lenient judges that the psychological argument seems unlikely to produce more than a heated standoff. Professor Yale Kamisar, one of the scrappiest combatants on the liberal side, has unearthed examples of breast-beating over judicial criminal-coddling and impending criminal anarchy that run as far back as the crusty days of law and order prior to World War I. But even though it can be shown that people blamed the courts for dangerous leniency in times when the cities were tame and judges were made of sterner stuff than they are now, there is a logic to the charge that the concentration of liberal decisions from the Warren Court during the 1960s did contribute to the deteriorating crime situation, and the charge is still made, even if it can never be proved. As Warren Burger put it before he became Chief Justice, if people think the law is ineffective, "the decent people experience a suppressed rage, frustration and bitterness and the others feel that they can 'get by' with anything."

While it is impossible to know if criminals were as impressed with their improved legal prospects as with the fact that a progressively smaller percentage of them were being caught as time went on, many noncriminals did seem to have been disheartened by what the Supreme Court was doing. Police reaction, especially to *Miranda*, was for a time almost paranoid. To many policemen the decision was a slap in the face, a declaration that police are more to be feared than criminals. Almost without exception, those who have observed *Miranda* in action and have talked to the police about it have found that the police believed that they had been hobbled far more than their actual performance indicated. Many of these observers came away concerned that the police might be letting down, slipping into a "what's the use?" attitude toward their job. This may pass with the realization that where police procedures are concerned, the Supreme Court's bark is worse than its bite, but knowledgeable officials have not dismissed it lightly. The F.B.I. was so concerned about the post-*Miranda* malaise among police that it published a how-to-comply-with-*Miranda* manual, which was bottomed on the principle that if the policeman's hand "is stayed by fear of a rule of law which he does not understand, he often will fail to stop, question, arrest, search and interrogate. The criminal will be left free to act, and human beings will pay the price of that neglect in blood and property." "This seeming anxiety of judges to protect every person from every consequence of his voluntary utterances is giving rise to myriad rules, sub-rules, variations and exceptions which even the most alert and sophisticated lawyers and judges are taxed to follow," Judge Burger warned; "Each time judges add nuances to these 'rules' we make it less likely that any police officer will be able to follow the guidelines we lay down."

There is some evidence that others not directly charged with enforcing the law have been touched by the same sense of frustration. According to the public opinion polls, the popular belief that the courts are not dealing effectively with crime has risen dramatically since *Miranda*, and this may have increased the seemingly growing reluctance of crime victims to press charges and of witnesses to testify.

However important these psychological by-products of the Supreme Court's pro-defendant rulings might have been, the Court's record has also had a healthy psychological effect, and it may well have outweighed all of the others. One impression that comes through the F.B.I.'s statistical overview of crime and punishment in the 1960s is a suspicion of the traditionalist belief that the be-all and end-all of the criminal process must be to discover truth about crime and bring to justice those who have committed offenses. The United States hedged heavily against this theory at the start, when it adopted the Bill of Rights. The experience of the past few years has added that in urban America it is currently almost impossible to stanch crime with raw enforcement power. When the F.B.I. reports that for every 100 reported crimes only 6 adults are convicted (and this includes guilty pleas to lesser offenses), and it is known that crimes are vastly under-reported but that convictions are not, then life is precarious indeed if only the threat of punishment stands between the citizen and crime.

That is why Chief Justice Warren's familiar question to prosecutors "But is it fair?" seemed so relevant to the times. It capsuled the belief that a vital element of the criminal justice system must be to operate within fair procedures and to preserve the dignity of those who come in contact with the system to the greatest possible extent. Warren's own preoccupation with the ninety young Negroes who were needlessly rounded up in Washington grew out of a persuasive example of the validity of this belief. For years the District of Columbia Police had unabashedly used dragnet tactics to haul likely suspects out of the ghettoes for questioning, until the first ominous ripples of Negro discontent forced the city to look into the situation in 1961. A study commission discovered that of 1,356 persons rounded up without probable cause and held for eight hours or more in 1960, only 16 were charged with any crime. Once the meager results of this system were balanced against the humiliation and rage that it caused, there was little opposition to the Government's ban on further dragnet arrests.

Of all the ironies surrounding the Supreme Court's efforts to reform American criminal justice, the most obvious is that *Miranda*, with all of its mechanistic concentration on cutting square procedural corners, hasn't greatly changed the rituals of police investigations, but the furor over the attempt seems to have had a salutary psychological effect on the public, and to some extent, on the police. The Court's attempt to force rigid procedures on the police, on pain of forfeiting convictions, has not worked out in practice. The police are getting by with a vast amount of noncompliance or half-hearted compliance with the rituals of *Miranda* and the restrictions of *Mapp*. As they discover how few cases are being lost as a result, the compliance may become still more casual. But the outrage over *Miranda* advertised the Supreme Court's message that individuals don't have to explain themselves to the authorities, and it seems unlikely that that impression can ever become widespread again. More important, the police custom of making cases in the "squealroom" seems to be dying. Persons who have observed post-*Miranda* interrogation have reported that the questioning is usually brief, casual, and not undertaken until a firm case has been made against the suspect. Some policemen are even taking a pained pride in their post-*Miranda* performance. Mickey McDaniel, the tough little Captain of Detectives of Davidson County, Tennessee, professes to believe that *Miranda* has been "a good thing" because it has reduced the temptation to rely on muscle to make a case. "Now you have to have something on him before you bring a man in," he says. "So you don't have to kick him around—if you bring him in, you've got him. It's better. Why should we have to police like we used to?"

Even if sentiments such as these are influenced by the realization that *Miranda* doesn't have the bite that was first feared, the long-term psychological impact does seem to have been beneficial—underscoring the possibility that the Supreme Court might have done better in the long run if it had relied more in *Miranda* on its role as constitutional teacher and propagandist, and had not attempted to police the police through the compulsion of an inflexible threat to include evidence. In retrospect, it appears that the most spectacular success of the Warren Court's due process revolution has been to create a climate of fairness about criminal justice. The Supreme Court's idealism proved contagious. Better people are now going into police work, prosecutors' offices and public defenders' careers. More money is being spent on law enforcement and criminal justice. The heavy-handed treatment of defendants that had been almost an assumption of the system has given way to a heightened and observable sensitivity among police, trial judges and appellate judges of the importance of fairness. Except for the lowest-rung criminal courts, which are generally more overwhelmed by their task in the wake of the criminal law revolution than before, there has been a discernible improvement in criminal justice that stands as a tribute to the Warren Court, only partially obscured by the charge that the police have been handcuffed.

Even if it is conceded that the Supreme Court's rulings have not seriously handicapped the police and that the psychological effect has been more to defuse the crime problem than to exacerbate it, there is still reason to ask if the American system of justice is not now suffering from an excess of due process. It is important that a suspect not be bullied into confessing, searched without cause or placed at a disadvantage by the procedures followed at his trial. But nice procedures can have a hollow ring to defendants who face long stretches in prison awaiting trial, pressures to plead guilty to end the wait, or incarceration (with scant efforts toward rehabilitation) years after the offense. It is also slight consolation to the public to know that the police have not been directly handicapped by the recent reforms, if the machinery of justice has been slowed to the point that it is incapable of removing criminals from society until years after they have been accused of a crime. That is why the earlier controversy over the effects of the Supreme Court's decisions is giving way to concern over the capacity of the urban courts to handle the rising volume of criminal cases under the present system. There have been increasing instances of procedural glue in the scales of justice, signs that the legal developments of the past decade can combine to gear down the machinery of justice into slow motion.

The problem seems most pressing in the urban areas, and is most noticeable in the Federal courts, where the reforms have taken root more rapidly and where the statistics are adequate to tell the story. They make it clear that more is happening than just an increase in the number of crimes to be processed. During the decade from 1958 to 1968, while the volume of criminal cases in the Federal courts was almost stable at about 30,000 prosecutions each year, and while the number of trial judges increased by one-third, the backlog of pending cases almost doubled. In one jurisdiction—Brooklyn—the average criminal indictment gathers dust for almost two years before trial. If there is an appeal, another two years usually passes. When this came to light, Chief Justice Warren, speaking with the insight of a former prosecutor, speculated aloud about the high cost of making innocent defendants wait that long for vindication—and of leaving the guilty ones free to raise their lawyers' and bondsmen's fees by committing more crimes. (William A. Johnson, an accused bank robber free on bail, hinted at the answer to Mr. Warren's question when he failed to show up in the Brooklyn courtroom on the morning of February 23, 1968, to stand trial—Johnson was robbing another bank that morning. Evidence later came to light to indicate that after Johnson was convicted of the first crime and was free on bail pending his appeal, and while he was still awaiting trial on the second bank robbery, he took part in a third bank robbery attempt, which failed.)

American justice has always been notoriously slow. In most European countries criminals would have served their time within the four years often required to put a felon behind bars in Brooklyn. But even by those lights, the recent freeze has been serious enough to cause alarm. What has apparently happened is that the time required to try the average case has increased, while fewer defendants are pleading guilty and more are appealing their convictions. This elongation of the criminal process seems to have been caused by the combined fall-out from three separate reforms: the proliferation of procedural advantages available to defendants, free counsel for poor defendants, and bail reform.

"No matter what your reaction to the Supreme Court's decisions, the attendant pre-trial, during-trial and post-conviction hearings make the trial of a felony twice as long and twice as difficult," says Saul S. Streit, Administrative Judge of the New York State Supreme Court. "We spend more time deciding which new legalisms by the Supreme Court have to be complied with than determining the guilt or innocence of a defendant." In a hard-fought case, this is often so. Frequently defense attorneys' objections to evidence, particularly when a search and seizure is being challenged, can be fought out in pre-trial hearings. But the admissibility of defendants' statements are usually hashed out at the trial, with the jury shuttling in and out of the courtroom as points are raised that are not for their ears. Often defense attorneys' strategy turns on winning these points; guilt or innocence is usually settled in short order after these preliminary issues are fought out. George L. Hart, a Federal judge who tries cases in the District of Columbia and thus has observed this phenomenon in its most potent form, told a Senate Subcommittee in 1969 that the new procedural rights declared by the higher courts in the previous decade had doubled the length of the average trial in the capital. In 1969 the patience of Massachusetts' highest court almost snapped when it was confronted with an appeal from a ten-day trial in which half of the time—occupying 500 of the 1,004 transcript pages—was spent "trying the police" as to whether or not the *Miranda* warnings had been given. Such cases are proof enough, the Massachusetts court grumbled, "why there is heavy and constantly increasing congestion in the jury trials of criminal cases."

Some judges in lower-level trial courts, where assembly-line justice has been a more frequent sin than overdeliberation, think that the Supreme Court's slowdown has its good points. Judge Joseph G. Kennedy, a thin, bespectacled Negro who deals daily with the crowds of shaggy hippies and turned-on Negroes who are herded before San Francisco's municipal court to answer for a wide range of petty malfeasances, has found that *Miranda* hasn't changed the outcome of many cases, because there's usually testimony that the arresting officers read the warnings from a "*Miranda* card." "Whether they did or not is a matter of evidence, so you're back where you were before *Miranda*. The only place that these decisions have made any perceptible effect is that it has slowed down the judicial process," he says. "This is not necessarily bad—all we've got is time—but it has forced us to take time to examine many things that they didn't bother with before."

As the Warren Court moved from its beachhead in criminal law reform in *Mapp* v. *Ohio* to the denouement of 1968, clearing away procedural anachronisms that had festered in the law for years, there were signs that the friction of change was causing some wear and tear on the criminal justice system. During this period the Court handed down more than 200 decisions on the subject of criminal law, many of which radiated shock waves through precedents that had slumbered for years. Each important new precedent raised new constitutional questions, which spawned new appeals, which produced fresh Supreme Court rulings. By the end of the 1968 term, many lawyers began to ponder the conservatives' familiar warning that the Supreme Court was becoming a super court of criminal appeals for the states—almost one-fourth of the appeals heard by the Court that year had been criminal cases. Sometimes further refinements to the Supreme Court's new doctrines were added in the lower courts. There developed a sense of disorientation about the criminal law, a negative emphasis that was called (usually by those who took a jaundiced view of the Supreme Court's work) the "Miranda syndrome." To some it appeared, as Judge Burger put it, that the courts were demanding "perfect" trials, rather than "fair" trials—and that the result could be the "impotent society."

Chief Justice Warren began to talk worriedly about the slowdown when it was just beginning, in the late 1950s. As his concern developed so did The Speech, a lecture on the "interminable and unjustifiable delays in our courts" that he delivered with dogged regularity over the next decade to meetings of legal scholars and judges. Warren agreed with most other experts that the pyramiding of more judges would not eliminate the problem; despite the rapid growth of the Federal judiciary, the backlog had continued to grow. He also agreed with them that a dangerous paralysis of justice could be avoided—if at all—only by scrapping the judiciary's quaint ways of conducting its business in favor of modern administrative techniques. But Warren never suggested, as did most of the others who discussed the problem, that criminal justice had become too complex, and that the Supreme Court was partially responsible.

Nobody had suggested that the due process revolution had been the major reason for what has happened, but most experts felt that it was an important contributing factor. "The Supreme Court must shoulder its share of responsibility," believes Dalmar Karlen, the Director of the Institute of Judicial Administration, for a situation that "is now perilously close to a breakdown of law enforcement and a collapse of civil justice." He has no quarrel with the fairness of the Court's decisions, but he feels that they were made with little or no thought of their impact on congestion and delay in the lower courts.

They have weakened the doctrine of *stare decisis* and, by increasing the uncertainty of litigation, have increased its volume. They have contributed to the feeling that anybody can get away with anything. They have sidetracked criminal trials away from the main issue of guilt or innocence into tangential inquiries as to the correctness of police and prosecution methods. They have increased the number of trials, especially trials by jury, and also the number of appeals. They have sanctioned collateral attacks upon judgments in great volume, and, in so doing, have created a new breed of legal experts in the convict population of our penitentiaries whose main therapy is thinking up new grounds for such attacks.

The Supreme Court's problem is that it must take constitutional questions as they come, doing justice as best it can as each case comes along. There is no apparent way to marshal, say, a three-year stack of constitutional issues and to gauge not only whether the claimants' rights are valid under the law, but also to decide which ones are of sufficient social benefit, considering their relative drag on the criminal justice system, to justify granting the defendants' claims.

An example of the Court's obliviousness to these considerations came in 1968 when the Court overturned the conviction of Thomas Earl Simmons, who had been found guilty of robbing a Chicago bank. Within hours after the stick-up, the F.B.I. had traced the getaway car to the home of a relative of Simmons. They searched the house and found a suitcase containing a gun holster, a sack similar to the one used in the robbery, and coin cards and bill wrappers from the bank that had been robbed. Simmons, having been identified as one of the bandits and charged with the crime, wished to challenge the constitutionality of the search and to move that the items found in the suitcase be barred from evidence at his trial. Here, he ran into a legal quirk that some scholars had criticized for years: In order to establish standing under the Court's decisions to complain that his Fourth Amendment rights had been violated when his relative's house was searched without a warrant, he had to admit at the pretrial hearing that the suitcase belonged to him. The judge allowed the contents of the valise in evidence anyway, holding that the F.B.I. men had been given consent to search the house. Worse yet from Simmons' viewpoint, his admission that the suitcase belonged to him was read to the jury at his trial. In ruling that a defendant's statements at a pretrial hearing to suppress evidence cannot later be used against him, the Court eliminated a source of unevenness in the enforcement of the Fourth Amendment's exclusionary rule. But in the process it opened an avenue for more motions to suppress evidence, by guaranteeing, as Hugo Black pointed out in a dissent, that a defendant can lie with impunity at either the pretrial hearing or the trial—claiming to own the item at the hearing and denying any knowledge of it at his trial—and neither story can come back to haunt the other. The issue was a very close one, but in terms of abstract justice the Court's decision (by a vote of 6 to 2), is defensible, if not altogether persuasive. Yet if this particular claim of right, with its built-in drag on the system, could have been considered in relation to competing constitutional values, it is possible that defendants would have been left to live with words spoken by them at pretrial hearings.

In one notable instance, the Supreme Court was reminded directly of the possible dilatory side effects of the quest for due process. Eddie Harrison of Washington, D.C., was accused in 1960 of the shotgun slaying of "Cider" Brown, a man well known in light-fingered Washington circles as a "fence" for stolen goods. Harrison gave three confessions, in which he admitted that he and two other eighteen-year-old youths went to Brown's house to rob him, and that Harrison fired the fatal shot when Brown resisted their entry into his home. Eight years later, having been convicted three times of murder and having succeeded in having the first two overturned, Harrison appealed to the Supreme Court on his third conviction. His complaint: that he had been denied his constitutional right to a speedy trial. The Court shrugged that contention off, noting that he had initiated the appeals that prolonged the litigation. But it then overturned the third conviction because the prosecution had used as evidence Harrison's testimony at his second trial that the confessions were untrue and that the shotgun had gone off accidentally. Since the confessions were later thrown out because they were obtained during an unreasonable delay in arraignment, Harrison's admission that he had fired the fatal shot, although accidentally, was ruled out by the Supreme Court on the ground that he would not have made the admission except to refute the illegal confession.

At a fourth trial, held in 1969, Harrison was convicted of murder again. (A witness, who consistently down through the years had failed to identify Harrison as the killer, recognized him at the fourth trial. Defense lawyers protested that the witness had simply come to know him through all those years of litigation.) This time, the Supreme Court let it stand. Even for litigious Washington, the murder of Cider Brown had produced a record of sorts for courtroom exertions. Between them, the three young men were the recipients of ten jury verdicts of guilty, all of which were overturned except Harrison's finale. (The first round of reversals got the boys off to a colorful start; their convictions were voided when it developed that

296 • *The Self-Inflicted Wound*

their trial attorney was Daniel Jackson Oliver Wendell Holmes Morgan, an ex-convict with a long and flamboyant record of practicing law without a license. Unmasked and jailed again, Morgan sued the Warden of Leavenworth Prison and beat the Justice Department in the lower courts until the Supreme Court finally ruled against him in 1969.)

Yet after nine years of laborious litigation and ten separate acts by courts in the interests of the defendants' rights, the Court of Appeals conceded that true justice had not been done. Joseph Sampson, the first of the three boys to win his freedom, had quickly shown Washington his heels. Orson White, who developed from a young tough into a level-headed adult in the eight years he spent in prison before the Government decided not to try him a fifth time, had become the type of solid citizen who held two jobs and the respect of the Government's prosecutors. At the end of his nine years of litigating, Harrison was also said by prison authorities to have been rehabilitated. The Court of Appeals had been confident enough of that that it released him on bail after his third reversal—an unusual move by an appellate court. Yet after his fourth conviction he still faced a twenty-year minimum term and because Federal courts do not have the power to reduce sentences, the Court of Appeals could only note in its opinion, by Warren Burger, the hope that the President would commute his sentence. The courts had outdone themselves in protecting Eddie Harrison's procedural rights, and in doing so had contributed to the bog in the District of Columbia courts, but they were not satisfied that they had done him justice. When it was over, having taken longer than would have been required in some countries to convict, punish and return him to society, there was some poignancy to his complaint that his rights were denied when he was allowed to delay things for so long. A few days before Harrison was to be returned to prison in 1970, to begin serving out his term a decade after his crime, President Nixon commuted his sentence to jail time served.

The dilatory effects of the recent procedural refinements have been magnified, in an unanticipated way, by the growing availability of counsel for the poor. *Gideon* v. *Wainwright* gave a life of its own to the idea that the Constitution gives poor defendants more than equal rights with the rich to sleep under the bridges of Paris. Public defender offices sprang up across the country. Where $2.6 million had been spent by the nation's 75 public defender offices to represent poor defendants in 1961, by 1968 there were more than 300 public defender offices, which spent $21.4 million to defend the poor. A similar development was taking place in the Federal courts, where Congress began in 1964 to make money available to pay private attorneys to represent the poor.

The result was to transform a national system of justice that had for years shuttled many accused felons through from arrest to prison either without legal counsel or with only the slapdash efforts of unpaid assigned attorneys. Over a period of two or three years in the mid-1960s, that ended. "Criminal justice had been conducted cafeteria style, with most poor defendants being pushed through pretty fast," says Junius Allison, Executive Director of the National Legal Aid and Defender Association. He believes that some slowdown in the system was inevitable as legal aid for the poor was beefed up. Suddenly the cafeteria line began to lag, as more and more defendants were in a position to sample the procedural goodies along the way. More than three-quarters of the defendants in most courts are poor, so the infusion of paid counsel—even though it is still spread thin and its clients complain that often it isn't combative enough—can exert tremendous leverage on the system. Nobody, as any appointed counsel can testify, can be as fierce in litigation as one who is not paying his own legal costs. So people who would have pleaded guilty before did not; motions that would not have been filed before were; appeals that would have been finessed were filed. Criminal justice was being homogenized, scandalously late, and suddenly the system had to digest a richer mix.

Bail reform had similar side effects. The purpose was to eliminate the "ransom" element of bail, which put the poor behind bars awaiting trial and rewarded the more affluent with freedom. Congress passed a law in 1966 that pegged defendants' freedom to reliability rather than means; if a person seemed likely to appear on the designated day for his trial, then he would be released without bail. The idea was just, and it caught on in communities across the country. But those who await the remote day of trial on the outside, free to consult with gratis counsel about ever-expanding constitutional defenses, are not the stuff of which *mea culpas* are made. Many were pleading guilty to misdemeanor charges, such as petty theft or simple assault.

Whatever the reasons, the freeze now seems to be on, and getting worse, in most large cities. The result is to force prosecutors to let chronic criminals facing serious charges plead guilty to misdemeanors carrying relatively brief prison terms. Less serious cases are often dropped altogether, and cases where the evidence is weak result in minor punishments or probation. The overall impact on a community's system of justice can be devastating. In New York City, the number of felony arrests rose from 29,257 in 1960 to 49,803 in 1967. Felony indictments increased only slightly, from 11,086 to 11,528. But convictions for felonies actually declined—from 3,361 to 3,296. The figures for robbery were even more startling. From 1960 to 1967, the number of reported robberies more than doubled, from 15,500 to 35,934. The number of convictions for robbery dropped, from 837 to 803. Not all of the offenders were going scot-free. The city's jails, where misdemeanor prisoners are kept, were bursting at the seams—while the state prisons were standing partially empty because the courts were not managing to grind out felony convictions.

Some defense lawyers even think that the trial logjam in many big-city courts can be a good thing. With prisons as nonrehabilitative as they are, a good argument can be made that people should not be sent to jail for relatively minor offenses. In more leisurely times prosecutors could spare the time and effort to send first-time petty criminals to jail, but in many cities the trial backlogs are so huge that the prosecutors are content to drop these "junk" cases or agree to probation after guilty pleas. Harry J. Subin, a New York University law professor who agrees that jammed court dockets can help prevent prosecutorial harshness, set out in the late 1960s to explore the possibilities of reducing trial delays in the Bronx by bringing only serious felony cases to trial. "We went from court to court, and found that they weren't trying anything but serious felonies already," Mr. Subin reported. The project was dropped.

In the one community where all the likely contributing factors converged—high crime, urban congestion and Federal jurisdiction—the impact was enough to send a shiver through the legal profession. In Washington, D.C., the criminal justice system almost ground to a halt.

The first signs appeared late in 1968, when it was noticed that the number of burglaries and robberies had roughly doubled from the previous year. Banks were robbed so frequently that timid souls feared to enter with their money, and by the year's end there had been 102 bank robberies, where there had been 29 the year before. Of the 67 suspects who were arrested, only 4 were brought to trial that year. A few others pleaded guilty. Most of the rest were on the street, and some were caught in later stick-ups. The previous year had been bad enough, with 56,598 reported "index" crimes, 9,181 arrests and only 940 convictions for index crimes. (An unknown number of those arrested had pleaded guilty to less serious offenses.) Even then, in 1967, things had begun to slow down; 2,283 cases were still pending at the end of the year.

Compared even to that record, 1968 was a disaster. Of the 65,982 index crimes reported, there were 14,125 arrests. Only 255 adults were convicted of index offenses. The year's end found 8,248 cases still pending. To those who were criminally inclined the gap between crime and punishment had become invitingly wide: with serious criminality hurtling along at a reported rate of almost 66,000 per year, the number of people being convicted each year for those same serious crimes was so small that they could be seated comfortably in one courtroom. (It would have been appropriate to gather them there—more than 90 percent of those convicted in felony trials in Washington elect to appeal, and more than 20 percent win reversals.) By early 1969 the situation had spawned some famous characters, including Tyrone Parker, who over the previous two years had been arrested successively for armed robbery, assault with a gun, armed robbery, assault with a board, armed robbery, robbery with a gun, bank robbery and bank robbery again. He was released after each arrest and had not been convicted of any of the offenses. Washington's reported crime rate, already high, continued to climb faster than the national average.

In February of 1969, emergency measures went into effect. First-degree murders and armed robberies were scheduled for trial first, then second-degree murder cases and unarmed robberies. Defendants accused of such nonviolent felonies as housebreaking, daytime burglary and narcotics violations saw their cases go to the bottom of the pile. Twelve of the District's fifteen District Judges pitched in to clear away the priority cases (the civil docket had to make do with the remaining judge power), and the city fathers pleaded with Congress for more judges, more prosecutors, more court space to take up the slack.

This was the crisis that gave the nation the term "preventive detention." President Nixon, fresh in office with a law-and-order mandate, promised the extra help but added a demand for a new type of law, alien to the presumption of innocence concept, but necessary, he said, to keep "hard-core" criminals out of circulation pending their trials. The idea is laced with moral and constitutional questions, but those who doubt the ability of the courts to dispense quick justice fear that it has a future.

An extremely high percentage of the total crime in the country is committed by a relative handful of repeaters. If a person has been arrested for burglary or a serious crime of violence, he will acquire, on the average, about nine other arrests to his credit. In the District of Columbia this has approached a revolving-door stage; more than one-third of the accused robbers released on bond were indicted for new crimes committed while they were free on bond. Yet psychologists say it is next to impossible to sift out those who would actually become repeaters from others with similarly odious backgrounds. It takes little imagination to see that some people would be "detained" as the price of being unwashed, unkempt, surly, black or perhaps just large and tough-looking.

The Eighth Amendment declares that "excessive bail shall not be required," but it does not say that all offenders must be given the chance to go free on bail. Bail has traditionally been denied in capital cases. In noncapital cases judges often practice preventive detention in fact, by setting bail so high that the defendants can't raise it. But this is actually a violation of the purpose of bail, which is supposed to be only a device to assure defendants' presence in court for trial. When a preventive detention law was passed in 1970 to authorize pretrial jailing of defendants in the District of Columbia thought likely to repeat their crimes, it became inevitable that the Supreme Court must eventually decide if the procedure is swift and fair enough to satisfy due process standards. While constitutional lawyers attuned to present concepts shake their heads over the prospect, the memory of the Supreme Court's approval of the internment of Japanese during World War II is too fresh to say what may constitutionally be done under the stress of runaway criminality.

The prospect that justice might become mired in its own procedures has thrown a shadow across the glittering reforms of the due process revolution, just when it seemed that the Supreme Court had won, that the police were adjusting to the changes and that the public was becoming resigned to them. The pulse of such events can often be felt in Washington, and there were many who perceived that attitudes changed, moderated, during the emotional turmoil that surrounded the Supreme Court in the spring of 1969. It all happened just as the word was circulating throughout the Capital that President Nixon was polishing a message to Congress which would surpass his get-tough preventive detention proposal. The President was planning to ask Congress to review the entire question of criminal suspects' rights, with an emphasis on *Miranda* v. *Arizona* and other cases that had expanded the privilege against self-incrimination. He planned to leave it to Congress to decide whether the Fifth Amendment should be amended or if other steps should be taken—an invitation that wise heads in Washington said could only prompt the anti-Court elements to pick up where they left off in 1968.

Nixon seemed about ready to make his move in early May, when *Life* magazine shattered the spell by making public the story of Abe Fortas' $20,000 fee. In terms of history, Fortas became the first member of the Supreme Court to resign under fire when the disclosure of his financial ties to the family foundation of Louis E. Wolfson, an imprisoned stock manipulator, forced him from the bench. But in terms of the psychology of the time, it meant far more. Fortas had been an outspoken liberal who explained his views in terms of the developing conscience of civilized men. His exercise of those views had produced the crucial fifth vote in *Miranda*. (Later, it was disclosed that on the day after *Miranda* v. *Arizona* was announced, Fortas flew to Florida for a rendezvous with Wolfson.) When he was forced from the bench, the public bile that had risen against the Warren Court began to recede. The man who had once been tapped to carry forward the liberal standard of the Warren era was gone; his departure had weakened, perhaps extinguished the liberal majority, and had shaken the Court's reputation. Almost instantly, pique toward the Court began to give way to concern for it.

President Nixon tried to help repair the damage by quickly appointing as Chief Justice Warren Burger, a man who could have been type-cast as The Down-To-Earth Judge. He was not well known to the public so Burger's image as a nominee had a one-dimensional cast that, while it unfairly minimized his intellectual qualities, did have a tranquilizing effect on the critics of the Court. A former Minnesota lawyer who had worked his way up by dint of sound Presbyterian virtues and solid Republic credentials, Burger projected a brand of Middle Western, middle-aged and middle-brow practicality that was the antithesis of Fortas' intellectual idealism. Burger had criticized the Warren Court's criminal decisions, not because they offended his concept of constitutional propriety, but because they outraged his sense of practicality. He did not argue, as some constitutional lawyers still do, that the Warren Court strayed from sound principles of federalism and constitutional theory when it rejected the fundamental fairness doctrine for the rigidities of selective incorporation. He complained instead that the Warren Court's technique did not work, that the exclusionary rule tended to hobble the police without protecting suspects, and that the Court should have used its rule-making power to experiment with the new procedures within the Federal system before it fastened them on the states. After he joined the Court these beliefs were to establish him quickly as the anchor man of the right wing where criminal suspects' rights were concerned. He had been appointed as a law-and-order judge, and nobody who approved of those qualities later complained of his performance.

Richard Nixon put his seal of approval upon the situation when he appeared personally to speak before the Supreme Court on the day of Earl Warren's retirement. Standing at the counsel's podium, the first President ever to make a speech in the Supreme Court, with Fortas' departure marked by an empty seat and Burger present for his swearing-in, Nixon reviewed the Warren legacy and pronounced it good. There had been "continuity with change," he said, and the nation needed both. There was no hint that anything done by the Warren Court should now be undone. After he finished, Warren Burger was sworn in as Chief Justice, and an unspoken event had occurred. The Supreme Court that Nixon had so profitably belabored was no more. His appointee now sat as Chief Justice, and he would have the opportunity to wipe out the liberal majority when he named a successor to Abe Fortas. The Supreme Court was quickly becoming the Nixon Court. Talk ceased within the Nixon administration about encouraging Congress to review the work of the Supreme Court on crime.

Shortly after Earl Warren announced his retirement, he disclosed that he would not return to California as reported, but that he would stay in Washington to assist the new Federal Judicial Center in its efforts to reduce court delay. The major changes in criminal law had been made, he said, and now it was far less pressing to define what the law means than to work out some way to put it more rapidly into effect.

What he was saying was that the reforms of the Warren era were fairly secure from direct attack by critics. What he was conceding was that they were vulnerable to the erosion of delay. By then it had become apparent that some of the Court's rulings were being honored in the breach, but these were only the few decisions that bore directly upon police practices. Most of the Court's reforms were widely approved, at least in legal and governmental circles, and they had obviously taken root. A period of consolidation and patching-up was in prospect, but American justice had been placed on a higher plateau and it seemed likely to remain at that level until there was some future opportunity for reform—either by the Supreme Court or at other levels.

What Earl Warren saw was that due process alone was not enough—that the criminal justice system must not only work fairly, it must also work. If not, preventive detention and perhaps more extreme antidotes to impotent justice could become commonplace in American justice, and make a mockery of all the reforms that have been made by the Warren Court.

XIII

Revolution and After

We have to choose, and for my part I think it is a less evil that some criminals should escape than that the government should play an ignoble part.

OLIVER WENDELL HOLMES

Several days after President Nixon nominated Warren Earl Burger to be Chief Justice, a politically oriented Washington restaurant with a puckish sense of humor listed a "Warrenburger" on its menu, priced at three cents.

The Warrenburger: One slice of bread and a glass of water.

The President must have been pleased to see his message had been so clearly understood: He had picked a law-and-order judge to lead the Supreme Court, and the nation could expect a sterner brand of justice in the future.

Mr. Nixon had gone to some pains to put this point across,

starting with the appointment itself. Prior to the nomination, Judge Burger had been known, when at all, for his criticism of judicial hair-splitting on behalf of criminal defendants and of Supreme Court actions that he thought had made criminal justice too cumbersome to protect the public. This was about all the press knew of the nominee on the night of his surprise nomination, and most of the headlines spread the word that a law-and-order judge had been named to succeed liberal Earl Warren.

The President drove the point home by calling in the press the next day to remind them that Burger's record as a lower court judge reflected Mr. Nixon's own distaste for the recent liberal trend on criminal suspects' rights.

With the Burger appointment, the President said he hoped that the trend would be reversed. Knowing that he would also have the opportunity to fill the vacancy created by Abe Fortas' resignation and anticipating that Hugo Black and William Douglas might not outlast his Presidency, Nixon obviously hoped to fulfill his campaign promise to turn the Supreme Court around on crime. This strategy became apparent in the Nixon administration's barren labors to seat Clement F. Haynsworth, Jr., and G. Harrold Carswell on the Supreme Court. Neither man had a track record as a law-and-order judge in the Burger mold, but senators who opposed them were accused of being soft on crime. The judge who was finally confirmed to fill the vacancy, Harry A. Blackmun, had earned his "strict constructionist" credentials by taking conservative positions on criminal suspects' rights.

It might well have been anticipated, as the Warren Court proceeded to make increasingly broad policy decisions, that eventually some of its actions would strike a sour note with the public and that a President would be elected on a pledge to try to undo what the Supreme Court had done. Presidents had feuded with the Supreme Court before, but never had a candidate won the office on the specific promise to use his appointive power to change the Court's direction on a particular issue. When Richard Nixon won on a pledge to appoint men who were "strict constructionists" on criminal issues, and when the new President pointedly began to appoint Justices who seemed to fit that description, the stage was set for an early test of a President's capacity to deliver on a promise to change the course of the Supreme Court.

At the outset, President Nixon was confronted with the famous unpredictability of Supreme Court nominees. The same frustrations that led Theodore Roosevelt to compare Oliver Wendell Holmes' backbone to a banana shortly after naming him to the Supreme Court have prompted other Presidents to gnash their teeth over the independence of the men who have recently donned Supreme Court robes. President Nixon's best hedge against this hazard was the likelihood that later in his term he would have more Court vacancies to fill.

However, the due process revolution is not so vulnerable as a few highly publicized 5 to 4 decisions might suggest. From the time of the *Mapp* decision in 1961 to Earl Warren's departure, the Supreme Court handed down more than 200 opinions on criminal issues. Some reaffirmed longstanding precedents. Others dealt with special problems—obscenity is the best example—that did not affect criminal justice as a whole. Some two dozen of these criminal rulings decided critical questions of federalism and criminal procedure, and thus established the direction of the due process revolution.

If the Justices of the Supreme Court saw any distinction between those decisions that were directed at the procedures to be followed inside the courtroom and those that were designed to police the police in the field, they did not discuss the subject in public. But once President Nixon set out to attack the Court's libertarian thrust by appointing Justices who would take a critical view of what had been done, a striking distinction emerged: with one possible exception, the in-court reforms were secure, but of the three major court doctrines for policing the police, two were vulnerable to attack.

Congress' fulminations over the 5 to 4 confessions decision planted the impression that the Warren majority was teetering on the brink throughout its criminal law revolution, but almost the opposite was true where the in-court reforms were concerned. Many of these were decided with no more than two Justices in dissent. These included the decisions that required free counsel for the poor at trials (9–0), established due process safeguards for youngsters in juvenile court proceedings (7–2), guaranteed jury trial rights in criminal contempt cases (7–2) and for petty offenses (7–2), required the physical presence of prosecution witnesses at state trials (9–0), forbade critical comment about the defendant's failure to take the stand (6–2), and barred the enforcement of gambling, narcotics and fire-arms statutes that required the filing of incriminating information (8–1).

The Court was more narrowly divided when it ruled out the exclusion of persons who oppose capital punishment from sitting on juries in capital cases (6–3), held that poor defendants must be furnished a free trial transcript (5–4) and free counsel (6–3) to aid them in their appeals, and ruled that the Federal procedure for testing the voluntariness of confessions must be followed in state trials (5–4). But the dissenters in these cases have long since acquiesced, if not approving the results, and none are considered even remotely likely to be reversed.

The single in-court reform that may be in doubt is the wide-open accessibility of the Federal District courts to state prisoners' habeas corpus pleas. The Warren Court split 5 to 4 on the question, and many judges and lawyers are aghast at the outpouring of jailhouse petitions that has followed. If this continues and the state post-conviction procedures improve, the Supreme Court might decide to narrow the Federal courts' availability to state convicts.

From all of this it was apparent that Richard Nixon's appointments would not cause the Supreme Court to retract any of the important reforms of in-court procedures that had occurred during the Warren years. They were not very controversial when they were announced, and in most cases a body of law had quickly developed in their wake that would have made it awkward to turn the clock back several years later.

Moreover, the Warren Court did not leave many criminal issues for others to decide. The notable exceptions are the constitutional status of bail and capital punishment; the limitations —if any—on states' power to initiate felony charges without grand jury indictments; the constitutional ramifications of plea bargaining; and the constitutionality of the common practice that permits prosecutors to disclose defendants' past criminal records if they testify in their own defense. Such issues are unlikely to inspire "Impeach Warren Burger" billboards, no matter how swashbuckling an approach the Burger Court might take.

It was the Supreme Court's efforts to police the police outside the courtroom that got it in trouble with the public, and this is where the Burger Court can be expected to backtrack, if at all. Not unexpectedly, the Court's decisions that extended the use of constitutional absolutes to regulate police searches, lineups and interrogation divided the Justices as bitterly as they did the nation at large. Even then, there were not as many 5 to 4 decisions as many critics seemed to believe.

Mapp v. *Ohio* was decided by a vote of 5 to 4. That margin has since become unimportant, though, because there is no serious prospect that the Court will take back its decision to suppress in state courts evidence that has been obtained in violation of the Fourth Amendment. If Federal officials have been able to live with this rule since 1914, it is not likely that the Supreme Court could be convinced that it stands in the path of law and order in the cities today. The Justices will undoubtedly continue to tinker with such details as the requirements for search warrants and the steps police must take to obtain valid consent for warrantless searches, but nobody expects the Burger Court to say that states may resume using illegally-obtained evidence if they wish.

Lawyers have proved so insignificant at lineups that *Wade* v. *United States* would have been accorded the obscurity it merited if it had not been announced at the height of the backlash against the *Miranda* v. *Arizona* ruling. When the Supreme Court handed down its *Wade* and *Stovall* decisions in June of 1967, Senator John L. McClellan's criminal law subcommittee was in the final throes of marshaling its testimony and indignation against the Supreme Court's interrogation decisions. To Senator McClellan, a lawyer in any part of a police station was equally odious, whether it was the interrogation room or lineup gallery. So the subcommittee tacked a final barb onto what was to become Title II of the Omnibus Crime Control Act of 1968, declaring that "the testimony of a witness that he saw the accused commit or participate in the commission of the crime for which the accused is being tried shall be admissible into evidence" in any Federal trial.

Without this, the *Wade* decision's exclusion of identifications made at lawyerless confrontations would probably not have been disturbed, even though three of the six Justices in the majority (Warren, Fortas and Clark) had been replaced on the Burger Court. The *Stovall* case's suppression of faulty show-up identifications was even more secure. Only Hugo Black dissented against that, as he did whenever the Court used a "fairness" application of the due process clause without reference to a specific portion of the Bill of Rights to strike down a police practice. Title II of the 1968 crime control statute only partially contradicts these rulings, as it precludes only the in-court identification of defendants based upon witnesses' at-the-scene observations. These would be admissible anyway, if the state could show that they were not tainted by an unconstitutional lineup or show-up. But since Congress did undertake, in its heavy-handed way, to overrule the *Wade* and *Stovall* decisions, the Supreme Court will eventually have to confront them again. This will be especially difficult because the statutory attack upon the identification rulings is associated with the far more troublesome question of what is to be done about *Miranda* v. *Arizona*.

If any of the handiwork of the Warren Court is likely to be discarded or greatly modified now that the Warren Era is over, it is the Court's novel approach to interrogation and confessions. The main risk to the lineup cases is that they will topple with the interrogation restrictions. *Miranda* v. *Arizona* bears many of the earmarks of a potential sacrificial lamb to the law-enforcement backlash: It was backed in the first instance by only five Justices (two of whom have since departed); its adverse impact on police effectiveness was magnified when the Court blundered and made it partially retroactive; Richard Nixon became committed to its demise on the way to the White House; and its underlying theory that rigid exclusionary rules can police the cop on the beat seems to have lost the confidence even of the Supreme Court's liberal Justices.

Subsequent events have shown that the Warren Court was wrong when it assumed that the police would get the message if it insisted that no confession would ever be admitted regardless of the circumstances unless, at the time of arrest, every suspect is warned of his rights. Despite the Court's painstaking efforts to anticipate all eventualities, situations continue to happen that expose the inherent difficulties of refusing to consider peculiar circumstances that might excuse a failure to give all of the warnings.

One famous incident was the interrogation of Senator Edward M. Kennedy by the Chief of Police of Edgartown, Massachusetts, on the day after the tragic drowning of a young secretary in Kennedy's car in the summer of 1969. Senator Kennedy was a lawyer himself, and a companion was a former United States Attorney. The police chief was so abashed by the necessity of questioning Senator Kennedy that he did not give any of the *Miranda* warnings. It was a vivid refutation of the Supreme Court's view that all statements made in police custody must be presumed to be the product of an intimidating atmosphere. If anyone was rattled it was the chief of police, and any concessions on Senator Kennedy's part were prompted by motives of his own. It would probably have been superfluous to inform the Senator of his right to counsel, but the *Miranda* opinion makes it clear that even lawyers must be told, before they are questioned "in custody," that they may remain silent and that anything they say may be used against them. Later, when Senator Kennedy appeared in court to plead guilty to leaving the scene of the fatal accident, his lawyer mentioned that there were defenses that could have been raised. Privately, the Senator's lawyers expressed the belief that in a case with no public opinion considerations, a successful effort to quash the statement might have been made.

In other situations, it would have simply been foolish for the police to give the *Miranda* warnings at the moment of arrest. A Texas Court, for instance, was faced with the case of a man who was collared by the police at night in the vicinity of a building that was being burgled. They quickly clapped handcuffs on the suspect's wrists and asked (without a *Miranda* warning) how many burglars were inside. He replied "just one," and the statement was later used to prove that he was in on the crime. When the judges are faced with the necessity of issuing a decision that they cannot explain rationally, they often fall back on a cloudy Latin term, as they did here. They ruled that the statement was admissible against the burglar as part of the *res gestae*—words that are spoken contemporaneously with the crime and thus becomes a part of it—even though the *Miranda* case clearly says that when a policeman arrests a suspect and wants information from him, he must first give the full warning.

When the Supreme Court announced the *Miranda* decision in 1966, the Justices knew that they would have to close loopholes as time went on. Otherwise, the police would quickly learn ways to get around the rule and to reduce it to an empty ritual. Justice Byron R. White, who had written bitterly of rape and murder to come in his *Miranda* dissent, pointed out in a little-noticed speech a few weeks later that subsequent decisions would determine how much bite the decision would really have. White realized that the aging liberal majority of the Warren Court could not remain intact much longer. He suggested five questions, yet to be answered, that would ultimately determine if the liberals would have their way in clamping down on police interrogation. As it happened, the Court managed to answer only one of them before events wiped out the liberal majority.

The *Miranda* opinion said that the warnings must be given after a suspect is taken into custody "or otherwise deprived of his freedom of action in any significant way." But it also stressed the evils of police station interrogation, which was said to be inherently coercive. This led to some wishful thinking among police that interrogation outside the station house might be all right. The Court quickly disabused them of those thoughts, holding that a suspected killer who was arrested in bed was then in custody and should have been warned before he was asked where he hid his gun.

But the more important questions listed by Byron White were still unanswered when Warren Burger became Chief Justice: If the police fail to give the *Miranda* warnings and a suspect's confession is inadmissible, is the prosecution also barred from using the weapon, the corpse, the subsequent admission that the police were able to obtain because they had the invalid confession? Can a tainted confession be used for such secondary purposes as to indict the defendant, contradict his testimony, assist the judge in sentencing or support a parole revocation? Does the *Miranda* rule require warnings or counsel at such information-gathering stages as psychiatrists' interviews or juvenile officers' talks with children? Most important of all, what must the prosecution show to prove that the defendant "voluntarily, knowingly and intelligently" waived his rights to silence and counsel before he talked?

Unwilling to say that a suspect must consult a lawyer before he can waive his rights to one, the Court had opted to play the waiver issue by ear. In the *Miranda* decision it placed a "heavy burden" on the prosecution to prove that any given suspect had waived his rights before he talked, and left it to future decisions to say in more detail what the police must specifically prove to validate a suspect's confession.

From the defense standpoint, this approach was satisfactory only under the assumption that the Warren majority would remain intact to continue turning the screw on the police. Previously, the Warren Court's impact on police practices had required more than a willingness to propound bold decisions. The Court had also been strong on follow-through. It constantly patched up landmark decisions, closed loopholes, blocked end-runs by the police, and in the process generated as much police frustration by the quantity of its criminal rulings as by their substance. So the entire process was vulnerable to the possibility that other winds might blow in the near future. As it turned out, the souring of public attitudes toward suspects' rights was hastened by *Miranda*, while the waiver loophole permitted lower courts to deal with confessions on virtually the same subjective grounds that *Miranda* had been designed to abolish.

Miranda changed little by declaring that confessions were invalid unless the suspect had "voluntarily" waived his rights. Voluntariness had been the test before *Miranda*, and the same "totality of the circumstances" standard would have to be used to test the voluntariness of a waiver that used to apply to the voluntariness of the confession itself. If anything, the Court complicated things by the further requirement that the waiver be "knowing and intelligent." There seems to be almost an inherent contradiction in the proposition that a person acts with intelligence when he waives rights that could save him from punishment. The Romans believed that "such is the nature of every confession that the one who confesses may be regarded as insane." But frequently the statements that get suspects in trouble are not full confessions, but inadvertent concessions or contradictions contained in self-serving conversations. Suspects may feel that they are being quite shrewd in talking to the police, but in the cold light of a subsequent trial it may seem that any intelligent person should have known better. As one harried New York judge has put it, the process of searching for intelligence in such matters is comparable to trying to decide in a divorce case if a man acted intelligently years before when in an ardent moment he proposed marriage.

On the subject of what makes a valid waiver, the *Miranda* opinion afforded only a few hints—some of which have been widely ignored by the lower courts. The opinion did say that neither silence by a suspect in response to the warnings nor the mere fact that the suspect later confessed can be taken as a valid waiver. It suggested that "an express statement that the individual is willing to make a statement and does not want an attorney" could be one. What the lower courts have done with this standard is a monument to the impotence of the Supreme Court to change police practices without first persuading the public and the bar that the old ways are unreasonable.

Nobody knew how many suspects should be expected to waive their rights, but it was reasonable to assume that many would not. In court, only 1 or 2 percent of the defendants in criminal trials reject free counsel and go it alone. With free counsel available during interrogation, there was every reason to feel that there would be many takers. Yet in the District of Columbia, the only city where the result has been tested, only 7 percent of the people arrested asked for counsel—so few that the program to provide free counsel was abandoned.

With so many suspects talking to the police despite the *Miranda* warnings, the lower courts have been caught in a conflict between their experience and the Supreme Court's logic. In the best Holmsian tradition, the law has followed experience. As logical as it might have seemed to the Supreme Court to declare a heavy presumption against the proposition that persons would voluntarily and intelligently waive their rights to counsel and silence, many criminal suspects seem to be doing so. Sometimes they give unambiguous waivers and sometimes they are more taciturn. To the lower courts, the result is heavy pressure to find that a person who has voluntarily talked to the police after a warning meant to waive his rights, whether he specifically said so or not.

The subtleties of the situation were demonstrated shortly after the *Miranda* case was announced, when the U.S. Court of Appeals for the Fourth Circuit, normally a favorable forum for defendants, upheld the confession of a suspect whom they said had impliedly waived his rights. Rufus Hayes had been arrested by F.B.I. agents at mid-day, taken to the local police station, warned fully of his rights, and permitted to make a telephone call. When he returned from making his call, the agents proceeded to question him, without ever asking him if he understood the *Miranda* warnings or if he desired counsel. He talked to them for about thirty minutes and in the process let some information slip that helped to convict him. Then he said he would talk no more and demanded to see his lawyer.

The Appeals Court held that Hayes' abrupt assertion of his rights showed that he understood and waived them when he previously talked to the agents. When the Supreme Court declined to review his appeal, it permitted—temporarily, at least—the spread of a doctrine that undercut the theory and express language of the *Miranda* decision. In the first place, it sanctioned subjective delving into the special circumstances of each confession, thus undercutting the objective rule that *Miranda* was supposed to create. It also encouraged courts to accept a subject's silence and confession in the wake of the *Miranda* warnings as proof that the subject waived his rights—a proposition that the Court expressly rejected in its opinion. Meanwhile, courts across the country have accepted silence as proof that rights were waived, often under circumstances much less persuasive than the *Hayes* case. Some courts have found implied waivers even after suspects refused to sign written ones. Other decisions have held that when suspects were warned at one interrogation session and kept silent, then talked at a later session when no warning was given, that the first warning had been waived and the statement would be used.

The last laugh in the *Miranda* episode was not had by its author, Earl Warren (who did not mention it when he later listed the three most important decisions of his tenure on the Court), but by Fred E. Inbau and John E. Reid, the authors of the interrogation manual that he quoted frequently and with disapproval in the *Miranda* decision. To show that secret interrogation was inherently coercive, even without the rubber hose or third degree, Warren exposed the techniques taught in that manual and others, which enable the police to bring psychological pressures to bear on the suspect to "persuade, trick, or cajole him out of exercising his constitutional rights." With this to recommend it, the manual became a best seller among police and a second edition had to be printed. "All but a few of the interrogation tactics and techniques presented in our earlier publication are still valid," the authors purred in their post-*Miranda* edition, adding that all that is required is to give the warnings, get a waiver, and proceed.

Not all lower courts have been niggardly about *Miranda* rights; some have observed the decision to the letter, and a few have given it expanded meaning—at times to their own grief. This has been one of the peculiar results of the Warren Court's swing from the ad hoc "fairness" approach to the technique of dealing with criminal procedure by means of constitutional absolutes. Since a constitutional right under the Bill of Rights is held to apply to all cases regardless of the circumstances, a lower court acts at its peril if it is swayed by the appealing circumstances of a given case to go beyond the Supreme Court's interpretation of a provision of the Bill of Rights. If it does so, the police who operate within the lower court's jurisdiction can find themselves stuck with the expanded rule in all situations.

This happened to the Supreme Court of Pennsylvania, which became distressed that individuals were waiving their *Miranda* rights because the required warnings apparently did not impress upon them the importance of asking for a lawyer's help. A vivid example of this came to the court's attention after Geraldine Taper of New Kensington, seventeen years old and immature of mind but not body, shot and killed the father of one of her two bastard children. The police effortlessly persuaded her to sign a waiver of rights and then a detailed statement about the shooting. This persuaded the Pennsylvania Supreme Court that the warnings had not given her enough information upon which to base an intelligent decision to waive her rights. So the Court ruled that in addition to the four *Miranda* warnings, a suspect should at least be told that "an attorney can inform him more fully of 'the nature of the charges, the statutory offenses included within them, the range of allowable punishments thereunder, possible defenses to the charges and circumstances in mitigation thereof, and all other facts essential to a broad understanding of the whole matter.' "

Later, it apparently dawned upon the Pennsylvania Justices that they had, in effect, tacked a long and complicated fifth warning onto the *Miranda* rule, which all policemen in Pennsylvania would thereafter have to recite to all suspects. Courts rarely withdraw opinions, once announced, but the Pennsylvania court quickly killed its opinion in *Taper* v. *Commonwealth*. The opinion by that name that subsequently appeared in the official law reporter made no mention of its unfortunate predecessor, but held simply that the totality of the circumstances showed that Miss Taper had not voluntarily waived her rights.

A few other state courts have also done the Supreme Court one better. (Because of a state court ruling, police in Tennessee have been issued new *Miranda* cards, bearing the additional warning that the suspect may stop talking at any time—a warning not required by the *Miranda* decision itself.) But more often, appellate courts have tended to skirt the Supreme Court's edicts and rely upon the sense of justice of their own juries and trial judges. This has produced a little-noticed legal development that could eventually take the edge off many of the Supreme Court's criminal decisions, including *Miranda* v. *Arizona*.

When the Supreme Court first began to set standards of criminal procedure on a broad scale, it did not make clear whether any violation of its rulings should automatically invalidate a conviction, or if in some instances minor constitutional errors could be excused as harmless. The early indications were that any error voided a conviction. If a defendant did not have a lawyer at his trial, or if a coerced confession had been used against him, or if the judge stood to gain a fee if he were found guilty, there would be no inquiry as to whether he would have been found guilty anyway; the conviction was void. But as the

Supreme Court pyramided procedural rules, some retroactively, pressures mounted to excuse some fluffs as harmless error. On a purely theoretical basis, there were good reasons for the Supreme Court to refuse to forgive any constitutional error as harmless, since this would tend to dilute the objective constitutional rules that it had gone to such pains to lay down. The deterrent effect of an exclusionary rule may well be watered down if violations may later be excused as harmless. Also, if lower courts are permitted to overlook constitutional violations that do not appear to have affected the jury's decision, then the Supreme Court can find itself back where it started, reviewing each conviction on its facts.

But again, the Supreme Court was in trouble because it had given some of its decisions partial retroactive effect. The Justices had no stomach for throwing out a series of convictions because police or prosecutors had done things that were later held to be unconstitutional—especially if the actions clearly did not affect the result. So the Justices temporized. In 1967 they held that a prosecutor's criticism of a defendant for not taking the stand, while unconstitutional, could be overlooked— but only if it were found to be harmless beyond a reasonable doubt.

Having risked public fury by imposing rigid procedures on the police, the Court had sanctioned a means by which they might be outflanked. It left open—to be decided on a case-by-case basis—which constitutional violations would be absolute and which could be overlooked if they were felt to be harmless to the victim. Lower courts pounced on that rationale to forgive a variety of lapses, and in 1969 the Supreme Court was faced with the problem again, this time in a more difficult context. At issue was a complicated legal question involving the joint trial of four robbery-murder suspects, in which the jury heard two defendants' confessions, which implicated a third defendant. If the third man had been tried separately, the confessions would have been hearsay and could not have been used against him. William O. Douglas, easily the all-time Supreme Court recordholder for siding with the defense, this time held for the state. Although it had been unconstitutional to try the men together and introduce the confessions, he found that the evidence against the third man was so overwhelming anyway that the miscue was harmless error. This produced an unusual phenomenon for the Warren Court—a dissent that castigated a Douglas opinion as a damaging blow to suspects' rights. Justice Brennan, joined by Chief Justice Earl Warren and Thurgood Marshall, warned that the capacity of *Mapp* v. *Ohio, Miranda* v. *Arizona, United States* v. *Wade* and other landmark cases to deter "the actions of both police and prosecutors, not to speak of trial courts, will be significantly undermined."

By 1968, the Supreme Court was experiencing the worst of two worlds. Holes were appearing in the constitutional safeguards it had thrown up around criminal suspects, yet the opinion polls revealed rising public ire over the restraints that had been placed on the police. In the spring of that year, with Election Day approaching and the crime index also on the rise, Congress reacted to the prevailing mood by enacting the Crime Control Act with its Title II, a piece of dubious statesmanship designed more to chastise the Supreme Court than to improve the law.

When Title II burst from the relative obscurity of the Senate Judiciary Committee onto the Senate floor in April of 1968, it was immediately seen as a bald Congressional attempt to rap the Supreme Court's knuckles over crime. Its provisions read like a catalogue of familiar grievances against the Warren Court:

First, it purported to reverse *Miranda* v. *Arizona* as a rule of evidence in Federal trials by declaring that any confession "shall be admissible in evidence if it is voluntarily given." Judges were instructed to take into consideration the police's failure to warn suspects of their rights, but the effect was an attempt to overrule the *Miranda* ruling by statute. Second, it included the similar effort to overrule *United States* v. *Wade*, by declaring that Federal judges should admit eyewitness testimony, regardless of circumstances. These two sections applied only to Federal courts, but it was assumed that state legislatures would pass similar laws if these were to get by the Supreme Court. Third, it overturned *Mallory* v. *United States*, by saying that no confession shall be rejected merely because it was obtained during a delay in bringing the defendant before a magistrate. Fourth, it abolished the jurisdiction of the Federal courts to review state convictions in habeas corpus proceedings. Fifth, it stripped away the jurisdiction of the Supreme Court and all other courts to overturn a state court's finding that a confession was voluntary or a state or Federal trial court's holding that an eyewitness identification was admissible.

Nothing quite so irregular had ever been aimed at the Supreme Court by Congress before. It was essentially an attempt to use a statute to reverse a string of Supreme Court decisions, most of which had been interpretations of the Constitution. According to long-standing principles of constitutional law, an amendment to the Constitution would have been required to accomplish most of its objectives. Of 212 legal academicians who answered a Senator's questionnaire about it, all said it was unconstitutional. The supporters of Title II made little effort to disguise their intent to blackjack the Court into changing its course. In private, Senator McClellan called it "my petition for a rehearsing" on *Miranda*. The Senate Judiciary Committee all but admitted as much when it formally reported the measure to the Senate floor. "After all," the Committee explained, "the *Miranda* decision itself was by a bare majority of one, and with increasing frequency the Supreme Court has reversed itself. The Committee feels that by the time the issue of constitutionality would reach the Supreme Court, the probability rather is that this legislation would be upheld."

Those were the sentiments of a committee that was dominated by Southern senators who had been nursing hurt feelings over the school desegregation decision of 1954 and who wanted to take it out on the Supreme Court over crime. Congress as a whole was not so aroused, yet it did approve Title II (watered down in two important respects). The fact that it did reveals much about the Warren Court, as well as much about the temper of Congress. The irony of Title II was that, while only future events can disclose if Congress was correct in thinking that the Supreme Court would so readily change its mind, the Supreme Court itself had created the impression that it might. Regardless of who was right on the bedrock question of individual rights versus public security, it was the Supreme Court —not Congress—that first took a casual view of the Constitution's static qualities. The Warren Court planted the idea that the Constitution could be changed with far less bother than anyone had realized, and thus the notion was spread that rights so easily created can just as easily be taken away.

The complaint most frequently heard about the Warren Court during the 1960s was that the Justices had taken it upon themselves to change the law according to their own notions—that they were legislating, making the law instead of interpreting it, usurping the powers of Congress and the states. Wise old heads knew that this complaint had been hurled at the Supreme Court (and other courts as well) since the days of John Marshall and before, and they knew that with times changing as rapidly as they were, there was more reason than ever for the Supreme Court not to be timid about changing the law.

But the gusto with which the Warren Court had done so struck some people as being unseemly. In its fifteen-year span the Warren Court reversed so many prior decisions that the number of such reversals in the Court's prior 165-year-old history was increased by almost one-half. Most of those rulings had the effect of changing the meaning of the Constitution, sometimes in ways that made people feel personally threatened by crime. Yet according to traditional constitutional theory, these decisions by a few Justices could be reversed only through the massive consensus required to put across a constitutional amendment. That would have been difficult enough, but the Bill of Rights had never been amended, and there was a historic taboo against breaking the ice. Finally, the Court's own willingness to do by judicial decision what historically could have been done only by constitutional amendment had made the amendment process seem obsolete, if not naive. The result was a public frustration about the Court that could be seen on every hand—the public opinion polls, the opposition to Abe Fortas' nomination as Chief Justice, and the astounding phenomena of Title II.

The seeds of Title II were first sown when the Supreme Court itself taught Congress to shortcut the tedious amending process —a lesson that proved to be short-sighted at a time when many of the Court's own decisions were unpopular. Having struggled for years to pass the Twenty-Fourth Amendment to eliminate poll taxes in Federal elections, Congress did it the easy way when it decided in 1965 to abolish the poll taxes that were still collected in a few states in local elections. It declared as an aside to the Civil Rights Act of 1965 that poll taxes discriminate against the poor and Negroes and that the Attorney General should bring suits to have those that remained declared unconstitutional. When the first suit reached the Supreme Court (as it happened, it was one brought by individual Negroes), the Justices obligingly reversed a prior ruling and abolished the poll tax, finding it a violation of the Fourteenth Amendment's ubiquitous equal protection clause.

Having vastly expanded its own powers through the use of the Fourteenth Amendment, the Supreme Court then did much the same for Congress. Under classical constitutional theory, Congress could enact only those laws that were necessary and proper to carry out powers delegated to the national government by the Constitution. Some of these—the war power, the taxing power and the power to regulate interstate commerce —had proved exceedingly elastic, but the Supreme Court could and did strike down laws on these subjects if the Justices determined that Congress had overstepped these bounds. From the Court's point of view, the important element was that when Congress purported to exercise these powers, the Court always had the last word. This clear judicial supremacy was jostled by the Court's own hand in 1966 when the Justices, straining to uphold a statute designed to put more Puerto Ricans on the voting rolls in New York, conceded some of its own authority to decide when an act of Congress is valid.

As commendable as it had been for Congress to relax New York's requirements that Spanish-speaking citizens must be literate in English in order to vote, there was one drawback— the Constitution grants the states and not Congress the general power to set voting requirements. This is limited by the premise that state voting standards are invalid if they discriminate unfairly against anyone, but here again Congress had a problem—the Supreme Court had already held that a requirement that voters be literate in English was not discriminatory. Still, the Supreme Court upheld the law and erased the English literacy requirement. Its reasoning: The Fourteenth Amendment gives Congress power to pass laws to enforce the amendment's safeguards. Courts have inherent power to do the same when violations are proved, so if the grant to Congress is to add anything to the strength of the amendment, it must carry with it an independent power on Congress' part to say when the amendment has been violated. Congress declared as a matter of fact in the 1965 law that the English literacy requirement *did* have the effect of diluting Spanish-speaking Americans' Fourteenth Amendment rights. Therefore, the Supreme Court must uphold the law if it can "perceive a basis" for Congress' conclusion that its law serves to enforce the Fourteenth Amendment.

In this way the Supreme Court neatly bootstrapped itself into a position to uphold Congress' finding that the English requirement violated the Fourteenth Amendment (the Justices "perceived" a probable belief by Congress that people who have the franchise are less likely to have their Fourteenth Amendment rights trampled), even though no court could cite evidence that it did.

This was, as Archibald Cox put it, "a strikingly novel form of judicial deference to constitutional power," and it was not long before the Court's critics in Congress were to throw these new precedents back at the Court with great glee. Title II was sufficient to reverse *Miranda* and *Wade*, they chuckled. Congress had found as a matter of fact that station-house interrogations were not inherently coercive and that lineups were not critical stages of criminal proceedings. As the Supreme Court had so recently said, "it is not for us to review the congressional resolution of these factors." The Supreme Court itself had been narrowly divided by these questions; surely, they said, it could "perceive a basis" for Congress' determination to the contrary.

Whether the Supreme Court can be hoist by its own petard in this fashion will eventually be decided by the Supreme Court when it reviews Title II. Its resourcefulness over the years in protecting its own turf suggests that some way will probably be found to avoid a complete reversal of both rulings. (In the same opinion that pledged the Justices' deference to acts passed by Congress in the name of the Fourteenth Amendment, the Court warned that it might renege if future acts of Congress cut back on rights already declared by the Supreme Court.)

But whether or not Congress succeeds in its attempts to reverse *Miranda* and *Wade* (there seems to be little reason why it cannot reverse *Mallory*, which was not a constitutional decision), the outcome will not be fatal to individuals' rights nor to the Supreme Court. One irony of Title II is that parts of it would have been a progressive expansion of suspects' rights if Congress had passed it prior to *Miranda*. It requires all of the elements of *Miranda* except the offer of free counsel, and it contains one feature that Miranda does not have—the statement that a suspect should be told the nature of the charges against him. The difference is that under Title II, the failure to comply with one of the elements does not invalidate a confession if it was otherwise voluntary.

If the Court swallows this Congressional attempt to roll back constitutional rulings by statute it will be an unfortunate precedent, but one that could fade with time. Far more dangerous to the Court as an institution is the threat that Congress would go beyond attacking particular decisions to strip away the Court's jurisdiction to consider broad classes of criminal cases. In the Senate Judiciary Committee's version of Title II, this was the intent of those sections designed to abolish the Federal courts' jurisdiction to review state convictions on habeas corpus proceedings or to overturn lower courts' rulings on confessions or lineup identifications. In the end, these provisions were eliminated from the measure and did not become law. But the threat posed by them remains a grave danger that hangs over the Supreme Court, one which could eventually confront the nation with a serious constitutional crisis over crime and the rights of individuals.

After almost two centuries of constitutional government, there are few loose ends that still seem capable of unraveling some of the fabric of the Constitution. One which does seem to have that potential is the apparent authority of Congress to regulate the Federal courts' jurisdiction to hear various types of cases. The problem is that the Constitution seems to give Congress the unqualified power to manipulate the jurisdiction of the Supreme Court and the inferior Federal courts. Congress, naturally enough, has accepted the Constitution at face value, since it seems to give the legislative branch this ultimate power over the otherwise independent judiciary. In speeches, statements, committee reports and other expressions of Congressional lore, it has been claimed that Congress has the ultimate power to add to or to subtract from the courts' authority to hear cases. The idea has become so deeply ingrained that even the Supreme Court has given lip service to it in unguarded moments.

Yet despite the seemingly clear words of the Constitution, reinforced by the Supreme Court's own rhetoric, it is inconsistent with the structure of the Government that Congress should have the power to bar the Supreme Court from reviewing selected questions of Federal law. With fifty state supreme courts and more than a dozen Federal appellate tribunals having independent authority to decide questions of Federal law, it is obvious that if the Supreme Court did not exist to maintain the uniformity and supremacy of Federal law, somebody would have to invent it. One of its essential functions is to see that the law of the United States means the same thing everywhere within its boundaries. From the standpoint of criminal defendants, also, it would seem to be a denial of due process to forbid any Federal court determination of constitutional rights. So the Court would have no alternative but to strike down any law designed to preclude it from reviewing certain Federal questions, even though the impression has been permitted to persist that Congress can accomplish this through its authority to control the Court's jurisdiction.

The apparent simplicity and symmetry of Article III of the Constitution obscures the complexity of this problem. Section 1 grants "judicial power" to the Supreme Court and the inferior courts that Congress chooses to create. Section 2 lists the types of cases that they can consider in exercising this judicial power, such as cases involving the United States, suits between citizens of different states, and—most relevant to the issue of criminal suspects' rights—controversies over the meaning of the United States Constitution. All of this, however, is subject to one proviso: "In all the . . . cases before mentioned, the Supreme Court shall have appellate jurisdiction, both as to law and fact, with such exceptions, and under such regulations as the Congress shall make."

A strong case can be made from these words alone that Congress has absolute power to control what the Supreme Court can hear. Events have reinforced the impression that it does. The first time Congress manipulated the Court's jurisdiction for the unabashed purpose of heading off an unwanted decision, it produced a ruling that has become a shorthand symbol for the proposition that Congress can do as it pleases with the Court's jurisdiction—*ex parte McCardle*. The setting, not unlike the present crime controversy, was the tension between the post-Civil War Congress and the courts as to how summarily justice could be visited on the former Confederates who opposed Reconstruction. William H. McCardle, an unreconstructed Mississippi newspaper editor, had been arrested in 1867 by military authorities and held for trial by a military commission. His articles were said to have committed offenses ranging from disturbing the peace to impeding reconstruction. He sought a writ of habeas corpus in the Federal Circuit court, pointing out that he was not in the service and could not be tried by a military tribunal. He lost there, but appealed to the Supreme Court under an 1867 statute that authorized appeals to the Supreme Court from decisions denying petitions for habeas corpus. At the arguments before the Supreme Court, McCardle's lawyer launched an assault on the constitutionality of the Reconstruction Acts, and it became apparent that the Supreme Court might well declare them unconstitutional in deciding McCardle's case. Congress moved swiftly. Before the Court could issue its decision, Congress repealed the 1867 law that permitted appeals to the Supreme Court in habeas corpus cases. "Without jurisdiction the court cannot proceed at all in any cause," the Court conceded. It unanimously dismissed McCardle's appeal, the Reconstruction Acts were spared, and the impression was created that in a pinch, Congress could resolve any conflict with the Supreme Court by limiting its jurisdiction.

So vivid was this impression that on occasion the Court itself paid lip service to it. In an 1881 decision in which it reaffirmed Congress' power to confine the Supreme Court review in admiralty cases to questions of law, the Court observed, with no apparent chagrin, that while its jurisdiction embraces the full judicial power of the United States, "actual jurisdiction under the power is confined within such limits as Congress sees fit to prescribe. . . . What those (appellate) powers shall be, and to what extent they shall be exercised, are, and always have been, proper subjects of legislative control. Authority to limit the jurisdiction necessarily carries with it authority to limit the use of the jurisdiction. Not only may whole classes of cases be kept out of the jurisdiction altogether, but particular classes of questions may be subjected to re-examination and review while others are not."

The Justices have not always been so complaisant about their powers. On several occasions they stated in dictum that Congress' authority over their jurisdiction had its limits. Once, when the Reconstruction Congress tried to bar ex-Confederates from suing the Government by means of an elaborate law that stripped the courts of jurisdiction to decide cases once certain facts about the plaintiff's disloyal background became known, the Supreme Court disregarded the law. This violated the separation of powers principle, the Court said, and some authorities have suggested that the same principle might apply if Congress tried to block the courts from considering particular questions entirely.

Still, the Supreme Court has never been confronted with the ultimate test—an act of Congress that purports to abolish the Court's jurisdiction to rule on a given subject. As sour as relations between the two branches have been at times, Congress has shied away from precipitating a struggle that it could win only at the price of upsetting the equilibrium between the two branches. In the decade before Title II was proposed, Congress had twice seriously considered measures of this type; once in a bill to strip away the Court's jurisdiction to review actions taken under the Government's loyalty-security program, and later in a proposal to bar the Court from considering certain reapportionment questions. Many members of Congress were down on the Supreme Court on both scores, but the bills failed by narrow votes because Congress had no taste for a constitutional crisis.

The same phenomenon developed when the Senate took up Title II. With the crime rate going up and the Supreme Court's stock going down, there was strong sentiment in Congress to chasten the Warren Court, but not at all costs. A compromise suggestion was quietly circulated through the Senate by Robert P. Griffin, the young Republican from Michigan who was to play a key role, only a few weeks later, in blocking Abe Fortas' confirmation as Chief Justice.

Nothing was said publicly about the strategy, so that when the voting on Title II got under way on May 21, 1968, it at first appeared that the Senate had panicked into an erratic, stunning assault on the Supreme Court. On the key vote, a motion to strike Title II from the bill, most observers had predicted a close vote. With wishful thinking firmly on the side of its opponents, there was some optimism that Title II would fall—though by a close enough vote to concentrate the Justices' thoughts on the problems of law enforcement.

Instead, the Senate voted to keep Title II by a startling 51 to 31 margin. Then, as the Senate voted section-by-section through Title II, a law-and-order bandwagon seemed to be rolling. A motion to strike the section reversing *Miranda* failed, 55 to 29. A similar vote on *Mallory* lost, 58 to 26. Then, without explanation, the Senate voted 52 to 32 to delete the section stripping the Court's jurisdiction to review state courts' rulings on confessions. Then just as inscrutably, the Senate voted 63 to 21 to keep the section reversing *Wade*.

The next vote was to be on a motion to strike the portion of the anti-*Wade* section that abolished the Federal courts' jurisdiction to review trial judges' decisions to admit eyewitness testimony. It appeared to be a part of the *Wade* provision that had just been approved. Senator Griffin, rising to point out the crucial distinction that it would strip away the Court's jurisdiction, tipped off the compromise strategy.

Referring to the sections that purported to reverse *Miranda* and *Wade*, he conceded that "Congress may fail in this effort when the Supreme Court reviews what we have done. Nevertheless, we are, with a clear and loud voice, giving the Supreme Court another opportunity to look at these questions—but after Congress has spoken." His purpose was to point out that this final clause involved "the question of whether Congress should take a much more drastic step and seek to limit the appellate jurisdiction of the U.S. Supreme Court." It was not necessary, he said, to argue if Congress can take such a step under Article

II of the Constitution. "I think the question is whether it would be the wise thing for Congress to do at this juncture in history," Senator Griffin said. Then he quoted a warning that had been sent in a letter from Francis Allen, Dean of the University of Michigan Law School:

> Stripping the Court of jurisdiction in certain types of cases because the members of Congress happen to disagree with the Court's view of the Constitutional commands is a step down a road that leads to fundamental alteration in the distribution of powers of the American system. Once a first step is taken along this path, it will be difficult to avoid other steps in the future. I regard Title II as fully as ominous an assault on the Supreme Court as the court-packing proposal of the 1930's. In some respects it may be a more insidious threat, for it is less forthright and candid, and its dangers less apparent to the public at large.

The Senate voted to strike that clause, 51 to 30. Then quickly, it voted 54 to 27 to strike the clause eliminating the Federal court's habeas corpus jurisdiction.

With the Supreme Court's jurisdiction left untouched, the remaining portions of Title II—John McClellan's "petition for a rehearing"—went on the books but not into effect. Attorney General Ramsey Clark circulated an order that Title II was to be ignored by the Justice Department; only evidence that squared with *Miranda* and *Wade* would be offered in evidence. Thus the Supreme Court would not have to face the question of Title II's constitutionality, because the law would not be invoked.

Richard Nixon changed that shortly after he became President. Attorney General John N. Mitchell passed the word that evidence could be used under the authority of Title II, whether the evidence comported with *Miranda* or *Wade* or not. Warnings were still to be given prior to questioning and lawyers were to be at lineups as a matter of policy. But in order to "salvage some cases which otherwise might be lost," when these steps were inadvertently overlooked, the evidence could be used. Thus it was assured that the Supreme Court would be confronted with the interrogation and lineup questions again, this time with a more conservative bench and the weight of Congress firmly against what the Warren Court had done.

Whatever the outcome, it was certain to be an anticlimax.

Suddenly, it was not a matter of great public importance that the Supreme Court was deciding cases in favor of defendants. It was as if the rebuke of Title II and Abe Fortas' defeat had been enough. Earl Warren stayed on for another year, and in that term the Supreme Court outdid itself in deciding cases on behalf of the accused. Of the twenty-six criminal decisions, the state won only eight. The next year, Warren Burger's first, almost one-third of the Court's docket involved suspects' rights, yet there was little public notice. Burger had once proposed avoiding the hazards of making police procedures on a case-by-case basis by substituting the Supreme Court's rule-making authority. He would have convened panels of advisers to help work out balanced rules of procedure which would become constitutional law only after they proved sound. He stopped talking about this after he became Chief Justice, and nobody noticed.

The fading of public tensions after Earl Warren left was a relief, but not a solution. The Senate's restraint had avoided one crisis, and the retirement of Earl Warren, coupled with Abe Fortas' departure, had prevented Richard Nixon from precipitating another one. Perhaps most crucial, it became known that the means chosen by the Warren Court to police the police —the exclusionary rule—was a nuisance but not a fully effective restraint.

This probably means that the post-Warren cooling-off period can be only an interregnum and not an end of the struggle by the Supreme Court to bring the police within the control of the Constitution. So long as no other means have been developed for some external controls over police conduct, it can only be a matter of time before the Supreme Court must undertake to enforce the same restraints again, but this time in a more effective form.

If the National Commission on the Causes and Prevention of Violence sees the future accurately, then the pressures of crime and racism that made the controversy over the Warren Court so volatile will be even more powerful as the years pass. Barring a radical change in national priorities, the Commission foresees lawlessness of such magnitude that the white middle class will retreat into guarded high-rise apartments and suburbs. Electronic alarms and vigilante patrols will keep out marauders from the slums. "High speed, patrolled expressways will be sanitized corridors connecting safe areas, and private automobiles, taxicabs, and commercial vehicles will be routinely equipped with unbreakable glass, light armor and other security features," it predicted. "Ghetto neighborhoods will be places of terror with widespread crime, perhaps entirely out of police control during night-time hours. Armed guards will protect all public facilities such as schools, libraries and playgrounds in these areas. Between the unsafe, deteriorating central city on the one hand and the network of safe, prosperous areas and sanitized corridors on the other, there will be, not unnaturally, intensifying hatred and deepening division. Violence will increase further, and the defensive response of the affluent will become still more elaborate," the Commission concluded.

If crime control is to take this paramilitary form, it seems inevitable that the Supreme Court will be drawn again into bitter controversy over citizens' right to be free from unlawful police power. Efforts by Federal judges to enjoin the police from aggressive patrol activities and systematic illegal searches would revive the charges that criminals were being coddled and the police handcuffed. Congress might feel it necessary to remove the Federal courts' jurisdiction to issue orders, and the long-avoided struggle for supremacy between the two branches would have come.

There is a tendency to minimize the threat of such a conflict, because the wounds suffered in the past were not, after all, so grievous. In each of the situations mentioned by Charles Evans Hughes—and in the Court's conflict with the New Deal—the Court was bloodied as it stood for property rights: rights to slaves, to tax havens, to hard money, and, in the 1930s, to the businessman's unencumbered use of his purse. In each instance, after the Supreme Court's defense of those rights was overcome, there was good reason to regret the Court's obdurance and a sense of relief that the Supreme Court had moved on to other concerns.

But a defeat over crime cannot be satisfactorily resolved as before, with the Court licking its wounds and moving on, wiser but not sadder, to other matters. When the Court found itself constantly at swordspoint with the other branches of the Government in the 1930s because it saw its role as a bulwark between the individual businessman and Government economic regulation (or interference, as the Court saw it), there was a way out, to the relief of one and all. The Court declared the Constitution irrelevant to substantive economic regulation, and the businessmen and the Government lived warily ever after.

Yet the Supreme Court cannot just get out of the business of shielding the individual from governmental police power. That is what the Bill of Rights—and the Supreme Court—is all about. So if Congress, state legislatures or city officials find it necessary to cut more and more deeply into individuals' rights in search of law and order, the Supreme Court may eventually have to take a stand and trust that the American public will swallow its fears and support the Court in a showdown with Congress. That is why there is an ominous void in the failure of any other institutions to come forward to help police the police. It has already been shown that nine men are not enough to do that, and to try again could produce an injury that would, unlike previous self-inflicted wounds, leave permanent scars.

Notes

Chapter I/ Crime and the Supreme Court

Page

1. William Howard Taft's quotation is from a commencement address at the Yale Law School in 1905. It is published in 15 Yale L. J. 1, at 16 (1905).
2. The de Tocqueville quotation is from *Democracy in America*, trans. by G. Lawrence (New York, Harper & Row, 1966), p. 137.
3. Hughes' lectures at Columbia were published in book form, *The Supreme Court of the United States* (New York, Columbia University Press, 1928). The quoted passages are from pp. 50–53.
6. Frankfurter's quotation is from his concurring opinion in *Adamson* v. *California*, 332 U.S. 46, at 67 (1947).
6. The Katzenbach quotation is from a celebrated letter from him to Chief Judge David L. Bazelon of the United States Court of Appeals for the District of Columbia, dated June 24, 1965. An exchange of letters between the two on the subject of a proposed Code of Pre-Arraignment Procedure then being considered by the American Law Institute was published in the *Washington Star* on August 4, 1965. The letters were reprinted in 56 Jour. Crim. Law, at 498 (1965). Katzenbach's "beat the rap" quotation is in 56 Jour. Crim. Law, at 502.
6. *Miranda* v. *Arizona*, discussed frequently in this book, is reported at 384 U.S. 436 (1966).
7. Dred Scott case is *Scott* v. *Sanford*, 60 U.S., (19 how), 393 (1857).
7. Friendly's statement was made at the American Law Institute meeting at the Mayflower Hotel in Washington, D.C., on Wednesday, May 18, 1966. It is printed in the *Proceedings of the 43rd Annual Meeting of the American Law Institute*, p. 250 (1966).
8. McClellan's peroration is printed at 114 Cong. Rec. 14155 (1968).

Chapter II/ The Politics of Crime

Page

10. George Wallace's quotation, from his all-purpose stump speech of the 1968 presidential campaign, was quoted by Fred J. Cooke in "There's Always a Crime Wave—How Bad is This One?" *The New York Times Magazine*, October 6, 1968, p. 39.

10. Charles I's warning was given in a letter to the House of Lords, May 12, 1628, published in William Cobbett, *Parliamentary History of England*, Vol. 2 (London, T. C. Hansard, 1808), pp. 351-52. Taft's statement is from his 1905 Commencement speech at Yale, published in 15 Yale L. J., at 15. The New York warning is quoted in Yale Kamisar's study of the "crime wave" syndrome in "Public Safety v. Individual Liberties: Some 'Facts' and 'Theories,' " 53 Jour. Crim. L. 171, at 172 (1962).

11. The crime statistics were published by the National Commission on the Causes and Prevention of Violence in its final report, *To Establish Justice, To Insure Domestic Tranquility* (Washington, D.C., U.S. Government Printing Office, 1969), pp. 18, 27.

12. McClellan's effective use of the crime index chart to flail the Supreme Court appears at 114 Cong. Rec. 14146 (1968).

13. The statement was made by Fortas before he became a Justice, in a CBS television documentary based on Anthony Lewis' book, *Gideon's Trumpet*, broadcast on October 7, 1964.

13. Rev. Shuttlesworth has also been in two civil cases before the Supreme Court, losing a school desegregation case, *Shuttlesworth v. Birmingham Board of Education*, 358 U.S. 101 (1958), and being a successful appellant in the landmark libel decision, *New York Times v. Sullivan*, 376 U.S. 254 (1964). Rev. Shuttlesworth's criminal appeals: *In re Shuttlesworth*, 369 U.S. 35 (1962); *Shuttlesworth v. Birmingham*, 373 U.S. 262 (1963); *Shuttlesworth v. Birmingham*, 376 U.S. 339 (1964); *Abernathy v. Alabama*, 380 U.S. 447 (1965); *Shuttlesworth v. Birmingham*, 382 U.S. 87 (1965); *Walker v. Birmingham*, 388 U.S. 307 (1967) (the appeal lost by Shuttlesworth) and *Shuttlesworth v. Birmingham*, 394 U.S. 147 (1969). This tally was compiled by James M. Nabrit, III, of the NAACP Legal Defense and Educational Fund, Inc., which represented Rev. Shuttlesworth in many of his court cases.

14. The riot figures are from *Hearings on Riots, Civil and Criminal Disorders Before the Permanent Subcommittee on Investigations of the Senate Committee on Government Operations*, 90th Cong., 1st Sess., pt. 1, facing p. 15 (1967).

14. The Hoover quotation is from his speech upon being given the "Sword of Loyola" Award, Chicago, November 24, 1964.

14. Murphy's statement was quoted in *The New York Times*, May 14, 1965, p. 39, col. 1.

15. Nixon's quotation, said to be from a typical stump campaign speech, was quoted by the *Wall Street Journal* on October 22, 1968, p. 20, col. 2.

15. Ramsey Clark's speech, made when he was Deputy Attorney General, was delivered on August 9, 1965, at the American Bar Association's annual convention in Miami, Florida.

15. The elder Clark made his statement on April 30, 1968, in a speech to the Los Angeles County Bar Association.
16. The dissent was published in the Commission's final report, *The Challenge of Crime in a Free Society* (Washington, D.C., U.S. Government Printing Office, 1967), pp. 303–08.
20. *Killough* v. *United States* is reported at 315 F.2d 241 (1962).
20. The Flores conversation was quoted to the United States Supreme Court on p. 6 of the State of California's unsuccessful petition for certiorari (review) in *California* v. *Flores*, 236 Cal. App. 2d 807, 46 Cal. Rptr. 412 (1965); *cert. denied*, 384 U.S. 1010 (1966).
21. Professor McCloskey's quotation is from his book, *The American Supreme Court* (Chicago, University of Chicago Press, 1960), p. 23.
24. *Katz* v. *United States*, 390 U.S. 347 (1967).
24. *McCray* v. *Illinois*, 386 U.S. 300 (1967).
24. *Warden* v. *Hayden*, 387 U.S. 294 (1967).

Chapter III/ THE DUE PROCESS REVOLUTION

26. Harlan Fiske Stone's quotation is from his dissent to the Supreme Court's decision holding the Agricultural Adjustment Act unconstitutional in *United States* v. *Butler*, 297 U.S. 1, at 78–78 (1936).
27. Judge Dunagan's remarks are quoted in Chief Justice Warren's concurring opinion in the Billie Sol Estes case, *Estes* v. *Texas*, 381 U.S. 532, at 566 (1965).
28. *Mapp.* v. *Ohio*, 367 U.S. 643 (1961).
28. Griswold's remark is from his article, "The Long View," 51 A.B.A.J 1017 (1965).
30. *Barron* v. *Baltimore*, 32 U.S. (7 Peter.) 243 (1833). The Marshall quotations are reported in 32 U.S., at 247, 250.
31. *The Slaughter House Cases*, 83 U.S. (16 Wall.) 36 (1873).
32. *Moore* v. *Dempsey*, 261 U.S. 86 (1923).
32. *Powell* v. *Alabama*, 287 U.S. 45 (1932).
32. *Brown* v. *Mississippi*, 297 U.S. 278 (1932).
32. Stewart's famous remark is from his concurring opinion in *Jacobellis* v. *Ohio*, 378 U.S. 184, at 197 (1964).
33. Cardozo's test was laid down in *Palko* v. *Connecticut*, 302 U.S. 319, at 328 (1937).
33. Frankfurter tried the "canons of decency" definition in *Adamson* v. *California*, 332 U.S. 46, at 67–68 (1947). The "sense of fair play and decency" definition and the "shocks the conscience" test were from *Rochin* v. *California*, 342 U.S. 165, at 172, 173 (1952).
34. The Illinois case: *Ciucci* v. *Illinois*, 356 U.S. 571 (1958).
34. The New York case: *Knapp* v. *Schweitzer*, 357 U.S. 371 (1958).
34. The New Jersey robbery case: *Hoag* v. *New Jersey*, 356 U.S. 464 (1958).
34. The New Jersey murder case: *Cicenia* v. *LaGay*, 357 U.S. 504 (1958).
35. The California case: *Crooker* v. *California*, 357 U.S. 433 (1958).
36. Way, "The Supreme Court and State Coerced Confessions," 12 JOUR. PUB. L. 53 (1963). The quotations are from pp. 61 and 63.
36. *Mallory* v. *United States*, 354 U.S. 449 (1957).
39. *Wolf* v. *Colorado*, 338 U.S. 25 (1949).

Page
39. *Irvine* v. *California*, 347 U.S. 128 (1954).
41. The quotation from *Mapp* v. *Ohio* is in 367 U.S., at 644.
43. Black's statement is found in 332 U.S., at 89-90.
43. Frankfurter's statement is in 332 U.S., at 6-7.
44. The 1965 case is *Pointer* v. *Texas*, 380 U.S. 400 (1965).
45. *Twining* v. *New Jersey*, 211 U.S. 78 (1908).
45. The "Julia" quip was made by Justice Robert Jackson in his dissenting opinion in *Everson* v. *Board of Education*, 330 U.S. 1, at 19 (1947).
45. *Gitlow* v. *New York*, 268 U.S. 652 (1925).
46. Cardozo's quotation from *Palko* v. *Connecticut* is in 319 U.S., at 325.
47. Clark's remarks about the moonshine case are from an interview, January 23, 1970 with the author.
49. Dr. King's disappointment in the Supreme Court came in the case, mentioned earlier, in which Rev. Fred L. Shuttlesworth lost his only criminal appeal to the Supreme Court: *Walker* v. *Birmingham*, 388 U.S. 307 (1967).
49. The Alabamians' quip about Black's robes was quoted in *The New York Times*, May 11, 1968, p. 21, col. 5.
50. Warren's familiar "But is it fair?" question is quoted in Anthony Lewis' profile of the Chief Justice in *The Justices of the United States Supreme Court 1789-1969*, Vol. IV, ed. by Leon Friedman and Fred L. Israel (New York, Chelsea House, 1969), p. 2725.
51. The commentary on Justice Douglas was made by Yosal Rogat in "Mr. Justice Pangloss," *The New York Review of Books*, October 22, 1964, p. 6, col. 2. The tally of Douglas' civil liberties decisions is found in the American Jewish Congress' publication, *The Civil Rights and Civil Liberties Decisions of the United States Supreme Court for the 1967-68 Term*, p. 90.
52. *Plessy* v. *Ferguson*, 163 U.S. 537 (1896).
52. *Schmerber* v. *California*.
52. Clark's "common sense" quotation is in 367 U.S., at 657.
53. Stewart's desire to be known only as a "good lawyer" is quoted in *The New York Times*, October 8, 1958, p. 1, col. 1.
55. *Benton* v. *Maryland*, 395 U.S. 784 (1969).
55. *Malloy* v. *Hogan*, 378 U.S. 1 (1964).
55. *Klopfer* v. *North Carolina*, 386 U.S. 213 (1967).
55. *Duncan* v. *Louisiana*, 391 U.S. 145 (1968).
55. *Pointer* v. *Texas*, 380 U.S. 400 (1965).
55. *Washington* v. *Texas*, 388 U.S. 14 (1967).
55. *Gideon* v. *Wainwright*, 372 U.S. 335 (1963).
55. *Robinson* v. *California*, 370 U.S. 660 (1962). This decision was handed down in June, before Goldberg joined the Court in October.
55. Black's lectures were published in a book entitled *A Constitutional Faith* (New York, Alfred A. Knopf, Inc., 1968). The quotation is on pp. 39-40.
56. Justice Brennan parsed the Bill of Rights into twenty-five separate safeguards in a speech entitled "The Bill of Rights as Restraints on State Power," delivered on October 6, 1967, at Canisius College, Buffalo, New York. His point was that many provisions had been made binding on the states before the Warren Court continued the process—and precipitated a public furor—with its criminal law rulings.
57. *Griffin* v. *Illinois*, 351 U.S. 12 (1956).

Page

57. Frankfurter's statement is from his article, "The Supreme Court and the Public," 83 FORUM 329, at 332-33, 334 (June 30, 1930).

58. Hughes' famous quotation, from an extemporaneous speech he made when he was Governor of New York, is discussed by Merlo J. Pusey in *Charles Evans Hughes* (New York, The Macmillan Company, 1951), pp. 204-05.

58. Professor Kurland's quotation is from his article "The Supreme Court 1963 Term—Foreword," 78 HARV. L. REV. 143, 176 (1964).

59. Roberts' statement is from the majority opinion in *United States* v. *Butler*, 297 U.S. 1, at 62 (1936).

59. Cardozo's remark that the "great generalities of the Constitution have a content and a significance that vary from age to age" is from his book *The Nature of the Judicial Process* (New Haven, Conn., Yale University Press, 1921), p. 17.

59. The Supreme Court's overruling decisions are tabulated in Vol. IV of *The Justices of the United States Supreme Court 1789-69*, pp. 3258-65.

59. Jackson's discussion of judicial infallibility was in his dissent in *Brown* v. *Allen*, 344 U.S. 443, at 540 (1953).

60. Black's interview was broadcast on December 3, 1968, on the CBS News Special, "Justice Black and the Bill of Rights."

60. White's statement, which he ad-libbed into a prepared address in Honolulu on August 3, 1967, is from the author's notes on the meeting. The statement was quoted in part in *The New York Times*, August 4, 1967, p. 60, col. 2.

61. The reference to Justice Schaefer in the *Miranda* decision is in 385 U.S., at 480.

62. The three lectures were published as law review articles: Friendly, "The Bill of Rights as a Code of Criminal Procedure," 53 CALIF. L. REV. 929 (1965); Schaefer, "Police Interrogation and the Privilege Against Self-Incrimination," 61 Nw. U. L. REV. 506 (1966); Traynor, "The Devils of Due Process in Criminal Detection, Detention, and Trial," 16 CATH. U. L. REV. 1 (1966).

64. Schaefer's quotation is from his article, "Federalism and State Criminal Procedure," HARV. L. REV. 1, at 26 (1956).

65. *United States* v. *Wade*, 388 U.S. 218 (1967).

65. The quotations from *Terry* v. *Ohio* are in 392 U.S., at 13-15.

66. Warren was quoted in *The New York Times*, September 30, 1968, p. 1, col. 4.

Chapter IV / THE MATHEMATICS OF CRIME

67. The text of the "frost notice" was quoted in the *Washington Post*, June 6, 1968, p. A1, col. 4.

68. Nixon's views on crime are stated in the text of a speech published in *The New York Times*, September 30, 1968, p. 41, col. 4.

69. The original source of Clark's remark about crime was an article in *The New York Times*, May 19, 1967, p. 23, col. 1.

69. Cipes' quotation from *The Crime War* (New York, New American Library, 1968) is from p. 7.

Page
69. Dr. Menninger was quoted in *The New York Times*, October 30, 1968, p. 49, col. 1.
69. Dr. Ohlin was quoted in an article in *The New York Times*, February 4, 1968, p. 1, col. 2. Dr. Sellin's quotation was in *Life* magazine, September 7, 1957, p. 49. Dr. Robison's statement appeared in *The New York Times* on July 27, 1965, p. 14, col. 3.
72. The quotation is from the report by the President's Commission on Law Enforcement and Administration of Justice, *The Challenge of Crime in a Free Society* (Washington, D.C., U.S. Government Printing Office, 1967), pp. 22-23.
73. Professor Wilson's quotation is from his chapter in the symposium edited by Kermit Gordon, *Agenda for the Nation* (Washington, D.C., Brookings Institute, 1968), p. 183.
73. The President's National Crime Commission reviewed much of the available data in the report of its Task Force on Assessment, *Crime and Its Impact—an Assessment* (Washington, D.C., U.S. Government Printing Office, 1967), pp. 21-23.
74. Professor Biderman's quotation is from his chapter in a symposium edited by Raymond A. Bauer, *Social Indicators* (Cambridge, Mass., The M.I.T. Press, 1966), p. 126.
74. Katzenbach's ire at Hoover's use of crime statistics was reported by a former Justice Department official, who prefers to remain anonymous.
76. The Crime Commission's remarks are quoted from *Crime and Its Impact—An Assessment*, p. 85.
76. The Webster City Story was reported in *The New York Times*, September 17, 1968, p. 38, col. 2. The Garnet, Kansas, article was reported in *The New York Times* (city ed.), October 22, 1968, p. 23, col. 3.
77. Examples of distortions in crime reporting are given in an article by Fred J. Cook, "There's Always a Crime Wave—How Bad Is This One?," *The New York Times Magazine*, October 6, 1968, p. 38.
78. The incident involving Chief Parker was related in a letter to the author, dated November 18, 1968, from Monroe E. Price, former Special Assistant to Secretary of Labor W. Willard Wirtz.
79. Daunt's remarks are from an interview with the author on February 20, 1969.
79. Hoover's statement was made in the press release issued on July 12, 1962, with the annual publication of Uniform Crime Report statistics, *Crime in the United States*.
80. Hoover's crime calculation was given in an end-of-the-decade interview as he looked—with evident disapproval—back at the events of the 1960s. Published in the *Washington Post*, December 28, 1969, p. A16, col. 1.
81. The vivid interpretation of the 1966 F.B.I. figures, which included such facts as the rape of a woman every 12 minutes, was published on January 2, 1968 by "Editorial Research Reports," which supplies facts and interpretations for newspaper editorial writers.
81. An example of Clark's reasoning concerning the threat of criminal violence is found in his testimony before the National Commission on Causes and Prevention of Violence, Washington, D.C., September 18, 1968.
82. The Republicans' statistical analysis was published in a press release

Page

of the House Republican Conference Task Force on Crime, May 5, 1968.

83. Ohlin's characterization of the crime rise was contained in an interview with the author that was reported in *The New York Times*, August 27, 1968, p. 1, col. 6.

84. Beattie's prior evaluation appeared in a critique of the F.B.I.'s Uniform Crime Reports, entitled "Aggressive Crimes," 364 *Annals of the American Academy of Political and Social Science*, pp. 73, 84 (1966). He took much of it back in testimony before the National Commission on Causes and Prevention of Violence on September 25, 1968.

85. The inflationary forces behind the rising crime statistics are discussed in the National Crime Commission's Report, pp. 5-6, and in its Task Force on Assessment's Report, pp. 25-28.

85. The probability figures are from the report of the Violence Commission's Task Force on Individual Acts of Violence, *Crimes of Violence*, p. 56. As of this writing, this task force report has not been published by the Government. The changing homicide picture in the District of Columbia was discussed in an article in the *Washington Star*, April 1, 1970, p. C1, col. 1.

85. Professor Wilson's gloomy prediction is from *Agenda for the Nation*, p. 206.

Chapter V / RACE, CRIME AND THE SUPREME COURT

86. Alexis de Tocqueville's quotation is from *Democracy in America*, trans. by Henry Reeve, Vol. II (New York, Alfred A. Knopf, Inc., 1945), p. 256.

87. Clark's quotation is from his testimony before the National Commission on Causes and Prevention of Violence, Washington, D.C., September 18, 1968.

89. The F.B.I.'s arrest statistics by race are found in *Crime in the United States—Uniform Crime Reports, 1967* (Washington, D.C., U.S. Government Printing Office, 1967), pp. 126-28.

89. Accounts of the NAACP chapter's anticrime efforts were reported in *The New York Times*, December 11, 1968, p. 49, col. 6; December 24, 1968 p. 25, col. 2.

91. The F.B.I.'s racial data were included in the draft report of the Violence Commission's Task Force on Individual Acts of Violence entitled *Crimes of Violence*, pp. 87-94. At this writing, the report has not been published by the Government. The results have been made available to the author. See p. 340.

93. The Philadelphia study is by Andre Normandeau, *Patterns and Trends in Robbery*. Unpublished Ph.D. dissertation, University of Pennsylvania, 1968.

93. The story of the young bandits appeared in the *Washington Star*, January 12, 1969, p. A10, col. 2.

94. Wolfgang's quotation is from his booklet *Crime and Race: Conceptions and Misconceptions* (New York, Institute of Human Relations Press, The American Jewish Committee, 1964).

94. Professor Miller's views were given in an interview on December 3, 1968.

URBAN ARREST RATES/100,000 BY RACE, 1964–67

	White		Negro	
		Total		Total
1964	*10–17 yrs.*	*(All Ages)*	*10–17 yrs.*	*(All Ages)*
Murder	1.3	2.8	12.2	38.6
Forcible Rape	4.1	4.8	45.7	47.2
Robbery	23.5	20.7	318.2	242.9
Aggravated Assault	32.3	38.4	274.6	451.0
Totals	61.2	66.7	650.7	779.7
1965				
Murder	1.1	3.0	15.6	45.3
Forcible Rape	4.1	5.0	64.3	56.8
Robbery	24.1	21.8	441.1	292.8
Aggravated Assault	33.7	39.8	308.2	453.5
Totals	63.0	69.6	829.2	848.4
1966				
Murder	1.5	3.2	19.6	48.0
Forcible Rape	4.3	5.4	56.5	56.9
Robbery	24.5	20.6	434.6	293.8
Aggravated Assault	38.3	42.9	302.0	441.1
Totals	68.6	72.1	812.7	839.8
1967				
Murder	1.3	3.1	22.3	53.9
Forcible Rape	4.9	5.4	60.0	59.9
Robbery	27.0	22.8	549.7	368.9
Aggravated Assault	40.6	45.7	335.7	477.3
Totals	73.8	77.0	967.7	960.0

Page

95. Philadelphia and Chicago results are found in the Normandeau dissertation. Also, in Menachem Amir, *Patterns in Forcible Rape.* Unpublished Ph.D. dissertation, University of Pennsylvania, 1965. The Stamford study is by Morris Allan Forslund, *Race and Crime,* a Ph.D. dissertation published by University Microfilms, Inc., Ann Arbor, Michigan. 1966.

95. The study by Sellin and Wolfgang, *Delinquency in a Birth Cohort,* will be published in 1970.

95. Sellin's quotation is from his foreword to Wolfgang's *Crime and Race: Conceptions and Misconceptions.*

96. The Wolfgang quotation is from an interview, December 13, 1968.

97. The Baltimore study is by Earl R. Moses, "Differentials in Crime Rates between Negroes and Whites Based on Comparison of Four Socio-Economically Equated Areas," *American Sociological Review,* Vol. 12, pp. 411–420.

Page
98. The murder statistics for Negroes are found in U.S. Department of Health, Education, and Welfare, Public Health Service, *Homicide in the United States 1950-1964*, Publication No. 1000-Series 20-NO. 6 (Washington, D.C., U.S. Government Printing Office, 1967).
99. The Tucker quotation is from the author's notes of his speech, delivered on August 6, 1967.
100. The Wilmington incident was reported in *The New York Times*, November 17, 1968, p. 80, col. 3, and on January 22, 1969, p. 26, col. 3. The Miami affair was reported in *The New York Times*, December 28, p. 21, col. 4.
100. Some of the legal and constitutional questions raised by police concentration on black neighborhoods are discussed in a Note, "Judicial Control of the Riot Curfew," 77 YALE L. J. 1560 (1968). The suburban policeman's quotation was reported in *The New York Times*, January 21, 1970, p. 30, col. 2.
101. The Katzenbach quotation is from his article, "Law and Order—Has the Supreme Court Gone Too Far?" *Look*, October 29, 1968, p. 28.

Chapter VI / RE-TRYING THE CONVICTED

102. The Brandeis quotation is from his dissent in *Burnet* v. *Coronado Oil and Gas Co.*, 285 U.S. 393, 406 (1932).
102. Young Bongiorno's letter is quoted from Judge Barnes' opinion in *Bongiorno* v. *Ragen*, 54 F. Supp. 973, at 975 (1944).
105. The Nebraska decision was *Case* v. *Nebraska*, 381 U.S. 336 (1965).
106. The growth in the number of habeas corpus proceedings in Federal District courts is traced in the *Hearings before Subcommittee No. 3 of the House Committee on the Judiciary*, 86th Cong., 1st. Sess., Ser. 2, p. 47 (1959), and in the *Administrative Office of the United States Courts, Report of the Director*, pp. II-52, 53 (1969).
107. The Reconstruction statute was the Act of February 5, 1867, Ch. 28, sec. 1, 14 Stat. 385, presently codified in 28 U.S.C. sec. 2241 (1958).
107. Holmes' quotation from *Moore* v. *Dempsey*, 261 U.S. 86 (1923), is at p. 91.
108. The 1953 decision was *Brown* v. *Allen*, 344 U.S. 443 (1953).
109. *Fay* v. *Noia*, 372 U.S. 391 (1963).
109. *Townsend* v. *Sain*, 372 U.S. 293 (1963).
109. Judge Parker's remark is reported in *Hearings on H.R. 5649 before Subcommittee No. 3 of the House Committee on the Judiciary*, 84th Cong., 1st Sess., p. 3 (1955).
110. The Conference of Chief Justices' Resolution is published at 25 *State Government*, p. 250 (1953).
110. Judge Desmond expressed his ire during a symposium on Federal Habeas Corpus at the University of Utah School of Law, May 1, 1964. His remarks are reported in 9 UTAH L. REV. 18, at 25 (1964).
111. The 1966 amendments are codified in Title 28 U.S.C. secs. 224(d), 2242 (Supp. 1966).
111. The Bar Association publication is *American Bar Association Project on Minimum Standards for Criminal Justice; Standards Relating to Sentencing Alternatives and Procedures*, p. 56 (1967).

Page
112. The recidivism estimate is the National Crime Commission's from its report *The Challenge of Crime in a Free Society*, p. 45.

112. Florida's post-*Gideon* experience was analyzed in Eichman, *Impact of the Gideon Decision upon Crime and Sentencing in Florida: A Study of Recidivism and Socio-Cultural Change*, Florida Division of Corrections, Research and Statistics Section, Research Monograph No. 2 (1966).

112. The California experiment was described by the President's Commission on Law Enforcement and Administration of Justice in its task force report *Corrections* (Washington, D.C., U.S. Government Printing Office, 1967), pp. 41, 42.

113. The A.B.A. committee's statement is found in its *Sentencing* report, p. 59.

114. A review of the litigious careers of the most successful Death Row writ-writers is given in Carter, "The Use of Federal Habeas Corpus by State Prisoners," 4 AMER. CRIM. QUART. 20 (1965).

115. *Witherspoon* v. *Illinois*, 391 U.S. 510 (1968).

115. The writ-writer case from Tennessee is *Johnson* v. *Avery*, 393 U.S. 483 (1969).

116. Bator's quotation is from his article "Finality in Criminal Law and Federal Habeas Corpus for State Prisoners," 76 HARV. L. REV. 441, at 452 (1963).

116. Judge Desmond's statement is quoted in 9 UTAH L. REV., at 43.

116. Friesen's suggestion was made in an interview with the author, November 21, 1968.

117. The sparse results of jailhouse writ-writing are revealed in H.R. Rep. No. 1293, 85th Cong., 2d Sess., p. 27 (1958).

117. Jackson's quotation is from his concurring and dissenting opinion in *Brown* v. *Allen*, 344 U.S. 443, at 537 (1953).

117. Snooks Jackson's case is reported in *Jackson* v. *Rundle*, 219 F. Supp. 538 (E.D. Pa. 1963).

118. James Byrnes' case is reported in *Byrnes* v. *Walker*, 217 F. Supp. 168 (E.D. La. 1963).

118. Fay Ward's case is reported in *Turner* v. *Ward*, 321 F. 2d 918 (10th Cir. 1963).

118. Brennan's quotation is found in 381 U.S., at 346.

119. The background information on Bongiorno's life after his hearing before Judge Barnes was obtained in a letter from Frank J. Pate, warden of Joliet Penitentiary, dated January 17, 1969; from a telephone interview with Bongiorno's court-appointed attorney in the Barnes hearing, Charles Liebman of Chicago, December 19, 1968; and from an interview on January 23, 1969, with Bongiorno's brother, Sgt. Anthony Bongiorno of the Chicago Police Department.

Chapter VII/ POLICING THE POLICE

122. Benjamin N. Cardozo's quotation is from *People* v. *Defore*, 242 N.Y. 13, 21; 150 N.E. 585, 587 (1926).

123. The study group that analyzed the Chicago riot was the Chicago Study Team of the National Commission on the Causes and Prevention

Page

of Violence, directed by Daniel Walker. Its report, *Rights in Conflict*, was published by Bantam Books, Inc., New York, in 1968; the observer who reacted to the scene was Tom Wicker, in a column in *The New York Times*, September 1, 1968, sec. IV, p. 10, col. 3.

123. Clark asked his question in his testimony before the National Commission on Causes and Prevention of Violence, Washington, D.C., September 18, 1968.

124. Brief for appellant, p. 2, *Bivens* v. *6 Unknown Agents of the Federal Bureau of Narcotics*, before the United States Court of Appeals for the Second Circuit. The appeal was dismissed in 402 F. 2d 718 (2d Cir. 1969). Certiorari granted, 38 U.S. L. WEEK 3507 (June 23, 1970).

125. The vignette about Chief Justice Warren's unsuccessful attempt to use criminal processes against offending officers was told by Jacob W. Landynski in his book *Search and Seizure and the Supreme Court* (Baltimore, Johns Hopkins Press, 1966), p. 139, n. 88.

126. Judge Burger explained his skepticism about the exclusionary rule in an article, "Who Will Watch the Watchman?," 14 AMER. U. L. REV. 1 (1964). He advocated instead the use of civilian-dominated police review boards to police the police.

127. Holmes' quotation is from his article "The Path of the Law," 10 HARV. L. REV. 457, at 469 (1897). The pitfalls of suing the police or the governments that employ them are discussed in a Symposium on Police Tort Liability, 16 CLEV.-MAR. L. REV. 397 (1967) and in an article by Caleb Foote, "Tort Remedies for Police Violations of Individual Rights," 39 MINN. L. REV. 493 (1955).

127. The results of the Los Angeles study were published in an article by James F. Coakley, "Restrictions in the Law of Arrest," 52 Nw. L. REV. 2, at 5 (1958). The many difficulties of attempting to enforce legal sanctions on the police are discussed in a book by Wayne R. LaFave, *Arrest: The Decision to Take a Suspect into Custody* (Boston, Little, Brown and Company, 1965), Ch. 20.

128. *Barr* v. *Matteo*, 360 U.S. 564, at 571 (1959).

128. Scherer's frustrations are detailed in the reports of his two futile lawsuits, *Scherer* v. *Brennan*, 266 F. Supp. 758 (N.D. Ill. 1966), *affirmed*, 379 F. 2d 609 (7th Cir. 1967), *cert. denied* 389 U.S. 1021 (1967); *Scherer* v. *Morrow*, 401 F. 2d 204 (1968), *cert. denied* 393 U.S. 1084 (1969).

130. *Weeks* v. *United States*, 232 U.S. 383 (1914).

131. Holmes' and Brandeis' joint sentiments were expressed in the dissent written by Brandeis in *Olmstead* v. *United States*, 277 U.S. 438, at 484 (1928).

131. Murphy's dissenting remarks are reported in 338 U.S., at 44.

132. Diploclo's statement is from an interview with the author, July 29, 1969.

133. *Alston* v. *United States*, 348 F.2d 72 (D.C. Cir. 1965).

133. *Massachusetts* v. *Painten*, 368 F. 2d 142 (1966); *cert. granted*, 386 U.S. 931 (1967); *cert. dismissed*, 389 U.S. 560 (1968).

133. The Paille incident was described in John Hersey's book, *The Algiers Motel Incident* (New York, Bantam Books, 1968), pp. 265–71, 285–86.

Page
134. The Traynor quotation is from *People* v. *Cahan*, 44 Cal. 2d 434, at 444; 282 P.2d 905, at 913 (1955).
134. Stewart made his statement in *Elkins* v. *United States*, 364 U.S. 206, at 217 (1960). A discussion of other nations' nonuse of the exclusionary rule is found in "The Exclusionary Rule Under Foreign Law," 52 JOUR. CRIM. L. 271 (1966).
135. Train's observation is from his book *Courts and Criminals* (New York, Charles Scribner's Sons, 1921), pp. 6–7.
136. The Columbia study is described in "Effect of *Mapp* v. *Ohio* on Police Search-and-Seizure Practices in Narcotics Cases," 4 COLUM. J. LAW and SOC. PROB. 87 (1968). Similar conclusions are reported by Sarah Barlow in "Patterns of Arrests for Misdemeanor Narcotics Possession: Manhattan Police Practices 1960–62," 4 CRIM. L. BUL. 549 (1969); and by Paul G. Chevigny, "Police Abuses in Connection with the Law of Searches and Seizures," 5 CRIM. L. BUL. 3 (1969).
137. The quotation is found in 4 COLUM. J. LAW and SOC. PROB., at 87.
138. Shriver's quotation is from an interview, February 4, 1968.
139. The quotation is from an article by Wayne R. LaFave and Frank J. Remington, "The Judge's Rule in Police Decisions," 63 MICH. L. REV. 987, at 1005 (1965).
140. The American Bar Foundation's study is by Lawrence P. Tiffany, Donald M. McIntyre, Jr., and Daniel L. Rotenberg, *Detection of Crime* (Boston, Little, Brown and Company, 1967), p. 117.
141. The observer's statement is from *Detection of Crime*, p. 13. A similar observation is expressed on pp. 183–84.
142. Jackson's conclusion was stated in his dissent in *Brinegar* v. *United States*, 338 U.S. 160, at 181 (1949).
144. *Terry* v. *Ohio*, 392 U.S. 1 (1968). The quoted passages from Warren's opinion are found on pp. 13–15.
145. The misfortune of the three youths in Philadelphia was recounted in *The New York Times*, December 30, 1969, p. 14, col. 3. Brennan's thoughts about the purposes of the exclusionary rule were given in a speech to the National Council on Crime and Delinquency, May 8, 1969.
145. Warren's quotation is in 392 U.S., at 15.
145. The statute is now codified at 42 U.S.C. sec. 1983 (1964).
146. *Hague* v. *CIO*, 307 U.S. 496 (1939).
146. McReynolds' dissenting statement is in 307 U.S., at 532.
147. *Dombrowski* v. *Pfister*, 380 I. S. 479 (1965).
148. The urban groups' statement was quoted in an article in *The New York Times*, February 28, 1969, p. 1, col. 1.
148. Carter's statement was quoted in *The New York Times*, August 25, 1967, p. 1, col. 1.
149. Sobeloff's description is from *Lankford* v. *Gelston*, 364 F. 2d 197, at 199–200 (4th Cir. 1966).
150. The statement about creating ad hoc police review boards through civil suits was made by Melvin Wulf, general counsel of the American Civil Liberties Union, in an interview on March 19, 1969.

Chapter *VIII*/ MIRANDA: SELF-INFLICTED WOUND

Page

153. Justice Jeremiah Smith's quotation is in Professor Paul A. Freund's book, *The Supreme Court of the United States* (Cleveland, The World Publishing Company, 1961), p. 28.
154. *Escobedo* v. *Illinois*, 378 U.S. 478 (1964).
155. Goldberg's quotation is in 378 U.S., at 492.
158. The horizontal interrogation occurred in *Orozco* v. *Texas*, 394 U.S., at 324 (1969).
159. The California Supreme Court first took the plunge by partially anticipating the *Miranda* rule in its 1964 decision, *People* v. *Dorado*, 61 Cal. 2d 264, 394 P. 2d 952 (1964). After a rehearing, another *Dorado* opinion was published at 62 Cal. 2d 338, 398 P. 2d 361 (1965). The Oregon court handed down a similar, but more limited, ruling in *Oregon* v. *Neely*, 239 Ore. 487, 395 P. 2d 557 (1964), followed by *Rhode Island* v. *Defour*, 206 A. 2d 82 (1965), and finally the Third Circuit's ruling in *Russo* v. *New Jersey*, 351 F. 2d 429 (3d Cir. 1965).
160. The first Frankfurter quotation is from *Watts* v. *Indiana*, 338 U.S. 49, at 54 (1949). The second is from *Colombe* v. *Connecticut*, 367 U.S. 568, at 571 (1961).
161. A thorough study of the law of confessions was published by the *Harvard Law Review* in the Spring of 1966 and cited by the Supreme Court in its *Miranda* opinion: "Developments in the Law—Confessions," 79 HARV. L. REV. 935 (1966).
161. *Mallory* v. *United States*, 354 U.S. 449 (1957).
162. *Betts* v. *Brady*, 316 U.S. 455 (1942).
163. *Massiah* v. *United States*, 377 U.S. 201 (1964).
164. The two 5-to-4 confessions cases were *Crooker* v. *California*, 357 U.S. 433 (1958) and *Cicenia* v. *Legay*, 357 U.S. 504 (1958).
165. The quotation from the majority opinion in *Crooker*, written by Justice Clark, is in 357 U.S., at 441.
167. Jackson's quotation is from *Watts* v. *Indiana*, 338 U.S. 49, at 59 (1949).
167. Various nations' police interrogation laws are discussed in a book by Gerhard O. W. Mueller, and Fre Le Poole-Griffiths, *Comparative Criminal Procedure* (New York, New York University Press, 1969), pp. 20–23, 29–84.
169. The Bator-Vorenberg statement is published at 66 COLUM. L. REVIEW 62, at 63 (1966) "Arrest, Detention, Interrogation, and the Right to Counsel: Basic Problems and Possible Legislative Solutions."
176. Fortas' statement about police interrogation is from *Hearings Before the Senate Committee on the Judiciary on the Nomination of Abe Fortas*, 89th Cong., 1st Sess., p. 42 (1965).
176. The statements by Fortas and the other Justices during the *Miranda* arguments are found in a book edited by Richard J. Medalie, *From Escobedo to Miranda* (Washington, D.C., Lerner Law Book Company, Inc., 1966) which contains a transcript of major portions of the oral arguments in the case. Fortas' "late in the day" remark is found at p. 99. His "great human adventure" quotation is at pp. 119–20.
177. Douglas' question, which does not appear in the Medalie book, is in

Page

the official transcript of the argument in the Supreme Court library.

177. Warren's quotation is from the official transcript. It appears in abbreviated form in *From Escobedo to Miranda*, p. 137.

178. Black's remark about the Model Code is reported in *From Escobedo to Miranda*, p. 123.

178. Warren's summation of the holding in *Miranda* is found in 384 U.S., at 444–45.

180. Warren's statements in support of his contention that stationhouse interrogation is "inherently compelling" are found in 384 U.S., at 447–55.

180. The development of the privilege against self-incrimination is traced in Lewis Mayers' book *Shall We Amend the Fifth Amendment?* (New York, Harper Brothers, 1959).

181. *Bram* v. *United States*, 168 U.S. 532 (1897).

182. Fortas' statement was made in an interview, April 27, 1967.

182. Arnaud's statement was made in an interview, July 28, 1967.

183. Vorenberg's statement was quoted in *The New York Times*, June 15, 1966, p. 1, col. 7.

183. Warren's quotation from the *Miranda* opinion is found in 384 U.S., at 478.

185. The Suarez affair was reported in *The New York Times*, February 21, 1967, p. 41, col. 2.

185. The judge who spoke of "nice people" was Chief Judge Wilbur K. Miller of the U.S. Court of Appeals for the District of Columbia, in his dissent in *Killough* v. *United States*, 315 F. 2d 241, at 265 (1962).

186. *Great Northern Railroad* v. *Sunburst Oil and Refining Co.*, 287 U.S. 358 (1932). Justice Walter V. Schaefer's analysis of the retroactivity problem in his Benjamin Cardozo Lecture, April 13, 1967, has been published as a book: *The Control of "Sunbursts": Techniques of Prospective Overruling* (New York, Association of the Bar of the City of New York, 1967).

187. *Linkletter* v. *Walker*, 381 U.S. 618 (1965).

187. *Griffin* v. *California*, 380 U.S. 609 (1965). The Supreme Court ruled on the retroactivity of *Griffin* in *Tehan* v. *Shott*, 382 U.S. 406 (1966).

189. *Johnson* v. *New Jersey*, 384 U.S. 719 (1966).

190. *Clemons* v. *Texas*, 398 S.W. 2d 563 (1965); *cert. denied*, 384 U.S. 1015 (1966).

192. The·Court ruled on the retroactivity of *United States* v. *Wade* in *Stovall* v. *Denno*, 388 U.S. 293 (1967).

193. The initial version of Clark's dissent was published in 34 U. S. L. WEEK at 4540, minus the afterthought that appears in the official version in 384 U.S. at 500.

Chapter IX/ SEARCHES: FROM CONFUSION TOWARD A RULE OF REASON

194. Felix Frankfurter's quotation is from his concurring opinion in *Chapman* v. *United States*, 365 U.S. 610, at 618 (1961).

195. Fortas' statement is published in *Hearings Before the Senate Committee on the Judiciary on the Nominations of Abe Fortas and Homer*

Page
Thornberry, 90th Cong. 2d Sess., pp. 170–71 (1968).

195. *Warden* v. *Hayden*, 387 U.S. 294 (1967). Fortas' quotation is from his concurring opinion in 387 U.S., at 312.

196. Thurmond's quotation is from the Fortas *Hearings*, 90th Cong., 2d Sess., p. 191 (1968).

197. Marshall's anecdote appeared in *The New York Times Magazine* (Sec. 6), December 10, 1967, p. 64.

199. *McCray* v. *Illinois*, 386 U.S. 300 (1967); *Terry* v. *Ohio*, 392 U.S. 1 (1968); *Spinelli* v. *United States*, 393 U.S. 410 (1969).

199. *Chimel* v. *California*, 395 U.S. 752 (1969).

200. *Gouled* v. *United States*, 255 U.S. 298 (1921).

203. Jackson's quotation is from *Johnson* v. *United States*, 333 U.S. 10, at 13–14 (1948).

204. The San Francisco figures were obtained in an interview on December 18, 1968, with Harry Green, Chief Division Clerk, Criminal Division, San Francisco Municipal Court. The Los Angeles figures were furnished to the Supreme Court by Keith C. Monroe, attorney for the petitioner in *Chimel* v. *California*, in the course of the oral arguments and later in written form. The remaining figures are from the book by Lawrence P. Tiffany, Donald M. McIntyre, Jr., and Daniel L. Rotenberg, *Detection of Crime* (Boston, Little, Brown and Company, 1967), pp. 99–100.

205. The statement about "limited" warrantless searches is Arthur Goldberg's, in *United States* v. *Vantresca*, 380 U.S. 102, at 106–07 (1965).

206. The clerk's statement is from *State* v. *Upchurch*, 267 N.C. 417, 148 S.E. 2d 259 (1966).

206. The two Prohibition era decisions were *Go-Bart Importing Co.* v. *United States*, 282 U.S. 344 (1931) and *United States* v. *Lefkowitz*, 285 U.S. 452 (1932).

206. *Harris* v. *United States*, 331 U.S. 145 (1947).

207. *Trupiano* v. *United States*, 334 U.S. 699 (1948).

207. *United States* v. *Rabinowitz*, 339 U.S. 56 (1950).

208. Stewart's quotation from the *Chimel* opinion is in 395 U.S., at 768.

209. The 1933 decision was *Nathanson* v. *United States*, 290 U.S. 41 (1933). The affirmation that the suspect "did receive, conceal, etc., narcotic drugs" was in *Giordenello* v. *United States*, 357 U.S. 480 (1958). The "reliable information from a credible person" affidavit was in *Aguilar* v. *Texas*, 378 U.S. 108 (1964).

210. *Spinelli* v. *United States*, 393 U.S. 410 (1969).

211. *Rovario* v. *United States*, 353 U.S. 53 (1957).

212. Douglas' statement is in 386 U.S., at 316.

212. Chevigny's statement about police prevarication is from his article entitled "Abuse of Police Power," *The Atlantic Monthly*, March, 1969, p. 128.

213. The 1886 case was *Boyd* v. *United States*, 116 U.S. 616 (1886). Bradley's statement appears at p. 630.

215. Brennan's quotation from the *Warden* v. *Hayden* opinion is found in 387 U.S., at 304.

216. *Jones* v. *United States*, 362 U.S. 257 (1960).

217. *Alderman* v. *United States*, 394 U.S. 165 (1969).

Chapter X/ IDENTIFICATION: LAWYERS AT LINEUPS

Page
221. The Felix Frankfurter quotation is from his book *The Case of Sacco and Vanzetti* (Stanford, Calif., Academic Reprints, 1954), p. 30.
222. *Williams* v. *United States* is reported at 345 F. 2d 733 (D.C. Cir. 1965).
223. Burger's "Disneyland" comment is in 345 F. 2d, at 736.
224. *United States* v. *Wade*, 388 U.S. 218 (1967); *Gilbert* v. *California*, 388 U.S. 263 (1967); *Stovall* v. *Denno*, 388 U.S. 293 (1967).
226. Borchard's book, published by Yale University Press, New Haven, in 1932, and Patrick M. Wall's book, *Eye-Witness Identification in Criminal Cases*, published by Charles C. Thomas, Springfield, Ill., in 1965, provide convincing examples of the hazards of eyewitness identification, some of which are mentioned in this chapter.
226. The gunflash identification is found in the Supreme Court of Florida's opinion in *Spires* v. *State*, 50 Fla. 121, 39 So. 181 (1905), in which the court upheld the identified man's death sentence.
226. The author represented Dawson in postconviction proceedings. Dawson's sentence was commuted to 99 years of imprisonment in 1963 by Governor Frank G. Clement.
229. The development of the law of identification in the United States is discussed by Daniel E. Murray in "The Criminal Lineup at Home and Abroad," 1966 UTAH L. REV. 610 (1966) and in a Comment, "Right to Counsel at Police Identification Proceedings: A Problem in Effective Implementation of an Expanding Constitution," 29 U. PITT. L. REV. 65 (1967).
233. The quotation from Clark's concurrence is found in 388 U.S., at 243.
237. Nixon's statement of the *Beasley* case is found in his 1968 campaign position paper on crime, "Toward Freedom from Fear." (*United States* v. *Beasley* was not reported.)
237. The *Kinnard* ruling, by United States District Judge Gerhard A. Gesell, was not published in an official law report. It was reversed after the Court of Appeals later took the opposite position and Kinnard was convicted in November of 1969.
238. *Russell* v. *United States*, 408 F. 2d 1280 (D.C. Cir. 1969).
239. Beaudin's statement is found in *Hearings Before the Subcommittee on Constitutional Rights of the Senate Committee on the Judiciary*, 91st Cong., 1st Sess. p. 65 (1969).
239. *Simmons* v. *United States* is reported at 390 U.S. 377 (1968).
241. The quotation from Black's dissent is found in 388 U.S., at 248.
241. White's quotation is found in 388 U.S., at 251.
241. Told by Webster to the author, October 28, 1969.
241. Gilbert's attorney, Luke McKissack of Hollywood, explained the aftermath in a letter to the author, dated April 7, 1970.
241. Weldon Holcomb, Wade's attorney, related in a telephone interview on November 2, 1969, that Wade left Texas without waiting for his second trial—or paying his lawyer's fee.
242. Told by Bridges to the author on October 29, 1969.
242. The San Francisco practice was explained to the author by Deputy Chief of Detectives John A. Engler on July 27, 1967. The case of the falsely accused attorney and other line-up incidents were uncovered

Page

by Frank T. Read of the Duke University Law School faculty and were included in his article, "Lawyers at Lineups: Constitutional Necessity or Avoidable Extravagence?" to be published by U.C.L.A. LAW REV.

243. Burger's lineup vignette can be found in the text of his address to the Ohio Judicial Conference, Columbus, Ohio, September 4, 1968.

243. The Frankfurter quotation is from his concurring opinion in *Adamson* v. *California*, 332 U.S., at 67.

244. The Brennan quotations are found in 388 U.S., at 239.

245. Senator Ervin's brief discussion of the lineup decisions is found in *Hearings Before the Subcommittee on Criminal Laws and Procedures of the Senate Committee on the Judiciary*, 90th Cong., 1st Sess., p. 908 (1967).

Chapter XI / POLICE EAVESDROPPING: LAW-ENFORCEMENT REVOLUTION

247. William Howard Taft's quotation is from *Olmstead* v. *United States*, 277 U.S. 438, at 468 (1928).

249. Upon the discovery of the listening device in his suite, Levinson sued the local F.B.I. agents and the Central Telephone Company for $4.5 million for invasion of privacy. The government then indicted Levinson and six colleagues for failing to pay taxes on money allegedly "skimmed" from the gaming tables. The publicity surrounding both actions quickly became too embarrassing for both sides, and they were mutually dismissed on March 27, 1968. The apparent compromise was reported in *The New York Times* on March 29, 1968, p. 22, col. 1.

249. The history of electronic surveillance is traced in a book by Samuel Dash, Richard F. Schwartz and Robert E. Knowlton, *The Eavesdroppers* (New Brunswick, N.J., Rutgers University Press, 1959), and in *American Bar Association Project on Minimum Standards for Criminal Justice: Standards Relating to Electronic Surveillance* (Tentative Draft, 1968).

251. *Olmstead* v. *United States*, 277 U.S. 438 (1928). Brandeis' dissenting statement is in 277 U.S., at 478. Holmes' "dirty business" quotation is in 277 U.S., at 470.

253. The section of the Communications Act that was construed as an antiwiretap law was 48 Stat. 1103 (1934), 47 U.S.C. Sec. 605 (1958).

254. The best summary of the types of surveillance devices known to be in use is in Alan F. Westin's book *Privacy and Freedom* (New York, Atheneum, 1967).

255. *Goldman* v. *United States*, 316 U.S. 129 (1942). The "spike mike" case was *Silverman* v. *United States*, 365 U.S. 505 (1961). The "thumb tack mike" case was *Clinton* v. *Virginia*, 377 U.S. 158 (1964).

256. The development of the "internal security" exception to the Federal Government's official antiwiretap policy is traced in an article by Athan G. Theoharis and Elizabeth Meyer, "The 'National Security' Justification for Electronic Eavesdropping: An Elusive Exception," 14 WAYNE L. REV. 749 (1968). The documents that revealed Attorney General Clark's role were discovered by Professor Theoharis in the

Page
Truman Library and were first published in an article by Theoharis in *New University Thought*, June, 1968, p. 16.

257. *Berger* v. *New York*, 388 U.S. 41 (1967).

257. Hoover's statement appears in *Hearings Before a Subcommittee of the House Committee on Appropriations*, 88th Cong., 1st Sess., p. 491 (1963).

257. The ex-F.B.I. agent is William W. Turner, whose story of the Bureau's eavesdrop activities appeared in "The Muckraker's Guide," a special edition of *Ramparts*, January, 1969, p. 51.

258. Robert Kennedy's comments and Hoover's allegations against him appear in *The New York Times*, December 11, 1966, p. 84, col. 1.

260. *Lopez* v. *United States*, 373 U.S. 427 (1963). The 1962 decision was on *Lee* v. *United States*, 343 U.S. 747 (1952).

263. *Baker* v. *Carr*, 369 U.S. 186 (1962).

264. The Osborn affair is reported in *Osborn* v. *United States*, 385 U.S. 323 (1966).

267. Clark's quotation from the Berger opinion is found in 388 U.S., at 63.

267. *Katz* v. *United States*, 389 U.S. 347 (1967).

268. Stewart's "people, not places" quotation is in 389 U.S., at 351.

268. His reassurance that the "legitimate needs of law enforcement" can be accommodated is in 389 U.S., at 356.

268. The Omnibus Crime Control and Safe Streets Act of 1968, Tit. III, 18 U.S.C. Secs. 2510-20 (Supp. 1969).

272. The quotations are from a memorandum filed by the Government in the case of the "Chicago Eight" conspiracy trial, *United States* v. *Dellinger*. It was supported by Attorney General Mitchell's affidavit that the transcripts of certain of the defendants' overheard conversations need not be disclosed to them because the surveillances were conducted in the course of investigations involving foreign intelligence or subversive domestic groups, and thus were not "illegal." The national security exception to Title III of the Omnibus Crime Control and Safe Streets Act of 1968 is found at 18 U.S.C. sec. 2511 (c) (Supp. 1969). Nixon's statement was reported in *The New York Times*, March 9, 1966, p. 24, col. 3.

274. The petition for Rehearing was filed in the case of *Ivanov* v. *United States*, 394 U.S. 165, *rehearing denied*, 394 U.S. 939 (1969). Stewart's reply was given in a concurring opinion to *Giordano* v. *United States*, 394 U.S. 310 (1969).

Chapter XII/ HANDCUFFING THE POLICE

276. Benjamin N. Cardozo's quotation is from *Snyder* v. *Massachusetts*, 291 U.S. 97, at 122 (1934).

276. The Yale incident is related in a brief note, "A Postscript to the *Miranda* Project, Interrogation of Draft Protesters," 77 YALE L. J. 300 (1967).

279. The District of Columbia study is reported in an article by Richard J. Medalie, Leonard Zeitz and Paul Alexander, "Custodial Interrogation in our Nation's Capital: The Attempt to Implement *Miranda*," 66 MICH. L. REV. 1347 (1968). The New York detective's garbled warning was reported in *The New York Times*, March 30, 1969, p. 49, col. 1.

Page
280. The defendant's hopeful remark about police error is found in 66 MICH. L. REV., at 1378.
280. The New Haven study is reported in a Note, "Interrogations in New Haven: The Impact of Miranda," 76 YALE L. J. 1519 (1967). A more readable version was published by one of the observers, Richard Ayres, as an article, "Confessions and the Court," in the *Yale Alumni Magazine*, December, 1968, p. 18.
280. The Pittsburgh study is reported in an article by Richard H. Seeburger and R. Stanton Wettick, Jr., "Miranda in Pittsburgh—A Statistical Study," 29 U. PITT. L. REV. 1 (1967).
281. Hogan's remarks are published in *Hearings Before the Subcommittee on Criminal Laws and Procedures of the Senate Judiciary Committee*, 90th Cong., 1st Sess., pp. 1120–23. The quoted passage is from p. 1121 (Washington, D.C., U.S. Government Printing Office, 1967).
284. Katzenbach's quotation is from an article by him, "Law and Order: Has the Supreme Court Gone Too Far?" *Look*, October 29, 1968, p. 29.
286. The F.B.I.'s advice was given in its manual, *Police Interrogation: The Miranda Rule* (F.B.I. National Academy, August, 1968), p. 9.
287. Burger's quotation is from his opinion in *Frazier* v. *United States*, decided by the Court of Appeals for the District of Columbia, March 14, 1969, No. 21, 426, unreported.
288. McDaniel's statement was made in an interview with the author, February 5, 1968.
291. Streit's quotation is from the *New York Post* (Magazine), June 28, 1969, p. 4, col. 2. The Massachusetts case is *Massachusetts* v. *Scott*, 245 N.E. 2d 415 (1969). The quotation is from p. 420.
292. Kennedy's statement is from an interview with the author, July 28, 1967.
293. The remarks by Karlen were made in a lecture delivered at the University of Birmingham, England, December 6, 1968.
294. *Simmons* v. *United States*, 390 U.S. 377 (1968).
295. *Harrison* v. *United States*, 392 U.S. 219 (1968). Harrison's release by President Nixon was reported in *The Washington Post*, February 3, 1970, p. A1, col. 6.
296. *Willingham* v. *Morgan*, 395 U.S. 402 (1969).
297. Allison's quotation is from an interview, July 16, 1969.
298. The New York Statistics are from the annual *Report of the New York State Joint Legislative Committee on Crime: Its Causes, Control and Effect on Society* (1968). Subin's remarks were made in an interview, January 6, 1970.

Chapter XIII/ REVOLUTION AND AFTER

305. The quotation by Oliver Wendell Holmes is from his dissenting opinion in *Olmstead* v. *United States*, 277 U.S. 438, at 470 (1928).
307. Counsel for the poor: *Gideon* v. *Wainwright*, 372 U.S. 335 (1963).
308. Juveniles' due process rights: *In re* Gault, 387 U.S. 1 (1967).
308. Jury trials in criminal contempt cases: *Bloom* v. *Illinois*, 391 U.S. 194 (1968).
308. Petty offenses: *Duncan* v. *Louisiana*, 391 U.S. 145 (1968).

Page
308. Confrontation with states' witnesses: *Pointer* v. *Texas*, 380 U.S. 400 (1965).
308. Comment on defendant's failure to take the stand: *Griffin* v. *California*, 380 U.S. 609 (1965).
308. Self-incrimination rights and gambling laws: *Marchetti* v. *United States*, 390 U.S. 39 (1968); firearms statute: *Haynes* v. *United States*, 395 U.S. 6 (1969); narcotics: *Leary* v. *United States*, 395 U.S. 6 (1969).
308. Capital punishment: *Witherspoon* v. *Illinois*, 391 U.S. 510 (1968).
308. Free transcript: *Griffin* v. *Illinois*, 351 U.S. 12 (1956).
308. Free appellate counsel: *Douglas* v. *California*, 372 U.S. 353 (1963).
308. Federal Fifth Amendment standards governing state trials: *Malloy* v. *Hogan*, 378 U.S. 1 (1964).
308. Habeas corpus: *Townsend* v. *Sain*, 372 U.S. 293 (1963).
309. The eyewitness provision of Title II is codified at 18 U.S.C. sec. 3503 (Supp. 1969). The Omnibus Crime Control Act, Public Law 90-351 (June 19, 1968), appears in scattered portions of the United States Code. Title II appears in its entirety at 18 U.S.C. secs. 3501-02 (Supp. 1969).
311. The Texas decision is *Hill* v. *Texas*, 420 S.W. 2d 408 (Tex. Crim. App. 1967).
312. White's speech, "Recent Developments in Criminal Law," was delivered before the Conference of Chief Justices in Honolulu, August 3, 1967.
312. The quotation from *Miranda* v. *Arizona* is reported in 384 U.S., at 444.
313. The remark of the Roman rhetorician Marcus Fabius Quintilianus is quoted by Helen Silving in her book *Essays on Criminal Procedure* (Buffalo, Dennis and Company, Inc., 1964), p. 258.
314. The quotation from *Miranda* v. *Arizona* is reported in 384 U.S., at 475.
315. *United States* v. *Hayes*, 358 F. 2d 375 (4th Cir. 1967).
316. The quotation from *Miranda* v. *Arizona* is reported in 384 U.S., at 455.
316. F. E. Inbau, *Criminal Interrogation and Confessions*, ed. John E. Reid (Baltimore, Williams & Wilkins Co., 1967).
317. The quotation is from the Supreme Court of Pennsylvania's opinion in *Commonwealth* v. *Tapper* which was issued on May 3, 1968, and reported in part at 36 U. S. LAW WEEK 2714. Several weeks later, a brief notice at 37 U. S. LAW WEEK 2020 announced that the opinion had been withdrawn. When *Commonwealth* v. *Taper*, 434 Pa. 71, 253 F. 2d 90 (1969) was finally reported officially a year later (with no mention that a previous decision had been written and withdrawn), the opinion was written by Chief Justice John C. Bell, Jr., the lone dissenter in the first version. He thus had the rare privilege of publishing a dissent and having it later become the majority position of the court in the same case.
317. The Court's initial harmless error decision was *Chapman* v. *California*, 386 U.S. 18 (1967).
319. Douglas' uncharacteristically elastic reading of the harmless error exception came in *Harrington* v. *California*, 395 U.S. 250 (1969).
319. The section of Title II that purported to reverse *Miranda* v. *Arizona* is codified at 18 U.S.C. sec. 3501 (Supp. 1969).
320. McClellan's private characterization of Title II was told to the author

Page

by a Senate staff official who worked on the legislation with the Senator. The statement by the Judiciary Committee majority is in the *Report, Senate Judiciary Committee, of the Omnibus Crime Control and Safe Streets Act of 1967*, p. 51, 90th Cong., 2d Sess. (1968).

322. The poll-tax provision was contained in the Voting Rights Act of 1965, Public Law 89-110, Sec. 10, August 6, 1965; 79 Stat. 442, 42 U.S.C. sec. 1973h (a)-(d), (Supp. I, 1965). The Supreme Court declared poll taxes in state elections unconstitutional in *Harper* v. *Virginia Board of Elections*, 383 U.S. 663 (1966).

322. Congress passed the statute designed to overturn New York's English literacy requirement as section 4(e) of the Voting Rights Act of 1965, codified at 42 U.S.C. sec. 1973b (e) (Supp. I, 1965). The Supreme Court upheld its constitutionality in *Katzenbach* v. *Morgan*, 384 U.S. 641 (1966).

323. Professor Cox's observation was made in an article, "Constitutional Adjudication and the Promotion of Human Rights," 80 HARV. L. REV. 91, p. 106 (1966). His article proved to be an impressive example of the occasional impact of scholarly writing on public policy: Senator Edward Kennedy read it and used its arguments to persuade the Senate in 1970 that it could constitutionally lower the voting age to eighteen by declaring that state laws to the contrary violate the Fourteenth Amendment rights of persons between eighteen and twenty-one years of age.

323. The Supreme Court's declaration of deference to "Congressional resolution" of certain constitutional questions is from *Katzenbach* v. *Morgan*, 384 U.S. at 653.

323. The Justices' hedge on their expansive view of Congressional power was buried in a footnote to Justice Brennan's opinion in *Katzenbach* v. *Morgan*, 384 U.S., at 651, n. 10.

326. *Ex Parte McCardle*, 74 U.S. (7 Wall.) 506 (1869). The quotation is found in 74 U.S., at 514.

327. The Supreme Court's generous statement of Congress's power is from a maritime case, *The Francis Wright*, 105 U.S. 381, at 385-86 (1881).

329. Senator Griffin's speech is recorded at 114 CONG. REC. 14180-81 (1968).

329. The Nixon Administration's new policy of enforcing Title II was reported in *The New York Times*, July 28, 1969, p. 1, col. 4.

331. The grim prediction by the National Commission on the Causes and Prevention of Violence was published in its final report, *To Establish Justice, To Insure Domestic Tranquility* (Washington, D.C., U.S. Government Printing Office, 1969), pp. 44-45.

List of Cases

Abernathy v. *Alabama*, 380 U.S. 447 (1965), 334
Adamson v. *California*, 332 U.S. 46, at 67, 68 (1947), 42, 44, 49, 57, 333, 335, 348
Aguilar v. *Texas*, 378 U.S. 108 (1964), 347
Alderman v. *United States*, 394 U.S. 165 (1969), 217, 347
Alston v. *United States*, 348 F 2D 72 (D.C. Cir. 1965), 343

Baker v. *Carr*, 369 U.S. 186 (1962), 263, 349
Barr v. *Matteo*, 360 U.S. 564, at 571 (1959), 128, 129, 343
Barron v. *Baltimore*, 32 U.S. (7 Peter.) 243 (1833), 30, 48, 335
Benton v. *Maryland*, 395 U.S. 784 (1969), 55, 336
Berger v. *New York*, 388 U.S. 41 at 63 (1967), 257, 266, 267, 268, 349
Betts v. *Brady*, 316 U.S. 455 (1942), 162, 171, 345
Bivens v. *6 Unknown Agents of the Federal Bureau of Narcotics*, 402 F 2D 718 (2d. Cir. 1969), 343
Bloom v. *Illinois*, 391 U.S. 194 (1968), 351
Bongiorno v. *Ragen*, 54 F. Supp. 973, at 975 (1944), 341
Boyd v. *United States*, 116 U.S. 616 (1886), 347
Bram v. *United States*, 168 U.S. 532 (1897), 181, 346
Brinegar v. *United States*, 338 U.S. 160, at 181 (1949), 344
Brown v. *Allen*, 344 U.S. 443, at 537, 540 (1953), 337, 341, 342
Brown v. *Mississippi*, 297 U.S. 278 (1932), 32, 35, 160, 335
Burnet v. *Coronado Oil and Gas Co.*, 285 U.S. 393, 406 (1932), 341
Byrnes v. *Walker*, 217 F. Supp. 168 (E.D. La. 1963), 342

California v. *Flores*, 236 Cal. App. 2D 807, 46 Cal. Rptr. 412 (1965); *cert.* denied, 384 U.S. 1010 (1966), 335
California v. *Stewart*, 384 U.S. 436 (1966), 156

Case v. Nebraska, 381 U.S. 336 (1965), 341
Chapman v. California, 386 U.S. 18 (1967), 352
Chapman v. United States, 365 U.S. 610, at 618 (1961), 346
Chimel v. California, 395 U.S. 752, at 768 (1969), 199, 207, 208, 346, 347
Cicenia v. LaGay, 357 U.S. 504 (1958), 335, 345
Ciucci v. Illinois, 356 U.S. 571 (1958), 335
Clemons v. Texas, 398 S.W. 2D 563 (1965); *cert. denied*, 384 U.S. 1015 (1966), 346
Clinton v. Virginia, 377 U.S. 158 (1964), 349
Colombe v. Connecticut, 367 U.S. 568, at 571 (1961), 345
Commonwealth v. Taper, 434 Pa. 71, 253 F 2D 90 (1969), 317, 352
Crooker v. California, 357 U.S. 433, 441 (1958), 335, 345

Dombrowski v. Pfister, 380 U.S. 479 (1965), 147, 148, 344
Douglas v. California, 372 U.S. 353 (1963), 351
Dred Scott, 7
Duncan v. Louisiana, 391 U.S. 145 (1968), 55, 336, 351

Elkins v. United States, 364 U.S. 206, at 217 (1960), 343
Escobedo v. Illinois, 378 U.S. 478 (1964), 63, 154–156, 158, 159, 165–167, 170–173, 175, 176, 178, 179, 181, 184, 190–192, 227, 232, 238, 344
Estes v. Texas, 381 U.S.· 532, at 566 (1965), 27, 335
Everson v. Board of Education, 330 U.S. 1, at 19 (1947), 336
Ex Parte McCardle, 74 U.S. (7 Wall.) 506, at 514 (1869), 326, 353

Fay v. Noia, 372 U.S. 391 (1963), 109, 341
Francis Wright, The, 105 U.S. 381, at 385–86 (1881), 353
Frazier v. United States, decided by the Court of Appeals for the District of Columbia, March 14, 1969, No. 21, 426, unreported., 350

Gault, 387 U.S. 1 (1967), 351
Gideon v. Wainwright, 372 U.S. 335 (1963), 13, 54, 55, 62–64, 112, 152, 158, 162–164, 171, 172, 188, 229, 234, 296, 336, 351
Gilbert v. California, 388 U.S. 263 (1967), 224, 227, 229, 231, 235, 238, 347
Giordano v. United States, 394 U.S. 310 (1969), 350
Giordenello v. United States, 357 U.S. 480 (1958), 347
Gitlow v. New York, 268 U.S. 652 (1925), 336
Go-Bart Importing Co. v. United States, 282 U.S. 344 (1931), 347
Goldman v. United States, 316 U.S. 129 (1942), 255, 349
Gouled v. United States, 255 U.S. 298 (1921), 195, 200, 214, 215, 346
Great Northern Railroad v. Sunburst Oil and Refining Co., 287 U.S. 358 (1932), 186, 346
Griffin v. California, 380 U.S. 609 (1965), 187, 189, 346, 351
Griffin v. Illinois, 351 U.S. 12 (1956), 57, 336, 351

Hague v. CIO, 307 U.S. 496 (1939), 344
Harper v. Virginia Board of Electors, 383 U.S. 663 (1966), 352
Harrington v. California, 395 U.S. 250 (1969), 352
Harris v. United States, 331 U.S. 145 (1947), 206–208, 347
Harrison v. United States, 392 U.S. 219 (1968), 351

Haynes v. *United States*, 395 U.S. 6 (1969), 351
Hill v. *Texas*, 420 S.W. 2D 408 (Tex. Crim. App. 1967), 351
Hoag v. *New Jersey*, 356 U.S. 464 (1958), 335

Irvine v. *California*, 347 U.S. 128 (1954), 39, 41, 125, 336
Ivanov v. *United States*, 394 U.S. 165, *rehearing denied*, 394 U.S. 939 (1969), 350

Jackson v. *Rundle*, 219 F. Supp. 538 (E.D. Pa. 1963), 342
Jacobellis v. *Ohio*, 378 U.S. 184, at 197 (1964), 335
Johnson v. *Avery*, 393 U.S. 483 (1969), 342
Johnson v. *New Jersey*, 384 U.S. 719 (1966), 154, 189, 191, 346
Johnson v. *United States*, 333 U.S. 10, at 13-14 (1948), 346
Jones v. *United States*, 362 U.S. 257 (1960), 216, 347

Katz v. *United States*, 389, 390 U.S. 347 (1967), 24, 267, 335, 349
Katzenbach v. *Morgan*, 384 U.S. 641, at 651, n. 10, 653 (1966), 352, 353
Killough v. *United States*, 315 F. 2D 241, at 265 (1962), 335, 346
Klopfer v. *North Carolina*, 386 U.S. 213 (1967), 55, 336
Knapp v. *Schweitzer*, 357 U.S. 371 (1958), 335

Lankford v. *Gelston*, 364 F. 2D 197, at 199-200 (4th Cir. 1966), 344
Leary v. *United States*, 395 U.S. 6 (1969), 351
Lee v. *United States*, 343 U.S. 747 (1952), 350
Linkletter v. *Walker*, 381 U.S. 618 (1965), 187, 346
Lopez v. *United States*, 373 U.S. 427 (1963), 260, 261, 264, 265, 349

Mallory v. *United States*, 354 U.S. 449 (1957), 36, 161, 162, 167, 173, 179, 282, 319, 324, 328, 335, 345
Malloy v. *Hogan*, 378 U.S. 1 (1964), 55, 336, 351
Mapp v. *Ohio*, 367 U.S. 643, 644 (1961), 28, 39, 44, 46, 48, 52, 62, 136, 137, 140, 155, 158, 172, 186, 187, 189, 192, 196, 198-200, 204, 205, 211, 212, 224, 227, 278, 288, 292, 307, 309, 319, 335, 336, 343
Marchetti v. *United States*, 390 U.S. 39 (1968), 351
Massachusetts v. *Painten*, 368 F. 2D 142 (1966); *cert. granted*, 386 U.S. 931 1967); *cert. dismissed*, 389 U.S. 560 (1968), 133, 343
Massachusetts v. *Scott*, 245 N.E. 2d 415 (1969), 351
Massiah v. *United States*, 377 U.S. 201 (1964), 166, 232, 238, 345
McCray v. *Illinois*, 386 U.S. 300 (1967), 24, 199, 211, 335, 346
Miranda v. *Arizona*, 384 U.S. 436, 444, 445, 447-55, 475, 478 (1966), 6-9, 11, 12, 14, 16, 20-24, 35, 52, 60-65, 132, 133, 137, 138, 143, 154-160, 163, 168-172, 175-189, 191-192, 219, 224, 227, 231-233, 238, 244, 245, 276-282, 284, 286-289, 291, 292, 301, 302, 309-317, 319, 320, 323, 324, 328, 329, 333, 345, 346, 350, 352
Moore v. *Dempsey*, 261 U.S. 86 (1923), 32, 107, 335, 341

Nathanson v. *United States*, 290 U.S. 41 (1933), 347
New York Times v. *Sullivan*, 376 U.S. 254 (1964), 334

Olmstead v. *United States*, 277 U.S. 438, at 468, 470, 478, 484 (1928), 251, 252, 255, 260, 261, 265, 268, 343, 348, 349, 351

Oregon v. *Neely*, 239 Ore. 487, 395 P. 2D 557 (1964), 345
Orozco v. *Texas*, 394 U.S., at 324 (1969), 344
Osborn v. *United States*, 385 U.S. 323 (1966), 265, 349

Palko v. *Connecticut*, 302 U.S. 319, at 325, 328 (1937), 46, 335, 336
People v. *Cahan*, 44 Cal. 2D 434 at 444; 282 P. 2D 905, at 913 (1955), 343
People v. *Defore* 242 N.Y. 13, 21; 150 N.E. 585, 587 (1926), 342
People v. *Dorado*, 61 Cal. 2D 264, 394 P. 2D 952 (1964); 62 Cal. 2D 338, 398
   P. 2D 361 (1965), 345
Plessy v. *Ferguson*, 163 U.S. 537 (1896), 52, 336
Pointer v. *Texas*, 380 U.S. 400 (1965), 55, 336, 351
Powell v. *Alabama*, 287 U.S. 45 (1932), 32, 235, 335

Rhode Island v. *Defour*, 206 A. 2D 82 (1965), 345
Robinson v. *California*, 370 U.S. 660 (1962), 55, 336
Rochin v. *California*, 342 U.S. 165, at 172, 173 (1952), 57, 335
Rovario v. *United States*, 353 U.S. 53 (1957), 211, 347
Russell v. *United States*, 408 F. 2D 1280 (D.C. Cir. 1969), 348
Russo v. *New Jersey*, 351 F. 2D 429 (3D Cir. 1965), 345

Scherer v. *Brennan*, 266 F. Supp. 758 (N.D. Ill. 1966), *affirmed*, 379 F. 2D
   609 (7th Cir. 1967), *cert. denied* 389 U.S. 1021 (1967), 343
Scherer v. *Morrow*, 401 F. 2D 204 (1968), *cert. denied* 393 U.S. 1084 (1969),
   343
Schmerber v. *California*, 384 U.S. 757 (1966), 52, 233, 336
Shuttlesworth, 369 U.S. 35 (1962), 334
Shuttlesworth v. *Birmingham*, 373 U.S. 262 (1963), 334
Shuttlesworth v. *Birmingham*, 376 U.S. 339 (1964), 334
Shuttlesworth v. *Birmingham*, 382 U.S. 87 (1965), 334
Shuttlesworth v. *Birmingham*, 394 U.S. 147 (1969), 334
Shuttlesworth v. *Birmingham Board of Education*, 358 U.S. 101 (1958), 334
Silverman v. *United States*, 365 U.S. 505 (1961), 349
Simmons v. *United States*, 390 U.S. 377 (1968), 239, 348, 351
Slaughter House Cases, The, 83 U.S. (16 Wall.) 36 (1873), 31, 32, 48, 107,
   335
Snyder v. *Massachusetts*, 291 U.S. 97, at 122 (1934), 350
Spinelli v. *United States*, 393 U.S. 410 (1969), 199, 210, 346, 347
Spires v. *State*, 50 Fla. 121, 39 So. 181 (1905), 348
State v. *Upchurch*, 267 N.C. 417, 148 S.E. 2D 259 (1966), 347
Stovall v. *Denno*, 388 U.S. 293 (1967), 224, 227, 229, 232, 235, 309, 310, 346,
   347

Tehan v. *Shott*, 382 U.S. 406 (1966), 346
Terry v. *Ohio*, 392 U.S. 1, at 13–15 (1968), 65, 144, 199, 337, 344, 346
Townsend v. *Sain*, 372 U.S. 293, 391 (1963), 109, 341, 351
Trupiano v. *United States*, 334 U.S. 699 (1948), 207, 347
Turner v. *Ward*, 321 F. 2D 918 (10th Cir. 1963), 342
Twining v. *New Jersey*, 211 U.S. 78 (1908), 45, 46, 55, 336

United States v. *Beasley*, 236, 348
United States v. *Butler*, 297 U.S. 1, at 62, 78–78 (1936), 335, 337

United States v. *Dellinger*, 350
United States v. *Hayes* 385 F. 2 375 (4th Cir. 1967), 315, 352
United States v. *Lefkowitz*, 285 U.S. 452 (1932), 347
United States v. *Rabinowitz*, 339 U.S. 56 (1950), 207, 208, 347
United States v. *Ventresca*, 380 U.S. 102, at 106-07 (1965), 347
United States v. *Wade*, 388 U.S. 218 (1967), 65, 191, 192, 219, 223, 224, 227–
   229, 231, 232, 234–238, 240, 242, 244, 245, 309, 310, 319, 323, 324, 328, 329,
   337, 346, 347

Vignera v. *New York*, 384 U.S. 436 (1966), 154

Walker v. *Birmingham*, 388 U.S. 307 (1967), 334, 336
Warden v. *Hayden*, 387 U.S. 294, at 304, 312 (1967), 24, 195, 199, 215, 265,
   335, 346, 347
Washington v. *Texas*, 388 U.S. 14 (1967), 55, 336
Watts v. *Indiana*, 338 U.S. 49, at 54, 59 (1949), 345
Weeks v. *United States*, 232 U.S. 383 (1914), 130, 131, 142, 206, 343
Westover v. *United States*, 384 U.S. 436 (1966), 154
Williams v. *United States*, 345 F. 2D 733 (D.C. Cir. 1965), 222, 347
Willingham v. *Morgan*, 395 U.S. 402 (1969), 351
Witherspoon v. *Illinois*, 391 U.S. 510 (1968), 115, 342, 351
Wolf v. *Colorado*, 338 U.S. 25 (1949), 39, 41, 46, 131, 172, 335

Index

abject poverty, 105
"absorption," 44
"abstention," 147
"accusatorial" system of justice, 159
Acheson, Dean, 67
Adamson, 42, 43, 44
Administrative Office of the United States Courts, 116
advisory opinions, 38
"aggressive patrol," 141
Agronsky, Martin, 60
Alabama, 32, 42, 49
alcoholics, chronic, 65
Allen, Francis, 329
Allison, Junius, 297
Alston, Tom E., Jr., 133
Amendments, first Eight, 45, 55
America, 85, 285, 287
American Bar Association, 23, 99, 112, 113, 120, 174
  Committee on Minimum Standards for Administration of Criminal Justice, 23
  Project on Minimum Standards for Criminal Justice, 174, 269
American Bar Foundation, 140, 141
American Civil Liberties Union, 148, 170

American Embassy in Moscow, 254
American justice, slowness of, 290, 291
American Law Institute, 62, 63, 169, 174, 175, 178
  Model Code of Pre-Arraignment Procedure, 174, 175, 178
American Nazis, 273
American ships, 38
Americans, 1, 2, 37, 58, 73, 75, 81, 92, 123, 197, 198, 227
amicus curiae, 170, 176
anti-Court elements, 301
anti-Negro elements, 148
antipoverty programs, 96
anti-Vietnam War protest, 277
anti-Wade section, 328
antiwar activists, 150
antiwar demonstrators, 122
antiwiretap law, 132, 253
apartheid, 99
"apartheid society," 96
arbitration, 151
arbitration systems, 56
Arizona, 156, 242
Arkansas, 32, 107, 108
armed robbery, 242
armed stickups, 93

Arnaud, Alfred G., 182
Arnold, Thurman, 139
"arrest" searches, 206
arrests, 19, 77, 89, 98
Ash, George, 133
Aspen, Colorado, 150
assault, 13, 77, 80, 83, 84, 98, 99, 228
  aggravated, 11, 77, 79, 87, 91, 98, 99
  by gun, 79
  felonious, 98
Associated Press, 89
Atlanta, 72
Austin, Texas, 76
Australia, 228
auto theft, 77, 80, 92

backlog of cases, 290, 293
bail, 239, 241, 297, 300, 301, 308
  bar against excessive, 56
  reform, 297
Baltimore, 68, 96, 149, 150, 215
bank robberies, 79
Barnes, Chief Judge John P., 102, 106, 119,
Bator, Professor Paul M., 115, 169, 174
Bazelon, Chief Judge David L., 237, 238
"Beasley case," 237
Beattie, Ronald H., 84
Beaudin, Bruce, 239
Beck, Adolf, 225, 226
Bell, Alexander Graham, 250
Berger, 266
Bertillon, Alphonse, 225
Bertillon system, 225
Bible reading, 2
Biderman, Albert D., 74
Big Brother, 22
Bill of Rights, 4, 5, 6, 17, 18, 29, 30, 31, 37, 41, 42, 43, 44, 45, 46, 47, 48, 52, 54, 55, 56, 57, 59, 130, 131, 142, 146, 159, 177, 212, 213, 217, 232, 243, 244, 255, 267, 287, 310, 316, 321, 332
Birmingham, Alabama, 49
Bivens, Webster, 123, 124, 126, 127, 129, 141, 142
Black, Justice Hugo L., 17, 42, 43, 44, 45, 47, 49, 55, 56, 60, 64, 125, 177, 178, 233, 234, 240, 260, 268, 294, 306, 310
black militants, 68, 259
Black Muslims, 259
blackmail, 262
Blackmun, Justice Harry A., 306
Blackstone, William, 59
Blakey, G. Robert, 269
"Blue Power," 148
Bongiorno, John, 102, 103, 104, 106, 113, 119, 120
Bongiorno, Sam, 102, 106
bookmaking, 210
bootleggers, 251
Borchard, Edwin M., 226, 232
Boston, 76, 94, 133
"Boston Strangler," 76
Boys Club of America, 273
Bradley, Justice Joseph P., 213
Brady, John, 115
Brandeis, Justice Louis D., 102, 131, 195, 251, 260
Brennan, Justice William J., Jr., 17, 47, 51, 52, 64, 118, 145, 147, 176, 178, 215, 233, 234, 235, 244, 250, 260, 261, 262, 265, 266, 274, 319
bribery, 23, 263, 264, 266
Bridges, Sheriff Ray, 242
Brief Against Death, 114, 115
British ships, 38
Bronx, the, 124, 298
Bronx County, 141
Brooklyn, 185, 290, 291
Brown, "Cider," 295
Buckley, William F., Jr., 114
"bug," 248, 251, 252, 254, 255, 258, 259, 267, 273
bugged olive, 254
"bugging," 22, 216, 217, 254, 255, 258, 266, 267
  court-approved, 268
Burger, Chief Justice Warren Earl, 9, 126, 129, 221, 222, 223, 243, 286, 287, 292, 296, 302, 303, 305, 306, 309, 312, 330
Burger Court, 129, 309, 310
burglar tools, 214
burglary, 77, 80, 81, 91, 118
bus drivers, 68
businessman's unencumbered use of his purse, 331

Byrnes, James, 117

California, 17, 39, 42, 43, 50, 68, 112, 114, 119, 134, 156, 303
  Bureau of Criminal Statistics, 84
  Court of Criminal Appeals, 21, 159
  State Bar, 61
  Supreme Court, 20, 21, 61, 172, 184
  University of, 35
Cambridge, 53, 94
Canada, 11, 228
Canada-to-Seattle bootleg operation, 251
Canons of Ethics, 234
Capital, the, 280, 282
capital punishment, 113, 308
  scruples against, 115
Capone, Al, 72, 257
Capone, Ralph, 257
car theft, 80
car wrecks, death in, 81, 84
Cardozo, Justice Benjamin N., 33, 46, 59, 122, 276
Carswell, G. Harrold, 306
Carter, Robert L., 148
Cassidy, Stanley, 189, 191
CBS News, 60
Central Intelligence Agency, 254
Central Telephone Company, 248
certiorari, petition for, 64, 103, 104, 108, 109, 110, 154, 169, 171, 172, 175, 187, 189, 190, 191, 264
Ceylon, 181, 182
Charles I, King, 10
Charybdis, 160
Chessman, Caryl, 114, 227, 228
Chevigny, Paul, 212
Chicago, 72, 76, 77, 95, 102, 103, 104, 115, 120, 122, 123, 125, 128, 141, 164, 171, 200, 201, 211, 215, 249, 271, 273, 274, 294
Chicago *Herald-American*, 103
Chicago Police Department, 128, 141
chicken stealing, 270
Cincinnati, 53
Cipes, Robert M., 69
city councils, 29
civil damages, 126, 131
civil liberty, 43

civil litigation, 163
civil rights, 147, 256
Civil Rights Act of 1871, 145
Civil Rights Act of 1964, 63
Civil Rights Act of 1965, 322
civil rights activities, 4, 13
civil rights militancy, 94
civil rights revolution, 13
Civil War, 3, 31, 73
civilian review board, 126
Clark, Attorney General Ramsey, 15, 69, 81, 82, 87, 123, 265, 266, 267, 329
Clark, Justice Tom C., 15, 46, 47, 52, 56, 188, 192, 193, 195, 232, 233, 234, 256, 257, 265, 266, 267, 268, 310
Clarke, Justice, 195
"classification interview," 19, 20
"clear and convincing evidence," 240, 241
Clemons, Johnny Lee, 190, 191
Cleveland, 40, 68
Clubb, Bruce E., 222, 223
"coddling criminals," 19, 25, 28, 111, 113, 120, 121, 134, 196, 220, 286, 331
coercion, 35, 62, 105, 108, 132, 154, 161, 162, 167, 175, 181, 187, 196, 240, 312, 316, 317, 323
Collins, 36
collusion, 38
color film, 245
Colorado, 26, 39
Columbia School of Social Work, 70
Columbia University, 3, 136
  School of Law, 55
communism, 11
Communists, 2, 73, 259
concentration camps, 50
Confederates, former, 326, 327
confessions, 19, 20, 21, 22, 23, 35, 36, 37, 62, 70, 117, 132, 133, 137, 138, 142, 143, 154, 155, 156, 157, 158, 159, 160, 161, 162, 163, 164, 165, 166, 170, 171, 172, 174, 175, 176, 177, 178, 179, 181, 182, 183, 184, 185, 186, 187, 189, 190, 192, 195, 196, 199, 203, 224, 227, 229, 231, 232, 240, 278, 280, 281, 282, 284, 295, 308, 310, 312, 313, 314,

confessions (*Cont'd.*)
   315, 317, 318, 319, 320, 324, 328
allegedly coerced, 35, 36
state court, 35
Congress, 1, 2, 9, 12, 22, 24, 46, 63,
   107, 110, 111, 145, 147, 162, 173,
   174, 244, 245, 249, 250, 253, 261,
   268, 269, 270, 282, 297, 300, 301,
   303, 307, 310, 319, 320, 321, 322,
   323, 324, 325, 326, 327, 328, 329,
   331, 332
Congress of Industrial Organizations,
   146
Connor, Eugene "Bull," 49
"consent" search, 203
Constitution of the United States,
   1, 2, 5, 6, 17, 27, 28, 30, 31, 38,
   39, 42, 43, 44, 52, 57, 58, 59, 60,
   64, 101, 103, 105, 107, 129, 130,
   131, 136, 146, 159, 161, 166, 178,
   181, 186, 192, 196, 244, 253, 296,
   320, 321, 322, 324, 325, 328, 329,
   330, 332
   Article II, 329
   Article III, 57, 325
constitutional crisis, likelihood of a,
   101, 151
constitutional error, 317, 318
constitutional law, 2
"continuity with change," 303
contraband, 214
"control," 206, 207
Convicting the Innocent, 226
convictions, overturned, 110
convictions, whether void, 317
convicts, 106, 108, 115, 116, 117
Coram Nobis, 104
Cosa Nostra, La, 217, 249, 269
counsel, court-appointed, 222, 223
county boards, 29
county courts, 29
Court of Appeals for the District of
   Columbia, 19, 20, 126, 133, 161,
   185, 221, 222, 237, 296
Court of Appeals for the Fifth Circuit, 230
Court of Appeals for the First Circuit, 133
Court of Appeals for the Fourth Circuit, 149, 215, 315

Court of Appeals for the Second
   Circuit, 23, 61, 129
Court of Appeals for the Sixth Circuit, 53
Court of Appeals for the Third Circuit, 159
Court of Criminal Appeal, 226
"Court of the Union," 58
Courts of Star Chamber and High
   Commission, 180
Cox, Archibald, 323
crime, 4, 11, 12, 13, 15, 29, 37, 38,
   48, 60, 68, 69, 70, 71, 72, 73, 74,
   75, 76, 77, 78, 79, 80, 81, 82, 83,
   84, 85, 86, 87, 88, 91, 92, 93, 94,
   95, 96, 97, 99, 100, 103, 104, 107,
   112, 120, 124, 125, 135, 141, 143,
   148, 156, 157, 159, 160, 162, 163,
   166, 167, 171, 172, 176, 183, 189,
   192, 196, 197, 202, 204, 205, 212,
   214, 215, 217, 219, 220, 225, 231,
   236, 237, 239, 241, 242, 245, 246,
   249, 251, 252, 253, 254, 255, 256,
   262, 267, 272, 279, 282, 283, 284,
   285, 287, 288, 289, 290, 294, 296,
   299, 300, 303, 306, 309, 311, 312,
   319, 320, 321, 324, 330, 331
"crime clocks," 81
crime control, 331
crime, interracial, 99
crime, Negro, 86–100
crime, organized, 24, 249, 250, 269
"crime rate," 80, 81, 82, 85, 327
crime, *reported*, 77, 78, 79, 121
"crime rise," 71, 73, 74, 75, 76, 78,
   79, 80, 82, 84, 85, 87, 91, 92
crime statistics, trends in, 79
crime, unreported, 77
"crime wave," 77
Crime in the United States, 88
Crime War, The, 69
crimes, property, 79, 80, 83, 84, 87,
   91
criminal anarchy, 286
criminal appeals, 103, 104, 105, 106,
   108, 109, 119
criminal cases, 29
criminal investigation, 157
criminal justice, 4, 6, 7, 17, 22, 30,
   42, 50, 113, 121, 147, 154, 155,

162, 163, 167, 222, 224, 232, 235, 237, 279, 283, 284, 285, 287, 288, 289, 292, 293, 294, 297, 299, 304, 306, 307
criminal justice revolution, 133
criminal law, 4, 5, 7, 10, 12, 13, 16, 27, 28, 29, 48, 49, 50, 60, 64, 103, 104, 133, 140, 142, 154, 165, 168, 171, 173, 175, 187, 195, 214, 223, 224, 225, 231, 240, 268, 284, 292, 303, 309
criminal law reform, 11
criminal law revolution, 14
criminal penalties, excessive, 111, 112
criminal procedure, 66
    code of, 61
    revolution in, 64
criminal prosecutions, 5
criminal suspects, 4
    constitutional safeguards of, 319
    rights, 31, 53, 301, 303, 306, 325
criminal trespass, 124
criminals, 33, 37
"critical" nature, 238
"critical stage," 162, 163, 229, 232, 233, 238, 239, 244
Crooker, John Russell, Jr., 165
"cruel and unusual" punishment, 119

Daley, Mayor Richard, 123
Daunt, Jerome, 78, 79
Davidson, County, Tennessee, 288
Davis, John F., 154
Dawson, Clayton, 226
Day, Justice William R., 130
death, risk of, 81
Death Row inmate, 113, 114, 115
defacto school segregation, 49
Democratic National Convention of 1968, 122, 125, 271
Democrats, 50
demography, 285
Depression, the, 146
Desert Inn, 248
Desmond, Chief Judge Charles S., 110, 116
"detectaphone," 254, 255
Dethmers, Chief Justice John R., 120
de Tocqueville, Alexis, 2, 86

Detroit, 72, 126, 133, 204
Diamond Cab Company, 215
Dick Tracy, 200
dignity, 37
Diplock, Lord Justice Kenneth, 132
"dirty business," 270
"Disneyland" contention, 223
District of Columbia, 29, 84, 100, 162, 169, 173, 222, 237, 242, 282, 291, 296, 300, 314
    bail agency, 239
    Police, 19, 288
Ditchley Park, England, 169
dope pushers, 136
dope traffic, 141
double-jeopardy prohibition, 46
Douglas, Justice William O., 17, 47, 50, 51, 64, 125, 177, 212, 217, 219, 233, 261, 265, 266, 306, 318, 319
draft cards, 277
dragnet arrests, 5, 160, 177, 184, 288
dragnet tactics, 288
Dred Scott decision, 3, 7
"dropsy" testimony (dropsies), 136, 137
drugs, 23
DuBois, W. E. B., 273
DuBois Club, 273
due process of law, 6, 31, 32, 33, 35, 43, 44, 45, 46, 52, 57, 106, 108, 119, 142, 181, 183, 186, 232, 235, 243, 289, 301, 304, 310, 325
"due process revolution," 6, 7, 8, 9, 16, 21, 24, 27, 28, 48, 49, 51, 52, 58, 64, 136, 157, 186, 218, 223, 224, 229, 232, 278, 279, 282, 283, 289, 293, 301, 307
Dulles, Allen, 67
Dumbarton Oaks, 192
Dunagan, Judge Otis T., 27, 28
Dunes, 248

East St. Louis, 72
eavesdrop doctrine, 250
eavesdrop scandals, 250
eavesdroppers, 254, 255
eavesdropping:
    court-approved, 264, 267, 270
    governmental, 249
    law-enforcement, 264, 266

Edgartown, Massachusetts, 311
egalitarianism, 6
1863 draft riots, 72
Eighth Amendment, 56, 119, 300
Eisenhower, President, 51, 53
Eisenhower period, crime in, 82
Election Day, 1968, 319
electrical surveillance, 251
electronic alarms, 330
electronic bugging, 249
electronic devices, 250, 272
electronic eavesdropping, 247, 249,
    250, 251, 257, 262, 269
electronic listening, 260
electronic spying, 268
electronic surveillance, 65, 250, 258,
    259, 261, 263, 264, 265, 268, 269,
    271, 272, 274
electronics, use of, 260
embezzling, 143
England, 11, 127, 132, 168, 171, 180,
    181, 196, 228
England's "Judges' Rules," 132, 133,
    142, 171, 182
England's robbery rate, 171
equal protection clause, 322
Ervin, Senator Sam J., Jr., 109, 158,
    195, 245
Escobedo, Danny, 164, 165, 166
"Escobedo Cases," 154, 172, 189
espionage, 23, 256, 259
Estes, Billie Sol, 26, 27, 28, 56, 188
European systems, 167, 168
Eustace, Texas, 230
exact look-alikes, 225
"exclusionary rule," 19, 24, 25, 29, 38,
    39, 47, 129, 130, 131, 132, 134, 139,
    140, 141, 142, 143, 144, 145, 150,
    152, 157, 158, 168, 172, 182, 186,
    187, 197, 199, 216, 217, 219, 234,
    240, 253, 294, 302, 310, 318, 330
executions, 113, 114
"exigent circumstances," 202, 203, 208
ex parte McCardle, 326
extortion, 258, 262
eyewitness identification, 199, 224,
    226, 237
eyewitness testimony, admissibility
    of, 319, 320, 328

"fear of strangers" syndrome, 81

Federal Bureau of Investigation, 4,
    11, 14, 29, 69, 70, 71, 73, 74, 75,
    77, 78, 79, 80, 81, 82, 83, 84, 87,
    88, 89, 90, 91, 92, 95, 98, 181, 182,
    207, 209, 210, 216, 217, 225, 230,
    248, 249, 252, 258, 259, 262, 273,
    276, 277, 278, 283, 284, 286, 287,
    294, 315
anti-Mafia bugs, 258, 260
bugs, 261
crime index, 4, 6, 11, 12, 13, 69, 70,
    73, 74, 75, 77, 78, 79, 80, 82, 83,
    84, 88, 89, 92, 278, 284, 285, 319
eavesdropping, 252, 257, 258, 261,
    262
"Top Hood" gangbusting pro-
    gram, 257
Uniform Crime Reports, 74, 77,
    285
Federal Bureau of Narcotics, 124
Federal Communications Act, 253
Federal District Court in Chicago,
    271
Federal District Court in New Or-
    leans, 147
Federal District Court in New York
    129
Federal Judicial Center, 303
Federal labor racketeering statutes,
    34
Federal law, 38
Federal officers, 37
Federal Rules of Criminal Procedure,
    161, 167
Federal wiretapping and bugging
    law, 267
felony cases, 283, 298, 299
felony charges, 308
female impersonator, 243
"ferreting out crime," 134
Fifth Amendment, 34, 37, 43, 45, 46,
    47, 48, 52, 55, 56, 60, 62, 159, 166,
    177, 179, 180, 181, 192, 196, 213,
    230, 233, 251, 301
"file 13," 78
fingerprinting, 225, 233
Finland, 11
First Amendment, 45, 46, 146, 147
Flores, Fausto Edward, 20, 21
Florida, 112, 226, 302
forgery, 207

forma pauperis, 154
Forslund, Morris A., 97
Fortas, Justice Abe, 9, 13, 17, 54, 64,
    67, 121, 158, 175, 176, 182, 184,
    194, 195, 196, 198, 199, 200, 212,
    214, 217, 234, 266, 301, 302, 303,
    306, 310, 321, 328, 330
"Foul-Smelling Rapist, The," 226
Founding Fathers, 57, 59, 201, 251
Fourteenth Amendment, 27, 31, 32,
    42, 43, 44, 55, 57, 63, 322, 323
Fourth Amendment, 24, 28, 37, 38,
    39, 41, 46, 47, 48, 65, 125, 127,
    129, 130, 132, 136, 142, 143, 144,
    195, 196, 197, 198, 199, 201, 202,
    203, 205, 207, 209, 210, 211, 212,
    213, 214, 215, 216, 217, 218, 220,
    251, 252, 253, 255, 260, 261, 263,
    265, 266, 267, 268, 274, 294, 309
Frankfurter, Justice Felix, 2, 6, 33,
    42, 43, 44, 45, 48, 52, 53, 57, 59,
    108, 160, 173, 174, 194, 221, 243
fraud, 207
free counsel, rejection of, 314
freedom of religion, 17
freedom of press, 17, 45
freedom of speech, 17, 45
freedom to search, 5
Fremont Hotel, 247
Freund, Professor Paul, 115
Friendly, Judge Henry J., 7, 61, 146
Friesen, Ernest C., Jr., 116
"fruit of the poisonous tree," 131, 132
"full and fair hearing, a," 109
"fundamental fairness," 6, 33, 34, 35,
    41, 42, 45, 52, 56, 63, 101, 142,
    231, 302, 310, 316

Gallup Poll, 8, 123
gambling. 23, 89, 98, 196
Garnett, Kansas, 76
"general search," 253, 267
Georgetown section, 67, 68
Georgetown University Law School,
    279
ghetto crime, 78
ghetto neighborhoods, 331
ghetto riots, 14
Gideon, Clarence Earl, 54, 112, 176
Gilbert, Jesse James, 231, 241
Gitlow, Benjamin, 45

Goldberg, Justice Arthur J., 17, 48,
    53, 54, 165, 166, 167, 175, 261
Goldwater, Barry, 8
Good Samaritan's burdens, 111
Gouled, Felix, 214
government agents, 23
government economic regulations,
    332
government informers, 23
Government's Big Ear, 271
grand jury indictments, 56
Grant, Stephen A., 124
Grant, President Ulysses S., 3
Great Writ, 113
Griffin, Senator Robert P., 328, 329
Griswold, Solicitor General Erwin
    N., 28, 62, 274
guilty pleas, 283

habeas corpus, petition for, 102, 103,
    104, 106, 107, 111, 113, 114, 115,
    119, 120, 147, 188, 189, 191, 195,
    215, 222, 232, 308, 320, 324, 326
habeas corpus jurisdiction, Federal
    Court's, 329
habeas corpus law, 111, 113, 116
Hague, "Boss" Frank, 146
"handcuffing the police," 19, 25, 28,
    29, 123, 151, 157, 196, 289, 331
"hard" evidence, 7
hard money, 331
Harlan, Justice John Marshall, 52,
    128, 174
Harlem, 89, 100, 218, 219
harmless error, 318, 319
Harriman, Averell, 67
Harris, George, 207
Harris, Patricia, 92
Harris Poll, 68
Harrison, Eddie, 295, 296
Hart, Judge George L., 291
Harvard, 42, 62, 69, 73, 115, 169, 173,
    174, 274
Harvard Law School, 173
Hauptmann, Bruno, 226
Hayden, Bennie Joe, 215
Hayes, Rufus, 315
Haynesworth, Clement F., Jr., 306
"heavy burden," 313
Henderson Novelty Company, 248
Henry IV, King, 127

heroin, 211
Hewes, Lieutenant, 149
Higginbotham, Judge A. Leon, 92
Hill, Virginia, 257
hippies, 150, 292
Hoffa, Teamster President James R., 23, 263, 264
Hogan, Frank S., 281
Holcomb, Weldon, 230
Holmes, Justice Oliver Wendell, 32, 107, 127, 131, 195, 251, 260, 305, 307
Holmsian tradition, 314
homicide, 14, 68, 79, 81, 84
homicide bureau, 281
"hoodlum," 72, 100
Hoover, J. Edgar, 11, 14, 71, 79, 80, 87, 88, 89, 257, 258
Hoover's Comet, 74
"hot pursuit," 38, 202, 215
Hotchkiss, 53
House Appropriations Committee, 257
House Government Operations Committee's Subcommittee on Legal and Monetary Affairs, 12
House Post Office and Civil Service Committee's Subcommittee on Census and Statistics, 12
housebreaking, 238
Housebreaking and Other Crimes, 68
How to Avoid Burglary, 68
How to Defend Yourself, Your Family and Your Home, 68
Hughes, Charles Evans, 3, 55, 58, 59, 331
Humphrey, Vice President, 68, 70, 82, 87, 99

identification, 224, 225, 226, 227, 228, 229, 230, 231, 232, 233, 234, 235, 236, 237, 238, 239, 240, 241, 242, 244, 245, 310
    false, 236
    faulty, 242, 243, 244
    in-court, 240, 241
    mistaken, 226, 232
    on-the-street, 237
identifying suspects, methods of, 224
illegal arrests, 143, 147

illegal eavesdropping, 19, 210, 262, 274
illegal lineups, 240
illegal police raids, 140
illegal police wiretapping, 251
illegal searches, 4, 11, 14, 38, 39, 62, 124, 132, 133, 136, 140, 141, 158, 187, 240, 255, 331
illegal showup, 241
illegally obtained evidence, 47, 130, 131, 132, 136, 137, 143, 172, 198, 206, 216, 217, 227, 309
Illinois, 34, 39, 104, 119
Illinois' Death Row, 115
Illinois State Penitentiary, 102
Illinois, Supreme Court of, 61, 104
Illinois, University of, 139
imprisonment, false, 124
Inbau, Fred E., 316
"incidents," 205, 207
"inclusion," 44
income tax deductions, 77
income tax law, 3
incriminating evidence, 203
incriminating statements, 143
"independent recollection," 241
India, 181, 182
Indiana, 39
individual rights, 245
"information," an, 56
informer systems, 23, 211, 212
informers, 65
innocence, presumption of, 37
"inquisitorial" system, 159, 160
Institute of Judicial Administration, 293
insurance claims, 77
International Association of Chiefs of Police, 75
interrogation curb, 282
interrogation, incommunicado, 180, 184
interrogation, in-custody, 183
interrogation manual, 316
interrogation procedure, 179
interrogation question, 329
interrogation, station-house, 180
interstate commerce, regulation of, 322
intimidation, 203

Jackson, John (Snooks), 117
Jackson, Justice Robert H., 39, 59, 117, 125, 142, 167, 168, 183, 203, 256
jailhouse petitions, 308
James, Jesse, 72
Japan, 11
Japanese, 50, 301
Japanese-Americans, 73
Jenner, Albert E., Jr., 115
Jersey City, 146
Jim Crow, 13
John Birch Society, 58
John Law, 13, 148
Johns Hopkins University, 96
Johnson, President Lyndon B., 54, 65, 74, 128, 173, 223, 266
Johnson, Sylvester, 189, 191
Johnson, William A., 290
Johnson, William Joe, 115
Joint Center for Urban Studies, 94
Joint Committee on Un-American Activities, 147
Joliet, Illinois, 102
Joliet Prison, 103, 106, 108, 113, 118, 119, 120
"joyriding," 80
judges, psychology of some, 208, 209
"judicial power," 1, 325
"judicial review," 57
"judicial self-restraint," 42
Julia, Lord Byron's, 45
"junk" cases, 298
Justice Department, 46, 125, 173, 174, 210, 214, 225, 253, 255, 256, 262, 263, 264, 266, 269, 270, 271, 272, 274, 277, 296, 329
 Criminal Division of, 125
 Office of Criminal Justice, 173
justices of the peace, 29
juvenile courts, 29

Kamisar, Professor Yale, 286
Kansas, 39, 140
Kansas City, 249, 273
Karlen, Dalmar, 293
Katzenbach, Attorney General Nicholas deB., 6, 15, 74, 75, 100, 258, 284
Kee, Al, 247, 248, 251, 252, 257

Kennedy, Senator Edward M., 311
Kennedy, President John F., 16, 17, 48, 53, 54, 68, 74, 248, 259
Kennedy-Johnson crime record, 82
Kennedy, Judge Joseph G., 292
Kennedy, Senator Robert, 249, 258, 259, 269
kidnapping, 258
Killough, James W., 19, 20
"Killough case," 20
King, Dr. Martin Luther, Jr., 13, 49, 99, 259, 272
King, Ross, 103
Kings County, New York, 281
Kinnard, Darnell R., Jr., 237
Ku Klux Klan, 49, 273
Kurland, Philip, 58

Labat, Edgar, 114
LaFave, Wayne R., 139
Lankford, Mrs., 149
larceny, 77, 80, 92
Las Vegas, 15, 248, 249, 257, 258, 260, 261, 262
law and order, 68, 73, 87, 95, 99, 148, 250, 285, 286, 300, 303, 305, 306, 309, 328, 332
"law and order" controversy, 71
"law and order with justice," 87
law enforcement, 6, 30, 31, 33, 52, 53, 60, 136, 139, 146, 156, 157, 159, 164, 166, 170, 171, 173, 174, 176, 178, 193, 196, 198, 202, 203, 206, 211, 224, 225, 234, 240, 243, 244, 245, 248, 250, 252, 262, 266, 268, 272, 278, 280, 281, 282, 284, 285, 289, 293, 310, 328
 national recoil against, 49
 reform, 19
lawful arrest, 38
lawless police snooping, 261
lawyerless defendants, 62
Leavenworth Penitentiary, 225, 296
legal aid for the poor, 296, 297
Legal Aid Society, 242
legal reform, 3
Legal Services Unit of the Office of Economic Opportunity, 148
legal tender case, 3
legislative branch, 324

legislatures, unfairly apportioned, 2
Levinson, Edward, 247, 248, 251, 252
Lewis, Duke Lee, 23
Life magazine, 69, 301
Lindbergh baby, 226
Lindsay, Mayor John V., 126
lineups, 19, 195, 223, 228, 230, 231,
    232, 233, 234, 235, 236, 237, 238,
    240, 241, 242, 243, 244, 245, 309,
    310, 329
  controlled stage, 236
  identification, 324
  "the lie-down," 243
liquor offenses, 196
literacy, 322
London, 94, 132, 225
Longview, Texas, 190
Los Angeles, 20, 35, 78, 127, 165, 204
Los Angeles County, 281
Louisiana, 114, 147
loyalty-security program, 327
Lumbard, Judge J. Edward, 23, 174
lynchings, 72

McCann, George, 237, 238
McCardle, William H., 326
McCarthy, Senator Joseph, 73, 74
McCarthy antisubversive scare, 54
McClellan, Senator John L., 8, 12, 16,
    267, 309, 320, 329
McCloskey, Robert G., 21
McCray, George, 211, 212
McDaniel, Mickey, 288
McReynolds, Justice James C., 146
Mafia, 216, 249, 257, 258, 259, 273
Magna Charta, 177
"Main Street, U.S.A.," 76
Manhattan, 219, 266
Mapp, Miss Dolree, 40, 41, 172
Mapp v. *Ohio*
  see exclusionary rules
  see illegal searches
  see state justice
marijuana, 85, 98, 197, 270
Marshall, Chief Justice John, 30, 48,
    57, 321
Marshall, Justice Thurgood, 197, 218,
    219, 319
Martin, Dean, 248
Maryland, 115, 185
Massachusetts, 291

Massiah, Winston, 163
Mayflower Hotel, 197
*mea culpa*s, 298
Memphis, Tennessee, 226
Menninger, Dr. Karl, 69
Menninger Clinic, 69
"mere evidence" rule, 24, 214, 215,
    253, 265
Mesa, Arizona, 76
Miami, 100, 249
Michigan, 140, 328
Michigan Law School, University of,
    329
Michigan Supreme Court, 120
microphone, 248, 250, 252, 254, 255,
    267, 268
Miller, Walter B., 94, 95
Milwaukee, 204
Minneapolis, 126
Miranda, Ernesto, 20, 64, 154, 156,
    191
"Miranda Cards," 137, 138, 317
"Miranda syndrome," 292
Miranda v. *Arizona*
  see confessions
  see incriminating statements
  see police interrogation
  see right to remain silent
  see right to counsel
  see self-incrimination
Mississippi, 32, 326
Missouri, 39
Mitchell, Attorney General John N.,
    270, 271, 273, 274, 329
Mobile County, Alabama, 242
Montrose Park, 192
moonshine case, 207
moonshine whiskey, 214
Morgan, Daniel Jackson Oliver
    Wendell Holmes, 296
Mormons, 73
Moses, Prof. Earl R., 96
muggings, 29, 68, 75, 77, 84, 93
mug-shots, 239
Muhammad, Elijah, 259, 272
municipal courts, 29
murders, 11, 29, 75, 76, 77, 79, 80,
    81, 82, 84, 87, 89, 91, 94, 98, 99,
    102, 103, 104, 133, 134, 262
Murphy, Justice Frank, 131
Murphy, Michael J., 14

narcotics, 57, 123, 124, 136, 137, 163, 196, 209, 210, 211, 212, 214
  addiction, 85
  addicts, crimes by, 141
  agents, 142
  arrest rate, 85, 98
  arrests, 136, 139
  charges, 98
  offenses, 28, 92
  smuggling, 262
  traffic, 23
Nashville, Tennessee, 137, 138, 263, 283
Nashville Police Department, 283
National Advisory Commission on Civil Disorders, 96
National Association for the Advancement of Colored People (NAACP), 89, 148, 218
  Legal Defense and Educational Fund, Inc., 148
  New York chapter of, 89, 100
National Commission on Causes and Prevention of Violence, 87, 88, 89, 90, 91, 92, 123, 330, 331
National District Attorney's Association, 170, 171
National Guard, 99
National Legal Aid and Defender Association, 297
"national security" cases, 274
national security investigations, 252
"national security" wiretapping, 259
Nebraska, 105
negligence suits, 127
Negroes, 13, 14, 32, 63, 65, 78, 85, 87, 88, 89, 90, 91, 93, 94, 95, 96, 97, 98, 99, 100, 107, 108, 126, 133, 144, 147, 148, 149, 150, 218, 225, 230, 288, 292, 322
  arrest rate, 13, 14, 89, 90, 91, 94, 95, 97, 98
  crime, as compared to whites, 90, 91, 92, 96, 97
  crime taboo, 90
  delinquency rates, 97
  high crime rate, 86, 88, 90, 92, 93, 94, 95, 97, 98, 99, 100
  narcotics arrests of, 98
  national crime rate for, 85
  neighborhoods, 78

policemen, 78
  problem of the, 12, 31
  rioting, 4, 14, 99, 100
  "stop and frisk" of, 98
neutral constitutional language, 59
Nevada, 39, 252
Newark, New Jersey, 150
New Deal, 50, 176, 331
New Frontier, 53
New Haven, Connecticut, 276, 280, 281
New Jersey, 17, 34, 39, 51, 114
New Jersey's Death Row, 189
New Kensington, Pennsylvania, 316
New Orleans, 114
New York (City), 11, 72, 77, 126, 136, 150, 204, 213, 249, 250, 254, 257, 298, 314, 322
  felony arrests in, 298
  felony convicts, 298
  felony indictments in, 298
  police department, 135
  public school children, 178
  reported robberies in, 298
New York County, 281
New York (State), 11, 34, 39, 45, 53, 110, 119, 267
  Attorney General of, 170
  Constitution of, 11, 250
  eavesdrop law, 266, 267
  Liquor Authority, 266
New York Telephone Company, 250
New York Times, The, 49, 69, 70, 74, 76, 100, 279
New York University Law School, 52, 298
Nine Old Men, 61
1984, 22, 259
Nisei, 73
Nixon, President Richard M., 9, 15, 16, 68, 70, 82, 87, 100, 121, 237, 267, 273, 284, 296, 300, 301, 302, 303, 305, 306, 307, 308, 310, 329, 330
Nixon administration, 84
Nixon Court, 303
Nobel Prize, 259, 273
nonviolent thefts of property, 80
nonwhites, 77, 92, 96
North Carolina, 109, 206
Norway, 11

"notice of intention," 281, 282
Notre Dame, 269
numbers runners, 136

obscenity, 307
O'Hare Inn, 128
Ohio, 39, 40
Ohio State Supreme Court, 40, 41, 53
Ohlin, Lloyd E., 69, 83
"Oklahoma Show-up," 229, 230
Olmstead, Roy, 251
Olney, Warren, 125
Omnibus Crime Control and Safe Streets Act of 1968, 9, 12, 65, 121, 162, 184, 268, 271, 309, 319
  Title II, 133, 309, 310, 319, 320, 321, 323, 324, 327, 328, 329, 330
  Title III, 268, 269, 270, 271, 272, 273
"on suspicion," 65, 144, 201
one-informer, one-conviction rule, 211
"order with justice," 87
"ordered liberty" standard, 46
Oregon appellate court, 159
Orwell, George, 22, 259
Osborn, Z. T. "Tommy," 23, 263, 264, 265
Ouachita, Louisiana, 117
outside surveillance, 254
Oxford, 52

Paille, Robert N., 133, 134
Painten, Donald M., 133
Palmer raids, 73
Paris, 94
Parker, Judge John J., 109
Parker, Tyrone, 299
Parker, Police Chief William, 78
Pearl Harbor, 73
penitentiaries, 103, 106, 110, 112, 115
Pennsylvania, 39, 317
Pennsylvania Supreme Court, 316, 317
"perceive a basis," 323
permissive eavesdrop law, 261
Perry Mason, 200
personal liberty, 213

personal security, 213
"persons, houses, papers, and effects," 197, 200
petitions, 106, 108, 109, 110, 111, 113, 115, 116, 117, 119, 120
petty claims courts, 56
petty larceny, 238
Philadelphia, 78, 83, 93, 95, 97, 99, 117, 126, 144, 145, 150, 159, 281
photographs, 236, 239, 240
Piersante, Detroit Police Chief Vincent, 281
Pittsburgh, 72, 280
Pittsburgh, University of, 280
Plainfield, New Jersey, 150
Playboy bunny club, 266
plea bargaining, 308
police, 4, 5, 7, 9, 16, 17, 18, 19, 21, 23, 24, 25, 29, 33, 37, 38, 39, 49, 50, 52, 56, 60, 62, 63, 65, 72, 77, 78, 79, 85, 87, 93, 94, 98, 100, 101, 117, 121, 123, 125, 126, 127, 129, 130, 131, 132, 133, 134, 135, 136, 137, 138, 139, 140, 141, 143, 144, 145, 146, 147, 148, 149, 150, 151, 152, 156, 157, 158, 159, 160, 161, 162, 163, 164, 165, 166, 167, 169, 170, 173, 175, 176, 177, 180, 182, 183, 184, 185, 186, 187, 190, 192, 193, 195, 196, 197, 198, 199, 201, 202, 203, 204, 205, 206, 207, 208, 209, 210, 211, 212, 213, 214, 215, 216, 217, 218, 219, 220, 222, 224, 227, 228, 229, 234, 235, 236, 237, 238, 239, 240, 242, 243, 244, 249, 250, 251, 252, 253, 254, 255, 260, 261, 262, 266, 267, 268, 269, 272, 275, 276, 278, 279, 280, 281, 282, 283, 284, 285, 286, 287, 288, 289, 291, 293, 301, 302, 303, 307, 309, 310, 311, 312, 313, 314, 315, 316, 317, 318, 319, 330, 331, 332
  agents, 23
  Baltimore, 149, 150
  brutality, 100, 123
  bugging, 255, 267
  Chicago, 122, 123, 125
  conduct, 134, 135, 140, 151, 155, 330
  constitutional limit on action, 48
  control, 126, 131, 132

discrimination, 98
District of Columbia, 133
eavesdropping, 250, 252, 253, 255, 257, 261, 266, 267, 269
impotence, 123
interrogation, 7, 19, 20, 21, 22, 37, 65, 132, 138, 152, 155, 156, 158, 159, 160, 161, 162, 163, 165, 166, 167, 168, 169, 171, 173, 174, 175, 176, 177, 178, 180, 181, 182, 183, 184, 185, 190, 235, 236, 240, 278, 280, 282, 309, 310, 312, 315, 316
in-the-field investigation, 236
intrusion, 214
lawlessness, 18, 217
limiting powers of, 3, 4, 5, 7
local, 4, 6, 7, 37, 125, 143, 253, 270
New York, 137
overreaching, 40
prohibition of oppressive action, 30
restrictions on questioning, 61, 62
review boards, 126, 151
"riot," 123
searches, 309
spying, 24
state, 4, 6, 37, 38, 41, 47, 48, 253
surveillance, 249
violations of law, 123, 124, 125, 127, 134, 145
violence, 87
wiretapping, 252, 254, 256, 261, 263, 269
police-community relations, 145
police-state methods, 224
politics, 2
poll taxes, elimination of, 321
polygamy, 73
Poor Peoples' Campaign, 68
Poret, Clifton, 114
pornography, 32, 191
post-arrest procedure, 7
post-Civil War Congress, 326
post-Warren cooling-off period, 330
post-World War I period, 73, 206
"poverty line," 97
prayers, 2
"preferred freedoms," 45
Presidency, 2, 9
President's Commission on Crime in the District of Columbia, 69

President's Commission on Law Enforcement and Administration of Justice, 69, 174
President's Commission on Urban Problems, 96
President's National Crime Commission, 15, 70, 71, 72, 75, 77, 78, 92, 139, 250, 269
"preventive detention," 100, 239, 300, 301, 304
Princeton, 52
privacy, individual, 37
privacy of premises, 219
privacy, threats to, 250
private papers, sanctity of, 212
private property, 213
"privileges and immunities" clause, 31
"probable cause," 202
procedural rights, 291
"process of absorption," 46, 56
Prohibition, 47, 206, 250, 251
pro-Negro image, 13
property rationale, 216
property rights, 331
prostitution, 89, 98
protective surveillance, 259
Providence, 249
public accommodations, equal use of, 63
public defenders, 64, 172, 173, 235, 289, 297
public opinion, 2, 3
public schools, 2
Puerto Ricans, 322

questioning, 158, 168, 169

race and crime, 88, 89, 90, 91, 92, 93, 94, 95, 96, 97, 98, 99, 100
racial crime trends, 90, 91, 92
racial disorders, 15
racial segregation, legal, 50
racial tensions, 3, 4
racism, 330
radical domestic groups, surveillance of, 271, 274
radio transmitter, 254
Ragen, Warden Joseph E., 106

rape, 11, 14, 29, 75, 76, 77, 79, 80, 81, 83, 84, 87, 91, 95, 99, 114, 118, 226, 243
reasonable search, 265
"reasonableness," 201, 219
recidivism rate, 89, 112, 113
Reconstruction, 326
  Acts, 326
  Congress, 107, 145, 327
"Red Light Bandit," 114
Red Scare, 73
Red's Taco House, 273
Reed, John E., 316
religious freedom, 45
Remington, Frank J., 139
Rent Stabilization, Office of, 128
replevin, 213
Republican Task Force on Crime, 82
res gestae, 312
res judicata, 103, 105, 108
retroactivity question, 186, 188, 189, 190, 191
Rhode Island appellate court, 159
right of privacy, 23
right to a fair trial, 235
right to assemble peaceably, 45
right to bear arms, 56
right to counsel, 6, 7, 47, 48, 63, 64, 65, 118, 132, 154, 155, 158, 162, 163, 164, 165, 166, 167, 177, 179, 181, 190, 191, 229, 231, 232, 234, 235, 236, 243, 277, 311, 314
right to remain silent, 37, 166, 179
riots, 76, 94, 99
Roberts, Burton B., 141
Roberts, Justice Owen, 59
robbery, 11, 14, 72, 77, 79, 80, 81, 83, 84, 87, 89, 91, 93, 95, 98, 99, 100, 117
Robison, Sophia M., 70
Rochester, 126
Roosevelt, President Franklin, 50, 256, 257, 259
Roosevelt, President Theodore, 307
Royal Courts of Justice, 132
Rube Goldberg nightmare, 198
Russell, Bobby, 238
Russians, 254

sabotage, 256, 259
Sacco and Vanzetti trial, 226

St. Louis, 150, 210
Sampson, Joseph, 296
Sands Hotel, 248
San Francisco, 39, 72, 204, 292
San Francisco police department, 138, 182, 242
sanitized corridors, 331
Santa Ana, California, 208
Scarlet O'Hara, 49
Schaefer, Justice Walter V., 61, 62, 64
Scherer, Anthony J., Jr., 128, 129
school desegregation decisions, 50, 58, 320
schools, slum, 49
Scotland, 181, 182
Scottsboro Boys, 32, 235
Scylla, 160
search warrants, 38, 40, 41, 199, 200, 201, 202, 203, 204, 205, 206, 207, 208, 209, 210, 214, 219, 236, 260, 309
searches, 19, 65, 195, 196, 197, 198, 199, 200, 201, 202, 203, 204, 205, 206, 207, 208, 209, 211, 212, 213, 214, 215, 216, 217, 219, 220, 224, 236, 240, 251, 252, 253, 265, 268, 291
Seattle, 251
Second Amendment, 56
Secret Service, 128
"security cases," 257
segregation, 2
segregationists, 50
seizures, 195, 196, 198, 201, 202, 205, 209, 213, 214, 236, 251, 252, 253, 255, 265, 268, 291
"selective incorporation," 44
Selective Service certificates, forged, 207
Selective Service Laws, 277
Selective Service violations, 28
self-confessed criminals, 184
self-incrimination, 6, 23, 37, 45, 47, 48, 52, 60, 159, 168, 178, 179, 180, 181, 196, 213, 229, 230, 233, 251, 278, 301
  "communicative," 233
  compulsory, 43
  "testimonial," 233
Sellin, Thorsten, 69, 95, 97

Senate, 121, 239, 245, 319, 327, 328, 329, 330
Senate Judiciary Committee, 239, 319, 320, 324
Senate Judiciary's hearings, 194
Senate Select Committee on Small Business, 12
Sevareid, Eric, 60
Seventh Amendment, 56
"show-up," 227, 228, 232, 236, 238, 240
faulty, 310
Shriver, Thomas A., 138
Shuttlesworth, Reverend Fred L., 13
"silver platter doctrine," 47
Simmons, Thomas Earl, 294
Simmons, 239
Sinatra, Frank, 248
Sixth Amendment, 44, 47, 48, 55, 64, 159, 163, 164, 165, 166, 179, 181, 212, 223, 230, 243
slaves, newly-freed, 31
slaves, rights to, 331
Smith, Edgar H., Jr., 114
Smith, Jeremiah, 153
snake handling, 270
Snyder, Jimmie, Jr., 114
Sobel, State Supreme Court Justice Nathan R., 281
Sobeloff, Judge Simon E., 149
South Vietnam, 100
Southern Conference Educational Fund, 147
soybean fertilizer tanks, 26
Spanish-speaking Americans, 323
"special circumstances," 162
Specter, Arlen, 281
Speech, The, 293
"spike mike," 255
Spinelli, William, 210
"squealrooms," 177, 288
Stamford, Connecticut, 95, 97
"standing" rules, 215, 216
Stardust, the, 248
State Chief Justices, Conference of, 58, 60, 120
"state courts," 29, 41, 46
State Department, 73, 74
State Governments, The Council of, 58
state judicial systems, 28

state justice, 31, 32, 37, 45, 46, 48, 57
state law, 37
state law-enforcement standards, 42
state legislatures, 1, 29
station-house interrogation, 323
statistical politics, 73, 74
Stewart, Justice Potter, 32, 52, 53, 134, 163, 188, 207, 264, 265, 268, 274
Stewart, Roy, 156, 191
stolen cars, 80
stolen property, 214
Stone, Justice Harlan Fiske, 26
stool pigeon system, 211
"stop and frisk" decision, 24, 25, 51, 62, 65, 141, 143, 144, 145, 157, 195, 199, 201, 217, 218, 219
Stovall, Theodore, 231, 235
Stratton, Governor William G., 119
Streit, Judge Saul S., 291
Suarez, Jose, 185, 186, 191
Subin, Harry J., 298, 299
"Sunburst" problem, 186
Supreme Court, 1–9, 11–25, 27–66, 70, 71, 78, 85, 88, 93, 100, 103–105, 107–118, 120, 121, 123, 125, 126, 128–131, 133–135, 137, 141–147, 151–199, 201, 202, 204–207, 209–215, 217–220, 223, 224, 227, 229, 231–236, 238–241, 243–246, 249–253, 255–257, 259–270, 274–276, 278, 279, 282–296, 301–315, 317–332
"suspects," 243
suspects' rights, 330
progressive expansion of, 324
Sweden, 112
Swedish Ombudsmen, 126

Taft, William Howard, 1, 10, 247
tape-recording, 175
Taper, Geraldine, 316, 317
tapping phones, 250
tax cheating, 143
tax havens, 331
taxing power, 322
Taylor, Telford, 176
telephones, 248, 250, 251, 252, 254, 255, 257, 258, 259, 267, 268, 272
television, 26, 27, 28
sports announcers, 254

Tennessee, 263, 317
Tennessee State Penitentiary, 115
Texas, 26, 27, 28, 35, 44, 311
Texas, University of, 76
thefts, 70, 77, 80, 93
Third Amendment, 56
"third degree," 22, 124, 159, 160, 180, 316
Thurmond, Senator Strom, 196
tort law, 127
tort litigation, 145
torts, 126, 151
"totality of the circumstances" test, 156, 161, 182, 227, 232, 313, 317
traffic courts, 29
Train, Arthur, 135
transistors, 254
transmitter, 260
Traynor, Chief Justice Roger J., 21, 61, 62, 134
trial judges, 289
trials, television coverage of, 26, 27, 28
Truman, President Harry S, 50, 59, 256, 257, 266
Truman administration, crime in, 82
Tucker, Sterling, 99
Twenty-Fourth Amendment, 321
Tydings, Senator Joseph D., 100
Tyler, Texas, 27, 230

"underlying circumstances," 209, 210
United Nations, 54
United Press International, 89
United States, 4, 11, 31, 38, 57, 61, 69, 71, 74, 75, 79, 81, 86, 107, 111, 112, 113, 127, 130, 167, 168, 174, 180, 204, 224, 227, 228, 284, 287, 325, 326
  District Court for the Northern District of Illinois, 102, 106
  Government Printing Office, 193
  Great Seal of the, 254
  Judicial Conference of the, 110, 111
  Marines, 67, 68
  Tariff Commission, 223
  trial courts, 106, 118, 251, 261
United States Code, 12
  Title 18, 124
United States Law Week, 5, 193

United States Reports, 34, 193
unlawful arrests, 124, 146
unlawful assaults, 124
unlawful police power, 331
unlawful possession, 212
unreasonable eavesdropping, 268
unreasonable searches, 23, 24, 28, 37, 125, 127, 129, 201, 209, 213, 251
Urban Coalition and Urban America, Inc., 148
Urban League, 99
urban riots, 272
Utah, 39, 118

Vanderbilt, Chief Justice Arthur T., 51
Veney, Earl, 149, 150
Veney, Samuel, 149, 150
Vick, Robert, 263, 264
videotape, 245
Vietcong, 100
Vietnam, war in, 97
  constitutionality of draft, 49, 53
vigilante patrols, 330
Vignera, 191
Vinson, Chief Justice Fred M., 207
violence, 4, 29, 68, 69, 71, 72, 76, 80, 81, 82, 83, 84, 90, 92, 93, 94, 272, 331
violent crime, decline of, 75, 79
violent crime, rise of, 70, 71, 72
"violent crimes," 80, 81, 82, 83, 84, 85, 88, 89, 91, 92, 99
Virginia, 114
voluntariness, 154, 156, 157, 160, 161, 164, 165, 181, 183, 190, 203, 308, 313
Vorenberg, James, 169, 173, 174, 183, 268

Wade, Billy Joe, 230, 231, 233, 234, 241
waiver of rights, 277, 278, 316, 317
waivers, 313, 314, 315
Wales, 11
Wallace, George C., 10, 68, 70, 86, 87, 88, 89, 90, 100, 121
Ward, Fay, Jr., 118
warrantless searches, 38, 39, 40, 146, 202, 207, 309
warrants, 253

Warren, Chief Justice Earl, 4, 9, 17,
    22, 47, 50, 56, 61, 64, 65, 120, 125,
    144, 145, 175, 177, 178, 180, 181,
    183, 188, 191, 192, 199, 233, 266,
    287, 288, 290, 292, 293, 303, 304,
    306, 307, 310, 315, 316, 319, 330
"Warrenburger," 305
Warren Court, 3, 4, 5, 6, 7, 9, 11, 16,
    17, 18, 19, 24, 44, 48, 50, 52, 53,
    59, 60, 101, 152, 157, 159, 174,
    186, 192, 199, 208, 210, 216, 220,
    224, 231, 245, 246, 247, 249, 256,
    257, 262, 266, 279, 283, 284, 286,
    289, 292, 302, 303, 306, 308, 310,
    313, 316, 319, 320, 321, 328, 329
Warren era, 219, 259, 285, 302, 303,
    310
"Warren majority," 17, 48, 52, 54, 59,
    63, 129, 175
Washington, D.C., 16, 17, 53, 54, 67,
    68, 72, 93, 100, 126, 157, 173,
    175, 177, 225, 237, 242, 248, 254,
    273, 274, 277, 279, 288, 295, 296,
    299, 300, 301, 303, 305
Washington Bar, the, 221, 222
Washington, President George, 38
Way, H. Frank, Jr., 35
Webster, Ronald, 241
Webster City, Iowa, 76
West, Will, 225
West, William, 225
Westover, 191

White, Justice Byron R., 53, 60, 210,
    217, 241, 312
White, Orson, 296
Wichita, Kansas, 204
Wigmore, John Henry, 140
Williams, Anthony, 222, 223
Williams, Edward Bennett, 248
Wilmington, Delaware, 99
Wilson, James Q., 73, 85
wiretapping, 22, 23, 24, 250, 251, 252,
    253, 254, 255, 256, 257, 258, 259,
    260, 262, 263, 267
wiretaps, 4, 5, 11, 131, 250, 251, 252,
    253, 255, 257, 258, 259, 260, 266,
    268, 269, 274
Wisconsin, 140
Wisconsin, University of, 139
Witherspoon, William C., 115
Wolfgang, Marvin E., 83, 93, 95, 96,
    97
Wolfson, Louis E., 302
World War I, 286
World War II, 4, 5, 73, 206, 214, 301
writ-writing binge, 110

Yale College, 53, 97, 276, 277, 278
Yale Law School, 53, 226, 277, 280
York, 126
Younger, District Attorney Evelle
    J., 281

Zeus, 2